Mentally Disordered Offenders

PERSPECTIVES FROM LAW AND SOCIAL SCIENCE

Perspectives in

Law &

Psychology

Series Editor: **BRUCE DENNIS SALES,** *University of Arizona, Tucson, Arizona*

Mentally Disordered Offenders

PERSPECTIVES FROM LAW AND SOCIAL SCIENCE

Edited by
John Monahan
University of Virginia
Charlottesville, Virginia
and
Henry J. Steadman
New York State Department of Mental Hygiene
Albany, New York

PLENUM PRESS · NEW YORK AND LONDON

Library of Congress Cataloging in Publication Data

Main entry under title:

Mentally disordered offenders.

(Perspectives in law and psychology; v. 6)
Bibliography: p.
Includes index.
1. Insanity—Jurisprudence—United States. 2. Mental health law—
United States. 3. Insane, Criminal and dangerous—United States. 4. Sex of-
fenders—United States. 5. Prisoners—Psychiatric care—United States. I.
Monahan, John, 1946– . II. Steadman, Henry J. III. Series.
KF9242.M46 1983   345.73'04   83-2329
ISBN 0-306-41151-2   347.3054

© 1983 Plenum Press, New York
A Division of Plenum Publishing Corporation
233 Spring Street, New York, N.Y. 10013

Printed in the United States of America

To Marge and Bernie Olsson
J.M.

To Carolyn
H.J.S.

Contributors

JERALDINE BRAFF
Special Projects Research Unit
New York State Department of Mental Hygiene

MICHAEL J. CHURGIN
School of Law
University of Texas

SHARON KANTOROWSKI DAVIS
Department of Behavioral Science
University of La Verne

GEORGE E. DIX
School of Law
University of Texas

ROBERT J. FAVOLE
Orrick, Herrington and Sutcliffe
A Professional Corporation

ELIOT HARTSTONE
URSA Institute

JOHN MONAHAN
School of Law
University of Virginia

GRANT H. MORRIS
School of Law
University of San Diego

HENRY J. STEADMAN
Special Projects Research Unit
New York State Department of Mental Hygiene

BRUCE J. WINICK
School of Law
University of Miami

Acknowledgments

We wish to acknowledge the considerable assistance of Professor David Wexler, who provided a meticulous critique of the legal chapters in this volume. For their advice and insight on the structure of our overall project, we thank our Advisory Board, consisting of Dr. Larry Clanon, Dr. Park Dietz, and Professor Sheldon Messinger, and particularly Lawrence Greenfeld, the project monitor of the National Institute of Justice grant (79–N1–AX–0126) that supported the writing of the contributors. Very thorough and very thoughtful editing of several of the social science chapters was done by Pamela Clark Robbins.

Contents

Introduction

In its narrowest sense, "mentally disordered offender" refers to the approximately twenty thousand persons per year in the United States who are institutionalized as not guilty by reason of insanity, incompetent to stand trial, and mentally disordered sex offenders, as well as those prisoners transferred to mental hospitals.

The real importance of mentally disordered offenders, however, may not lie in this figure. Rather, it may reside in the symbolic role that mentally disordered offenders play for the rest of the legal system. The 3,140 persons residing in state institutions on an average day in 1978 as not guilty by reason of insanity (see Chapter 4), for example, are surely worthy of concern in their own right. But they represent only 1% of the 307,276 persons residing in state and federal prisons in the same period (U.S. Dept. of Justice, 1981). From a purely numeric point of view, the insanity defense truly is "much ado about little" (Pasewark & Pasewark, 1982). The central importance of understanding these persons, however, is that they serve a symbolic function in *justifying* the imprisonment of the other 99%. The insanity defense, as Stone (1975) has noted, is "the exception that proves the rule." By exculpating a relatively few people from being criminally responsible for their behavior, the law inculpates all other law violators as liable for social sanction. Likewise, the true importance of incompetence to stand trial may be not in the 6,420 persons institutionalized as such in 1978 (see Chapter 2), but rather in the fact that the right to be present at trial—in this case, psychologically as well as physically "present"—is supported for the vastly larger number of competent defendants.

We have planned this volume to balance and juxtapose the concerns of the lawyer with those of the social scientist and accordingly have chosen as contributors a mix of lawyers, sociologists, and psychologists. This choice reflects our belief that in the area of mentally disordered offenders, as in many others, each has a great deal to learn from the other, both in terms of the nature of the contributions that the other can make and in terms of the limitations inherent in those contributions.

For those whose primary interests are in the law of mentally disordered offenders, social science can provide a factual foundation on which to build the law. Law, as the National Science Board (1969, p. 35) has stated, is based on "an underlying set of assumptions about how people act and how their actions can be controlled." The assumptions appear to be of two types. Some are *descriptive* of human behavior or personality ("how people act,") and some are *consequential* ("how their actions can be controlled") (Monahan & Loftus, 1982). Both types of assumptions are made in the law of mentally disordered offenders. The law makes the descriptive assumption that some people are unable to communicate with their attorneys (incompetence); others cannot tell right from wrong (insanity); others are predisposed by psychological disorder to commit sex offenses (mentally disordered sex offenders); and still others cannot be treated for their psychological pains in prison, but require placement in a mental hospital (prison transfers). The law also makes the consequential assumption that *if* mental health treatment is provided *then* at least some mentally disordered offenders will shed their special status: the incompetent will become fit to be tried, the insane and mentally disordered sex offender will no longer be "dangerous" and can be released, and the transferred prisoner can be returned from the hospital to the prison. It is insight into the reality of these descriptive and consequential assumptions that social science—and *only* social science—can offer the law.

For those whose primary interests are in the scientific study of mentally disordered offenders, knowledge of the law is essential in two ways. Those social scientists who study mentally disordered offenders as an end in themselves—that is, as worthy of study and intervention in their own right—are dependent upon the law both for the definition of their subject matter and for setting the substantive and procedural constraints on attempts for remedial intervention. The periodic recommendations by social scientists to "abolish" one or another of the classifications, procedures, or facilities for mentally disordered offenders often flaunt the reality that legal principles such as the Constitution dictate that some of these categories must exist. For those social scientists who study mentally disordered offenders primarily as sources of insight into more general principles of human behavior—who study mentally disordered sex offenders not because of their intrinsic interest but because their behavior may generate hypotheses about human sexuality in other contexts, for example—the law is likewise germane. The manner in which legal rules have evolved over the centuries regarding incompetence to stand trial and the insanity defense provide a powerful commentary on the centrality of notions of "fairness" and "responsibility" in human affairs.

This book grew out of a project to understand mentally disordered offenders both in their own right and in the context of larger issues in the criminal justice and mental health systems. We chose one of the nations's foremost legal scholars on each of the four areas that comprise mentally disordered offenders and commissioned each to do a comprehensive state-of-the-law review and analysis of unresolved legal issues. We and our colleagues then began a comprehensive search of the social science literature in each area, evaluatively reviewed it, and gave priority to the unanswered empirical questions.

We developed two surveys to assist in the analyses presented in this book. One was an examination of legal statutes as of January 1, 1980, in the 50 states in each of the four legal classifications. It is presented in our final chapter. The other was a telephone and mail survey of the forensic directors in each state plus the District of Columbia and the federal system concerning the number of persons admitted to state facilities and residing there on any given day in 1978 as one of the four categories of mentally disordered offenders. Numerous follow-ups allowed us to obtain a 100% response rate. The relevant aspects of these data are reported in each of the social science chapters.

Both the legal and social science chapters were written according to a standard format from which the authors deviated where they believed appropriate. For the legal chapters, that format consisted of addressing (1) the rationale and history of the particular mentally disordered offender status in the law; (2) the various legal criteria or "tests" that are used to determine who qualifies for the status; (3) the legal procedures necessary to invoke the status (hearings, trials, etc.); (4) the rights of the individual mentally disordered offender while he or she resides in that status; (5) the legal procedures necessary for terminating the status; (6) the legal consequences of having once resided in the status; and, finally, (7) the authors were asked to detail what they saw as the central legal issues that remained to be resolved in the next decade.

The social science chapters were structured more simply, since there is less social science research than there is legal commentary on each of the topics. In each chapter, we provided (1) an overview of social science approaches to the given mentally disordered offender status; (2) the results of our national survey of the incidence of the status's invocation;

(3) a critical review of existing social science research; and (4) a prioritized agenda of essential research yet to be done if social science is to provide the kind of factual information necessary for intelligent decision making in the area.

We have ordered our paired chapters according to the degree of penetration into the legal system represented by each mentally disordered offender status. Thus an individual accused of a crime who is also believed to be mentally ill can first be found incompetent to stand trial; then, if competent, can be acquitted of the crime by reason of insanity; then, if found sane, and if the crime qualifies, can be diverted to a mental hospital as a mentally disordered sex offender, and finally if found guilty of any crime can be transferred with appropriate certification from a prison to a mental hospital for treatment.

We will not rehearse here the arguments and observations presented in the chapters to come. Our hope is that this volume will serve as both a reference point and a catalyst for further understanding a group of persons that raise some of the most vexing problems confronting the mental health and criminal justice systems.

JOHN MONAHAN
HENRY J. STEADMAN

I

INCOMPETENCY TO STAND TRIAL

Incompetency to Stand Trial

DEVELOPMENTS IN THE LAW

BRUCE J. WINICK

LEGAL RATIONALE AND HISTORY OF THE INCOMPETENCY STATUS

The incompetency doctrine has common law origins, going back at least to mid-seventeenth century England (Group for the Advancement of Psychiatry 1974, pp. 912–915). Blackstone wrote that a defendant who became "mad" after the commission of an offense should not be arraigned "because he is not able to plead . . . with the advice and caution that he ought" and should not be tried, for "how can he make his defense?" (Blackstone 1783, p. 94; *see also* Hale 1736, pp. 34–35). Some have traced the common law prohibition on trying the incompetent defendant to the ban against trials *in absentia* (Foote 1960, p. 834; *see, e.g.,* *Frith's Case* 1790; *Kinloch's Case* 1746). Others have traced the origins of the doctrine to the difficulties resulting when a defendant frustrated the ritual of the English common law trial by remaining mute instead of pleading to the charge. Without such a plea, the trial could not go forward. In such cases the English court was obliged to determine whether the defendant was "mute by visitation of God" or "mute of malice." If "mute of malice," the defendant was subjected to a form of medieval torture—the *peine forte et dure*—in which increasingly heavier weights were placed upon his chest in an effort to compel him to plead. The category

BRUCE J. WINICK ● School of Law, University of Miami, Coral Gables, Florida 33124.

"mute by visitation of God," the members of whom were spared this painful ritual, originally encompassed the "deaf and dumb," but gradually was expanded to include "lunatics." At the discretion of the Chancellor, a jury could be impaneled to conduct an inquest into the defendant's competency (Group for the Advancement of Psychiatry 1974, pp. 887–88, 912–13; Slovenko 1977, p. 168).

Various standards for determining competency relating to the defendant's cognitive disabilities emerged. An early formulation came in *Firth's Case* (1790, p. 318), in which the court stated that:

> no man shall be called upon to make his defense at a time when his mind is in that situation as not to appear capable of so doing for, however guilty he may be, the inquiring into his guilt must be postponed to that season, when by collecting together his intellects, and having them entire, he shall be able so to model his defense as to ward off the punishment of the law.

The common law approach was followed by early American courts. In *United States v. Lawrence* (1835, p. 891), involving an assault on President Jackson, the court stated that "in case a man, in a frenzy, . . . is put upon his trial; and it appears to the court, upon his trial, that he is mad, the judge, in his discretion, may discharge the jury of him, and remit him to gaol, to be tried after the recovery of his understanding."

In an 1898 case (*United States v. Youtsey*, p. 941), the incompetency doctrine received constitutional recognition, the court holding that "[i]t is not 'due process of law' to subject an insane person to trial upon an indictment involving liberty or life." Gradually, the competency standard expanded from one focusing mainly on cognitive capacity to encompass as well the defendant's communicative abilities. Thus, a 1906 case (*United States v. Chisolm*, p. 287) stated the test as follows:

> [A] person, though not entirely sane, may be put to trial in a criminal case if he rightly comprehends his own condition with reference to the proceedings, and has such possession and control of his mental powers, including the faculty of memory, as will enable him to testify intelligently and give his counsel all the material facts bearing upon the criminal act charged against him and material to repel the incriminating evidence, and has such poise of his faculties as will enable him to rationally and properly exercise all the rights which the law gives him in contesting a conviction.

The modern formulation of the competency standard, stressing both cognitive and communicative capacity, is taken from the Supreme Court's opinion in *Dusky v. United States* (1960). In *Dusky*, the Court approved as a standard for federal cases whether the defendant "has sufficient present ability to consult with his lawyer with a reasonable degree of rational understanding—and whether he has a rational as well as factual understanding of the proceedings against him" (p. 402).

Although the common law origins of the incompetency doctrine may have become obsolete in view of Supreme Court decisions affording defendants a right to the assistance of counsel (Gobert 1973, p. 660), the modern doctrine is justified as a means of protecting the integrity of the adversarial criminal proceeding through promotion of the accuracy, fairness, and dignity of the trial process (Brakel & Rock 1971, p. 408; Harvard Law Review 1967, pp. 457–59). The Supreme Court has characterized the prohibition on trying an incompetent defendant as "fundamental to an adversary system of justice" (*Drope v. Missouri* 1975, p. 172). Without a defendant capable of understanding the nature of the proceedings and of assisting in his defense, our adversary system would make little sense. In order to safeguard the accuracy of criminal adjudication, competency requires, at a minimum, that the defendant be able to provide his counsel with facts necessary to construct a defense. Moreover, to exercise his rights at trial, the defendant must have the ability to confer intelligently with counsel, to testify coherently, and to follow and evaluate the evidence presented (Harvard Law Review 1967, p. 457). Insisting on competency thus serves both societal and individual interests in accurate and fair adjudication.

Moreover, the appearance of fairness, insured by insisting on a defendant capable of exercising control over the conduct of his defense, is essential to the legitimacy of our criminal process. The requirement of a threshold level of defendant competency in a system committed to the adversarial model of adjudication is indispensable to command the respect and confidence of the community in the criminal justice system. Competency also is required to preserve the integrity and dignity of the legal process. A defendant behaving bizarrely or remaining passive and uncomprehending throughout the proceedings may destroy the decorum of the court (Harvard Law Review 1967, p. 458). Finally, it is essential to the philosophy of punishment that a defendant understand why he is being punished (Harvard Law Review 1967, p. 458).

For these reasons all American jurisdictions follow the practice of holding incompetent to stand trial defendants who are found to be, as a result of mental illness, incapable of understanding the proceedings against them or of assisting in their own defense. (For a compilation of statutory provisions, *see* Favole 1983.) The determination of incompetence suspends the criminal proceedings while the defendant is remanded for mental health treatment designed to restore him to sufficient competence to stand trial. Not only is the practice universally followed, but it is deemed to be constitutionally required. In *Pate v. Robinson* (1966, pp. 378, 385), in dicta that is frequently cited, the Supreme Court noted that the failure to observe procedures adequate to protect a defendant's right not to be tried or convicted while incompetent to stand trial would deprive him or her of the due process right to a fair trial.

THE COMPETENCY STANDARD

Although terminology varies widely (*see* Favole 1983), all jurisdictions follow in substance the *Dusky* standard, the test approved by the Supreme Court for use in federal cases (*Dusky v. United States* 1960). Under this standard, it is not sufficient that "the defendant [is] oriented to time and place and [has] some recollection of events" (p. 402). Rather, the "test must be whether he has sufficient present ability to consult with his lawyer with a reasonable degree of rational understanding—and whether he has a rational as well as factual understanding of the proceedings against him" (p. 402). A number of statutes adopt the *Dusky* formulation verbatim. Most simply define an incompetent defendant as one who, as a result of mental disease or defect, lacks the capacity to understand the proceedings against him or her or to assist in his or her defense (*see* Favole 1983). The *Dusky* test is deemed the minimum constitutional standard to be applied in determining competency (*e.g., Bruce v. Estelle* 1973, p. 1042; *Noble v. Sigler* 1965, p. 677) and all jurisdictions construe their respective statutory formulations in conformity with it.

Several states supplement the general formulation with more detail. For example, New Jersey, in a statute adapted from the American Law Institute's Model Penal Code, specifies that:

> [A] person shall be considered mentally competent to stand trial on criminal charges if the proof shall establish: (1) that the defendant has the mental capacity to appreciate his presence in relation to time, place and things; and (2) that his elementary mental processes are such that he comprehends: (a) that he is in a court of justice charged with a criminal offense; (b) that there is a judge on the bench; (c) that there is a prosecutor present who will try to convict him of a criminal charge; (d) that he has a lawyer who will undertake to defend him against that charge; (e) that he will be expected to tell to the best of his mental ability the facts surrounding him at the time and place when the alleged violation was committed if he chooses to testify and understands the right not to testify; (f) that there is or may be a jury present to pass upon evidence adduced as to guilt or innocence of such charge or, that if he should choose to enter into plea negotiations or to plead guilty, that he comprehends the consequences of a guilty plea and that he be able to knowingly, intelligently, and voluntarily waive those rights which are waived upon such entry of a guilty plea and (g) that he has the ability to participate in an adequate presentation of his defense. (New Jersey Statutes Annotated § 2C:4-4)

A similar elaboration of the test is contained in an oft-cited federal case (*Wieter v. Settle* 1961).

As it is mental health evaluators who typically apply the competency standard, there have been several attempts in the literature to develop a "checklist" for clinicians in their examination for competency (*e.g.*, Bukataman, Foy, & deGrazia 1971; Robey 1965). The most comprehensive competency assessment instrument was developed by McGarry and his colleagues under a grant from the National Institute of Mental Health (Laboratory of Community Psychiatry 1973; Lipsitt, Lelos, & McGarry 1971). The McGarry checklist, an attempt to objectify the competency evaluation by use of an instrument with numerical ratings, has been used by experts in a number of states. The checklist approach is controversial, and some rating instruments have been criticized for built-in bias (Brakel 1974). In an attempt to standardize the evaluation process, Florida recently mandated a variation on the checklist approach, although without numerical ratings (Florida Rule of Criminal Procedure 3.211(a)(1)). Under this new approach, the competency evaluator must consider and analyze in his report the defendant's mental condition as it affects each of the following factors:

(i) Defendant's appreciation of the charges;
(ii) Defendant's appreciation of range and nature of possible penalties;
(iii) Defendant's understanding of the adversary nature of the legal process;
(iv) Defendant's capacity to disclose to attorney pertinent facts surrounding the alleged offense;
(v) Defendant's ability to relate to attorney;
(vi) Defendant's ability to assist attorney in planning defense;
(vii) Defendant's capacity to realistically challenge prosecution witnesses;
(viii) Defendant's ability to manifest appropriate courtroom behavior;
(ix) Defendant's capacity to testify relevantly;
(x) Defendant's motivation to help himself in the legal process;
(xi) Defendant's capacity to cope with the stress of incarceration prior to trial. (Florida Rule of Criminal Procedure 3.211(a)(1))

Such a specification of relevant factors should do much to reduce the tendency of some evaluators to confuse competency with legal insanity (Hess & Thomas 1963; Matthews 1970, p. 85; Roesch & Golding 1980, pp. 16–17; Stone 1975, pp. 202–03), or with diagnosis of psychosis. (Matthews 1970, p. 86; McGarry 1969, p. 50; Roesch & Golding 1980, p. 18; Vann & Morganroth 1964, p. 84). An incompetency determination should not be equated with an inquiry into criminal responsibility (*Bruce v. Estelle* 1973; *Martin v. Estelle* 1977; *Wolcott v. United States* 1969). The primary issue relating to an incompetency appraisal is not the defendant's mental condition at the time of the offense—the focus of the legal insanity inquiry—but rather his condition at the time of trial. Indeed, a defendant may not have been mentally ill at the time of the alleged offense, but nevertheless be incompetent to stand trial.

A diagnosis that the defendant is "mentally ill" does not in itself justify a finding of incompetence (*Hall v. United States* 1969; Robey 1965, p. 617; *United States v. Horowitz* 1973). To satisfy the test, the defendant's illness must render him incapable of understanding the nature of the proceedings against him and assisting in his defense. A defendant can be severely mentally ill, even overtly psychotic, and still be competent (Robey 1965, p. 617; *e.g., Feguer v. United States* 1962). A diagnosis of psychosis or the existence of particular descriptive symptoms is therefore not dispositive of the legal question of competence to stand trial (Kentucky Law Journal 1978, p. 676; *e.g., United States v. Adams* 1969). Moreover, the presence of some mental disorder or a prior admission to a mental institution should not alone serve as proof of incompetence (*Newman v. Missouri* 1974). Nor should the competency standard be confused with the legal criteria for involuntary commitment to a mental hospital under a state's civil commitment statute.

Even if a defendant is competent to stand trial, the issue of his competency to participate at other stages of the criminal proceeding may arise. Thus, before accepting a plea of guilty or nolo contendere, the court may be obligated to determine the defendant's competence to plead (*e.g., Suggs v. LaVallee* 1978; *United States v. Masthers* 1976). In making this determination most courts employ the same standard used for determining competence to stand trial (*e.g., Allard v. Helegmoe* 1978; *Malinauskas v. United States* 1974; *People v. Heral* 1976), although a minority require a higher degree of competence to plead guilty (*Sieling v. Eyman* 1973; *see* Duke Law Journal 1974). Similarly, when a defendant seeks to waive counsel and represent himself, the court must determine his competence to do so. The standard of competence to waive counsel is considered stricter than the general standard for competence to stand trial. (*United States ex rel. Konigsberg v. Vincent* 1975; *Westbrook v. Arizona* 1966).

INVOKING THE INCOMPETENCY STATUS

Raising the Issue

Virtually every defendant who seems mentally ill at the time of the criminal proceedings will be ordered examined for competence. The issue typically is raised at arraignment or other initial appearance, but may be raised at any point in the criminal process (Harvard Law Review

1967, p. 454; Stone 1975, pp. 200–01). Indeed a defendant may be competent at the commencement of his trial, but become incompetent during the proceedings. The Supreme Court has cautioned that "a trial court must always be alert to circumstances suggesting a change that would render the accused unable to meet the standards of competence to stand trial" (*Drope v. Missouri* 1975, p. 181). Even where the issue arises for the first time at sentencing, the trial court must inquire into the issue before rendering sentence (*Wojtowicz v. United States* 1977, p. 790).

In practice, the issue of the accused's competence is most frequently raised on motion by the defendant's counsel. The prosecutor also may bring the issue to the court's attention by seeking a determination of competency. Someone removed from the court proceeding may initially identify the problem. For example, the arresting officer may indicate in his arrest report that the individual appears to be mentally ill. A defendant's family or friends may disclose a prior history of mental health problems; jail officials may comment on a defendant's bizarre behavior in detention. In such cases, counsel for the defense or for the state typically will inquire further and seek from the court an evaluation of the defendant's competency.

On occasion, the court will raise the issue itself. Indeed, the Supreme Court has held that a trial judge has a duty to raise the issue *sua sponte* when the evidence before the court raises a bona fide doubt as to the defendant's competency (*Drope v. Missouri* 1975; *Pate v. Robinson* 1966). Trial and conviction in such circumstances, without a determination of competency, even where the defendant does not raise the issue, violates due process, requiring reversal of any conviction obtained (*Drope v. Missouri* 1975; *Pate v. Robinson* 1966). Whenever reasonable grounds exist to question the defendant's competence, the court thus usually will order a formal evaluation. The Supreme Court has recognized that there are "no fixed or immutable signs which invariably indicate the need for further inquiry to determine fitness to proceed; the question is often a difficult one in which a wide range of manifestations and subtle nuances are implicated" (*Drope v. Missouri* 1975, p. 180).

The Competency Examination

Location of Evaluation

Once the court decides that competency evaluation is necessary, expert evaluators—usually psychiatrists but increasingly psychologists as well—are appointed to examine the defendant. Although several states authorize the examination to be performed on an outpatient basis (*e.g.*, Florida Rule of Criminal Procedure 3.210(b)(3); *Marcey v. Harris* 1968; Maryland Code Annotated Article 59, § 23; Massachusetts General Laws Annotated Chapter 123, § 15), in most jurisdictions the evaluation is performed in a hospital setting. (Halleck 1980, p. 229; Janis 1974, p. 728). Inpatient evaluation is unnecessary for all but a fraction of defendants (Bluestone & Melella 1979, p. 172; deGrazia 1974, p. 436 n. 14; Goldstein 1973, p. 1146; Roesch & Golding 1980, pp. 202–04; Stone 1975, pp. 209–20; Winick 1974, p. 2), is often unduly stigmatizing, and takes considerably longer than evaluation in a jail or a court clinic (Bluestone & Melella 1979, p. 176; Burt & Morris 1972, p. 88; Group for the Advancement of Psychiatry 1974, p. 906; Halleck 1980, pp 229–30; Wexler 1976, pp. 39–41). In addition, for those defendants who would otherwise be released on bail or other pretrial release provision, hospital evaluation necessitates a deprivation of liberty that usually is unnecessary. As a result, such defendants may attack their hospitalization for evaluation as a violation of the "least restrictive alternative" doctrine (*see* Chambers 1972; p. 16, *infra*), arguing that the state interest in performing a competency evaluation, however compelling, usually can be accomplished on an outpatient basis (Kaufman 1972, pp. 473–77; Mental Health Law Project 1978, pp. 622–23).

Period of Evaluation

Inpatient competency evaluation often has taken a lengthy period, usually more than 30 and sometimes as many as 80 days (Burt & Morris 1972, p. 88; Wexler 1976, p. 38). The Supreme Court's landmark competency decision in *Jackson v. Indiana* (1972) placed substantive due process limits on the duration of such commitments for evaluation, but specified only that they last no more than a "reasonable" time. With adequate resources, competency evaluation reasonably can be performed within several days or weeks (Burt & Morris 1972, p. 88). One court has specified a 60-day limit on evaluation (*State ex rel. Walker v. Jenkins* 1974, p. 357), and several states by statute have specified 20-day or other similar limits (*e.g.*, Florida Rule of Criminal Procedure 3.210(b); Ohio Revised Code Annotated § 2945.371(B)–(C)).

Presence of Counsel or Defense Psychiatrist at Examination

The examiner and the defendant are generally the only people present at the examination, although in some states attorneys for the state and for the defendant are permitted to be present (*e.g.*, Florida Rule of Criminal Procedure 3.210(b)). Most courts have rejected the contention that the competency examination is a critical stage in the proceedings for Sixth Amendment purposes and therefore subject to the right to counsel (*e.g., Davis v. Campbell* 1979; *United States ex rel. Stukes v. Shovlin* 1972; *United States v. Fletcher* 1971; *but see Thornton v. Corcoran* 1969, pp. 701–02). The Supreme Court recently held that a competency evaluation at which inquiry will extend to issues other than competency is a critical stage for Sixth Amendment purposes (*Estelle v. Smith* 1981). The psychiatrist in the case used the defendant's statements in the examination as the basis for his testimony, at a penalty hearing to determine whether the defendant should receive the death penalty, that the defendant was dangerous. The Court held that the defendant was entitled to consult with counsel prior to the interview on whether to submit to the examination, but indicated that the Sixth Amendment did not require the presence of counsel at the examination itself. On a related issue, several cases have rejected the contention that the defendant has the right to the presence of his own evaluator at the examination (*Proctor v. Harris* 1969; *United States v. Fletcher* 1971; *contra, State v. Whitlow* 1965).

Form of Examination

The examination may take several forms and last anywhere from about one-half hour to many hours. Regardless of the form of examination used, the examiner must apply the *Dusky* standard or its equivalent. The examiner typically performs a standard mental health evaluation of the defendant, including the taking of a history of the individual and a mental status examination. Sometimes a physical examination is performed as well, although this is rarely necessary for competency evaluation. In some cases court clinics or hospitals use a competency checklist or other assessment instrument (*see* p. 7, *supra*). Occasionally the evaluator, in probing the defendant's ability to assist his counsel in making a defense, will consult with defense counsel to determine the nature of the defense contemplated (Bukatman, Foy, & deGrazia 1971, pp. 1228–29).

Fifth Amendment Issues Relating to the Evaluation

Numerous decisions have concluded that a routine examination by a court-appointed expert does not violate the Fifth Amendment privilege against self-incrimination or require *Miranda* warnings (*e.g., Collins v. Auger* 1977; *Davis v. Campbell* 1979; *United States v. Albright* 1968; *United States v. Bohle* 1971; *United States v. Greene* 1974; *United States v. Handy* 1971; *United States v. Trapnell* 1974). The Supreme Court recently held that if the defendant's statements at the examination are to be used for any purpose other than determining his competency, he must be given *Miranda* warnings concerning this possible use (*Estelle v. Smith* 1981). If he objects, then the defendant still must submit to the examination, but the use of his statements will be restricted to determining his competency (*id.*). Thus, the Fifth Amendment does not bar a forced examination, but would prohibit the use at trial of incriminating statements made by the defendant during the examination. The expert examiner may testify concerning the defendant's mental status, but statements made by the defendant during the examination may not be introduced into evidence on the issue of guilt (*Lee v. County Court* 1971; Florida Rule of Criminal Procedure 3.211(e); *Gibson v. Zahradnick* 1978; United States Code, Title 18, § 40–44; *United States v. Alvarez* 1975; *United States v. Baird* 1969; *United States v. Reifsteck* 1976). Moreover, as the statements of a defendant required to submit to the examination are compelled within the meaning of the Fifth Amendment (*Estelle v. Smith* 1981), not only is their use for purposes of establishing the individual's guilt prohibited, but also derivative evidence to which such statements provide links or leads may not be used (Berry 1973; *Blaisdell v. Commonwealth* 1977, pp. 198–99). As the Fifth Amendment is implicated, such statement should not be admissible for purposes of impeachment (*Blaisdell v. Commonwealth* 1977, p. 198; *see Mincey v. Arizona* 1978).

The mental health professional performing the examination, as he is court-appointed, does not have a psychiatrist–patient or psychologist–patient relationship with the defendant. As a result, although the expert will not be required to give *Miranda* warnings in an examination in which the defendant's statements will be limited to the determination of his competence, professional ethics may dictate that he disclose to the defendant the limits of confidentiality in the examination.

BAIL OR PRE-TRIAL RELEASE DURING PERIOD OF EVALUATION

As a matter of practice, few defendants are granted bail or pre-trial release once an evaluation has been ordered (Burt & Morris 1972, p. 88; Roesch & Golding 1980, pp. 108–09; Slovenko 1977, p. 197). Some statutes, however, specifically contemplate that a defendant may be released on bail or on his own recognizance during the evaluation period (*e.g.*, Ohio Revised Code Annotated § 2945.371(D)). Other statutes, although a distinct minority, provide specifically that a motion for competency evaluation "shall not otherwise affect the defendant's right to pre-trial relase" (Florida Rule of Criminal Procedure 3.210(b)(3)).

The mere filing of a motion for competency evaluation should not necessarily affect the freedom from custody of a defendant either already on bail or other pre-trial release or seeking such release. The provisions specifically authorizing bail provide that the court may order the defendant to appear at a designated place for evaluation as a condition of release (Florida Rule of Criminal Procedure 3.210(b)(3); Ohio Revised Code Annotated § 2945.371(B)). The automatic no-bail policy still followed in practice in many jurisdictions seems clearly inconsistent with the Supreme Court's opinion in *Stack v. Boyle* (1951, p. 5), construing the Eighth Amendment's prohibition on excessive bail to require that restrictive bail be justified as "relevant to the purpose of assuring the presence of the defendant" at trial. Unless the defendant's mental condition (or some other factor) suggests he will not appear for subsequent proceedings, or for evaluation as to his competency, pre-trial release is appropriate, and should be made available on the same basis as with other defendants (*see* Burt & Morris 1972, p. 88; Gobert 1973, p. 671; Mental Health Law Project 1978, pp. 620–21; *United States v. Curry* 1969).

THE COMPETENCY HEARING

After the experts have completed their evaluation of the defendant, they typically prepare written reports for submission to court, with copies to the attorneys for the state and the defense. If the reports are unanimous in their conclusions as to competence, the prosecution and defense may stipulate to accept them, in which case a formal hearing may be avoided in most states. If not, a hearing will be held at which the attorneys have an opportunity to offer evidence and examine the witnesses, including the examining experts. A statute permitting the court summarily to determine competency based on the examiners' reports if neither counsel contested them was held to deny due process to a defendant who himself wished to contest the reports (*State ex rel. Matalik v. Schubert* 1973). The court held that due process requires a prompt and meaningful hearing for the determination of competency, including the right to counsel, notice of the hearing, the right to introduce evidence contradicting the examiners' reports, and sworn testimony subject to cross-examination (*id.*).

In most jurisdictions the competency issue is decided by the court, although some permit a jury determination (Slovenko 1977, p. 168). The right to jury trial is not held to apply (*Hall v. United States* 1969; *United States v. Holmes* 1971, p. 267; *United States v. Huff* 1969), even where a jury is used in civil commitment (*State ex rel. Matalik v. Schubert* 1973; *but see Gomez v. Miller* 1972; Gobert 1973, p. 673).

The ultimate determination of the defendant's competence is within the discretion of the trial judge. Although the court need not follow the recommendations of the appointed experts, it generally does so. In fact, the literature documents the tendency of judges rarely to disagree with recommendations of mental health professionals (Rosenburg & McGarry 1972, pp. 1092–95; Steadman 1979; pp. 54, 56; Vann & Morganroth 1965, pp. 2–3,9). Notwithstanding this tendency to defer to the "expert," the cases emphasize that the competency decision is not a psychiatric judgment, but a legal one that must be reached independently by the judge (*United States v. Davis* 1966, p. 256; *United States v. Makris* 1976, p. 908; *United States v. Sermon* 1964, p. 974).

The states follow differing approaches on the question of who bears the burden of proof with respect to competency. In some states, where defendant seeks a finding of incompetence, the burden of proof is on the defense and must be carried by a preponderance of the evidence (*e.g.*, *Brown v. State* 1971, p. 71). In other states the burden of proving incompetence is placed on the defense regardless of who raises the issue (*e.g.*, *State v. Aumann* 1978). Other jurisdictions impose the burden on the prosecution of showing, by a preponderance of the evidence, that the defendant is competent (*People v. Carl* 1977; *United States v. DiGilio* 1976, p. 988; *see* Iowa Law Review 1979). Some have suggested that the court, rather than either of the parties, should bear the burden of determining competence. (Pizzi 1977, pp. 55–57, 66). The Mental Health Law Project has suggested that the party asserting incompetency should bear the burden of proof by a preponderance of the evidence (Mental Health Law Project 1978, p. 264).

DISPOSITION AND LEGAL RIGHTS OF THE INCOMPETENT DEFENDANT

DISPOSITION

If the court determines that the defendant is competent to stand trial, the criminal proceedings are resumed. If, however, the defendant is found incompetent, the defendant is remanded for psychiatric treatment designed to restore him to competence. Although a number of states authorize treatment of the incompetent defendant on an outpatient basis (*e.g.*, Florida Rule of Criminal Procedure 3.212(c); Illinois Revised Statutes Chapter 38, § 1005-2-2; Kansas Code of Criminal Procedure § 22-3303; Maryland Code Annotated Article 59, § 24), many still provide for automatic hospitalization. In the early 1970s the overshelming majority of states automatically committed the incompetent defendant (Brakel & Rock 1971, pp. 415, 444–50, Table 11.2; Janis 1974, p. 729), and 19 states and the District of Columbia still do (Roesch & Golding 1979, p. 357).

This practice of automatic hospitalization is questionable as a matter of policy and may be unconstitutional under the "least restrictive alternative" doctrine (Stone 1975, p. 212; Wexler 1976, pp. 40–41; *see United Staes v. Klein* 1963). For further discussion of the implications of the "least restrictive alternative" principle on competency commitment, see p. 16, *infra*.

RIGHT TO TREATMENT

The purpose of court-ordered mental health treatment for the incompetent defendant is to restore him to sufficient competence to stand trial, not necessarily to cure him of his mental illness. As the purpose of commiting the defendant found incompetent to stand trial is treatment designed to restore him to capacity, the Supreme Court in the landmark case of *Jackson v. Indiana* (1972, p. 738) held that such commitment must be justified by treatment that makes it substantially probable "that he will attain that capacity in the foreseeable future." If such treatment is not forthcoming or if treatment would not afford the defendant a substantial probability of restoration to competence, then commitment violates substantive due process (*Jackson v. Indiana* 1972, p. 738).

Jackson thus provides support for the argument that defendants committed on the basis of trial incompetence have a constitutional right to treatment (Gobert 1973, pp. 684–85; Mental Health Law Project 1978, p. 625). If treatment afforded at the state hospital is inadequate to achieve the goal of expeditious restoration to competence, then such hospitalization can be attacked as a violation of the defendant's constitutional right to treatment (*see Wyatt v. Stickney* 1972), as well as his Fourteenth Amendment right to liberty (*see O'Connor v. Donaldson* 1975). Unfortunately, many state hospital forensic wards, grossly understaffed and underfunded, do not meet this standard (Gobert 1973, pp. 663–64). In fact the Supreme Court itself recognized this in *Jackson*, expressing "substantial doubts about whether the rationale of pre-trial commitment—that care or treatment will aid the accused in attaining competency—is empirically valid given the state of most of our mental institutions" (p. 735).

RIGHT TO THE LEAST RESTRICTIVE ALTERNATIVE: COMMUNITY ALTERNATIVES TO HOSPITALIZATION OR HOSPITALIZATION IN LESS THAN A MAXIMUM SECURITY INSTITUTION

Although several states authorize outpatient treatment of an incompetent defendant in community mental health facilities or private treatment by a mental health professional (*e.g.*, Florida Rule of Criminal Procedure 3.212(b)(1),(c); Illinois Revised Statutes, Chapter 38, § 1005-2-2; Ohio Revised Code Annotated § 2945.38(D)), many follow a practice of automatic commitment of such defendants to state institutions, typically maximum-security institutions for the "criminally insane." As mental hospitalization involves a massive deprivation of the fundamental right to liberty (*Addington v. Texas* 1979; *Humphrey v. Cady* 1972; *Jackson v. Indiana* 1972; *Vitek v. Jones* 1980), such confinement may be justified only if necessary to accomplish a compelling state interest. Even though the state interest in treating the defendant in order to restore him to trial competence is compelling, in many cases hospitalization is not necessary to accomplish this (Group for the Advancement of Psychiatry 1974, p. 907; Stone 1975, p. 212; Wexler 1976, pp. 40–41). Under the "least restrictive alternative" doctrine (*see Ashe v. Robinson* 1971; Chambers 1972; *Covington v. Harris* 1969, p. 623; *Davis v. Watkins* 1974, p. 1203; *Kesselbrenner v. Anonymous* 1973, p. 905; *Welsch v. Likens* 1974), where outpatient treatment is at least as effective as hospitalization in effecting a particular defendant's restoration to trial competence, hospitalization, involving a greater deprivation of the defendant's constitutional rights, would seem constitutionally offensive (*DeAngelas v. Plant* 1980; Janis 1974, p. 738; Steinberg 1978, pp. 11–20).

Even where hospitalization is required because of the lack of available outpatient treatment programs or where outpatient care is deemed less efficacious, hospitalization in a maximum-security institution for the "criminally insane" is itself constitutionally suspect. Since incompetent defendants at the pre-trial stage of their proceedings have not been convicted or sentenced, they may not be punished consistent with due process (*Bell v. Wolfish* 1979) or placed in correctional institutions, at least absent a finding of dangerousness (Mental Health Law Project 1978, p. 626). Rather, they ordinarily should be treated at civil facilities under the supervision of a state department of mental health, rather than a department of corrections (Mental Health Law Project 1978, p. 626; Wexler 1976, pp. 40–41). Most incompetent defendants are nondangerous (*see* Stone 1975, p. 212) or have never been adjudicated to be dangerous pursuant to procedures comparable to those required for involuntary commitment on this basis for civil patients. To require hospitalization in a maximum-security institution absent such a finding would thus seem violative of equal protection (*Johnson v. Brelje* 1979; *see Baxtrom v. Herold* 1966; Gobert 1973, p. 673; *Jackson v. Indiana* 1972), as well as the least restrictive alternative principle.

RIGHT TO REFUSE TREATMENT

A growing body of recent case law and commentary recognizes the right of competent mental patients and prisoners to refuse mental health treatment (*e.g.*, Friedman 1975; *Kaimowitz v. Dept. of Mental Health* 1973; *Knecht v. Gillman* 1973; Plotkin 1977; *Rogers v. Okin* 1980; Schwitzgebel 1979; Shapiro 1974; Wexler 1973; Winick 1981). Such a right has been derived from a variety of constitutional sources: a First Amendment right to be free of interference with mental processes (*e.g.*, *Kaimowitz v. Dept. of Mental Health* 1973; *Rogers v. Okin* 1979; *Scott v. Plante* 1976), the right to privacy protected by Fourteenth Amendment substantive due process (*Davis v. Hubbard* 1980; *Kaimowitz v. Dept. of Mental Health* 1973; *Rennie v. Klein* 1978; *Rogers v. Okin* 1979), Fourteenth Amendment procedural due process (*e.g.*, *Rennie v. Klein* 1979; *Scott v. Plante* 1976; *Winters v. Miller* 1971), the First Amendment right to the free exercise of religion in the case of religious-based refusals of treatment (*Dyer v. Brooks* 1976; *In re Boyd* 1979; *Winters v. Miller* 1971), and the right to be free of cruel and unusual punishment protected by the Eighth Amendment (*e.g.*, *Knecht v. Gillman* 1973; *MacKey v. Procunier* 1973). The Supreme Court, in a 1982 case involving the right of civilly committed patients to refuse psychotropic drugs, avoided the opportunity of addressing the right to refuse question (*Mills v. Rogers* 1982).

Even if a defendant found incompetent to stand trial has a fundamental right, derived from one or more of these constitutional sources, to refuse treatment, the state may nonetheless be able to insist that the defendant accept treatment. Even fundamental constitutional rights are not absolute and in appropriate cases must be subordinated to overriding state interests. Here the justification for imposed treatment is accomplishment of the state's interest in restoring the defendant to competency so that he may be tried. The state's substantial interest in bringing to trial defendants accused in good faith and on probable cause of violating its laws—an interest in "the integrity of its criminal justice system" '(Shapiro 1974, p. 300 n.215) and therefore at the very core of its police power (*see Kelley v. Johnson* 1976, p. 247)—would seemingly be counted as sufficiently compelling to outweigh the defendant's interest in refusing treatment necessary to restore him to competency (Winick 1977, pp. 812–13).

However, a defendant, by invoking the "least restrictive alternative" principle, may be able to challenge imposition of a particular treatment on the basis that alternative treatment methods that intrude less on his consitutional rights should be tried before a more intrusive technique is used (*In re Boyd* 1979, p. 753; *Rennie v. Klein* 1978, p. 1146; *Rogers v. Okin* 1980; Winick 1977, p. 813; Winick 1981, pp. 376–83). In *Rennie v. Klein* (1978), the court applied the least restrictive alternative doctrine in the context of a mental patient's attempt to refuse a particular therapy, permitting the patient to resist antipsychotic medication. The court found that lithium plus an antidepressant drug, to which the patient raised no objection, presented a less intrusive treatment program than the antipsychotic medication proposed by the hospital, and ordered that the hospital attempt treatment with lithium and the antidepressant before antipsychotic medication could be administered. As *Rennie* illustrates, applying the least restrictive alternative principle to choices of therapy involves difficult empirical questions concerning the efficacy of the various treatment techniques (*see* Roth & Applebaum 1982), as well as substantial value judgments concerned with the ranking of the various treatments in terms of their respective intrusions on constitutional rights. (For an attempt to rank the various therapies on a continuum, *see* Winick 1981.) Of course, in applying the least restrictive principle, only therapies that are regarded as likely to be effective in restoring a particular defendant to competency would be considered as alternatives that would accomplish the state's compelling interest (Winick 1977, p. 813).

The right to refuse treatment issue in the competency context is likely to be asserted frequently by defendants seeking to refuse psychotropic drugs, continuation of which, psychiatrists predict, is necessary to maintain the defendant's competence (Winick 1977, pp. 808–14). One court has suggested that a defendant restored to competency by drugs could assert a right to discontinue them and waive in advance his due process objection to trial while incompetent should discontinuation deprive him of his competence (*State v. Hayes* 1978; *see* Winick 1977, p. 814).

Right of Incompetent Defendant to Attack Indictment or Raise Certain Defenses

Although at common law the criminal process was suspended once the defendant was found incompetent, today some states permit a limited continuation of the proceedings to determine whether the prosecution has sufficient admissible evidence to bring the defendant to trial for the crime charged (Kentucky Law Journal 1978, p. 677; *see, e.g.,* California Penal Code § 1368.1). Four states permit a type of provisional trial in which a defendant may present a defense to the charges and the court may dismiss the indictment (Roesch & Golding 1979, pp. 362–63).

As it is the pending charge that serves as the justification for requiring the incompetent defendant to undergo treatment and frequently hospitalization, at a minimum the defendant's attorney should be permitted, even during the period of his client's incompetence, to attack the indictment or otherwise to raise defenses that may be determined without his client's presence and participation. Unfortunately, attorneys, particularly overworked public defenders (who frequently represent the incompetent defendant), tend to lose track of their incompetent clients following commitment (Gobert 1973, p. 666; Golten 1972, p. 408). Even though the criminal proceedings are suspended by the defendant's adjudication of incompetence, counsel has a continuing responsibility to protect his client's rights (American Bar Association Code of Professional Responsibility, E.C. 2–31). The Supreme Court in *Jackson v. Indiana* (1972, p. 741), recognized counsel's continuing responsibility, stating that "[w]e do not read this court's previous decisions to preclude the states from allowing, at a minimum, an incompetent defendant to raise certain defenses such as insufficiency of the indictment, or make certain pretrial motions through counsel."

Counsel for an incompetent defendant should thus be encouraged to make all possible motions on his client's behalf that are susceptible of determination without his client's personal participation and presence (Model Penal Code § 4.06(3)). A number of states have statutorily recognized the ability of counsel to attack the indictment or raise certain defenses (*e.g.*, California Penal Code § 1368.1; New York Criminal Procedure Law § 730.60(4)). Purely legal issues that can be considered on pretrial motion, such as sufficiency of the indictment or information, the constitutionality of the statute under which the defendant is charged, and challenges to the composition of the grand jury, should be raised whenever possible (*see* Foote 1960, p. 841). Moreover, motions to suppress evidence, to controvert a search warrant, or to challenge identification testimony often can be made and resolved without the defendant's personal participation. Such motions may result in the dismissal of charges against the defendant, thereby depriving the state of its basis for hospitalizing him or ordering him treated in an outpatient facility and requiring that the defendant either be released from treatment or be civilly committed (Janis 1974, p. 731).

TERMINATING THE INCOMPETENCY STATUS

PERIODIC REVIEW

Until about 15 years ago defendants hospitalized for incompetency to stand trial received what in effect was an indeterminate sentence of confinement in a security mental hospital (Gobert 1973, p. 685; Wexler 1976, p. 38). Of course, if it became apparent that a defendant was restored to competency, he would be returned to court. But many defendants were never restored to competency and some that were remained institutionalized for lengthy periods, their improvement either not coming to the attention of hospital staff or being ignored by them. McGarry's study of defendants in Massachusetts committed as incompetent to stand trial revealed that few had ever been returned to trial as competent, although many, on examination, were found to be so (1969, pp. 50–51). At one hospital, there appeared to be a bias against returning defendants to trial, the presumption being that a patient was incompetent until he demonstrated his competence. This perhaps common attitude of hospital staff was compounded by the generally prevailing lack of clinical resources at such facilities. Indeed, these maximum security facilities are "typically the worst institution in the state" (Stone 1975, p. 209). These "hospitals" were (and to some extent still are) little more than grim store-houses in which treatment was grossly inadequate. (Brooks 1974, pp. 397–99; Matthews 1970, p. 134). Defendants committed to such institutions as incompetent to stand trial typically were confined for lengthy periods, often exceeding the maximum sentence for the crime alleged (Engelberg 1967, p. 165; Hess & Thomas 1963, p. 716; Special Committee 1968, pp. 72–73), and occasionally lasting a lifetime (Harvard Law Review 1967, p. 456; Hess & Thomas 1963, pp. 717–18; McGarry, Curran, & Kenefick 1968, p. 44; Special Committee 1968, pp. 214–15; Stone 1975, p. 203).

As a result of a 1972 Supreme Court decision, this picture has changed drastically. In *Jackson v. Indiana* (1972), the Court ruled unconstitutional the indefinite confinement of defendants committed as incompetent to stand trial pursuant to procedures and standards that differed substantially from those employed for the commitment of civil mental patients. The Court held that equal protection was violated by treating the incompetent defendant differently than the civilly committed patient, rejecting the contention that pending criminal charges or the determination of incompetency could justify differential treatment. The Court also held that the commitment of the defendant, a mentally defective deaf mute whose restoration to competency was thought unlikely, violated substantive due process. "[A]t the least," the Court held, "due process requires that the nature and duration of commitment bear some reasonable relation to the purpose for which the individual is committed" (p. 737). As a result, the Court held that a defendant committed solely on account of his incapacity to stand trial "cannot be held more than a reasonable period of time necessary to determine whether there is a substantial probability that he will attain that capacity in the foreseeable future" (pp. 737–38). The Court further required that any continued confinement of an incompetent defendant must be based on a probability that he will be returned to trial and could only be justified by progress toward that goal. If no substantial probability exists that a defendant will be restored to competency within the foreseeable future, or if the treatment provided does not succeed in advancing him toward that goal, then, the Court held, the state either must institute customary civil commitment proceedings, if it wishes to detain the defendant further, or must release him (p. 738).

Jackson has resulted in a substantial revision of incompetency commitment procedures in many states. Some state procedures have been revised to mandate as conditions of hospitalization not only a finding of incompetence, but also a prediction that hospitalization will result in a restoration to competency within a reasonable time. Moreover, many require periodic review of the defendant's progress toward restoration to competence (*e.g.*, California Penal Code § 1370; Florida Rule of Criminal Procedure 3.212(b); Ohio Revised Code Annotated § 2945.38). Many states, however, have not as yet effectively responded to *Jackson*. A 1979 survey found that almost one-half of the jurisdictions still permitted indefinite commitment without requiring periodic review (Roesch & Golding 1979, p. 357). Substantial statutory change in many states is thus needed to comply with the constitutional requirements of *Jackson*. For discussion of a recently revised Florida statute and court rule providing extensive procedures for the disposition of the incompetent defendant, *see* Winick and DeMeo (1980).

DURATIONAL LIMIT ON INCOMPETENCY COMMITMENT

How long is the maximum period that a defendant may be hospitalized based on incompetency to stand trial? In *Jackson*, the Supreme Court declined "to prescribe arbitrary time limits" in view of the lack of evidence in the record before it (p. 178). Knowledgeable observers have suggested that six months should be more than sufficient time within which to restore most defendants to competence, as this is the maximum length of time normally required to treat most civilly committed patients in hospitals (Burt & Morris 1972, pp. 90–92; Group for the Advancement of Psychiatry 1974, p. 907; Roesch & Golding 1980, pp. 208–09; Stone 1975, p. 212). In their view, after six months the vast majority of incompetent defendants will either be restored to competence or it wll be clear that such restoration is unlikely (*id.*). An additional six-month period is suggested for a small residual category of defendants not clearly permanently incompetent and for whom an additional period of treatment seems promising (Group for the Advancement of Psychiatry 1974, p. 908; Stone 1975, pp. 212–13).

Although most states do not impose such a durational limit on incompetency commitment, several have statutes limiting the term either to a "reasonable period" or to a term of 6, 12, 15, or 18 months (Janis 1974, p. 731; Roesch & Golding 1979, p. 357; Slovenko 1977, p. 174). Several state courts have judicially imposed similar time limits (*e.g.*, *State ex rel. Haskins v. County Court* 1974). The federal practice has been an 18-month period (*see Cook v. Ciccone* 1970; *Drendel v. United States* 1968). After this period has expired, any further hospital commitment must be in accordance with the state's civil commitment statute or with a special statute for incompetent defendants containing substantially similar standards. (*But see Altman v. Hofferber* 1980.)

One court has held that the state has no legitimate interest in incompetency commitment beyond the maximum sentence term authorized for the offense charged, and that confinement beyond this point would therefore violate due process (*In re Banks* 1979). Some states provide by statute that incompetency commitment may not exceed a maximum sentence for the offense charged (Slovenko 1977, p. 174; *e.g.,* Louisiana Code of Criminal Procedure Article 648; Massachusettes General Laws Ch. 123, § 16(f); *State ex rel. Deisinger v. Treffert* 1978), or a portion of such maximum sentence, such as two thirds (New York Code of Criminal Procedure § 730.50(5)). In New York a defendant charged with a misdemeanor may be committed for no longer than 90 days (New York Code of Criminal Procedure § 730.50(1)). Such a durational limit on commitment in misdemeanor cases is especially important as without it a real hardship can be imposed on minor offenders who are increasingly subjected to the incompetency commitment route (*see* Dickey 1980). In addition, some states, recognizing that once charges have been dropped, the rationale for incompetency commitment no longer exists, require that the defendant be released or civilly committed if the indictment is dismissed (Janis 1974, p. 731).

PSYCHOTROPIC MEDICATION AND COMPETENCY

Psychotropic medication is perhaps the most widely used and most effective treatment technique for the psychiatric conditions resulting in incompetence to stand trial (Group for the Advancement of Psychiatry 1974, p. 901; Hollister 1972; Winick 1977). As a result, many defendants adjudicated incompetent and treated either in the hospital or in the community will be restored to competency by use of these drugs. Many will require ongoing medication to maintain their competence. Yet some courts, mistakenly assuming that psychotropic drugs produce a "chemical sanity" that is unacceptable for participation in a trial, automatically prohibit the return for trial of defendants under the influence of such drugs (Winick 1977, pp. 774–76). This automatic approach, however, has been rejected by the appellate courts to have considered the issue (*e.g., People v. Dalfanso* 1974; *State v. Hampton* 1969; *United States v. Hayes* 1979), as well as by a number of recent statutes (*e.g.*, Florida Statutes § 925.22(1); Ohio Revised Code Annotated § 2945.37). It was also recently criticized by the Task Panel on Legal and Ethical Issues of the President's Commission on Mental Health (1978, pp. 1459–60).

Of course, if the medication does not succeed in restoring the defendant to competence, or if its side effects materially interfere with his ability to understand the nature of the proceedings or to assist in his defense, then he should not be deemed competent (Winick 1977, p. 815; *e.g.*, *Whitehead v. Wainwright* 1978). A defendant brought to trial on psychotropic medication should, if he wishes, receive an explanatory jury instruction regarding such medication and its effects (Burt & Morris 1972, p. 86; Group for the Advancement of Psychiatry 1974, p. 904). Such an instruction would be particularly appropriate in the case of a defendant raising an insanity defense. The jury, observing the defendant in an artificially calm state—the bizzarre symptoms of his mental illness kept in check by the medication—might otherwise find it difficult to believe he was mentally ill at the time of the crime (*see In re Pray* 1975; *State v. Jojola* 1976; *State v. Murphy* 1960). For discussion of a defendant's ability to refuse psychotropic medication which psychiatrists believe is necessary to maintain his competence, *see* pp. 16–18 *supra*; Winick 1977, pp. 808–14).

LEGAL CONSEQUENCES OF AN INCOMPETENCY ADJUDICATION

RETURN TO TRIAL, RELEASE, OR CIVIL COMMITMENT

Under *Jackson v. Indiana* (1972), a defendant adjudicated incompetent must, within a reasonable period of time, either be restored to competence and returned to trial, civilly committed pursuant to the state's civil commitment statute, or released. If restored to competency and returned to trial, the criminal proceedings will be resumed. If civilly committed, the same standards and procedures applicable to civil mental patients must be followed (*but see Altman v. Hofferber* 1980). Many permanently incompetent defendants will meet the criteria for civil commitment and accordingly will be hospitalized. Once committed, they will enjoy the same rights (right to treatment, right to least restrictive alternative, right to refuse treatment, right to communicate, etc.) as other patients. Where criminal charges for such permanently incompetent defendants have not been dismissed (in the majority of jurisdictions), such civil commitment may be accompanied by criminal detainers or hold orders, frequently leading to confinement in secure wards or institutions (Wexler 1975, pp. 41–42).

DISMISSAL OF CHARGES

Although *Jackson v. Indiana* (1972) imposed a durational limit on incompetency commitment, on the facts before it the Court declined to require the dismissal of criminal charges following the termination of the period of incompetency commitment (pp. 739–40). The Court, did, however, recognize that in some cases dismissal might be required on either speedy trial or due process grounds (p. 739). Although some states provide for a dismissal of charges (*e.g.*, Ohio Revised Code Annotated § 2945.38(G)), and several permit the courts to dismiss the charges if so much time has passed that a new trial would be unjust (Janis 1974, p. 732; *e.g.*, Hawaii Revised Statutes § 704–406(2)), most jurisdictions continue to leave the criminal charges outstanding (Roesch & Golding 1979, p. 363). In fact, several states permit the refiling of charges against a defendant whose charges were dismissed and who subsequently is declared competent to stand trial (Florida Rule of Criminal Procedure 3.214(a); Florida Statutes § 925.24). Most jurisdictions will decline to dismiss charges, or will provide for their possible revival if dismissed, out of a concern expressed by one judge who commented that "[t]his court is aware of many criminal cases where defendants have made seemingly miraculous recoveries after pending criminal charges have been dropped" (*United States v. Lancaster* 1976, p. 229).

Shortly after *Jackson v. Indiana* (1972) was decided, Florida revised its rules of criminal procedure to provide that defendants who were permanently incompetent would be adjudicated not guilty by reason of insanity (Florida Rule of Criminal Procedure 3.210(a)(5) (1972)). As a not guilty by reason of insanity acquittal is frequently a desirable one for defendants charged with serious crimes who lack other defenses, and as the insanity defense rarely succeeds with juries, defendants in Florida responded behaviorally to this change in rule by remaining clinically and legally incompetent for lengthy periods. The rule thus produced a "contingency structure" inducing continued incompetency on the part of some defendants who sought to take advantage of the "secondary gains" of continuing to play the sick role (*see* Wexler 1976, p. 41; Wexler 1981, pp. 121–22). This rule was changed in 1977 and Florida law now permits the dismissal of charges against a defendant who remains incompetent after a lengthy period (five years in the case of a felony; one year in the case of a misdemeanor), but provides that such charges subsequently may be refiled against a defendant who later is retored to competence (*see* Winick & DeMeo 1980, pp. 59–61).

SPEEDY TRIAL AND DUE PROCESS LIMITS ON THE INCOMPETENCY COMMITMENT

Although declining to require a dismissal of charges against a permanently incompetent defendant, the Supreme Court in *Jackson v. Indiana* noted that such dismissal might be justified in particular cases on grounds of the Sixth Amendment right to a speedy trial or for denial of due process inherent in holding pending criminal charges indefinitely over the head of one who never will have a chance to prove his innocence (1972, pp. 739–40). In at least some cases in which a defendant is brought to trial after a lengthy period of incompetency, a speedy trial defense might well be successful. Although few cases raise the issue, assertions of the defense in this context are likely to increase.

The leading Supreme Court speedy trial decision adopted a balancing test for determining violation of the right (*Barker v. Wingo* 1972). Four factors were identified by the Court to be considered on a case-by-case basis: the length of the delay, the reason for the delay, the defendant's assertion of his right, and prejudice to the defendant. Under the first factor there must be a sufficient period of delay to trigger further inquiry. A period in excess of one year certainly would seem sufficient. Once such a period has passed, the courts, under the second *Barker* factor, must inquire into the reason for the delay. In this regard, *Barker* distinguished between "deliberate" attempts by the government to hamper the defense, which "should be weighted heavily against the government," a "more neutral reason such as negligence or overcrowded courts," which "should be weighted less heavily," and a "valid reason, such as a missing witness," which "should serve to justify appropriate delay" (pp. 530–32). A reasonable period of evaluation and treatment for competence to stand trial traditionally has been deemed a valid reason excusing delay (*e.g., Germany v. Hudspeth* 1954; *Johnson v. United States* 1964; *United States v. Cartano,* 1970; *United States v. Lancaster* 1976). However, unreasonable periods of delay should not be excused. In this connection, the courts have recognized that the "primary responsibility for bringing [a defendant] to a speedy trial rest[s] squarely on the state . . . [and that a requested competency evaluation does] not shift, in whole or in part, the state's continuing responsibility to try [the defendant] speedily" (*McGraw v. State* 1976, p. 50). The prosecution "may not justify a delay merely by citing the defendant's incompetence" (*United States v. Geelan* 1975). "The government must carefully and vigilantly protect the interests of both the incompetent individual and society" (*id.*). As the period of hospitalization for incompetence lengthens, the prosecutor's burden increases (*id.* at 589). Thus the prosecutor should bear a greater responsibility to see that a defendant committed as incompetent is not simply forgotten but is returned for trial as expeditiously as possible.

The third *Barker* factor is the defendant's assertion of his right to a speedy trial. Although nonassertion of the right does not constitute waiver, the Court recognized that failure to assert the right "will make it difficult for a defendant to prove that he was denied a speedy trial" (p. 532). The final factor cited by *Barker* is prejudice to the defendant, although the Court "expressly rejected the notion that an affirmative demonstration of prejudice was necessary to prove a denial of the constitutional right to a speedy trial" (*Moore v. Arizona*, 1973, p. 26). Moreover, "where the defendant has established a prima facie case of denial of the speedy trial right, the burden is on the state to show that the defendant has not been prejudiced by the delay" (*Prince v. Alabama* 1975, p. 707). "[P]rejudice is immaterial where consideration of the other three factors—length of delay, defendant's assertion of his right, and reasons for the delay—coalesce in the defendant's favor" (*Hoskins v. Wainwright* 1973; *Prince v. Alabama* 1975, p. 707).

Barker identified three types of prejudice against which the speedy trial right was designed to protect: oppressive pre-trial incarceration, anxiety and concern of the accused, and the possibility that the defense will be impaired (pp. 532–33). Clearly, any period of unnecessary hospitalization constitutes oppressive pre-trial detention within the meaning of *Barker*. And, as already noted, the maximum security facilities to which incompetent defendants are sent are "typically the worst institutions in the state" (Stone 1975, p. 209). They frequently provide such poor care, restrictive custody, deprivations, hardships, and indignities that many inmates would prefer a prison setting (*see* Brakel & Rock 1971, p. 407; Steadman 1979, pp. 8–9; *United States ex rel. Schuster v. Herald* 1969).

In addition, periods of unnecessary hospitalization would certainly provoke considerable anxiety and concern. Concern about the outcome of pending charges on the part of defendants hospitalized for incompetence has been recognized to be antitherapeutic, potentially posing an overwhelming obstacle to the patient's improvement (Group for the Advancement of Psychiatry 1974, p. 905). The final type of prejudice mentioned in *Barker*—the possibility of impairment of the defense— although usually the most serious type, is not one that must necessarily be shown to make out a violation of the speedy trial right (*Moore v. Arizona* 1973, pp. 26–27). Lengthy incompetency commitment may well, however, impair the defendant's ability to defend. A defendant hospitalized for a lengthy period far from family, friends or counsel, necessarily making difficult the gathering of evidence, location and interviewing of witnesses, and similar trial preparation, may well be hampered in the making of a defense (Winick 1977, p. 804). A defense of sanity, often appropriate for the defendant so mentally ill as to be declared incompetent, is especially hampered by the passage of time, making difficult the proof of defendant's mental state at the time of the crime (*United States v. Geelan* 1975, p. 589; *United States v. Morgan* 1977, pp. 497–98; *Williams v. United States* 1957, pp. 22–24). As a result of factors such as these, some courts have granted dismissals for violation of the right to speedy trial in cases involving incompetent defendants confined for lengthy periods (*United States v. Pardue* 1973; *Williams v. United States* 1957; *see United States ex rel. von Wolfersdorf v. Johnson* 1970; *United States v. Jackson* 1969). In a recent case involving more than six years of oppressive pretrial delay during which an incompetent defendant underwent repeated periods of remission and relapse, a Florida court sidestepped the speedy trial question, but ordered a dismissal of charges on due process grounds (*Garrett v. State* 1980).

SENTENCE CREDIT FOR TIME SPENT HOSPITALIZED FOR INCOMPETENCY

A defendant adjudged incompetent to stand trial and committed to a hospital for treatment may spend a considerable period of time in the facility before he is restored to competence and returned for trial. Most jurisdictions credit such time spent hospitalized against sentence (*e.g.*, California Penal Code § 1375.5; Ohio Revised Code Annotated § 2945.38(I)), although a minority do not (*e.g.*, *Dalton v. State* 1978). Even where such sentence credit is not explicitly provided by statute, it is likely that at least some sentencing judges and parole boards take this factor into account (*see* Kentucky Law Journal 1978, p. 678; Steadman 1979, p. 98–99).

DEVELOPING LEGAL ISSUES FOR THE 1980s

A considerable number of the legal rights, both statutory and constitutional, that defendants involved in the incompetency process have or arguably should have, are rarely asserted by such defendants or their counsel. Even though almost 10 years have passed since the Supreme Court's decision in *Jackson v. Indiana* (1972), placing substantial constitutional limits on the state's power to commit the incompetent defendant, these limitations are not faithfully followed in many areas (Slovenko 1977, p. 174). Neither judicial decisions nor the statutory pronouncements of the legislature are self-executing. Incompetent defendants often are unaware of their rights or lack the initiative or resources to assert them. Defense counsel all too frequently neglect their incompetent clients once they have been committed.

As a result, many of the rights discussed in this chapter are theoretical only at this point. However, developments in the 1980s may well change this. Increasing attention is being given to the needs of mental patients for adequate legal representation. Special mental health advocacy programs providing counsel and paraprofessional assistance to patients are burgeoning, although proposals by the Reagan administration to end federal funding of the Legal Services Program and to reduce budgetary support to social programs may reverse this trend. Moreover, the Civil Rights Attorney's Fees Awards Act of 1976 (United States Code, Title 42, § 1988), by authorizing attorney's fees and costs for prevailing parties in civil rights actions, will encourage members of the private bar to take up the causes of mental patients, including those in the criminal justice system. In addition, recent federal legislation, signed into law on May 23, 1980, authorizes a larger role for the United States Department of Justice in safeguarding the civil rights of institutionalized patients where state institutions have systematically infringed patients' rights (Public Law 96–247).

Litigation asserting the rights of defendants in the incompetency process thus is likely to increase in the coming years. In addition to enforcing the durational limits of *Jackson v. Indiana*, thereby considerably reducing the period of time defendants spend hospitalized for examination or treatment for incompetency, it can be anticipated that such law suits will address, in particular, the developing constitutional rights to treatment, to the least restrictive alternative, and to refuse treatment.

The least restrictive alternative principle will be asserted to require that competency evaluation be performed on an outpatient basis in most cases (*see* pp. 9–10, *supra*). In a related development, it can be anticipated that more defense attorneys will assert their clients' right to bail or other pre-trial release during the period of competency evaluation (*see* pp. 12–13, *supra*). Such release will be conditioned on the defendant's appearance at a court clinic or at the office of a court-appointed evaluator for competency evaluation. In response, courts, legislatures, or mental health departments will require the establishment or expansion of specialized forensic mental health services or court clinics to perform competency screening and outpatient evaluation (*see* Mental Health Law Project 1978, pp. 621–22). Since outpatient evaluation can be performed on a more expeditious and economical basis, freeing inpatient facilities for treatment of defendants requiring hospitalization, these changes already have been accomplished in some areas without the pressure of litigation (*see* Winick 1974, pp. 1–2). With the increase in outpatient evaluation, it can be anticipated that less reliance will be placed on psychiatrists as evaluators. Psychologists are increasingly appointed by courts as examiners, and multidisciplinary teams, including social workers, paraprofessional mental health workers, and perhaps lawyers and criminal justice specialists, will be used (Bukatman, Foy & DeGrazia 1971; Laben, Kashgarian, Nessa, & Spencer 1977; Laboratory of Community Psychiatry 1973, p. 64; Mental Health Law Project 1978, p. 622; Roesch & Golding 1980, pp. 205–06). The evaluation process also will more frequently use competency assessment instruments or other means of standardizing examination criteria, reducing considerably the confusion that often prevailed in the past as well as the tendency of reports to the court to be conclusionary only. The coming years thus may witness a substantial restructuring of the way competency evaluation is performed, as well as an increase in its quality.

The least restrictive alternative principle also will be asserted to defeat automatic commitment to state mental hospitals of defendants adjudicated incompetent. Considerations of constitutionality, therapeutic efficacy, and economy coalesce to favor outpatient treatment for many incompetent defendants presently hospitalized. In response, courts, legislatures, or mental health departments will require the creation or expansion of community alternatives to hospitalization for the treatment of incompetent defendants who are not considered dangerous. Community mental health centers and outpatient hospital programs will be pressured to accept the criminal patients they traditionally have excluded. Group homes and other specialized therapeutic residential programs for forensic patients will be established. The deinstitutionalization process that has been gaining momentum in recent years in the civil mental health delivery system, thus will affect institutions for forensic patients as well (Wexler 1976, p. 4). Increasing numbers of incompetent defendants will be treated in the community or in civil wards or institutions rather than in maximum-security correctional facilities (*see* p. 15–16, *supra*).

The partial deinstituitionalization of forensic hospitals and wards will have the effect of considerably improving these facilities. To the extent that these frequently overcrowded facilities will experience a reduction in patient census, their limited resources can be used more effectively to restore to competence more expeditiously those defendants requiring hospitalization. Of course, this hoped-for reduction in patient census may never come about even if a comprehensive network of community alternative facilities for competency evaluation and treatment is established. In a trend that may continue and intensify in the 1980s, more rigorous standards and expanding procedural safeguards for civil commitment have made the formerly easy civil hospitalization of the mentally ill more difficult (Dickey 1980; Halleck 1980, p. 227; Winick 1977, p. 776). One unintended consequence has been increased use of the criminal process and diversion through the incompetency commitment as an alternative method of providing treatment for mentally ill individuals who commit minor crimes, which previously would not have been dealt with criminally (Dickey 1980; Geller & Lister 1978; Group for the Advancement of Psychiatry 1974, p. 885; Halleck 1980, pp. 227–28; McGarry 1969, p. 49; Winick 1977, p. 776). Thus, the numbers of defendants found to be incompetent might well increase substantially, guaranteeing a continuation of overcrowded and understaffed forensic institutions. In such a case, and perhaps in any event, large class action right-to-treatment law suits can be anticipated on behalf of incompetent defendants committed to such facilities, resulting in court-ordered improvements (*e.g., Johnson v. Brelje* 1979; *State v. Twyman* 1980; *see* p. 15, *supra*).

With increasing attention being paid to the developing right to refuse treatment, it can be anticipated that right-to-refuse law suits also will be filed in the incompetency context (*see* pp. 16–18, *supra*). The trend in civil mental hospitals toward institutional review boards, detailed guidelines on the administration of psychotropic drugs and other intrusive treatment techniques, and internal and external review mechanisms to monitor informed consent and treatment adminstration thus will be applied as well to forensic facilities for the incompetent defendant (*see* Mental Health Law Project 1978, p. 632).

As psychotropic medication becomes more accepted by the judiciary in the treatment of defendants found incompetent to stand trial, the number of courts insisting on a defendant who is competent without medication will diminish (*see* pp. 22–23, *supra*). The vast majority of incompetent defendants could rapidly be returned to competence through use of these drugs and other modern psychiatric treatment techniques (Group for the Advancement of Psychiatry 1974, p. 901). As a result, their judicial acceptance should make a six-month period for restoration to competence a reasonable goal for virtually all incompetent defendants. With the use of these drugs, few civil patients, suffering from identical conditions, require more than six months of hospitalization.

Trial of defendants competent on medication will, however, spawn new problems. Judges and parole boards will become increasingly concerned with the prospect that such defendants, following either conviction and sentence or acquittal by reason of insanity, will discontinue medication necessary to keep their psychopathology in remission. Concern with the potential danger to community safety resulting from such drug discontinuation following release likely will lead to statutes authorizing a conditional release status under which defendants will be required to continue their medication and report periodically to drug clinics. Such forms of conditional release will, in turn, raise complex right-to-refuse-treatment issues.

As defense attorneys become more sophisticated concerning the rights of their incompetent clients, it also can be anticipated that more vigorous representation will be displayed throughout the incompetency process. Certainly the speedy trial defense will be raised more frequently for defendants hospitalized for lengthy periods due to incompetency (*see* pp. 25–27, *supra*). In addition, counsel increasingly will attack the indictments under which their incompetent clients are held or otherwise raise defenses capable of determination without their clients' presence or participation (*see* pp. 18–19, *supra*). More vigorous representation, accompanied by the increasing legal sophistication of evaluators and hospital staff, will result in an incompetency process much more respectful of defendants' rights than traditionally has been the case.

It has been proposed that the incompetency plea be abolished altogether (Burt & Morris 1972). Proponents of abolition would substitute a trial continuance of no more than six months, during which the state would be obligated to commit resources to help the defendant regain his competency. If competence is not restored within the six-month period, however, the state would be required either to dismiss the criminal charges or to bring the defendant to trial, even though incompetent, pursuant to specialized procedures designed to compensate in some measure for the defendant's trial disabilities. The defense would be accorded broader discovery, the prosecution would bear a higher burden of proof, and special jury instructions would be provided. In addition, a more liberal provision for the setting aside of a verdict would be available should new evidence emerge (Burt & Morris 1972, pp. 93–95).

The abolition proposal runs directly counter to the Supreme Court's dictum in *Pate v. Robinson* (1966, pp. 378, 385), reiterated in many cases, that conviction of an incompetent defendant would violate due process. Although Burt and Morris argue that this dictum is easily discardable (1972, p. 76), no jurisdiction has as yet adopted the proposal and, as a result, no court has ruled on the issue.

Perhaps more likely in the way of state experimentation is the provisional trial or "acquittal only" trial that Massachusetts and three other states authorize (Massachusetts Laws Annotated Ch. 123; *see* Roesch &

Golding 1979, pp. 356–57, 362–63, 369–70). Such a trial would give the defendant some opportunity to face his charges even though incompetent. If acquitted, he would be vindicated of the charges. If convicted, he would at least have the opportunity of recording testimony in evidence, alleviating much of the hardship stemming from faded memories, unavailable witnesses, and stale evidence, should a future trial be necessary (*see* Gobert 1973, pp. 686–87). For similar reasons, the prosecution also might welcome the opportunity of preserving testimony for possible future use, although as the prosecutor has everything to lose and very little to gain in such a provisional trial, it is likely that the prosecutor will not initiate the procedure. Empirical examination is needed of the extent to which such provisional trials have occurred in the four states that authorize them and whether the benefits of such a provisional trial system outweigh the added costs.

A variation on the provisional trial proposal is the suggestion that the trial take place prior to a determination of competency, which would occur only if the defendant is convicted (Janis 1974, p. 737; Roesch & Golding 1980, pp. 213–16). If the defendant is found incompetent, the verdict would be set aside. One advantage of this proposal is that the defendant's behavior during trial might provide a firmer basis on which to gauge competency than exclusive reliance on clinical testimony and prediction. However, the cost of conducting these trials, many of which would be set aside, would be considerable. Such costs could be minimized by reserving the provisional trial for defendants for whom treatment has not succeeded in effecting a restoration to competency in a six-month or similar period.

Notwithstanding some experimentation with the provisional trial and similar innovations, it is likely that the overwhelming number of jurisdictions will continue the incompetency status in its traditional form and that none will abolish it altogether. The principal developments of the 1980s thus should be procedural reforms fulfilling the promise of *Jackson v. Indiana,* increased litigation asserting and securing the rights of incompetent defendants, and a general movement of the competency evaluation and treatment process from the hospital to the community.

CASES CITED

1. Addington v. Texas, 441 U.S. 418 (1979).
2. Altman v. Hofferber, 167 Cal. Rptr. 854, 616 P.2d 836 (Calif. Sup. Ct. 1980).
3. Allard v. Helgemoe, 527 F.2d 1 (lst Cir. 1978).
4. Ashe v. Robinson, 450 F.2d 681 (D.C. Cir. 1971).
5. Barker v. Wingo, 407 U.S. 514 (1972).
6. Baxstom v. Herold, 383 U.S. 107 (1966).

7. Bell v. Wolfish, 441 U.S. 520 (1979).
8. Blaisdell v. Commonwealth, 364 N.E.2d 191 (Mass. 1977).
9. Brown v. State, 345 So.2d 68 (Fla. 1971).
10. Bruce v. Estelle, 483 F.2d 1031 (5th Cir. 1973).
11. Collins v. Auger, 428 F. Supp. 1079 (S.D. Iowa 1977).
12. Cook v. Ciccone, 312 F. Supp. 822 (W.D. Mo. 1970).
13. Covington v. Harris, 419 F.2d 617 (D.C. Cir. 1969).
14. Dalton v. State, 362 So.2d 457 (Fla. 4th DCA 1978).
15. Davis v. Campbell, 465 F. Supp. 1309 (E.D. Ark.), aff'd in part & rev'd in part on other grounds, 608 F. 2d 317 (8th Cir. 1979).
16. Davis v. Hubbard, 506 F. Supp. 915 (N.D. Ohio 1980).
17. Davis v. Watkins, 384 F. Supp. 1196 (N.D. Ohio 1974).
18. DeAngeles v. Plaut, 5 Mental Disability L. Rep. 9 (D. Conn. 1980).
19. Drendel v. United States, 403 F.2d 55 (5th Cir. 1968).
20. Drope v. Missouri, 420 U.S. 162 (1975).
21. Dusky v. United States, 363 U.S. 402 (1960).
22. Dyer v. Brooks, 1 Mental Disability Law Reporter 122 (Marion County [Or.] Cir. Ct., 1976).
23. Estelle v. Smith, 451 U.S. 454 (1981).
24. Feguer v. United States, 302 F.2d 214 (8th Cir.), cert. denied, 371 U.S. 871 (1962).
25. Frith's Case, 22 How. St. Tr. 307 (1790).
26. Garrett v. State, 390 So.2d 95 (Fla. 3d DCA 1980), review denied, 399 So.2d 1146 (Fla. 1981), cert. denied, 102 S. Ct. 544 (1981).
27. Germany v. Hudspeth, 209 F.2d 15 (10th Cir.), cert. denied, 347 U.S. 946 (1954).
28. Gibson v. Zahradnick, 581 F.2d 75 (4th Cir.), cert. denied, 439 U.S. 996 (1978).
29. Gomez v. Miller, 341 F. Supp. 323 (S.D.N.Y. 1972), aff'd, 412 U.S. 914 (1973).
30. Hall v. United States, 410 F.2d 653 (4th Cir.), cert. denied, 396 U.S. 970 (1969).
31. Hoskins v. Wainright, 485 F.2d 1186 (5th Cir. 1973).
32. Humphrey v. Cady, 405 U.S. 504 (1972).
33. In re Banks, 88 Cal. App. 3d 864, 152 Cal. Rptr. 111 (1979).
34. In re Boyd, 403 A.2d 744 (D.C. 1979).
35. In re Pray, 133 Vt. 253, 336 A.2d 174 (1975).
36. Jackson v. Indiana, 406 U.S. 715 (1972).
37. Johnson v. Brelje, 482 F. Supp. 125 (N.D. Ill. 1979).
38. Johnson v. United States, 333 F.2d 371 (10th Cir. 1964).
39. Kaimowitz v. Dep't of Mental Health, Civ. No. 73-19434–AW (Wayne County [Mich.] Cir. Ct., July 10, 1973).
40. Kelley v. Johnson, 425 U.S. 238 (1976).
41. Kesselbrenner v. Anonymous, 33 N.Y.2d 161, 305 N.E.2d 903, 350 N.Y.S.2d 889 (1973).
42. Kinloch's Case, 18 How. St. Tr. 395 (1746).
43. Knecht v. Gillman, 488 F.2d 1136 (8th Cir. 1973).
44. Lee v. County Court, 27 N.Y.2d 432, 318 N.Y.S.2d 705, 267 N.E.2d 452, cert. denied, 404 U.S. 823 (1971).
45. Malinauskas v. United States, 505 F.2d 649 (5th Cir. 1974).
46. Marcey v. Harris, 400 F.2d 772 (D.C. Cir. 1968).
47. Martin v. Estelle, 546 F.2d 177 (5th Cir. 1977).
48. McGraw v. State, 330 So.2d 48 (Fla. 1st DCA), overruled, 332 So.2d 705 (1976).
49. Mills v. Rogers, 102 S. Ct. 2442 (1982).
50. Mincey v. Arizona, 437 U.S. 385 (1978).
51. Moore v. Arizona, 414 U.S. 24 (1973).

52. Noble v. Sigler, 351 F.2d 673 (8th Cir. 1965), *cert. denied*, 385 U.S. 853 (1966).
53. Newman v. Missouri, 394 F. Supp. 83 (W.D. Mo. 1974).
54. O'Connor v. Donaldson, 422 U.S. 563 (1975).
55. Pate v. Robinson, 383 U.S. 375 (1966).
56. People v. Dalfanso, 24 Ill. App.2d 748, 321 N.E.2d 379 (1974).
57. People v. Carl, 58 App. Div.2d 948, 397 N.Y.S.2d 193 (3d Dep't 1977), *rev'd on other grounds*, 46 N.Y.2d 806, 413 N.Y.S.2d 916, 386 N.E.2d 828 (1978).
58. People v. Heral, 62 Ill.2d 329, 342 N.E.2d 34 (1976).
59. Prince v. Alabama, 507 F.2d 693 (5th Cir.), *cert. denied*, 423 U.S. 876 (1975).
60. Proctor v. Harris, 413 F.2d 383 (D.C. Cir. 1969).
61. Rennie v. Klein, 462 F. Supp. 1131 (D.N.J. 1978).
62. Rennie v. Klein, 476 F. Supp. 1294 (D.N.J. 1979), *aff'd in part, modified in part & remanded*, 653 F.2d 836 (3d, (eb blanc). Cir. 1981).
63. Rogers v. Okin, 478 F. Supp. 1342 (D. Mass. 1979), *aff'd in part*, 634 F.2d 650 (1st Cir. 1980), *vacated & remanded*, 102 S.Ct 2442 (1982).
64. Rogers v. Okin, 634 F.2d 650 (1st Cir. 1980), *vacated & remanded*, 102 S. Ct. 2442 (1982).
65. Scott v. Plante, 532 F.2d 939 (3rd Cir. 1976) *vacated & remanded*, 102 S. Ct. 3474 (1982).
66. Sieling v. Eyman, 478 F.2d 211 (9th Cir. 1973).
67. Stack v. Boyle, 342 U.S. 1 (1951).
68. State v. Aumann, 265 N.W.2d 316 (Iowa 1978).
69. State v. Hampton, 253 La. 399, 218 So.2d 311 (1969).
70. State ex rel. Haskins v. County Court, 62 Wis.2d 250, 214 N.W.2d 575 (1974).
71. State v. Hayes, 389 A.2d 1379 (N.H. 1979).
72. State v. Jojola, 89 N.M. 489, 553 P.2d 1296 (Ct. App. 1976).
73. State ex rel. Deisinger v. Treffert, 85 Wis.2d 257, 270 N.W.2d 402 (1978).
74. State ex rel. Matalik v. Schubert, 57 Wis.2d 315, 204 N.W.2d 13 (1973).
75. State v. Murphy, 56 Wash.2d 761, 355 P.2d 323 (1960).
76. State v. Twyman, Case No. 75-525 CFA (Cir. Ct., 17th Jud. Cir. [Fla.], March 27, 1980).
77. State ex rel. Walker v. Jenkins, 203 S.E.2d 353 (W. Va. 1974).
78. State v. Whitlow, 45 N.J. 3, 210 A.2d 763 (1965).
79. Suggs v. LaVallee, 570 F.2d 1092 (2d Cir. 1978).
80. Thornton v. Corcoran, 407 F.2d 695 (D.C. Cir. 1969).
81. United States v. Adams, 297 F. Supp. 596 (S.D.N.Y. 1969).
82. United States v. Albright, 388 F.2d 719 (4th Cir. 1968).
83. United States v. Alvarez, 519 F.2d 1036 (3rd Cir. 1975).
84. United States v. Baird, 414 F.2d 700 (2d Cir. 1969), *cert. denied*, 396 U.S. 1005 (1970).
85. United States v. Bohle, 445 F.2d 54 (7th Cir. 1971).
86. United States v. Cartano, 420 F.2d 362 (1st Cir.), *cert. denied*, 397 U.S. 1054 (1970).
87. United States v. Chisolm, 149 F. 284 (5th Cir. 1906).
88. United States v. Curry, 410 F.2d 1372 (4th Cir. 1969).
89. United States v. Davis, 365 F.2d 251 (6th Cir. 1966).
90. United States v. DiGilio, 538 F.2d 972 (3rd Cir. 1976), *cert. denied*, 429 U.S. 1038 (1977).
91. United States v. Fletcher, 329 F. Supp. 160 (D.D.C. 1971).
92. United States v. Geelan, 520 F.2d 585 (9th Cir. 1975).
93. United States v. Greene, 497 F.2d 1068 (7th Cir. 1974), *cert. denied*, 410 U.S. 986 (1975).
94. United States v. Handy, 454 F.2d 885 (9th Cir. 1971), *cert. denied*, 409 U.S. 846 (1972).
95. United States v. Hayes, 589 F.2d 811 (5th Cir.), *cert. denied*, 444 U.S. 847 (1979).
96. United States v. Holmes, 452 F.2d 249 (7th Cir. 1971), *cert. denied*, 405 U.S. 1016 (1972).
97. United States v. Horowitz, 360 F. Supp. 772 (E.D. Pa. 1973).

98. United States v. Huff, 409 F.2d 1225 (5th Cir. 1969).
99. United States v. Jackson, 306 F. Supp. 4 (N.D. Cal. 1969).
100. United States v. Klein, 325 F.2d 283 (2d Cir. 1963).
101. United States ex rel. Konigsberg v. Vincent, 526 F.2d 131 (2d Cir. 1975), cert. denied, 426 U.S. 937 (1976).
102. United States v. Lancaster, 408 F. Supp. 225 (D.D.C. 1976).
103. United States v. Lawrence, 26 F. Cas. 887 (D.C. Cir. 1835).
104. United States v. Makris, 535 F.2d 899 (5th Cir. 1976).
105. United States v. Morgan, 567 F.2d 479 (D.C. Cir. 1977).
106. United States v. Pardue, 354 F. Supp. 1377 (D. Conn. 1973).
107. United States v. Reifsteck, 535 F.2d 1030 (8th Cir. 1976).
108. United States ex rel. Schuster v. Herald, 410 F.2d 1071 (2d Cir. 1969).
109. United States v. Sermon, 228 F. Supp. 972 (W.D. Mo. 1964).
110. United States ex rel. Stukes v. Shovlin, 464 F.2d 1211 (3rd Cir. 1972).
111. United States v. Trapnell, 495 F.2d 22 (2d Cir. 1974).
112. United States ex rel. von Wolfersdorf v. Johnston, 317 F. Supp. 66 (S.D.N.Y. 1970).
113. Vitek v. Jones, 445 U.S. 480 (1980).
114. Welsch v. Likins, 373 F. Supp. 487 (D. Minn. 1974).
115. Westbrook v. Arizona, 384 U.S. 150 (1966).
116. Whitehead v. Wainwright, 447 F. Supp. 898 (M.D. Fla. 1978).
117. Wieter v. Settle, 193 F. Supp. 318 (W.D. Mo. 1961).
118. Williams v. United States, 250 F.2d 19 (D.C. Cir. 1957).
119. Winters v. Miller, 446 F.2d 65 (2d Cir.), cert. denied, 404 U.S. 985 (1971).
120. Wojtowicz v. Unites States, 550 F.2d 786 (2d Cir. 1977).
121. Wolcott v. United States, 407 F.2d 1149 (10th Cir. 1969).
122. Wyatt v. Stickney, 344 F. Supp. 373 (M.D. Ala. 1972), aff'd sub nom. Wyatt v. Aderholt, 503 F.2d 1305 (5th Cir. 1974).
123. Youtsey v. United States, 97 F. 937 (6 Cir. 1899).

REFERENCES

Berry, F. D. Self-incrimination and the compulsory mental examination: A proposal. Arizona Law Review, 1973, 15, 919–37.

Blackstone, W. Commentaries. Vol. 4 (9th ed.). London, 1783.

Bluestone, H., & Melella, J. A study of criminal defendants referred for competency to stand trial in New York City. Bulletin of the American Academy of Psychiatry and Law, 1979, 7, 166–78.

Brakel, S. J. Presumption, bias, and incompetency in the criminal process. Wisconsin Law Review, 1974, 1974, 1105–30.

Brakel, S. J., & Rock, R. S. The mentally disabled and the Law (rev. ed.). Chicago: University of Chicago Press, 1971.

Brooks, A. D. Law, psychiatry and the mental health system. Boston: Little, Brown & Co., 1974.

Bukataman, B. A., Foy, J. L., & deGrazia, E. What is competency to stand trial? American Journal of Psychiatry, 1971, 127, 1225–29.

Burt, R. A., & Morris, N. A proposal for the abolition of the incompetency plea. University of Chicago Law Review, 1972, 40, 66–95.

Chambers, D. Alternatives to civil commitment of the mentally ill: Practical guides and constitutional imperatives. Michigan Law Review, 1972, 70, 1107–1200.

deGrazia, D. Diversion from the criminal process: The 'mental-health' experiment. *Connecticut Law Review*, 1974, *6*, 432–528.

Dickey, W. Incompetency and the nondangerous mentally ill client. *Criminal Law Bulletin*, 1980, *16*, 22–40.

Duke Law Journal. Competence to plead guilty: A new standard. *Duke Law Journal*, 1974, *1974*, 149–74.

Engleberg, S. L. Pre-trial criminal commitment to mental institutions: The procedure in Massachusetts and suggested reform. *Catholic University Law Review*, 1967, *17*, 163–214.

Favole, R. J. Mental disability in the American criminal process: A four-issue survey. Chapter 9, in this volume.

Foote, C. A comment on pre-trial commitment of criminal defendants. *University of Pennsylvania Law Review*, 1960, *108*, 832–46.

Friedman, P. R. Legal regulation of applied behavior analysis in mental institutions and prisons. *Arizona Law Review*, 1975, *17*, 39–104.

Geller, J. L., & Lister, E. D. The process of criminal commitment for pre-trial psychiatric examination: An evaluation. *American Journal of Psychiatry*, 1979, *135*, 53–60.

Gobert, J. J. Competency to stand trial: A pre- and post-Jackson analysis. *Tennessee Law Review*, 1973, *40*, 659–88.

Goldstein, R. L. The fitness factory. Part I: The psychiatrist's role in determining competency. *American Journal of Psychiatry*, 1973, *130*, 1144–47.

Golten, R. J. Role of defense counsel in the criminal commitment process. *American Criminal Law Review*, 1972, *10*, 385–430.

Group for the Advancement of Psychiatry, Committee on Psychiatry and Law. *Misuse of psychiatry in the criminal courts: Competency to stand trial.* New York: Group for the Advancement of Psychiatry, 1974.

Hale, M. *Pleas of the crown.* London, 1736.

Halleck, S. L. *Law in the practice of psychiatry: A handbook for clinicians.* New York: Plenum Medical Book Company, 1980.

Harvard Law Review. Incompetency to stand trial. *Harvard Law Review*, 1967, *81*, 454–73.

Hess, J. J., & Thomas, T. E. Incompetency to stand trial: Procedures, results and problems. *American Journal of Psychiatry*, 1963, *119*, 713–20.

Hollister, L. W. Psychotropic drugs and court competence. In L. M. Irvine & T. B. Brelje (Eds.), *Law, psychiatry and the disordered offender.* Springfield, Ill.: Charles C Thomas, 1972.

Iowa Law Review. Should the burden of proving incompetence rest on the incompetent? *Iowa Law Review*, 1979, *64*, 984–99.

Janis, N. R. Incompetency commitment: The need for procedural safeguards and a proposed statutory scheme. *Catholic University Law Review*, 1974, *23*, 720–43.

Kaufman, J. Evaluating competency: Are constitutional deprivations necessary? *American Criminal Law Review*, 1972, *10*, 465–504.

Kentucky Law Journal. The identification of incompetent defendants: Separating those unfit for adversary combat from those who are fit. *Kentucky Law Journal*, 1978, *66*, 666–706.

Laben, J. K., Kashgarian, M., Nessa, O. B., & Spencer, L. D. Reform from the inside: Mental health center evaluation of competency to stand trial. *Journal of Community Psychology*, 1977, *5*, 52–62.

Laboratory of Community Psychiatry, Harvard University. *Competency to stand trial and mental illness.* DHEW Pub. No. (HSM) 73–9105, Rockville, Md.: National Institute of Mental Health, Center for Studies of Crime and Deliquency, 1973.

Lipsitt, P. D., Lelos, D., & McGarry, A. L. Competency for trial: A screening instrument. *American Journal of Psychiatry*, 1971, *128*, 105–09.

Matthews, A. R., Jr. *Mental disability and the criminal law: A field study.* Chicago: American Bar Foundation, 1970.

McGarry, A. L., Curran, W. J., & Kenefick, D. P. Problems of public consultation in medical legal matters. *American Journal of Psychiatry,* 1968, *125,* 42–47.

McGarry, A. L. Demonstration and research in competency for trial and mental illness: Review and preview. *Boston University Law Review,* 1969, *49,* 46–61.

Mental Health Law Project. Legal issues in state mental health care: Proposals for change—incompetence to stand trial on criminal charges. *Mental Disability Law Reporter,* 1978, *2,* 617–50.

Pizza, W. T. Competency to stand trial in federal courts: Conceptual and constitutional problems. *University of Chicago Law Review,* 1977, *45,* 21–71.

Plotkin, R. Limiting the therapeutic orgy: Mental patients' right to refuse treatment. *Northwestern University Law Review,* 1977, *72,* 461–525.

Robey, A. Criteria for competency to stand trial: A checklist for psychiatrists. *American Journal of Psychiatry,* 1965, *122,* 616–22.

Roesch, R., & Golding, S. *Competency to stand trial.* Urbana: University of Illinois Press, 1980.

Roesch, R., & Golding, S. Treatment and disposition of defendants found incompetent to stand trial: A review and a proposal. *International Journal of Law and Psychiatry,* 1979, *2,* 349–70.

Rosenberg, A. H., & McGarry, A. L. Competency for trial: The making of an expert. *American Journal of Psychiatry,* 1972, *128,* 192–96.

Roth, L. H., & Applebaum, P. S. What we do and do not know about treatment refusals in mental institutions. In A. E. Doudera & J. P. Swazey (Eds.) *Refusing treatment in mental health institutions—Values in conflict.* Ann Arbor, Mich.: Aupha Press, 1982.

Schwitzgebel, R. K. *Legal aspects of the enforced treatment of offenders.* DHEW Pub. No. (ADM.) 79–831, Rockville, Md.: National Institute of Mental Health, Center for Studies of Crime and Deliquency, 1979.

Shapiro, M. H. Legislating the control of behavior control: Autonomy and the coercive use of organic therapies. *Southern California Law Review,* 1974, *47,* 237–356.

Slovenko, R. The developing law on competency to stand trial. *Journal of Psychiatry and Law,* 1977, *5,* 165–200.

Special Committee on the Study of Commitment Procedures and the Law Relating to Incompetence of the Association of the Bar of the City of New York. *Mental illness, due process and the criminal defendant.* New York: Fordham University Press, 1968.

Steadman, H. J. *Beating a rap? Defendants found incompetent to stand trial.* Chicago: University of Chicago Press, 1979.

Steinberg, M. I. Summary commitment of defendants incompetent to stand trial: A violation of constitutional safeguards. *St. Louis University Law Journal,* 1978, *22,* 1–24.

Stone, A. A. *Mental health and law: A system in transition.* DHEW Pub. No. (ADM) 76-176, Rockville, Md.: National Institute of Mental Health, Center for Studies of Crime and Deliquency, 1975.

Task Panel Report. *Legal and ethical issues, President's Commission on Mental Health.* Sprinfield, Va.: National Technical Information Service, 1978.

Vann, C.R., & Morganroth, E. Psychiatrists and the competence to stand trial. *University of Detroit Law Journal.* 1964, *42,* 75–85.

Vann, C. R., & Morganroth, E. The psychiatrist as judge: A second look at the competence to stand trial. *University of Detroit Law Journal,* 1965, *43,* 1–12.

Wexler, D. B. *Criminal commitments and dangerous mental patients: Legal issues of confinement, treatment, and release.* DHEW Pub. No. (ADM) 76-28650, Rockville, Md.: National Institute of Mental Health, Center for Studies of Crime and Delinquency, 1976.

Wexler, D. B. *Mental Health Law: Major Issues.* New York: Plenum Press, 1981.

Wexler, D. B. Token and taboo: Behavior modification, token economies and the law. *California Law Review,* 1973, *61,* 81–109.

Winick, B. J. Legal limitations on correctional therapy and research. *Minnesota Law Review,* 1981, *65,* 331–422.

Winick, B. J. *Statement before the New York Legislature Select Committee on Mental and Physical Handicap.* Unpublished, January 17, 1974.

Winick, B. J. Psychotropic medication and competence to stand trial. *American Bar Foundation Research Journal,* 1977, *1977,* 769–816.

Winick, B. J., & DeMeo, T. L. Competence to stand trial in Florida. *University of Miami Law Review,* 1980, *35,* 31–76.

2

Defendants Incompetent to Stand Trial

HENRY J. STEADMAN AND ELIOT HARTSTONE

The inadequate state of empirical knowledge about the special offender populations analyzed in this book is epitomized by the research on defendants found incompetent to stand trial (IST). This group, which comprises about 32% of the admissions of mentally disordered offenders (Steadman *et al.*, 1981), is the group for which the largest body of research exists. Yet, as we shall see in this chapter, even this is quite inadequate. It is inadequate in understanding: (1) how incompetency currently is working across various jurisdictions; (2) trends over time in the use of incompetency either within or across jurisdictions; and (3) how appropriate public policy, clinical practices, and legal statutes might be developed.

Our approach to reviewing the research about the ISTs will be to assess what is known at each step in the pathways leading from arrest to an incompetency determination and, for some defendants, to recidivism. This sequential, or process approach seems useful as a device to most clearly articulate the informational gaps that exist. The chapter first will highlight some of the findings from the national mail survey described in Chapter 1. A second section will review the existing data in this processual framework. These will provide some trend data when compared

HENRY J. STEADMAN • Special Projects Research Unit, New York State Department of Mental Hygiene, 44 Holland Avenue, Albany, New York 12229.   ELIOT HARTSTONE • URSA Institute, Pier 1½, San Francisco, California 94111.

to Scheidemandel and Kanno's 1967 data. Finally, we will indicate some of the major research needs in this area.

Before proceeding to the research data it may be useful to summarize quickly what is meant by incompetency to stand trial and its rationales within the American judicial system elaborated in the previous chapter. It is instructive to note that in some jurisdictions the competency issue is discussed as fitness to proceed with trial. Such fitness involves three major components: (1) the defendant's ability to understand the charges; (2) the defendant's ability to cooperate rationally with an attorney in his or her own defense; and (3) the defendant's ability to understand the judicial process. The requirements, which are derived from English common law, were articulated by the United States Supreme Court in a landmark 1960 decision, *Dusky v. United States* (362 U.S. 405, 1960) (cf. Chapter 1). What is required is a determination whether a defendant "has sufficient present ability to consult with his lawyer with a reasonable degree of rational understanding, and whether he has a rational as well as factual understanding of the proceedings against him" (p. 402).

The requirements are seen as sufficiently important that the Supreme Court, in *Pate v. Robinson* (383 U.S. 375, 1966), mandated that the judge, prosecutor, and defense attorney had an obligation to raise these issues if they had any doubt about the defendant's abilities. Were they not raised, a mistrial could be declared even after conviction. As Stone (1975) has noted, the strict adherence to these standards is precipitated by demands of our legal system to: (1) guarantee the accuracy of the criminal proceeding; (2) guarantee the fairness of the trial; (3) maximize the efficacy of punishment for both individual deterrence and retributive catharsis of society as a whole; and (4) preserve the dignity of the judicial process.

THE SCOPE OF THE PROBLEM: OUR NATIONAL SURVEY

As we indicated above, one reason for the amount of research on ISTs relative to the other groups of mentally disordered offenders is their number. The first indication of how large a segment the ISTs are was Scheidemandel and Kanno's 1969 report from a 1967 national survey. They reported that 52% of all mentally disordered offenders were IST. This often cited figure really overestimates their number, however, since persons being evaluated for competency were included. This evaluation group amounts to 14% of the total number of mentally disordered offenders. We feel strongly that it is inappropriate to include defendants being evaluated for competency among mentally disordered offenders just as it would be inappropriate to include all persons arrested as prison admissions. Rather, it is much more accurate to note that Scheidemandel and Kanno found a total of 6,927 admissions to primary facilities as adjudicated mentally disordered offenders of which 1,527 (22%) were IST. To inflate this latter figure with 4,282 defendants admitted for competency evaluations badly overestimates the actual adjudications in this category.

To develop data on admission trends for ISTs, one next would have to rely on Stone's report of some unpublished 1972 National Institute of Mental Health (NIMH) data that reported 8,825 males were admitted in 1972 as incompetent to stand trial. This figure would seem to include evaluations, also. Otherwise, it would have been a fivefold increase over 1967. While Goldstein's (1973) New York City data and Geller and Lister's (1978) Worcester, Massachusetts data suggest that the use of incompetency is increasing, especially where evaluation may permit the rapid and secure detention of persons who marginally may meet the involuntary commitment standards, these observations seem insufficient to explain the huge differences between the 1972 and 1967 data cited. Rather, it would seem that Stone's 1972 data include admissions for competency evaluation.

The most recent data available on ISTs are those collected as part of our national mail survey described in Chapter 1. These deal only with persons *adjudicated* as IST. In 1978, there were 6,420 admissions in the 50 states plus the federal system and the District of Columbia. These admissions occurred in 256 facilities. Of these facilities, 32 were "specialty" institutions and the remaining 224 were specially designated forensic units, regular mental hospitals, or correctional facilities to which small numbers of ISTs were committed. On any given day in the United States in 1978 there were 3,400 defendants in these mental health or correctional facilities adjudicated as incompetent to stand trial.

Using a 25% figure (Roesch & Golding, 1980; Steadman, 1979) to extrapolate to evaluations for incompetency from actual incompetency adjudications would result in approximately 25,000 defendants having been evaluated in 1978. Not surprisingly, the vast majority of those adjudicated were males (92.5%). Making any interpretations of these data exceedingly difficult is the fact that 12 states were unable to identify specifically women among the ISTs. However, there is no reason to expect that those states that were unable to identify women would have significantly different proportions than those that reported, so the 7.5% figure mentioned above is one that would seem accurate for the United States as a whole.

It should be clear in both absolute and relative senses that ISTs are an important group and one that may be becoming even more important.

Their potentially increasing importance may be related to current speculations on the impact of more restrictive mental health codes which make it more difficult for police to get persons admitted to mental hospitals for lower level criminal or nuisance behavior. It is claimed that, as a result, evaluations for incompetency are invoked after arrest only to have the arrest charges dropped after the initial evaluation period expires. In this way rapid and secure detention is facilitated without the necessity of a criminal court hearing. Obviously much more research on these issues is needed before such trends could be confirmed on local or national levels. Regardless, ISTs are a group of considerable size and the scope of problems they present is substantial.

ASSESSING COMPETENCY

Since incompetency to stand trial involves impediments to proceeding with a criminal trial as a result of mental disease or defect that impairs the rational comprehension of and participation in the legal process, it is not surprising that judicial decisions on this matter depend heavily on expert witnesses. As we will see below, the level of agreement between the court and the expert witness in the United States is so high as to make the determination of competency virtually a medical one. It is medical in that the dominant paradigm for investigating competency is a medical/illness one. Depending on the jurisdiction, psychologists, as well as psychiatrists, may be called on for expert testimony. However, the basic focus remains mental disease or defect and how this may impair the defendant's involvement in the court process. As we will see later in this section, one of the major thrusts of recent revisions in competency evaluations has been to introduce inputs from a variety of other professionals and paraprofessionals at the initial screening phases. Regardless, there continues to be heavy reliance on psychiatrists for the competency assessment.

Until Robey's 1965 article, clinical evaluations for competency were the archetype of clinical decision making. With no specific guidelines, a mental health professional typically would see a defendant for 30 minutes or less and on vague criteria recommend whether he or she could proceed with a trial. What such assessments often produced was grave confusion between competency to stand trial and criminal responsibility and between mental illness and fitness (Hess & Thomas, 1963; McGarry, 1973). Robey suggested for the first time that there may be a specific set of items that routinely should be covered and from which a final determination of competency could emerge. The set of 20 items cut across both clinical and legal criteria. Each item was checked as "OK," "Mental Illness," or "Intellectual Deficiency." However, no quantification was suggested to calculate any summary score that might indicate varying levels of confidence that the clinician had in the defendant's ability to stand trial. Although Robey's checklist was widely distributed and often reprinted,[1] there never was any systematic research on its reliability or validity.

The next published checklist to assess competency was offered by Bukatman (Bukatman, Foy, & DeGrazia, 1971). This checklist has had much the same history as Robey's, although not gaining nearly the visibility of its predecessor. It was developed from clinical experience. Its reliability and validity were never determined before publication and no reports on its reliability and validity were produced after its publication.

In sharp contrast to the Robey and Bukatman checklists was the work of McGarry and colleagues (1973). Their two well-known competency assessment instruments were developed very systematically between 1966 and 1970. Working with various samples of defendants being evaluated for competency, they devised two instruments that were heavily tested for interrater reliability. Their training sessions with nonphysicians as well as psychiatrists produced interrater reliability scores of .84. One test was called the Competency Screening Test (CST) and the other the Competency Assessment Instrument (CAI). The first was a 22-item sentence completion test and the second a 13-item assessment of the level of cognitive incapacity on major legal criteria. The work on these instruments is much more systematic than on the other assessment instruments, but it concentrated almost entirely on questions of reliability rather than validity. As they note, "although the interrrater reliability of the CAI has now been demonstrated, its validity remains to be adequately established" and "this limited demonstration hardly suffices to establish the validity of those two instruments" (McGarry, 1973, p. 37).

The most recent research on competency assessment is that of Shatin (1979). His work grew from McGarry's in that it examined the question of the validity of the CST as compared to regular clinical assessments and it took a 5-item subscale from the CST to determine its relationship to the entire 22-item scale. He concluded that the 5-item subscale had a very high relationship to the total scale (Rho = .92) and the subscale classified 17 of the 21 patients the same as the clinical examinations did. He recommended the use of the 5-item subscale as a tool for quick, initial competency screening.

---

[1]McGarry (1973) states that Robey reported to him that over 2,600 copies had been distributed and over 50 permissions to reprint had been given.

One change in competency assessment practices precipitated by McGarry's work was a decentralization and demedicalization of preliminary screening evaluations in some states, primarily Tennessee, Ohio, and North Carolina. The Tennessee experience has been lucidly described by Laben (1977). By means of the CAI nonmedical staff, such as social workers and paraprofessionals, performed initial screening in regional units. This was in contrast to a central state hospital being the site of evaluations conducted by psychiatrists. These developments were broad in impact and more enduring than any intense use of the McGarry instruments in final evaluations and as information included in competency hearing reports (Schreiber, 1979).

Currently there is limited interest in systematic research on these assessment questions. Much of the general disinterest in these assessment questions appears to be the preference for clinical assessment within the medical profession over a more statistical approach implicit in the instruments reviewed here. The extent to which this also is indicative of judical recalcitrance is uncertain. While it may be "good form" to report MMPI and IQ scores in court reports, there seem to be few jurisdictions where clinicians are expected, or dare, to include competency evaluation scores from any of these instruments in their reports. Thus, both ideological and practical considerations contribute to the limited research on this topic area both in the past and in the present.

JUDICIAL DETERMINATIONS OF INCOMPETENT TO STAND TRIAL

The Hearing Process

After arrest, arraignment, and psychiatric evaluation, if a defendant is believed to be incompetent to stand trial, the next step is a competency hearing. It is at this hearing that the individual is formally adjudicated incompetent to stand trial. As noted above, of all those defendants for whom the question of competency is raised after their arrest, only about 25% actually reach the point of receiving a formal competency hearing.

Although some data have been collected on judicial decision making, the formal procedures incorporated in a competency hearing rarely have been explored and described systematically. Furthermore, little is known on how such procedures vary from state to state. A chapter of our earlier work (Steadman, 1979) described in detail the procedure and context of hearings in New York. With regard to examining and evaluating judicial decision making at competency hearings, two recurring findings in the existing literature are particularly relevant. First, these hearings typically appear to perform a perfunctory task of "rubber stamping" earlier clinical evaluations. And second, the clinicians evaluating the competency of the defendant, who are relied on by the judge, frequently are unclear with regard to the legal criteria for competency.

In the New York State study referred to above, 129 competency hearings were observed in 1971 and 1972. The average length of time for these hearings was 10 minutes. Furthermore, 35% of these hearings were conducted within three minutes time. The brevity with which they were conducted appears to result from the almost complete reliance of the judge on the determination made by the psychiatrists who evaluated the defendant prior to the trial. Our study found that when the psychiatrists decided a defendant was incompetent, the judge supported that decision 92% of the time (Steadman, 1979). Similar findings of concurrence with incompetency assessments were reported in Massachusetts (92%) (McGarry, 1965) and in the United States District Court in Lexington, Kentucky (88%) (Pfeiffer, Eisenstein, & Dabbs, 1967). Roesch and Golding (1980) reported their North Carolina results were in this same high range. The rate of judicial concurrence with psychiatric assessments of the defendant being competent to stand trial also has been found to be high but lower than for an incompetency finding (Roesch & Golding, 1980). Consistent with these findings was the result of a questionnaire distributed to judges in North Carolina (Roesch & Golding, 1980) where it was found that 35% of the judges responding stated they *never* disagreed with the evaluation recommendation and the remaining 65% said that they only rarely or occasionally disagreed.

This judicial reliance on psychiatric testimony would not be so alarming if evidence indicated that psychiatrists or other clinicians had a clear and accurate understanding of what it means legally to be incompetent to stand trial. In fact, the existing data strongly suggest the opposite conclusion. As Roesch and Golding stated, "many evaluators misunderstand the distinction between competency and responsibility.... Unfortunately, these standards are sometimes confused and may lead to the evaluation of competency in terms of presence or absence of psychosis" (Roesch & Golding, 1980, p. 50). This concern that clinical evaluations frequently use criminal responsibility and competency to stand trial interchangeably without apparent knowledge of the major distinctions between these two legal statutes also has been supported by Pfeiffer, Eisenstein, and Dabbs (1967) and Hess and Thomas (1963).

Clearly the research shows a high level of concurrence between medical recommendations and judicial determinations of incompetency. The extent to which such agreement may be appropriate is entirely unclear from the data. Rather than inappropriate deference or outright default, it may be that the 25% of defendants who raise the issue of competency and are found incompetent by clinicians are those who are truly unfit to proceed. On the other hand, without some validating criterion against which to compare both clinical and judicial findings, there is a hint of excessive deference to expert medical testimony on what is fundamentally a legal issue. The extent to which one explanantion is more accurate than the other awaits more rigorous research.

CHARACTERISTICS OF PERSONS FOUND INCOMPETENT TO STAND TRIAL

Within the research literature on incompetency, there is an astonishing lack of information about persons who are found incompetent to stand trial. Frequently, efforts to gather data on this population have collected information on all persons referred for competency evaluations without separating out those who are determined to be incompetent to stand trial (e.g., Pfeiffer *et al.*, 1967; Cooke, Johnson, & Pogany, 1973; Laczko, James, & Alltrop, 1970). In order to develop an understanding of persons found incompetent to stand trial, the research that would appear to be most useful are studies that: (1) compare persons found incompetent to those persons found competent to stand trial, or (2) compare persons found incompetent to stand trial to the general population, the prison population, or the mental hospital population. Empirical studies allowing for such comparisons are rare.

The only study that compares in detail the background characteristics of those persons found incompetent to stand trial to those determined to be competent was the previously referred to Roesch and Golding study (1980). It compares a sample of 130 persons released between 1971 and 1975 from the state's maximum security prison after having regained their competency to a matched group of 140 competent defendants evaluated for competency between 1965 and 1975. These data reveal that incompetent defendants when compared to competent defendants were somewhat more likely to be black (46% to 36%) and unmarried (75% to 69%), and were significantly younger (29.6 to 36.2 mean age) and less educated (6.9 and 8.7 mean years of school) (Roesch & Golding, 1980, p. 147). Furthermore, incompetent defendants had experienced significantly more prior hospitalizations than competent defendants and also were significantly more likely to be defined as psychotic both at the time of initial diagnosis (89% to 20%) and at the final diagnosis (94% to 27%). Some additional studies also have suggested a strong relationship between psychotic diagnoses and incompetency (e.g., Cooke, 1969; McGarry, 1965). It is uncertain whether persons who are determined to be incompetent to stand trial are more likely to be psychotic than competent defendants or, more simply, that clinicians routinely diagnose those persons they think are incompetent to stand trial as being psychotic.

The only other study that provided basic background data on persons found incompetent to stand trial was our earlier work (Steadman, 1979). It examined background characteristics of all 539 males found incompetent to stand trial between September 1, 1971 and August 31, 1972 in New York State. Like the incompetent defendants studied by Roesch and Golding, the New York incompetent defendants differed from the general population in that they were disproportionately unmarried (83% versus 35% of the general population), black (46% compared to 12%), and less educated (9th grade mean attainment compared to 12th grade). In addition, this study found persons incompetent to stand trial to be rarely or irregularly employed (85%); usually having prior hospitalization in state mental hospitals (82% for an average of 29 months); and frequently arrested for prior offenses (73%). In sum, as we noted in that study, "overall, the demographic picture of these incompetent defendants is one of marginal individuals with much less than average education and few useful job skills. Most have few community ties, either through employment or family. An unusually high proportion have never been married. They appear to be a marginal group, many of whom have been and continue to shuttle back and forth between mental hospitals and prisons" (Steadman, 1979, p. 30).

DETENTION AND LEGAL DISPOSITION OF PERSONS FOUND INCOMPETENT TO STAND TRIAL

Of perhaps more importance than the question concerning who is found incompetent to stand trial, are the questions regarding what happens to persons after they are adjudicated incompetent. Answers certainly are needed to questions such as: Which incompetent defendants get hospitalized and which ones do not? How long are such defendants hospitalized pre-trial? Do incompetent defendants spend more or less time in hospitals than they would have spent in prison? What happens to those persons who are restored to competency when they are returned to the courts? As with other areas concerning incompetency, little systematic data exists.

DETENTION

A theme receiving much support in earlier research pertaining to length of hospitalization of persons found incompetent to stand trial was that they frequently were hospitalized for excessively long periods of time and that it was not unusual for persons found incompetent to stand trial to receive the equivalent of a life sentence. Evidence generating this conclusion was found initially by Hess and Thomas (1963) in their study in Michigan and supported by the Massachusetts work of McGarry and Bendt (1969), and in Illinois by Tuteur (1969). Based on these studies, the Group for Advancement of Psychiatry (GAP) in 1974 concluded that although the incompetency defense was designed to provide due process protection for defendants, "all too frequently a determination of incompetence becomes a lifetime sentence to a hospital for the criminally insane" (GAP, 1974, p. 905).

The conclusion drawn by GAP and others that incompetent defendants usually receive excessive hospitalization appears to be suspect, however, since all of the data supporting these conclusions resulted from the examination of records of persons who were at the time of study hospitalized in special security hospitals. The earlier studies rarely had followed a cohort of incompetent defendants from the incompetency determination to date of discharge. The only study prior to the GAP report that did examine this issue with cohort data was Vann's (1965). His data revealed a wide variation in the length of hospitalization experienced by incompetent defendants ranging from 3 months to 10 years. Vann noted that to a large extent this variation was explained by the seriousness of the pending charges.

The data presented in two recent studies (Steadman, 1979; Roesch & Golding, 1977) were fundamentally consistent with Vann's findings. In our 1979 study we found that incompetent defendants who had not been indicted, and typically were charged with less serious crimes, averaged one year in a state mental hospital prior to being released to the community or to the court. Incompetent defendants who had been indicted and who usually were charged with more serious crimes averaged slightly over two years in a state mental hospital before their release to the community or the court. Roesch and Golding (1980) found the average length of hospitalization for their North Carolina cohort of incompetent defendants to be approximately 2.6 years. Persons charged with murder (3.7 years) and rape (2.3) averaged the longest hospitalizations. Based on these studies it would appear the GAP conclusion that incompetent defendants frequently recieved "life time sentences" to mental hospitals is a myth supported by nonsystematic data collection and perpetuated by conventional wisdom. This is not to say, however, that some individuals found incompetent to stand trial were and are not excessively hospitalized and detained inappropriately. Perhaps the best study depicting such abuses was presented by McGarry and Bendt (1969), who on careful psychiatric evaluations found 56 of 219 incompetent defendants hospitalized in Bridgewater State Hospital in Massachusetts to be competent to stand trial. These 56 persons had averaged 4.3 years of hospitalization. The two most recent studies by Roesch and Golding and by Steadman, however, strongly suggest such abuses are currently much less frequent. It would appear that the amount of time incompetent defendants spend hospitalized is quite similar to the time they would have spent in the criminal justice system. As we stated in detail in *Beating a Rap*, when one considers the informal but ubiquitous process of "plea bargaining" and the amount of maximum sentence a convicted offender usually serves after receiving "good time" and parole consideration, "it appears that the length of time most of these (incompetent) defendants are off the streets is quite similar to what would have resulted had they remained in jail" (Steadman, 1979, p. 104).

Legal Disposition

The research examining ultimate disposition of criminal charges is quite contradictory. The major contradiction concerns the conviction rate of persons returned to court after having regained competency. In our earlier work (Steadman, 1979), we compared 88 incompetent defendants returned to stand trial in three New York City counties between November 1971 and November 1972 to 88 nondiverted criminal defendants. These data revealed that the incompetent felony defendants were significantly more likely to be convicted than nondiverted criminal defendants (93% to 80%). Consistent with this finding was the New York City Bar Study (1968) which found that 79% of all incompetent defendants returned to court were convicted. However, in contrast to these findings, Matthews's (1970) study of 21 persons charged with homicide and restored to competency found 18 (86%) of these defendants had their charges dismissed, one (5%) was found to be NGRI, and only two persons (9%) were convicted (both for manslaughter). McGarry's (1969) study of 71 incompetent defendants returned to court in Massachusetts found only 33 (46%) were convicted. Geller and Lister's work at Worcester State Hospital in Massachusetts found that only 28% of the 83 cases (primarily misdemeanors) commited to that hospital as incompetent ultimately resulted in conviction. Furthermore, Roesch's (1977) work in North Carolina found incompetent defendants returned to court were convicted at a rate of 64% as opposed to 82% for persons evaluated by psychiatrists to be competent to stand trial. Clearly more research and data are needed before any conclusory statement can be made on this issue.

Data on sentencing practices, while far less contradictory than data on conviction rates, are too preliminary for a strong conclusion to be made. Only two studies (Roesch & Golding, 1980; Steadman, 1979) have gathered sentencing data on comparison groups. Both of these suggest that incompetent defendants tend to receive less severe sentences. Roesch and Golding's North Carolina study compared the type of sentence given (prison vs. nonprison) and the average length of prison sentence for incompetent defendants returned to court and persons who had been evaluated as competent at the time of their evaluation. Although the differences between these groups rarely were statistically significant, for each offense category incompetent defendants were less likely than competent defendants to be sentenced to prison (57% to 72% overall), and with one exception (assault), incompetent defendants also received less severe prison sentences than competent defendants (Roesch & Golding, 1980, pp. 165–167). Although the differences in sentencing practices frequently were sizable, the small number of subjects in the study prevented all but two cells (type of placement for property crimes; length of sentence for violent offenses other than murder, rape, and assault) from being significant. Our earlier study (Steadman, 1979) produced findings quite similar to those of Roesch and Golding. We found incompetent defendants were sentenced to prison less often than criminal defendants staying within the criminal justice system (41% to 50%). Furthermore, the differences in sentencing practices were found for both crimes against person (52% to 67%) and to lesser extent, property and drug crimes (30% to 38%). Unfortunately, no other studies have been conducted that compare sentences given to incompetent versus competent defendants.

There are, however, three other studies that while providing no comparison group, do provide some information on the sentences given to incompetent defendants. The New York City Bar (1968) found two-thirds of the IST convictions studied in New York State in 1964 produced guilty pleas, typically for a reduced charge where the sentence was to "time served." Vann's study in Erie County, New York, produced similar findings where in the majority of cases the court allowed the time spent in a criminal mental hospital to substitute for a prison sentence. McGarry (1969) found only 14 of 33 incompetent defendants convicted (42.4%) received prison sentences. While these rates are useful, they really tell us nothing about how incompetent defendants fare relative to other groups in the same jurisdictions. As yet all we can say is that there is some indication that Roesch and Golding's (1980) conclusion about property offenders is generalizeable to most ISTs: "These defendants were significantly more likely to receive a suspended sentence, usually because defendants were given credit for time spent in the hospital. This time often exceeded the prison sentence which could have been given" (1980, p. 174).

Thus, while data on the impact of an incompetent assessment on ultimate court conviction is left unanswered by the existing research, the data clearly indicate that judges tend to give incompetent defendants returned to court less severe sentences when convicted. This difference in sentence would appear to be based on the time spent hospitalized prior to conviction which is equivocated by judges to incarceration times. Another explanation of these data is that the judges see the "mental illness" associated with incompetency as somehow mitigating culpability of the alleged criminal actions (Monahan & Ruggerio, 1980). Regardless of cause, the data suggest dispositional differences for defendants diverted as incompetent as compared to other criminal defendants.

POST-RELEASE RECIDIVISM RATES AND REHOSPITALIZATION

Only two studies examine the issue of post-release recidivism and rehospitalization, Mowbray's in Michigan (1979) and our study in New York referred to above (Steadman, 1979). Mowbray's study followed-up 222 persons discharged from the State Department of Mental Health after being rendered competent to stand trial during fiscal years 1972 and 1973. Mowbray collected follow-up data on both state rehospitalization and arrests. The data revealed that 55% of the sample reentered Michigan state hospitals. One-third of the 223 readmissions by these 222 persons were criminally related, and two-thirds were voluntary admissions or involuntary civil commitments. Most of the forensic readmissions were related to the IST charge that brought them into the study but, as Mowbray pointed out, even if these rehospitalizations were excluded, the rehospitalization rate still would be 50%. The mean time from discharge to readmission was 10.7 months for forensic and 1.5 months for the civil commitments. It should be noted that such immediate civil commitments may have resulted from judges dropping charges on the condition of the defendant accepting civil hospitalization.

With regard to subsequent criminal involvement, 32% of Mowbray's sample had one or more subsequent arrests (14% committing crimes against person, 25% committing crimes against property). The mean time from release to arrest was about 17 months, ranging from two weeks to 4½ years. Sixteen percent of the sample had one or more subsequent convictions. The average sentence for those 20 persons convicted was approximately 10 years. These data, along with the finding that 80% of this population never went to jail, caused Mowbray to conclude that while the mental health services given to this population were effective in returning these persons to court in a reasonable time, "in terms of overall outcomes, the present system of dealing with ISTs is a miserable failure. . . . In terms of preparing the individual to adapt to society or of protecting society, the present method of dealing with those adjudicated incompetents is unsuccessful" (Mowbray, 1979, p. 38). Mowbray goes on to suggest that rather than placing these persons for inappropriately long stays as in the past, they are now restored to competency and then forgotten about and returned to the community before they are ready to return.

It should be noted here that the two goals posited by Mowbray for incompetency (i.e., protection of society and helping an individual adapt to society) were not among those mentioned by us earlier in this chapter. Rather, the legal bases of incompetency rest on due process legal protections that are quite incidental to the treatment and societal protection goals mentioned by Mowbray. These latter goals are probably quite consistent with many expectations of the general population, but they are distortions of the legal underpinnings of incompetency.

Our earlier work (Steadman, 1979) also examined the issue of rehospitalization and recidivism by examining the post-release experiences of 411 persons found incompetent between September 1, 1971, and August 31, 1972 and subsequently returned to the community by June 30, 1974. These 411 incompetent defendants averaged 18 months in the community during the follow-up. Of these 411 persons, 44% were rehospitalized. Rehospitalization was found to be strongly related to whether the person had any hospitalization history prior to the incompetency determination and how extensive that history had been. The percentage of persons rehospitalized ranged from 22% of those with no prior hospitalizations to 57% for those with three or more prior hospitalizations.

With regard to rearrest, our study found 44% ($N = 182$) of the subjects to be arrested at least once. Nine of the defendants were arrested once, 33 were arrested twice, and 50 were arrested at least three times. Less than 15% of the subjects were arrested for violent crimes.

The similarities in these two studies' findings suggest similar conclusions. Clearly, incompetent defendants are prone to rearrest just as are the general criminal population. The recidivism rates found by Mowbray (32%) and by us (44%) are relatively consistent with the figures usually produced in follow-up studies of prison inmates (Glaser, 1969; Kassebaum, Ward, & Wilner, 1971). Furthermore, the recidivism rate of incompetent defendants appears to be considerably higher than the subsequent arrest rate of released mental hospital patients, 9.8% (cf. Steadman et al., 1978). Both studies also revealed only a small minority of incompetent defendants were subsequently arrested for violent crimes against persons. Further, these two studies suggest that about half of the population subsequently return to state mental hospitals.

Clearly, then, these two studies show that persons found incompetent to stand trial are not "rehabilitated" in either the usual criminal justice or mental health sense of the word. Although Mowbray feels these data indicate the inappropriate handling of persons found incompetent to stand trial, it is our position that these data should not be used to evaluate the use of the incompetency to stand trial status or the treatment provided to this group. As we stated in our earlier work (Steadman & Cocozza, 1979),

> The justification for this [incompetency to stand trial] is that the defendant does not possess the mental abilities to participate rationally in a trial. There is nothing in the statutes or mental health treatment goals that suggests that recidivism rates should be the measure of the program's success. . . . Incompetency diversion is intended to maintain a balance between the rights of the state and the rights of the individual to due process. (p. 124)

With this research on recidivism we have exhausted the empirical data on the persons in and the effects of the incompetency to stand trial machinery in the United States. What there is quite clearly points to very socially and economically disadvantaged persons who have been consistently in jails and mental hospitals. They no longer are detained for life. Rather, after periods quite similar to experiences in the criminal justice system, they return to the community to begin the cycle again.

Before these or any other conclusions can be applied to jurisdictions beyond those few that have generated the data reviewed here, much more work is needed. Furthermore, only a very few of many critical questions about the practices and impacts of incompetency have been empirically addressed thus far. In the final section of this chapter we will concentrate primarily on additional problem areas for which negligible data may exist and/or those that were suggested by the materials just reviewed.

MAJOR RESEARCH NEEDS

As we explicate the most critical areas that could profit most from research attention, we will present them in the order of the priority we place on them. Priorities may vary from jurisdiction to jurisdiction depending, for example, on the extent to which a given jurisdiction's procedures and facilities are similar to those in another area for which research data now exist. For example, if a defense attorney wishes to assess the costs and benefits of suggesting a client be evaluated for competency, he or she may be able to make an informed recommendation to a client if the attorney knows the state's statutes, procedures, facilities, and practices are similar to those in New York, Michigan, or North Carolina, where good empirical data have been developed. With such real needs as these in mind, we offer the following list of topics that could benefit from research.

Processing from Arrest until Evaluation for Competency

Beyond anecdotes, almost nothing in regard to competency is known about what transpires pre-trial between the defendant and the arresting officer(s), the defendant and the jailer, the defendant and his or her attorney, the defendant and the prosecution, or any of the possible permutations of these relationships. The research that has been done both on incompetent defendants and on the processes for determining competency begins at the point the defendant is brought in for screening for competency. What occurs prior to this has never been systematically recorded. Clearly the parties involved in any given case engage in considerable negotiation. Such negotiations are especially problematic when we recall the discrepancy reported by Mowbray (1969) and Steadman and Braff (1975) between the charges of defendants found incompetent and those of all statewide arrests or of inmates in state prisons. The incompetent defendants in both instances had more serious charges on the whole. Why? One can only speculate. This speculation, however, would seem to center on the bargaining process, possibly in lieu of a straightforward plea bargain. For example, are district attorneys more willing to plea bargain in cases of violent crime after community reactions simmer down or after some retribution is obtained via maximum security mental hospitalization? Do defense attorneys project this as happening regardless of the validity of the perception, and, therefore, request competency evaluations? No study has yet been undertaken to document what the negotiation processes are and how they may be related to the seriousness of the pending criminal charges.

Not only are the negotiations carried out and bargains struck between the defense attorney and the prosecution or the defense attorney and his or her client, but also there are key decisions that also may involve negotiation between the defendant and the police and jail personnel with whom the defendant is in contact immediately after arrest. Although the folklore is that incompetency is almost always raised by the defense attorney or by an arraigning judge, whether this is the case has not been empirically documented. Even if it overtly is, to what extent is the question initially posed to the attorney by the jail staff? The whole set of interactions from the point of arrest to admission for initial competency evaluation is an empirical void. The research designs that would be required to generate such data are complex and costly. Nevertheless, they are truly critical if we are to have a full understanding of the real role of incompetency practices in the American criminal justice and mental health systems. As it stands we have at most only a partial picture until a greater research emphasis is placed on the events prior to competency evaluations. An accurate understanding of the practices surrounding incompetency determinations is most hindered by the total absence of systematic study of the early stages in the incompetency process.

THE IMPACT OF JACKSON

From the standpoint of legal precedent there was no mental health case law in the 1970s of greater importance than *Jackson v. Indiana* (406 U.S. 715, 1972), which set an upper limit on the maximum detention of ISTs when they were not expected to become competent. Unless there is a "reasonable probability" that within the "foreseeable future" a defendant can proceed with a trial, continued retention requires using the mental health statutes for involuntary commitments. In any casebook on mental health law, *Jackson* receives elaborate consideration, and quite appropriately so. However, it is also probable that *Jackson's* notoriety from a case law perspective is extremely misleading in terms of its actual impact on mental health facilities and the processing of ISTs.

There has been no systematic research on the actual impact of *Jackson* in any jurisdiction. What adaptations have states really made? What are *Jackson* hearings? How many such hearings actually occur in any given year? To what extent does the impact of *Jackson* resemble that of the 1966 revision of the New York Mental Hygiene Law that Kumusaka (1972) found to result in patients being released once they indicated they would contest the psychiatric report? Are clinicians similarly avoiding *Jackson* hearings in ways that would not be apparent simply from studying *Jackson* hearings? Has *Jackson* lowered the number of ISTs in the system? What have been the impacts of patients successfully petitioning for release or transfer under *Jackson*? In fact, how often does a *Jackson* petition result in outright release because a defendant does not meet civil commitment standards? Does the presence of *Jackson* impede or enhance treatment for ISTs?

These and other questions remained untouched by the probes of the research community. It is quite possible that the considerable legal interest in the precedent of *Jackson* is much ado about nothing as far as real impact on the processing of ISTs. The extent to which this landmark legal decision has affected patients, staff, and the legal and mental health systems is as yet unknown and warrants much attention.

The Costs of Raising the Issue

There is a strong suggestion in the work of Cook, Pogany, and John-ston (1974), reviewed above, that the courts may act differently, in terms of sentencing, to persons who have had a mental health evaluation. Their sample was comprised of both incompetent defendants and NGRIs. Examining only the group of incompetent defendants in New York, we found that, as compared to defendants who remained in the criminal jus-tice system, those adjudicated as incompetent to stand trial were more often convicted although sentenced less often to prison (Steadman, 1979). The extent to which these two studies may be generalized is an important question both from the standpoint of court and prosecutorial practices and from the defense attorney's actual advice to a client.

In dealing with the question of the impact of mental health evalu-ation and diversion, it is important to note that the two studies just men-tioned deal with two somewhat distinct questions. The first deals with the impact of simply being referred for evaluation, regardless of whether or not the defendant is found incompetent. The second centers on the question of what differences occur if the defendant is found incompetent to stand trial as compared to defendants who are handled entirely within the criminal justice system. Both questions are significant, but they may be very different, albeit important, questions.

Links of Incompetency to Insanity Acquittal

A set of questions very closely allied to those just raised about the impact of incompetency evaluation and adjudication relate to an ultimate disposition of NGRI. It has been popular to suggest that an incompetency determination, and possibly even requests by an attorney for evaluation, is little more than the first step in an insanity plea. As we have previously mentioned (Steadman, 1979), a major goal in the preliminary screening of one large New York City hospital was to prevent the admission to the psychiatric prison ward of persons who clearly were not incompetent to stand trial. This stance was predicated on the belief that many attorneys simply wished to have a mental health admission and evaluation as part of a defendant's record, feeling that it would strengthen the evidence favoring an insanity acquittal. The three studies with data to address these questions reviewed earlier did not support these views.

Mowbray (1979) found that among 200 defendants released from mental health facilities after treatment 13% were found NGRI. Interest-ingly, those charged with murder had a significantly higher probability of receiving this disposition than less serious offenders. Among the 539 cases we studied in New York (Steadman, 1979), only 2% were acquitted by reason of insanity. The total number of persons acquitted by reason of insanity in New York during the period in which these defendants were NGRI was about 135, and 11 cases from our sample comprise but 8% of the total. Roesch and Golding (1980) report that 1 of 137 defendants referred for competency evaluations was found NGRI. Thus, from the three studies with data on these questions, there is no support that incompetency is a necessary or sufficient prelude to an NGRI disposition. A very small percentage of all incompetency cases were so disposed of and those that were NGRI made up a small proportion of all insanity acquittals. However, the studies represent but three jurisdictions at three time periods. The links between incompetency and insanity acquittals are quite different in other jurisdications. To what extent and in what ways we are again left to speculate about. These are important questions deserving comprehensive research attention.

WOMEN AND YOUTH

The major research and policy questions that emerge from the consideration of women and youth relate to the infrequent use and/or availability of both the plea and special facilities after such determinations. As we saw above in the data from our recent national survey, there are few women who are found incompetent to stand trial. Further, many states are unable to identify how many women are found incompetent. This in large part results from the lack of discrete programs for them. As opposed to their male counterparts in most states, female defendants found incompetent to stand trial are placed in a general purpose mental health or correctional facility where they may be distinguished within the existing treatment program only by their legal status. An intriguing question that arises from the lack of discrete programs is whether women are receiving unequal protection under the law. Do they have equal access to appropriate facilities for treatment if found incompetent? Do they have equal access to the plea? That is, if no programs exist for women, is the court equally willing to entertain the competency examination petition? Do women have access to clinicians who are suitably specialized in forensic issues to sort out the questions of competency from those of mental illness? To begin to answer some of these questions a careful look at the processing of the women IST is needed. None now exists. Our national survey but hints at what may be some hidden problems. A very focused examination across a variety of jurisdictions could be most profitable.

The questions of equal protection also relate to youth. New York, for

example, revised its statutes effective September 1, 1979 to allow a finding of incompetency to stand trial for juveniles. In the first 16 months, 4
youths were found IST. To what extent this small number represents limited needs or system resistance to a complex set of new procedures is
entirely unclear. Further, as we suggested in our discussion on *Jackson*,
it may be that this statutory revision had the effect of increasing mental
health services pre-trial through the more frequent use of other avenues
that had previously existed but were little used. That is, to look at the
direct impacts of any statutory revision that served only 4 juveniles may
underestimate badly the real impact of the change.

In dealing with juvenile incompetency to stand trial there are
numerous legal issues that may stimulate legal scholars. Meantime, however, some empirical assessments of the impact of legislation in those few
jurisdictions that have introduced incompetency for juveniles would
help frame such legal analyses. Further, it may be instructive to delve
into the mental health services for youth in the family court system to
evaluate the extent to which incompetency legislation may impact in the
future and the extent to which it is currently needed to protect this often
disadvantaged population. We know almost nothing about the functioning of incompetency to stand trial for youth and women.

THE VALIDITY OF COMPETENCY SCREENING INSTRUMENTS

This area is one where some of the needed work is underway. As we
discussed earlier in this chapter, the work that went into developing the
two McGarry screening instruments (McGarry & Bendt, 1973) concentrated heavily on interrater reliability, avoiding most validity questions
beyond the instruments' face validity, which is widely disputed (Schreiber, 1978). It remains to be determined whether independent clinical
assessments and judicial findings validate the items on either the CAI or
the CST. A significant step toward answering these questions is underway under the direction of Jan Schreiber, Stephen Golding, and Ronald
Roesch. Using data from Boston and Chicago, they will compare decisions of an expert panel representing the "state of the art" in competency
assessments; the actual outcomes of a set of cases; and the evaluations by
the CST and the CAI. This is a most significant step, but more will be
needed. What is the situation in nonmetropolitan areas? How might
validity vary as the make-up of the expert panel was varied across dis-
ciplines? What implications does the push toward initial screening by
paraprofessionals in decentralized locations have for the mix on expert
panels? Certainly, within any one study only so many factors can be
manipulated adequately. Thus, it is encouraging to see the work of

Schreiber, Golding, and Roesch, but their efforts should be seen as an impetus to other researchers rather than as an effort likely to produce a full set of answers to the complex questions.

DESCRIPTION OF DEFENDANTS EVALUATED AND FOUND INCOMPETENT

As we noted a number of times in our review of the research, very few studies have adequately described the samples that were studied. Also, only the Roesch and Golding (1980) study contains a detailed comparison of defendants who were found competent versus those who were found incompetent. From the descriptions of the ISTs that are available, it seems that there is considerable similarity across jurisdictions. These defendants have substantial arrest records and many prior hospitalizations and have almost no community roots. How this group compares to all those for whom the competency question is raised is entirely unclear. One might speculate, in fact, that they vary greatly. If, as Roesch (1980) and we (Steadman, 1979) have argued, the question of competency often is raised as a dispositional ploy when competency is not really doubted, it may be that the more socially and economically advantaged within the evaluation group are consistently screened out. Regardless, the analysis of almost every question posed in the research needs section would benefit from descriptive data.

Although there is more information on incompetency issues than the others covered in this book, "more" is not enough. This is a large group of individuals utilizing many beds in public facilities, subject to many unknown legal and clinical practices that warrant empirical analysis on ethical, fiscal, and jurisprudence grounds.

THE ROLE OF DANGEROUSNESS

The role of the psychiatrist as an expert witness predicting the probabilities of future violent behavior have been the focus of much discussion (Monahan, 1981; Rappaport, Lassen, & Hay, 1967) and some research (Steadman & Cocozza, 1979; Steadman & Morrissey, 1980). That these issues should be mentioned in a research agenda for incompetency to stand trial is an indication of an ongoing miscarriage of the legal system. In fact, one of our longitudinal studies of the inaccuracy of psychiatric predictions of dangerousness followed a change in New York's Criminal Procedure Law as it related to incompetency (cf. Steadman, 1979).

In 1971 New York decided to remove from the Department of Correctional Services the responsibility for care and detention of all ISTs, with one exception. Those defendants who were charged with a felony and were indicted would not necessarily go to the Department of Mental Hygiene, as would all misdemeanors and unindicted felony defendants.[2] Rather, a determination of dangerousness would be made by the court based on the testimony of two psychiatrists. Those found dangerous would continue to be treated in a maximum security mental hospital under the auspices of Corrections. As we detailed elsewhere (Steadman, 1979), this arrangement was thought to be unconstitutional after two years, since unconvicted defendants were being detained in Correctional Department facilities. In fact, that such constitutional considerations ever entered consideration is inappropriate since dangerousness should never have been linked to determinations of competency in the first place. Arguably, it has a role in an assessment for release on bail for outpatient evaluation. This clearly coincides with the 1981 Reagan proposal for an assessment of dangerouness in any bail decision. However, this issue is quite distinct from the inclusion of considerations of dangerousness in reports on competency *per se*. Such questions involve only *Dusky* cognitive standards among which dangerousness is conspicuously absent.

The issue of incompetency revolves around the defendant's capacity to work with an attorney and understand the court process and his or her criminal charge(s). Such issues do not involve dangerousness. Yet, in fact, when one talks with the clinicians who regularly prepare the court reports on competency, one is told that, "sure, in many cases we comment on the patients' dangerousness" or "the judges require that we give them some opinion on dangerousness." The extent to which such demands are operative and met needs to be examined. The hows and whys of such practices demand attention because of the impropriety of such linkages. A determination of competency should be entirely outside the question of dangerousness. If such a prediction is a core part of the court's determination, remedial action is warranted. We know very little about the role that estimations of dangerousness may play in the incompetency determinations.

REFERENCES

Bukatman, B. A., Foy, J. L., & DeGrazia, E. What is competency to stand trial? *American Journal of Psychiatry*, 1971, *127*, 1225–1229.

----

[2]Implicit in the New York State Criminal Procedure Law revision that became effective on September 1, 1971, were assumptions that (1) those defendants who had the highest probability of being violent would be charged with the most serious offenses, and (2) defendants with the most serious offenses would be indicted by a grand jury before the question of competency to stand trial was adjudicated. In New York, a trial cannot proceed on a felony charge without an indictment from a grand jury.

Cooke, G. The court study unit: Patient characteristics and difference between patients judged competent and incompetent. *Journal of Clinical Psychology*, 1969, *25*, 140–143.

Cooke, G., Johnson, N., & Pogany, E. Factors affecting referral to determine competency to stand trial. *American Journal of Psychiatry*, 1973, *130*, 870–875.

Geller, J. L., & Lister, E. D. The process of criminal commitment for pretrial psychiatric examination: An evaluation. *American Journal of Psychiatry*, 1978, *135*, 53–60.

Glaser, D. The effectiveness of a prison and parole system (abridged ed.). New York: Bobbs-Merrill, 1969.

Goldstein, R. L. The fitness factory. Part I: The psychiatrist's role in determining competency. *American Journal of Psychiatry*, 1973, *130*, 1144–1147.

Group for the Advancement of Psychiatry. Misuse of psychiatry in the criminal courts: Competency to stand trial, 1974, *8*, report 89.

Hess, J. H., Jr., & Thomas, H. E. Incompetency to stand trial: Procedures, results, and problems. *American Journal of Psychiatry*, 1963, *119*, 713–720.

Kassebaum, G., Ward, D., & Wilner, D. *Prison treatment and parole survival*. New York: Wiley, 1971.

Kumasaka, Y. The lawyers role in involuntary commitment—New York's experience. *Mental Hygiene*, 1972, *56*, 21–29.

Laben, J. K., Kashgarian, M., Nessa, D., & Spencer, L. D. Reform from the inside: Mental health center evaluations of competency to stand trial. *Journal of Community Psychology*, 1977, *5*, 52–62.

Laczko, A. L., James, J. F., & Alltrop, L. B. A study of four hundred and thirty court-referred cases. *Journal of Forensic Sciences*, 1970, *15*, 311–323.

McGarry, A. L. Competency for trial and due process via the state hospital. *American Journal of Psychiatry*, 1965, *22*, 623–631.

McGarry, A. L. Demonstration and research in competency for trial and mental illness: Review and preview. *Boston University Law Review*, 1969, *49*, 46–61.

McGarry, A. L. *Competency to stand trial and mental illness*. Washington, D.C.: U.S. Government Printing Office, 1973.

McGarry, A. L., & Bendt, R. H. Criminal vs. civil commitment of psychotic offenders: A seven year follow-up. *American Journal of Psychiatry*, 1969, *125*, 93–100.

Monahan, J. *The clinical prediction of violent behavior*. Washington, D.C.: U.S. Government Printing Office, 1981.

Monahan, J., & Ruggerio, M. Psychological and psychiatric aspects of determinate sentencing. *International Journal of Law and Psychiatry*, 1980, *3*, 143–154.

Mowbray, C. T. A study of patients treated as incompetent to stand trial. *Social Psychiatry*, 1979, *14*, 31–39.

New York City Bar Association, Special Committee on the Study of Commitment Procedures and the Law Relating to Incompetents. *Mental illness, due process, and the criminal defendant*. New York: Fordham, 1968.

Pfeiffer, E., Eisenstein, R. B., & Dabbs, E. G. Mental competency evaluations for the federal court: I. Methods and results. *The Journal of Nervous and Mental Disease*, 1967, *144*, 320–328.

Rappaport, J. R., Lassen, G., & Hay, N. B. A review of the literature of the dangerousness of the mentally ill. In J. Rappaport (Ed.), *The Clincal Evaluation of the Mentally Ill*. Washington, D.C.: American Psychiatric Association, 1967.

Robey, A. Criteria for competency to stand trial: A checklist for psychiatrists. *American Journal of Psychiatry*, 1965, *122*, 616–622.

Roesch, R., & Golding, S. L. *A systems analysis of competency to stand trial procedures: Implications for forensic services in North Carolina*. Urbana, Ill. University of Illinois Press, 1977.

Roesch, R., & Golding, S. L. *Competency to stand trial.* Urbana, Ill. University of Illinois Press, 1980.

Scheidemandel, P. L., & Kanno, C. K. *The mentally ill offender: A survey of treatment programs.* Baltimore: Gavamond/Pridemork, 1969.

Schreiber, J., Golding, S. L., Roesch, R., & Heller, M. Evaluation of competency assessment procedures. Grant proposal to National Institute of Mental Health, 1979.

Shatin, L. Brief form of the competency screening test for mental competence to stand trial. *Journal of Clinical Psychology,* 1979, *35,* 464–467.

Steadman, H. J. *Beating a rap? Defendants found incompetent to stand trial.* Chicago: University of Chicago Press, 1979.

Steadman, H. J., & Braff, J. Crimes of violence and incompetency diversion. *Journal of Criminal Law and Criminology,* 1975, *66,* 73–78.

Steadman, H. J., & Cocozza, J. J. The dangerousness standard and psychiatry: A cross national issue in the social control of the mentally ill. *Sociology and Social Research,* 1979, *63,* 649–670.

Steadman, H. J., Monahan, J., Hartstone, E., Davis, S. K., & Robbins, P. C. Mentally disordered offenders: A national survey of patients and facilities. *Law and Human Behavior,* 1982, *6,* 31–38.

Steadman, H. J., & Morrissey, J. The statistical prediction of violent behavior: Measuring the cost of a civil libertarian versus a public protectionist model. *Law and Human Behavior,* 1981, *5,* 1–12.

Stone, A. A. *Mental health and law: A system of transition,* Washington, D.C.: U.S. Government Printing Office, 1975.

Tuteur, W. Incompetency to stand trial, A survey. *Corrective Therapy and Journal of Social Therapy,* 1969, *15,* 73–79.

Vann, C. R. Pre-trial decision-making: an analysis of the use of psychiatric information in the administration of criminal justice. *University of Detroit Law Journal,* 1965, *43,* 13–33.

II

ACQUITTAL BY REASON OF INSANITY

3

Acquittal by Reason of Insanity

DEVELOPMENTS IN THE LAW

GRANT MORRIS

INTRODUCTION

Our criminal law is premised on this assumption: Because an individual has the ability to choose between socially acceptable and socially unacceptable behavior, he or she can be held responsible for conduct that violates the law. Thus, an individual who chooses to commit a crime is morally blameworthy and therefore an appropriate subject for punishment. The insanity defense developed as a device to exclude from criminal responsibility people whom society views as not blameworthy. A severely mentally disordered individual is not considered blameworthy because he or she lacks the capacity (free will) to form the intent to commit a criminal act.

Modern formulations of the test of insanity are derived from the 1843 case of *Daniel M'Naghten*.[1] M'Naghten shot and killed the secretary to the British prime minister, mistaking the secretary for the prime minister. At his trial, M'Naghten proved that he had acted under a delusion that the Tory party was persecuting him. M'Naghten's inability to control his conduct resulted in an acquittal by reason of insanity. In response

[1]M'Naghten's Case, 10 CLARK & FIN. 200, 8 ENG. REP. 718 (1843).

GRANT MORRIS • School of Law, University of San Diego, San Diego, California 92110.

to that decision, the House of Lords, utilizing advisory opinions received from common law judges, formulated a new, more restrictive insanity defense. The insanity defense was limited to instances in which the accused "was labouring under such a defect of reason, from disease of the mind, as not to know the nature and quality of the act he was doing; or, if he did know it, that he did not know he was doing what was wrong."[2] Although this test focuses on the defendant's cognitive capacity, a majority of American jurisdictions today utilize a test of insanity that also excuses from criminal responsibility defendants who are unable to control their conduct due to mental disorder.[3]

Because the purpose of the insanity defense is to identify those individuals who are not criminally blameworthy, one would expect that an individual who successfully pleaded the insanity defense would not be equated with criminally blameworthy, sentence-serving convicts. Historically, however, the person found not guilty of crime by reason of insanity (NGI) was disposed of in a manner that stigmatized him or her as both criminal and mentally ill—twice-cursed, as mad and bad. For

---

[2]*Id.* at 210, 8 ENG. REP. at 722.

[3]In some states, the M'Naghten rule has been supplemented by an "irresistible impulse" test. "The irresistible impulse doctrine is applicable only to that class of cases where the accused is able to understand the nature and consequences of his act and knows it is wrong, but his mind has become so impaired by disease that he is totally deprived of the mental power to control or restrain his act." Thompson v. Commonwealth, 193 Va. 704, 70 S.E.2d 284, 286 (1952). By statute in Georgia, a person is not guilty of a crime if he acted "because of a delusional compulsion as to such act which overmastered his will to resist committing the crime." GA. CODE § 26–703 (1978). Similarly, in Colorado, a person whose legal insanity is manifested "by irresistible impulse or otherwise" is not accountable for his behavior. COLO. REV. STAT. § 16–8–101 (1978).

The American Law Institute (ALI), in its Model Penal Code, proposed an insanity test formulation that combines, in modern language, the cognitive factor of M'Naghten and the control factor of irresistible impulse:

> (1) A person is not responsible for criminal conduct if at the time of such conduct as a result of mental disease or defect he lacks substantial capacity either to appreciate the criminality [wrongfulness] of his conduct or to conform his conduct to the requirements of law.
> (2) As used in this Article, the terms "mental disease or defect" do not include an abnormality manifested only by repeated criminal or otherwise anti-social conduct.

MODEL PENAL CODE § 4.01 (Proposed Official Draft 1962). The ALI test, with minor modifications, has become the predominant test of criminal responsibility in the United States.

example, Daniel M'Naghten was sent to Broadmoor, where he remained for 22 years, until his death in 1865. During that time, no court ever examined his mental condition to determine the propriety of his continued confinement in that mental institution.[4]

Although much legislative, judicial, and scholarly attention has been directed to revising the technical language utilized in the various formulations of the insanity defense, until recently little attention has been focused on reforming the system of disposing of those who successfully assert the defense. Without such reform, however, the insanity defense no longer can be justified as an instrument to determine criminal responsibility. In this chapter, I will examine three major NGI dispositional issues: mandatory, indeterminate commitment; release criteria and procedures; and conditions of confinement. With each, I will focus on whether recent developments signify that needed reform has occurred or is occurring.

POST-INSANITY ACQUITTAL COMMITMENT ISSUES

MANDATORY, INDETERMINATE COMMITMENT

Many people erroneously assume that the insanity defense is frequently pleaded and often successful. A college student sample estimated that of the 22,102 felony indictments in Wyoming, 8,151 utilized the NGI plea and that 44% of those were successful. In fact, only 102 persons made the plea and only one was successful.[5] Only 278 individuals were adjudicated NGI in New York State between April 1, 1965, and June 30, 1976.[6] Nevertheless, societal concern that the insanity defense will unleash a horde of criminally blameless defendants to prey on the public resulted in the enactment of laws to ensure that insanity acquittees are automatically committed to mental institutions at the end of their criminal trials. Many states mandated indeterminate commitment on a

---

[4]Benham v. Edwards, 501 F. Supp. 1050, 1057 (N.D. Ga. 1980).
[5]PASEWARK, PANTLE, & STEADMAN, *The Insanity Plea in New York State, 1965–1976*, 51 N.Y. ST. B.J. 186, 186–87 (1979).
[6]*Id.* A federal official estimates that fewer than 100 NGI acquittals occur in the more than 50,000 federal criminal cases brought annually. Dershowitz, *Abolishing the Insanity Defense: The Most Significant Feature of the Administration's Proposed Criminal Code—An Essay,* 9 CRIM. L. BULL. 434 (1973).

finding of NGI while others made indeterminate commitment easily achievable under a variety of procedures and standards.[7]

Automatic indeterminate postacquittal commitment assumes that the criminal trial proved that the defendant should be institutionalized. This assumption would be warranted only if the trial had established that the defendant committed the criminal act, that he or she was insane at the time of the act and continues to be insane. The trial, however, does not establish these facts. When the insanity defense has been raised, the jury is not generally called upon to make an express finding that the defendant committed the underlying criminal act and would have been found guilty of the crime had he or she not been found insane. Moreover, half the states place the ultimate burden of proof on the prosecution and an insanity acquittal in those jurisdictions establishes only that the jury had a reasonable doubt about whether the defendant was sane.[8]

Even if a jurisdiction required that the jury determine specifically that the defendant committed the criminal act and that the defendant had been insane at the time it was committed, an indiscriminately applied presumption that the defendant's insanity continues at the time of disposition is not logical. A criminal defendant may not stand trial unless he or she is mentally competent.[9] Although the test of incompetency differs from the test of insanity, the fact that the trial was held at all undermines an inflexible presumption of continued insanity.[10] The defendant's mental disorder, existing at the time of the criminal act, may well have dissipated since that time, at least to the extent that the disorder affects defendant's cognitive ability to understand.[11] Additionally, an insanity acquittal is a determination of irresponsibility for a specific crim-

---

[7]*See* statutes compiled in Note, *Commitment Following an Insanity Acquittal*, 94 HARV. L. REV. 605 n. 4 (1981); GERMAN & SINGER, *Punishing the Not Guilty: Hospitalization of Persons Acquitted by Reason of Insanity*, 29 RUTGERS L. REV. 1011, 1076–79 (1976); G. MORRIS, THE INSANITY DEFENSE: A BLUEPRINT FOR LEGISLATIVE REFORM 93–94, 97–126 (1975); AMERICAN BAR FOUNDATION, THE MENTALLY DISABLED AND THE LAW 430–43 (table 11.1) (rev. ed.) Brackel & Rock, eds., 1971).

[8]A state-by-state analysis of the burden of proof issue is presented in G. MORRIS, *supra* note 7, at 91–92, 97–126.

[9]Pate v. Robinson, 383 U.S. 375 (1966).

[10]A. GOLDSTEIN, THE INSANITY DEFENSE 144 (1967) (footnotes omitted).

[11]In Dusky v. United States, 362 U.S. 402 (1960), the Supreme Court ruled that in federal prosecutions, the test of a defendant's competency is whether defendant "has sufficient present ability to consult with his lawyer with a reasonable degree of rational understanding—and whether he has a rational as well as factual understanding of the proceedings against him." *Id.*

inal act committed in the past. That determination does not justify a presumption that the insanity acquittee would be criminally irresponsible for other criminal acts that might be committed in the future.[12]

Other possible justifications for mandatory, indeterminate commitment also are dubious. Automatic commitment is not needed to discourage the fabrication of insanity defense pleas.[13] In fact, a mandatory, indeterminate commitment statute improperly discourages legitimate insanity pleas by those who are criminally blameless but who are unwilling to risk indeterminate commitment in a mental institution for the certainty of a fixed prison sentence.

The existence of habeas corpus or other release proceedings after commitment is not an adequate safeguard justifying automatic, indeterminate commitment on NGI acquittal. Some states require the insanity acquittee to wait a year[14] or more[15] before he or she may initiate a release proceeding. The burden of proof in these proceedings and in habeas corpus proceedings usually is placed on the patient who seeks release. The United States Court of Appeals for the District of Columbia Circuit has noted that in cases involving psychiatric testimony—which is often unclear and confused—the burden of proof allocation can be outcome determinative.[16] These obstacles clearly make habeas corpus or other patient-initiated release proceedings an inadequate substitute for a hearing prior to any hospitalization order.

A defendant who pleads the insanity defense should not, by that plea alone, be estopped from claiming that he or she is no longer mentally ill. The "estoppel" argument focuses on the antisocial act that was committed by the NGI defendant and erroneously construes that act as a criminal act.[17] Although in many jurisdictions a defendant who asserts an insanity defense may be admitting the commission of an act, the

---

[12]Note, *supra* note 7, at 611–12.

[13]In Lynch v. Overholser, 369 U.S. 705 (1962), the United States Supreme Court ruled that a mandatory, indeterminate commitment statute could not be applied to an insanity acquittee who had not affirmatively asserted the insanity defense. In dictum, the Court opined, "Congress might have considered it appropriate to provide compulsory commitment for those who successfully invoke an insanity defense in order to discourage false pleas of insanity." *Id.* at 715.

[14]UTAH CODE § 77–24–16 (1953).

[15]A recently repealed Indiana statute required an insanity acquittee to wait two years after commitment to initiate a release proceeding. *See* statutes listed in AMERICAN BAR FOUNDATION, *supra* note 7, at 430–43 (table 11.1).

[16]Waite v. Jacobs, 475 F.2d 392, 395 (D.C. Cir. 1973).

[17]*See, e.g.,* State v. Kee, 510 S.W.2d 477, 480–81 (Mo. 1974).

defendant is not admitting the commission of a *criminal* act.[18] His or her current mental condition, and not the past act alone, must be examined at the conclusion of the criminal trial to determine whether mental hospitalization is now appropriate.

Some courts have ruled that the commission of an antisocial act establishes that the insanity acquittee is dangerously mentally ill and should be subjected to automatic indeterminate commitment.[19] These decisions fail to account for insanity acquittals in which the defendant was charged with a nonviolent crime. Additionally, other mentally ill individuals who were alleged to be dangerous nevertheless were accorded the procedural and substantive protections of the civil commitment process. Individuals found morally blameless in criminal trials should be entitled to no less protection.[20]

RELEASE AND DISCHARGE FROM COMMITMENT

Insanity acquittees have been disadvantaged in the criteria and procedures utilized for release from confinement. As of 1976, 18 states utilized release criteria that were more restrictive for insanity acquittee patients than for civilly committed patients.[21] Some states view NGI commitment as therapeutic in purpose and focus on the individual's mental condition. They require that he or she be "restored to sanity," or "cured," or "no longer mentally ill," or "entirely and permanently recovered" in order to be eligible for release.[22] Because some mental illnesses, including schizophrenia, can last a lifetime, a requirement that the patient's illness be cured can lead to lifelong confinement.

Other states view the NGI commitment as a form of preventive detention and focus on the dangerousness of the individual. They require that he or she no longer be dangerous in order to be eligible for

---

[18]*See, e.g.,* People v. Chavez, 629 P.2d 1040, 1047 (Colo. 1981): "A plea of not guilty by reason of insanity is a plea in the nature of confession and avoidance. . . . By asserting it the defendant admits the acts charged, but denies criminal culpability."

[19]*See, e.g.,* State *ex rel.* Schopf v. Schubert, 45 Wis. 2d 644, 173 N.W.2d 673, 677 (1970), *overruled prospectively by* State *ex rel.* Kovach v. Schubert, 64 Wis. 2d 612, 219 N.W.2d 341 (1974), *appeal dismissed,* 419 U.S. 1117, *cert. denied,* 419 U.S. 1130 (1975).

[20]For a more detailed critique of the arguments supporting automatic, indeterminate commitment, *see* German & Singer, *supra* note 7, at 1017–25.

[21]GERMAN & SINGER, *supra* note 7, at 1080–83. The insanity acquittee release criteria were less restrictive than for civilly committed patients in only five states. *Id.*

[22]*See, e.g.,* CAL. PENAL CODE § 1026.1 (West Supp. 1981). An insanity acquittee "shall be released . . . only (a) upon determination that sanity has been restored."

release.[23] Thus, a patient who is not mentally ill is denied release if he or she is dangerous. Some states, focusing on both the mental condition and the dangerousness of the individual, require a restoration to sanity and a lack of dangerousness for eligibility for release.[24] Strangely, a few states used to permit release either if the patient was sane *or* if he or she was not dangerous.[25] Theoretically, under such an arrangement a dangerous person would be released if he or she was sane; an insane person would be released if found not dangerous.

The sanity criterion and the dangerousness criterion, as they are utilized in release statutes, have been criticized for their ambiguity.[26] For example, does a statute requiring that the patient be "restored to sanity" mean that the person must be cured of mental illness completely or only that the mental condition be improved to the extent that it no longer meets the insanity test utilized by the state in its insanity defense? Does a statute requiring that the individual be "no longer dangerous" mean

[23]*See, e.g.,* DEL. CODE ANN. Title 11 § 403(b) (1979). An insanity acquittee "shall be kept . . . until . . . the public safety will not be endangered by his release."

KAN. STAT. ANN. § 22-3428 (Supp. 1980). "[I]f the [insanity acquittee] patient [is not] a danger to the patient's self or others or property of others . . . the patient [shall be] discharged or conditionally released."

ME. REV. STAT. ANN. Title 15 § 104–A (Supp. 1981). An insanity acquittee "may be released or discharged [if] without likelihood that he will cause injury to himself or to others due to mental disease or mental defect."

N.J. CODE OF CRIMINAL JUSTICE 2C:4-9 (1981). An insanity acquittee may be released or discharged if this can be accomplished "without danger to himself or others."

WASH. REV. CODE §§ 10.77.150, 10.77.200 (1979). An insanity acquittee may be released or discharged if this can be accomplished "without substantial danger to other persons, or substantial likelihood of committing felonious acts jeopardizing public safety or security."

WIS. STAT. ANN. § 971.17(2) (West 1980). An insanity acquittee may be released or discharged if this can be accomplished "without danger to himself or herself or to others."

[24]*See, e.g.,* IOWA CODE ANN. § 813.2 Rule 21(8) (1979). An insanity acquittee shall be "retained in custody until he or she demonstrates good mental health and is considered no longer dangerous to the public peace and safety or to himself or herself."

A repealed Wisconsin statute provided that an insanity acquittee was to be discharged if he was "sane and mentally responsible [and] not likely to have a recurrence of insanity or mental irresponsibility as will result in acts which but for insanity or mental irresponsibility would be crimes." WIS. STAT ANN. § 957.11(4) (1958), repealed 1969. In *In re* Treglown, 38 Wis. 2d 317, 156 N.W.2d 363, 367 (1968), the Wisconsin Supreme Court construed the statute to require confinement of the insanity acquittee beyond the full recovery of the patient's mental illness.

[25]*See* discussion in A. GOLDSTEIN, *supra* note 10, at 150. The states cited by Goldstein—Kansas, Minnesota, Vermont, and Washington—no longer utilize the "sanity or not dangerous" formulation.

[26]A. GOLDSTEIN, *supra* note 10, at 146–54.

that there must be no recurrence of the same criminal act, or any criminal act, or any threatening conduct, or even something less? Obviously, a strict construction of the statutory language can result in extended confinement for the insanity acquittee.

Vague release criteria are frequently accompanied by procedural barriers to release. Involuntary commitment for the typical mental patient ends when the treating doctor concludes that the patient's mental condition no longer warrants inpatient hospitalization. Not so, however, for the typical insanity acquittee. Many states require that he or she obtain a court order of discharge.[27] In essence, the patient must convince both the treating doctor and the court that his or her mental condition satisfies the release criteria. In some instances, courts have rejected the unanimous judgment of several psychiatrists that the patient was ready for release.[28] Although society may feel more secure knowing that a judge may overrule medical judgment favoring discharge, one wonders whether the insanity acquittee is being treated fairly. In many states, civil commitment is limited to those mentally ill individuals who have engaged in dangerous behavior prior to hospitalization.[29] Nevertheless, those individuals are entitled to discharge without court intervention

---

[27]GERMAN & SINGER, *supra* note 7, at 1076–79, list 25 states plus the District of Columbia that do not provide for insanity acquittee patients to be administratively discharged.

[28]*See, e.g.,* United States v. Ecker, 543 F.2d 178 (D.C. Cir. 1976), *cert. denied,* 429 U.S. 1063 (1977); *In re* Flemming, 431 A.2d 616 (Me. 1981); State v. Taylor, 158 Mont. 323, 491 P.2d 877 (1971). *See also* State v. Montagne, 510 S.W.2d 776 (Mo. Ct. App. 1974) (court rejected testimony of the sole psychiatrist); United States v. Harris, Crim. No. F–1976-79 (D.C. Super. Ct. Jan. 30, 1981) as reported in 5 MENTAL DIS. L. RPTR. 82 (1981) (court rejected expert testimony that insanity acquittee did not have, and never had, mental disease or defect in the absence of evidence indicating that patient's mental condition had changed since the time he committed the criminal act).

[29]Overt dangerous behavior has been required as a prerequisite for involuntary civil commitment in the following statutes: ALA. CODE tit. 22 § 22–52-10 (Supp. 1981); CAL. WELF. & INSTN. CODE §§ 5260, 5300 (West 1972); HAW. REV. STAT. § 334–1 (1976 & Supp. 1981); MASS. GEN. LAWS ANN. ch. 123, § 1 (West Supp. 1981); NEB. REV. STAT. § 83–1009 (1976); N.C. GEN. STAT. § 122–58.3 (1974) (repealed 1974); WIS. STAT. ANN. §§ 51.15(1), 51.20(1)(a) (West Supp. 1981).

See Lessard v. Schmidt, 349 F. Supp. 1078 (E.D. Wis. 1972), *vacated and remanded for a more specific order,* 414 U.S. 743, *order on remand,* 379 F. Supp. 1376 (1974), *vacated and remanded on other grounds,* 421 U.S. 957 (1975), *order reinstated on remand,* 413 F. Supp. 1318 (1976); Lynch v. Baxley, 386 F. Supp. 378 (M.D. Ala. 1974); Bell v. Wayne Co. Gen. Hosp., 384 F. Supp. 1085 (E.D. Mich. 1974); Dixon v. Attorney General, 325 F. Supp. 966 (M.D. Pa. 1971). Other cases are collected and discussed in Comment, *Overt Dangerous Behavior as a Constitutional Requirement for Involuntary Civil Commitment of the Mentally Ill,* 44 U. CHI. L. REV. 562, 569–74 (1977).

and approval. What distinguishes the insanity acquittee from the civilly committed patient so as to justify such discrimination in release procedures?

When a civilly committed patient seeks to obtain release through a habeas corpus proceeding, the law requires proof by a preponderence of the evidence that the individual is entitled to release. However, when an insanity acquittee seeks release, some courts have imposed the far more onerous burden of proof beyond a reasonable doubt.[30] Some authors have asserted that such a burden is practically impossible to meet because it requires the individual to prove a negative, that is, that he or she is not now dangerous and will not be dangerous in the future.[31] Is it conceivable that an insanity acquittee who has been kept continuously in maximum security confinement will be able to prove beyond a reasonable doubt that he or she will not be dangerous to society if freed?

Although the criminal trial that resulted in an insanity acquittal is concluded by that verdict, many states continue the authority of the criminal trial judge to decide matters of commitment and release for the insanity acquittee.[32] States often require that the prosecutor or district attorney be notified of and participate in release hearings initiated by the insanity acquittee patient.[33] In my opinion, release proceedings should not be considered as a continuation of the criminal case. Because the insanity acquittal is a determination that the person is not legally blameworthy, neither the prosecutor nor the criminal trial judge has an appropriate interest to pursue or role to play in the release proceeding involving an insanity acquittee. The criminal trial may have established that the insanity acquittee committed a criminal act. That act may be rel-

---

[30]*See, e.g.,* Chase v. Kearns, 278 A.2d 132, 137–38 (Me. 1971); State v. Shackford, 262 A.2d 359, 365–66 (Me. 1970); State v. Taylor, 158 Mont. 323, 491 P.2d 877, 882 (1971), *cert. denied,* 406 U.S. 978 (1972); State *ex rel.* Barnes v. Behan, 80 S.D. 370, 124 N.W.2d 179, 181 (1963).

[31]GERMAN & SINGER, *supra* note 7, at 1064.

[32]*See, e.g.,* N.J. CODE OF CRIMINAL JUSTICE 2C:4-8, 2C:4-9 (1981); N.Y. CRIM. PRO. §§ 330.20(6) (13) (McKinney 1981); OHIO REV. CODE § 2945.40(A) (Baldwin 1981); WASH. REV. CODE §§ 10.77.110, 10.77.200 (1979); WIS. STAT. ANN. § 971.17(2) (West 1980). As of 1976, 20 states required a hearing before the committing court in order for an insanity acquittee to obtain release, GERMAN & SINGER, *supra* note 7, at 1076–79.

[33]*See, e.g.,* KAN. STAT. ANN. § 22–3428 (1980 Supp.); N.Y. CRIM. PRO. § 330.20(18). (McKinney 1981); OHIO REV. CODE § 2945.40(F) (Baldwin 1981); WASH. REV. CODE § 10.77.200 (1979); WIS. STAT. ANN. § 971.17(2) (West 1980). As of 1976, 19 states required notice to the prosecutor before an insanity acquittee could be released. GERMAN & SINGER, *supra* note 7, at 1076–79.

evant evidence to be considered on the issue of whether the insanity acquittee's mental condition has improved to the extent that the person is now ready for release. The release decision, however, focuses on the individual's current mental condition and need not be made by the judge who sat at the criminal trial.

A doctor who can require his or her patient to continue taking antipsychotic medication and undergo outpatient treatment may be willing to release the patient from institutional confinement. Thus, civilly committed patients often are able to obtain conditional release from hospitalization even when their mental states do not permit full discharge. Some jurisdictions, however, deny insanity acquittee patients this opportunity.[34] Even when conditional release is available, some states require court approval before the insanity acquittee patient may be released.[35] Judges who are willing to grant conditional release often impose restrictions that are unrelated to the patient's mental condition and treatment needs. In this respect, a conditional release policy for an insanity acquittee patient often parallels the criminal parole process. If an insanity acquittee violates a condition of release, some states permit his or her summary rehospitalization without according procedural protections in the readmission process.[36]

Some states provide for a periodic judicial review of all involuntary civil commitment orders. As with an initial commitment order, the state has the burden of establishing a basis for continuing commitment. Thus, the requirement of periodic judicial review prevents a patient from being detained indefinitely on an outdated evaluation of his or her mental condition. Unfortunately, even in those states that have provided periodic

---

[34] As of 1976, only 18 states had statutory conditional release provisions for insanity acquittees. GERMAN & SINGER, *supra* note 7, at 1076-79. At least five others provided for conditional release of insanity acquittees under statutes applicable to civilly committed patients. *Id.* at 1068 n. 271. *See also* State v. Carter, 64 N.J. 382, 316 A.2d 449 (1974), in which the court created a right of conditional release for insanity acquittees, although none existed in the New Jersey statutes. The various states' criteria for conditional release are listed at 64 N.J. 382, 401-2 n. 10-12, 316 A.2d 449, 460 n. 10-12.

[35] *See, e.g.,* KAN. STAT. ANN. § 22-3428(3) (1980 Supp.); ME. REV. STAT. ANN. Title 15 § 104A(2) (Supp. 1981); N.Y. CRIM. PRO. § 330.20(12) (McKinney 1981); OHIO REV. CODE § 2945.40(D)(4) (Baldwin 1981); WASH. REV. CODE § 10.77.150 (1979).

[36] *See, e.g.,* KAN. STAT. ANN. § 22-3428b (1980 Supp.) (The individual is also subject to contempt of court proceedings.); ME. REV. STAT. ANN. Title 15 § 104B (Supp. 1981); WIS. STAT. ANN. § 971.17(3) (1973). As of 1976, only eight states provided statutorily for a right to a hearing upon revocation of conditional release. GERMAN & SINGER, *supra* note 7, at 1076-79.

review for civilly committed patients, a similar commitment review policy has not been adopted for insanity acquittees.[37]

CONDITIONS OF CONFINEMENT

In addition to the easy commitment and difficult release problems confronting insanity acquittees, they have been disadvantaged during their confinement in mental institutions. In most jurisdictions, the insanity acquittee is placed in a special maximum security ward or institution where all "criminally insane" or forensic patients are housed.[38] Investigations conducted in the 1960s and 1970s revealed inhumane and morally reprehensible conditions at these facilities which supported the conclusion that treatment is virtually nonexistent and that "patients" are merely warehoused. For example, a United States district court noted that only 3% of the patients at Farview State Hospital, Pennsylvania's maximum security hospital for the criminally insane, received any therapeutic-psychiatric treatment.[39]

The Final Report of the Ionia State Hospital Medical Audit Committee described a patient's life inside Michigan's maximum security mental institution:

> The absolutely apathetic, empty existence that these men lead on the wards and the groping efforts which they follow to busy themselves with nothing, is terrible to behold. There was obviously little about which to be hopeful.
>
> The over concern for security is evident everywhere, and this reflects the poor understanding of the mission of the hospital, the culture which surrounds the hospital, and the lack of training for the security attendant staff. As one passes from building to building, one begins to feel somewhat like a mole. Obviously, it is not necessary to pass through the miles of tunnels in order to go from one building to another. It is impossible to believe

---

[37]GERMAN & SINGER, *supra* note 7, at 1073–74. The state of Washington requires a professional examination of each insanity acquittee's mental condition at least once every six months. WASH. REV. CODE § 10.77.140 (1979). This examination, however, does not automatically trigger a court review of the patient's status. *But see* R.I. GEN. LAWS § 40.1-5.3-4(f) (Supp. 1981). The director of the Rhode Island Department of Mental Health is required to petition the court to review the condition of a committed insanity acquittee every six months.

[38]*See* MORRIS, *"Criminality" and the Right to Treatment*, 36 U. CHI. L. REV. 784 (1969) for a discussion of these various categories of patients, for example, persons found incompetent to stand trial, dangerous civil patients, defective delinquents, and so forth, whom the author denominates "mentally ill, non-criminal criminals."

[39]Dixon v. Attorney General, 325 F. Supp. 966, 969 (M.D. Pa. 1971). "We cannot avoid the conclusion that medical-psychiatric treatment of inmates at Farview was grossly inadequate." *Id.*

that this is the best way to provide security. The psychological oppressiveness of this system, in itself, makes it worthy of modification.[40]

A study of the Arizona State Hospital found that "the true daily existence of the bulk of the patients is one of idleness and inactivity, occasionally sprinkled with staff and other patient contact."[41] Though the situation was described as "relatively bleak" for almost all patients, the report stated that forensic patients, who are housed on the maximum security ward, experienced the worst conditions. Among those described in the 1969–1970 Annual Report of the Arizona State Hospital were: obsolete, crowded buildings, lack of proper treatment facilities, critical staff shortages, and high staff turnover. "Under these conditions the primary medical treatment is chemotherapy. Appropriate rehabilitation, counseling, and education cannot even be attempted."[42]

Insanity acquittees who have been civilly committed to the Arizona State Hospital, as well as all patients confined on the maximum security unit, are on special classification. Requests for privileges for special classification patients must be approved by their residence unit, by the Special Classification Committee (SCC), and by the hospital superintendent. The Arizona State Hospital study reported that hospital staff members were disappointed by the SCC's reluctance to grant privileges—even when a request received the strong endorsement of staff members in closest contact with the patient. SCC approval was most difficult to obtain for requests involving off-grounds passes or other patient contact with the community.[43]

The security orientation of hospital administrators who deal with insanity acquittee patients is attested to in a report prepared for the California Department of Mental Hygiene by Professor Herbert L. Packer.[44]

---

[40]A. DUKAY, M.D. et al. Final Report of the Ionia State Hospital Medical Audit Committee 17 (Unpublished Report, 1965). For a more extensive description of "patient activities" as reported in the Ionia Medical Audit, see Morris, Mental Illness and Criminal Commitment in Michigan, 5 U. MICH. J. L. REFORM 1, 11–13 (1971).

[41]WEXLER, SCOVILLE et al. The Administration of Psychiatric Justice: Theory and Practice in Arizona, 13 ARIZ. L. REV. 1, 235 (1971).

[42]Arizona State Hospital, 1969–70 Annual Report (August 14, 1970) as cited in Wexler, Scoville et al., id. at 235.

[43]WEXLER, SCOVILLE et al., id. at 219–20.

[44]Memorandum from Herbert L. Packer to Norman C. Lindquist, August 16, 1966, on file with the author. Portions of the Packer Report and subsequent memoranda commenting on the report were published in Morris, The Confusion of Confinement Syndrome Extended: The Treatment of Mentally Ill Non-Criminal Criminals in New York. 18 BUFF. L. REV. 393, 425–26 (1969).

Although the department had explicit statutory authority to transfer insanity acquittee patients between mental hospitals, it had not developed any criteria for determining fitness for transfer. Insanity acquittees were routinely housed in Atascadero, California's maximum security mental institution. In Professor Packer's judgment, Atascadero's treatment staff tended to rely too heavily on the seriousness of the patient's underlying criminal act in determining the length of stay. For example, Atascadero employed an unwritten rule precluding insanity acquittee patients who had been charged with murder from being considered for release until they had been confined at Atascadero for a minimum of 10 years.[45]

S. W. Morgan, M.D., Superintendent and Medical Director of Atascadero, responded to the criticism of the Packer Report,[46] and, according to Professor Packer, Dr. Morgan's "comments explicitly reject almost all of the recommendations for change made in the [Packer Report]."[47] The superintendent's attitude toward the "unwritten 10-year rule" criticism illustrated the security orientation of his facility. In addition to admitting that patients acquitted of murder were not considered for release for 10 years, Dr. Morgan revealed that they were not considered even for transfer out of Atascadero to a less secure facility for 10 years.[48] Dr. Morgan was unwilling to accept Professor Packer's suggestion that Atascadero should consider the nature of the alleged offense only to the extent that it is relevant in deciding the likelihood of recovery from mental illness. In Dr. Morgan's opinion, dangerousness of the underlying offense should be given "top priority."[49]

More recently, the California Supreme Court described Atascadero's physical appearance as more like a prison than a hospital—evidencing all the stigmata of punishment rather than treatment. The court con-

---

[45]Memorandum from Herbert L. Packer to Norman C. Lindquist, August 16, 1966, at 8–9. A similar policy precluded insanity acquittee patients who had been charged with assault from being considered for release until they had been confined at Atascadero for a minimum of three years. Memorandum from S. W. Morgan, M.D. to E. F. Galioni, M.D., October 7, 1966, at 4, on file with, the author.

[46]Memorandum from S. W. Morgan, M.D., Superintendent and Medical Director, to E. F. Galioni, M.D., Deputy Director, Division of State Services, October 7, 1966.

[47]Memorandum from Herbert L. Packer to Norman E. Lindquist, November 28, 1966, at 1, on file with the author.

[48]Memorandum from S. W. Morgan, M.D., to E. F. Galioni, M.D., October 7, 1966, at 4.

[49]Id. at 5.

cluded by agreeing with the characterization of Atascadero as "a sanitary dungeon."[50]

A researcher studying the records of an institution for the criminally insane located in a midwestern state confirmed that institution's security orientation. He found that the staff's decision to release patients was not significantly affected by demonstrated improvement in patients' mental condition.[51]

Inadequacies in treatment and undue security orientation are illustrated by comparing the release potential of patients confined in maximum security facilities with that of other mental patients who are confined in non-maximum security facilities within the same jurisdiction. In 1965, the median stay of patients in New York's maximum security facility for criminal order patients was a minimum of six to seven *years*. The average length of hospitalization in New York's civil state mental hospitals was four *months*.[52]

Although conditions at some maximum security facilities may have been ameliorated over the years,[53] conditions that a civilized society should find intolerable nevertheless continue to be tolerated. In 1981, the United States Court of Appeals for the Third Circuit characterized as "subhuman" living conditions at the maximum security wing of New Jersey's Trenton Psychiatric Hospital. For 24 years, the insanity acquittee plaintiff had been exposed to

> poor plumbing with leaking pipes covering the floor with inches of water; inoperative sinks and toilets; inadequate ventilation; absence of windows or inoperative windows; inability during seven months of the year to go into the yard for fresh air; inoperative radiators resulting in indoor temperatures below 50°; summer temperatures reading 105° due to absence of ventilating equipment; for a time availability of showers only once a week; and absence of hot running water in sinks in the cells. As to many of these gross physical deficiencies the testimony was not even disputed.[54]

---

[50]People v. Burnick, 14 Cal. 3d 306, 319, 535 P.2d 352, 360–61, 121 Cal. Rptr. 488, 496–97 (1975).
[51]PIPERNO, *Indefinite Commitment in a Mental Hospital for the Criminally Insane: Two Models of Administration of Mental Health*, 65 J. CRIM. L. & CRIM. 520, 526 (1974).
[52]MORRIS, *supra* note 38, at 790.
[53]For example, legislation was enacted in 1976 transferring the jurisdiction of New York's maximum security mental hospitals from the Department of Correctional Services to the Department of Mental Hygiene. N.Y. Sess. Laws 1976, ch. 766, § 4, effective April 1, 1977.

Dr. Al Rucci, currently Medical Director of Atascadero State Hospital in California, stated that persons found NGI of murder are no longer detained for 10 years or for any other specified period before they are transferred or released from that facility. Telephone conversation with Al Rucci, M.D., June 24, 1981.
[54]Scotte v. Plante, 641 F.2d 117, 128 (3d Cir. 1981), *appeal pending*.

In such an environment, one could anticipate that treatment of the patient's mental condition would also be grossly deficient. It was. Expert and lay testimony and hospital records revealed

> that no staff member worked with plaintiff individually on a regular basis; that neither a psychiatrist nor a psychologist has seen him individually on any regular basis in the twenty-four years of his confinement; that ten years after his confinement a staff physician filed a report that there was no reason to bother trying to treat him; that recently a treatment team was established, but it met with him for only ten to fifteen minutes a month; and finally, that he had not received any psychiatric counseling for almost a year and a half prior to trial. Indeed, it is undisputed that Trenton Psychiatric Hospital lost its hospital accreditation several years ago partly because the treatment offered its inmates was merely custodial and not therapeutic.[55]

Because insanity acquittees are perceived as unpredictable and dangerous, the public is afraid of them.[56] Understandably, this fear creates a desire that insanity acquittees receive certain and lengthy post-trial confinement. Nevertheless, authors have concluded that the only adequate explanation for the atrocious conditions endured by insanity acquittees during their confinement is a societal motivation for retribution—a motivation that is usually considered appropriate only for those who have been convicted of crime and who are being subjected to punishment.[57] In the Trenton State Hospital case, the records disclosed that the patient had not engaged in violent behavior and was not a management problem. Because no treatment or security reason existed to justify subjecting the patient to the severe deprivations encountered in the maximum security ward, the court concluded that his confinement there amounted to punishment in violation of the due process clause.[58]

A New York judge recently characterized institutions for the criminally insane "as relics of abhorance of misdeeds of bygone eras."[59] Although they should have faded away with an increased sensitivity of the times, unfortunately they have not.[60] One major researcher examined problems inherent in maximum security institutions and changes in

---

[55]*Id.* at 132.

[56]STEADMAN & COCOZZA, *Selective Reporting and the Public's Misconceptions of the Criminally Insane,* 41 PUB. OPIN. Q. 523, 532 (1978).

[57]GERMAN & SINGER, *supra* note 7, at 1074. A retributive motivation has also been suggested to explain why insanity acquittees have received fewer procedural protections in the commitment process. Note, *supra* note 7, at 617–25.

[58]Scotte v. Plante, 641 F.2d 117, 128–29 (3d Cir. 1981), *appeal pending.*

[59]*In re* Rose, 109 Misc. 2d 960, 441 N.Y.S.2d 161, 163 (Sup. Ct., Kings Co. 1981).

[60]*Id.*

treatment philosophy and concluded "that new, large security and other special institutions ought simply not to be constructed."[61]

RECENT JUDICIAL AND LEGISLATIVE ACTIVITY FOCUSING ON POST-INSANITY ACQUITTAL COMMITMENT ISSUES

Recently, courts and legislatures have begun to examine NGI mandatory, indeterminate commitment statues, release criteria and procedures, and conditions of confinement. Although reform efforts have achieved some measure of success, they have encountered continued resistance from those who fear insanity acquittees or who desire to punish them.

MANDATORY, INDETERMINATE COMMITMENT

In *Bolton v. Harris*,[62] the United States Court of Appeals for the District of Columbia Circuit, in construing the District's mandatory, indeterminate commitment statute, recognized the limitations of a verdict of not guilty by reason of insanity. In the opinion, Chief Judge Bazelon relied on the United States Supreme Court case of *Baxstrom v. Herold*[63] for the principle that "the commission of criminal acts does not give rise to a presumption of dangerousness which, standing alone, justifies substantial difference in commitment procedures and confinement conditions for the mentally ill."[64] Thus, to institutionalize an insanity acquittee without affording him the procedural safeguards established under the civil commitment scheme constituted a denial of equal protection of the laws. The court rejected the argument, which had also been rejected by the Supreme Court in *Baxstrom*, that expeditious commitment of various categories of nonconvict mentally ill persons is somehow justified because of the dangerous or criminal propensities of the individuals involved.

[61]D. WEXLER, CRIMINAL COMMITMENTS AND DANGEROUS MENTAL PATIENTS: LEGAL ISSUES OF CONFINEMENT, TREATMENT, AND RELEASE 53–55 (1976).

[62]395 F.2d 642 (D.C. Cir. 1968).

[63]383 U.S. 107 (1966). In *Baxstrom*, the Supreme Court held unconstitutional a statute that authorized an administrative decision continuing the maximum security confinement of mentally ill convicts upon expiration of their criminal sentences. Although confinement pursuant to that statute was deemed a civil commitment, mentally ill ex-convicts were denied both a jury review on the question of civil commitability and court hearings on the issue of dangerous mental illness, a prerequisite for confinement in a maximum security mental institution.

[64]395 F.2d 642, 647 (D.C. Cir. 1968).

The *Bolton* court also utilized *Specht v. Patterson*[65] as precedent for its decision. In *Specht*, the United States Supreme Court held that a person convicted of taking indecent liberties (maximum sentence of 10 years) could not be sentenced under the Colorado Sex Offenders Act (sentence of one day to life) without a full hearing. The imposition of the indeterminate sentence required a new finding of fact that was not an ingredient of the offense charged at trial; that is, that the defendant, if at large, constituted a threat of bodily harm. Without the requisite hearing, sentencing pursuant to the Sex Offenders Act violated the defendant's constitutional right to due process of law.

Relying on *Specht*, the court in *Bolton v. Harris* found the District of Columbia mandatory commitment statute constitutionally suspect for failing to provide a hearing on the issue of present mental condition. A verdict of acquittal by reason of insanity signifies only that the jury had a reasonable doubt about the defendant's sanity at the time of the act that served as the basis for the criminal prosecution. To preserve the statute's constitutionality, the court construed it to authorize a temporary detention of the insanity acquittee to examine into his current mental condition. Upon completion of the examination period, a new hearing must be held to determine if the insanity acquittee's mental condition meets the criteria for involuntary civil commitment.

The highest state appellate courts in New York,[66] Indiana,[67] Arizona,[68] Wisconsin,[69] Michigan,[70] and New Jersey[71] have used similar reasoning and reached similar results in construing their NGI commitment statutes. The Fifth Circuit Court of Appeals, in cases applying Florida law[72] and Louisiana law,[73] and federal district courts in South Dakota[74] and Georgia[75] also found constitutional violations in the summary, indeterminate commitment of insanity acquittees. Mandatory, indeterminate commitment following an NGI verdict is being supplanted by the

---

[65]386 U.S. 605 (1967).

[66]People v. Lally, 19 N.Y.2d 27, 224 N.E.2d 87, 277 N.Y.S.2d 654 (1966); People *ex rel.* Henig v. Commissioner of Mental Hygiene, 43 N.Y.2d 334, 372 N.E.2d 304, 401 N.Y.S.2d 462 (1977).

[67]Wilson v. State, 259 Ind. 375, 287 N.E.2d 875 (1972).

[68]State v. Clemons, 110 Ariz. 79, 515 P.2d 324 (1973).

[69]State *ex rel.* Kovach v. Schubert, 64 Wis. 2d 612, 219 N.W.2d 341 (1974), *cert. denied,* 419 U.S. 1130 (1975).

[70]People v. McQuillan, 392 Mich. 511, 221 N.W.2d 569 (1974).

[71]State v. Krol, 68 N.J. 236, 344 A.2d 289 (1975).

[72]Powell v. Florida, 579 F.2d 324 (5th Cir. 1978).

[73]Jackson v. Foti, 670 F.2d 516 (5th Cir. 1982).

[74]Allen v. Radack, 426 F. Supp. 1052 (D.S.D. 1977).

[75]Benham v. Edwards, 501 F. Supp. 1050 (N.D. Ga. 1980).

requirement of a new hearing to determine the insanity acquittee's current mental condition.

The New Jersey experience illustrates a remarkable reversal of position by that state's highest court. New Jersey's mandatory, indeterminate NGI commitment statute authorized detention of a patient until he was "restored to reason." In 1972, the New Jersey Supreme Court construed this statute as prohibiting an insanity acquittee's release until his underlying illness was "cured" or "neutralized."[76] Two years later, the court retreated from its Draconian position by authorizing conditional release of insanity acquittee patients.[77] In 1975, the court held unconstitutional the state's mandatory, indeterminate commitment statute and overruled its 1972 decision to the extent that the earlier case required cure or neutralization of the insanity acquittee's underlying illness prior to release.[78] The court rejected the argument that insanity acquittees constitute an exceptional class of persons in whose confinement the state has a special interest. For indeterminate commitment of an insanity acquittee, the court required a new hearing at which the state must establish the person's mental illness plus dangerousness—the same standard utilized for civil commitment of any other person in New Jersey.

The highest state appellate courts in Missouri,[79] Delaware,[80] and Kansas[81] have rejected the *Bolton* analysis and upheld automatic, indeterminate commitment statutes. The Missouri court relied on a Wisconsin case[82] that was overruled[83] two months after the Missouri court decision.

In Missouri[84] and Delaware,[85] unlike the District of Columbia at the time of the *Bolton* decision,[86] the burden of proving insanity at the criminal trial is placed on the defendant. The NGI acquittal signifies more

---

[76]State v. Maik, 60 N.J. 203, 287 A.2d 715 (1972), *overruled by* State v. Krol, 68 N.J. 236, 344 A.2d 289 (1975).

[77]State v. Carter, 64 N.J. 382, 316 A.2d 449 (1974).

[78]State v. Krol, 68 N.J. 236, 344 A.2d 289 (1975).

[79]State v. Kee, 510 S.W.2d 477 (Mo. 1974).

[80]*In re* Lewis, 403 A.2d 1115 (Del. 1979).

[81]*In re* Jones, 228 Kan. 90, 612 P.2d 1211 (1980).

[82]State *ex rel.* Schopf v. Schubert, 45 Wis. 2d 644, 173 N.W.2d 673 (1970), *overruled prospectively by* State *ex rel.* Kovach v. Schubert, 64 Wis. 2d 612, 219 N.W.2d 341 (1974), *appeal dismissed*, 419 U.S. 1117, *cert. denied*, 419 U.S. 1130 (1975).

[83]State *ex rel.* Kovach v. Schubert, 64 Wis. 2d 612, 219 N.W.2d 341 (1974), *appeal dismissed*, 419 U.S. 1117, *cert. denied*, 419 U.S. 1130 (1975).

[84]Mo. Stat. Ann. § 552.030(7) (Supp. 1981).

[85]Del. Code Ann. Title 11 § 401(a) (1979).

[86]In 1970, Congress amended the District of Columbia statute to require that at trial a defendant's insanity be established affirmatively by a preponderance of the evidence. D.C. Code § 24–301(j) (1973).

than the jury's reasonable doubt of the defendant's sanity; the verdict is an affirmative finding of insanity at the time of the criminal act.[87]

In my opinion, an affirmative finding of criminal conduct resulting from mental disorder may justify a short-term commitment to inquire into the defendant's present mental condition. However, the finding does not justify a presumption of continuing insanity sufficient to permit automatic, indeterminate commitment without any evaluation of the insanity acquittee's present mental condition. Even though both New Jersey[88] and Wisconsin[89] treat insanity as an affirmative defense with the burden of proof on the defendant, the supreme courts in those states agreed with Judge Bazelon's analysis in *Bolton:* "A defendant who was insane for the purpose of responsibility at the time of the offense may not be insane for the purpose of civil commitment at the time of the verdict."[90] Although the *Bolton* rationale was enhanced by the District's placement of the burden of proof on the prosecution, the decision does not rest solely on that justification. Because present commitment is predicated upon a finding of present insanity, *Bolton* appropriately relied upon *Specht* for the requirement of a new hearing on this new finding of fact.

In its decision prohibiting automatic, indeterminate commitment of insanity acquittees without a hearing to determine present mental condition, the Wisconsin Supreme Court relied on the precedents of *Humphrey v. Cady*[91] and *Jackson v. Indiana*,[92] two United States Supreme Court cases decided subsequent to *Bolton*. In *Humphrey*, the United States Supreme Court ruled that a sex offender could not be confined for treat-

---

[87]Even though Kansas places on the prosecution the burden of proving defendant's sanity, the Kansas Supreme Court in upholding the state's mandatory, indeterminate commitment statute cited approvingly decisions in Missouri and Delaware. Although a mandatory, indeterminate commitment statute may be more supportable in states—such as Missouri and Delaware—where insanity is an affirmative defense, apparently the Kansas Supreme Court did not consider the distinction in reviewing the Kansas statute. *In re* Jones, 228 Kan. 90, 612 P.2d 1211, 1226–27 (1980).

[88]State v. DiPaglia, 64 N.J. 288, 315 A.2d 385 (1974).

[89]WIS. STAT. ANN. § 971.15(3) (1971). Under Wisconsin law, the defendant has the option of choosing the ALI-Model Penal Code formulation of the insanity test or the *M'Naghten* formulation. Schleisner v. State, 58 Wis. 2d 605, 207 N.W.2d 636 (1973); State v. Schoffner, 31 Wis. 2d 412, 143 N.W.2d 458 (1966). The statute establishes the insanity defense as an affirmative defense whenever a defendant chooses the ALI-Model Penal Code formulation.

[90]Bolton v. Harris, 395 F.2d 642, 647 (D.C. Cir. 1968).

[91]405 U.S. 504 (1972).

[92]406 U.S. 715 (1972).

ment beyond his maximum sentence without the jury trial accorded to other persons undergoing civil commitment. In *Jackson*, the United States Supreme Court invalidated a statute permitting an indeterminate, and potentially lifetime, commitment of a mentally defective deaf mute who had been found incompetent to stand trial. Extending its *Baxstrom* principle to nonconvicts, the Court stated: "If criminal conviction and imposition of sentence are insufficient to justify less procedural and substantive protection against indefinite commitment than that generally available to all others, the mere filing of criminal charges surely cannot suffice."[93] The state denied incompetent criminal defendants equal protection of the laws by subjecting them to a more lenient commitment standard and to a more stringent release standard than that generally applicable to all others undergoing the civil commitment process who were not charged with criminal offenses.

Although the United States Supreme Court has not considered a case involving the constitutionality of an NGI mandatory, indeterminate commitment statute, in *Jackson* the Court cited with approval *Bolton* and other decisions that extended civil commitment procedural protections to insanity acquittees. Mentally incompetent criminal defendants are still subject to trial, conviction, and punishment. Insanity acquittees have been found legally blameless and are not subject to prosecution or punishment for their past conduct. The procedural protections extended to incompetent criminal defendants in *Jackson* logically should be extended to nonconvict insanity acquittees.

In 1980, the United States Supreme Court ruled that notice and an adversary hearing are required prior to the transfer of a sentence-serving prisoner from a state prison to a mental hospital.[94] The Court identified a liberty interest of convicts protected by the due process clause of the Fourteenth Amendment: "A criminal conviction and sentence of imprisonment extinguish an individual's right to freedom from confinement for the term of his sentence, but they do not authorize the State to classify him as mentally ill and to subject him to involuntary psychiatric treatment without affording him additional due process protections."[95] Obviously, if sentence-serving convicts may not be confined in a mental hospital without notice and an adversary hearing, insanity acquittees are entitled to no less protection.

Elimination of mandatory, indeterminate commitment should be accompanied by a recognition that insanity acquittees possess no special

[93]*Id.* at 724.
[94]Vitek v. Jones, 445 U.S. 480 (1980).
[95]*Id.* at 493–94.

status and that for purposes of involuntary mental hospitalization they are to be treated as all other citizens. The Supreme Court of North Carolina accepted this view in stating: "A verdict of not guilty by reason of insanity constitutes a full acquittal, and an NGI 'is thus entitled to all the constitutional rights of one acquitted upon any other ground.'"[96] A special committee of the Association of the Bar of the City of New York recently asserted: "The wall separating acquittees as a group apart from all other civil patients is a throwback to separating mentally ill with 'proven criminal tendencies as shown by their past criminal records,' a category discredited in *Baxstrom* by the Supreme Court and thereupon abolished by the Legislature."[97] Because insanity acquittees are no longer within the criminal justice system, the committee recommended that New York's laws be amended to assure that the same civil commitment procedures utilized for involuntary hospitalization of other patients be utilized for insanity acquittees. Once committed, the insanity acquittee is to be entitled to complete civil patient status.[98]

A pre-*Baxstrom* decision of the United States Supreme Court, read in the context of *Baxstrom* and post-*Baxstrom* developments, also lends support to the position that insanity acquittees are to be equated with all other citizens for purposes of involuntary hospitalization. In *Lynch v. Overholser*,[99] the Court held that the District of Columbia's mandatory, indeterminate commitment statute could not be applied to an insanity acquittee who had not affirmatively relied on the insanity defense[100] but who was, nevertheless, acquitted on that grounds. If commitment is warranted for this individual, in the Court's view the civil commitment provisions provided the appropriate recourse.[101] Although in *Lynch* the Court construed a statute in accordance with its belief about Congress' intention, the Court noted that the interpretation freed the statute "from not insubstantial constitutional doubts."[102] If *Baxstrom* and its progeny

---

[96]*In re* Tew, 280 N.C. 612, 618, 187 S.E.2d 13, 17 (1972), *quoting In re* Boyette, 136 N.C. 415, 419, 48 S.E. 789, 791 (1904).

[97]ASSOCIATION OF THE BAR OF THE CITY OF NEW YORK, MENTAL ILLNESS, DUE PROCESS AND THE ACQUITTED DEFENDANT 9 (1979).

[98]*Id.* at 12.

[99]369 U.S. 705 (1962).

[100]In a proper case, the court may inject the insanity defense. Whalem v. United States, 346 F.2d 812 (D.C. Cir.), *cert denied*, 382 U.S. 862 (1965). However, sound reasons may exist for the court to decline raising the defense over defense objections. United States v. Wright, 627 F.2d 1300 (D.C. Cir. 1980).

[101]Lynch v. Overholser, 369 U.S. 705, 720 (1962).

[102]*Id.*, at 711.

eliminate mandatory, indeterminate commitment for all insanity acquittees by requiring an evaluation of current mental condition prior to indeterminate confinement, *Lynch* suggests that commitment can be accomplished only through recourse to the civil commitment provisions.
Lynch himself was adjudicated NGI. He was as presumptively dangerous
as any other insanity acquittee. The only difference between Lynch and
any other insanity acquittee is that he did not affirmatively assert the
insanity defense. The Supreme Court ruled that confinement could not
be made easier for Lynch, or release more difficult for him, than it was
for any other individual in society who had not become involved in the
criminal justice system. Thus, because Lynch is indistinguishable from
other insanity acquittees on the questions of current mental condition
and potential dangerousness, insanity acquittees who asserted the insanity defense should be entitled to the full civil commitment protections
accorded to Lynch and to other insanity acquittees who resisted that
defense. Statutes in several states now provide for the civil commitment
process to be used for post-trial confinement of insanity acquittees.[103]

RELEASE AND DISCHARGE FROM COMMITMENT

A civil commitment approach following an insanity acquittal solves
the problems of appropriate confinement and appropriate release of
insanity acquittees. In holding that mandatory, indeterminate commitment is inappropriate, several courts explicitly ruled that insanity acquittees are subject to civil commitment and that the statutes governing
release of civilly committed patients shall likewise govern the release of
insanity acquittees.[104] For example, the Indiana Supreme Court utilized
an equal protection analysis to extend to insanity acquittees the state's
civil commitment guarantees of convalescent leave, judicial authority to
revoke, terminate, or amend the original commitment order, habeas corpus release, transfer of veterans to a federal hospital, and hospitalization
in the district of the patient's residence.[105]

Although use of the civil commitment device following insanity
acquittal is warranted, problems remain with such an approach. One
problem concerns the way in which civil commitment is invoked. Rarely

---

[103]*See, e.g.*, N.C. GEN. STAT. § 15A–1321 (1978); OHIO REV. CODE ANN. § 2945.40(A) (Baldwin
   1981). (However, restrictions are placed on the conditional release of those insanity
   acquittees who are civilly committable.).
[104]People v. McQuillan, 392 Mich. 511, 221 N.W.2d 569 (1974); State v. Clemons, 110 Ariz.
   79, 515 P.2d 324 (1973); Wilson v. State, 259 Ind. 375, 287 N.E.2d 875 (1972).
[105]Wilson v. State, *id.* at 384, 287 N.E.2d at 881.

have courts ruled that insanity acquittees are entitled to the same pre-commitment hearing afforded other individuals prior to mental hospi-talization.[106] In most jurisdictions, the insanity acquittee may be detained temporarily for an evaluation of his present mental condition to deter-mine whether involuntary civil commitment is justified.[107] The length of these detentions varies although 60 days is not uncommon.

A long evaluation period for insanity acquittees may be inappro-priate. For example, California imposes a 90-day confinement period for insanity acquittees charged with violent crimes.[108] Confinement is not only authorized for 90 days, it is required for that period. The trial court has no discretion even to order outpatient treatment.[109] This 90-day eval-uation period is inconsistent with the 72-hour maximum evaluation period prescribed by California law for involuntary hospitalization of mental patients generally.[110] If a three-day evaluation is sufficient to determine whether certification for intensive treatment is appropriate for other civil patients, mandating an additional 87 days confinement for insanity acquittees is extreme and may be unconstitutional. The United States Supreme Court has ruled that even if involuntary confinement is initially permissible, a mental patient's detention cannot constitutionally continue after his mental condition no longer meets the statutory criteria for commitment.[111]

Even if a state utilizes equal periods of evaluational confinement, the

---

[106]See, e.g., State ex rel. Kovach v. Schubert, 64 Wis. 2d 612, 219 N.W.2d 341 (1974), appeal dismissed, 419 U.S. 1117, cert. denied, 419 U.S. 1130 (1975); Wilson v. State, 259 Ind. 375, 287 N.E.2d 875 (1972).

[107]See, e.g., People v. Chavez, 629 P.2d 1040 (Colo. 1981) (180 days); State v. Krol, 68 N.J. 236, 344 A.2d 289 (1975) (60 days); People v. McQuillan, 392 Mich. 511, 221 N.W.2d 569 (1974) (60 days); Bolton v. Harris, 395 F.2d 642 (D.C. Cir. 1968) (length will vary with the individual case).

[108]CAL. PENAL CODE § 1026(b) (West Supp. 1982). CAL. PENAL CODE § 1026.2 (West Supp. 1982) provides that no hearing on an application for release of an insanity acquittee "shall be allowed until the person committed shall have been confined for a period of not less than 90 days." Further applications for release are not permitted until one year from the date of the hearing on a preceding application. In re Franklin, 7 Cal. 3d 126, 496 P.2d 465, 101 CAL. RPTR. 553 (1972), the California Supreme Court ruled that the required 90-day confinement period is not violative of due process or equal protection of the laws. The court noted that the ninety-day period is well within the six-month period recommended by the Model Penal Code. MODEL PENAL CODE § 4.08 (Proposed Official Draft 1962).

[109]People v. Froom, 108 Cal. App. 3d 820, 166 Cal. Rptr. 786 (3d Dist. 1980).

[110]CAL. WELF. & INST. CODE §§ 5152, 5213 (West 1972).

[111]O'Connor v. Donaldson, 422 U.S. 563 (1975).

problem is not alleviated if the period is excessive for both groups.[112] Use of lengthy observational periods for mentally ill people has been criticized as improperly allowing involuntary treatment without an adjudication of the threshold question of whether they are even civilly committable.[113] The most reasonable solution is to limit the evaluation to a short time, perhaps 72 hours, and to apply this limitation to insanity acquittees and all others being considered for civil commitment.

To avoid undue deprivation of liberty, outpatient examinations should be ordered in situations in which an inpatient evaluation is unnecessary. In fact, if an individual's current mental condition has been fully evaluated during a pre-trial detention, and if that evaluation has not become stale due to the length of the trial or other factors, then a hearing on the propriety of civil commitment can be conducted without any delay for another evaluation. Nevertheless, expeditious handling of post-criminal trial procedures should not result in the elimination of the separate civil commitment hearing as sometimes occurs when a court sits as trier of fact in both the insanity defense trial and the civil commitment proceeding.[114] A separate hearing is needed to ensure that the insanity defense is fully considered on its own merits. The issue of criminal responsibility should not be compromised by dispositional considerations introduced into the criminal trial itself.

In the civil commitment process, the burden of proof is placed on the state to demonstrate that detention of a mentally ill person is warranted; the individual is not required to demonstrate that detention is unwarranted. "Freedom, in short, is presumptively his, to be taken from him only if exceptional circumstances are proved to exist."[115] If civil commitment is utilized for the insanity acquittee, he or she should be entitled to this protection. Unfortunately, some courts and legislatures have been unwilling to so provide. For example, Congress, anxious about *Bolton's* limitation on automatic commitment of insanity acquittees, amended the District's NGI commitment statute to distinguish insanity acquittees from others subject to civil commitment. At a civil commitment hearing in the District of Columbia, the government bears the bur-

---

[112]AMERICAN BAR FOUNDATION, *supra* note 7, at 47–48, lists temporary or observational hospitalization periods ranging from three to 180 days. Some states provide for indefinite observational confinement.

[113]Kendall v. True, 391 F. Supp. 413 (W.D. Ky. 1975); Bell v. Wayne County Gen. Hosp., 384 F. Supp. 1085 (E.D. Mich. 1974); Morris, *Civil Commitment in a Suburban County: An Investigation by Law Students.* 13 SANTA CLARA LAW. 518, 532–34 (1973).

[114]People v. Thiem, 82 Ill. App. 3d 956, 403 N.E.2d 647 (1980).

[115]A. GOLDSTEIN, *supra* note 10, at 160.

den of proving by clear and convincing evidence that the individual's condition meets the commitment standard.[116] In contrast, Congress authorized a temporary, automatic commitment of insanity acquittees[117] with a "release hearing" to be conducted within 50 days of that confinement.[118] At that "release hearing," the insanity acquittee bears the burden of proving by a preponderance of the evidence that he is entitled to release.[119] Similarly, California and Colorado, with a 90-day and 180-day evaluational commitments respectively, statutorily require insanity acquittees to establish by a preponderance of the evidence their eligibility for release at hearings conducted at the conclusion of the evaluation period.[120] Although the Georgia statute is silent on the burden of proof issue,[121] the Supreme Court of Georgia imposed the preponderance burden on insanity acquittees at release hearings.[122]

Shifting the burden of proof to the insanity acquittee has been criticized as an inappropriate attempt to restore mandatory, indeterminate commitment. As one author noted, when the burden of proof is placed on the insanity acquittee, he is accorded

> no more substantial opportunity . . . to obtain his release than is already available by means of a habeas corpus or a contested release proceeding. In all three proceedings, the patient has the burden of proving that he has recovered his sanity and is not likely to be dangerous to himself or others,

---

[116]D.C. CODE § 21–545(b) (1973) as construed in *In re* Nelson, 408 A.2d 1233 (D.C. Ct. App. 1979). The District of Columbia Court of Appeals stated that it was bound by the United States Supreme Court decision in Addington v. Texas, 441 U.S. 418 (1979). In *Addington*, the Court ruled that for civil commitment decisions, a clear and convincing burden of proof satisfies the minimum constitutional requirements of due process. *See* discussion in text at note 128, *infra*. Prior to *Addington*, the United States Court of Appeals for the District of Columbia Circuit ruled that proof beyond a reasonable doubt was required to civilly commit persons in the District. *In re* Ballay, 482 F.2d 648 (D.C. Cir. 1973).

[117]D.C. CODE § 24–301(d)(1)(1973).

[118]*Id.* §24–301(d)(2).

[119]*Id.*

[120]CAL. PENAL CODE § 1026.2 (West Supp. 1982). An identical predecessor statute was upheld in *In re* Franklin, 7 Cal. 3d 126, 496 P.2d 465, 101 Cal. Rptr. 553 (1972). COLO. REV. STAT. § 16–8–115(2) (Supp. 1981), upheld in People v. Chavez, 629 P.2d 1040 (Colo. 1981).

[121]GA. CODE § 27–1503 (1978).

[122]Clark v. State, 245 Ga. 629, 266 S.E.2d 466 (1980). However, in Benham v. Edwards, 501 F. Supp. 1050 (N.D. Ga. 1980), the court ruled that a presumption of continuing insanity cannot be relied upon to justify placement of the burden of proof on the insanity acquittee. The court required the state to initiate a commitment hearing at which it must sustain the burden of proving, by clear and convincing evidence, that the insanity acquittee's mental condition presently meets the involuntary civil commitment criteria.

even though the District has never shown the insanity acquittee, unlike the civil patient, to be presently insane.[123]

Legislation that imposes the burden of proof on the insanity acquittee is vulnerable to a new *Bolton*-type challenge.[124] Such legislation "reflects a punitive gloss derived from his previous criminal behavior. [T]his extra, punitive basis for commitment [permits] an abbreviated, more burdensome release hearing, resulting, arguably, in a less valid finding of mental illness and dangerousness than the civil commitment process would yield."[125]

Because the interests considered in insanity acquittee commitments are identical to those in civil commitments—community security versus individual liberty—the burden of proof and other procedural protections should be identical.[126] As Judge J. Skelly Wright noted, "*Bolton* and *Baxstrom* stand for a basic proposition that a proven history of past dangerousness or illness, while certainly admissible in evidence, may not be used as an excuse to abrogate or change well recognized standards, including burden of proof in civil commitment proceedings, or their equivalent, to determine present dangerousness or illness."[127]

In *Addington v. Texas*,[128] the United States Supreme Court noted that civil commitment constitutes a significant deprivation of liberty and can engender adverse social consequences for the individual. For these reasons, due process requires the state to justify confinement by proof greater than a mere preponderance of the evidence. At a minimum, due process requires a "clear and convincing" standard of proof. Although *Addington* did not involve an insanity acquittee, the civil commitment proceedings in that case were instituted after the individual had been arrested and charged with assaulting his mother.

State appellate courts in New Jersey[129] and Maryland[130] and a United States District Court in Georgia,[131] jurisdictions that prior to *Addington* had required the state to justify commitment of insanity acquittees by a

---

[123]Note, *Commitment of Persons Acquitted by Reason of Insanity: The Example of the District of Columbia*, 74 COLUM. L. REV. 733, 744–45 (1974) (footnotes omitted).

[124]Jones v. United States, 396 A.2d 183, 186 n.3 (D.C. Ct. App. 1978), *opinion vacated on rehearing*, 411 A.2d 624 (D.C. Ct. App. 1980).

[125]*Id.* at 188 n. 8.

[126]State v. Krol, 68 N.J. 236, 271, 344 A.2d 289, 308 (1975) (Clifford, J., dissenting in part).

[127]United States v. Brown, 478 F.2d 606, 613 (D.C. Cir. 1973) (Wright, J., dissenting).

[128]441 U.S. 418 (1979).

[129]*In re* Scelfo, 170 N.J. Super. 394, 406 A.2d 973 (1979).

[130]Williams v. Superintendent, 43 Md. App. 588, 406 A.2d 1302 (Md. Ct. of Sp. Appeals, 1979).

[131]Benham v. Edwards, 501 F. Supp. 1050 (N.D. Ga. 1980).

preponderance of the evidence, read *Addington* to require clear and convincing proof for insanity acquittees as well as civil committees. The New Jersey court expressed "no hesitancy in concluding that the standard of proof established in the *Addington* case should have . . . application to all persons who have been acquitted by reason of insanity."[132] Two of three trial court decisions in New York have applied the *Addington* standard to insanity acquittees.[133] The third case did not even discuss the potential applicability of the *Addington* decision.[134]

The supreme courts of Washington[135] and Hawaii[136] also have rejected, *sub silentio*, *Addington's* applicability to insanity acquittees.[137] The Supreme Court of Washington cited with approval a pre-*Addington* New Jersey case and did not clearly articulate a rationale for its decision. The court merely noted that it was "dealing with a most imprecise area of human behavior and . . . [was] attempting to predict future conduct of a particular individual."[138] Because of these factors, "it is unreal to insist that the statutory elements be proved beyond a reasonable doubt or by clear, cogent and convincing evidence."[139] *Quaere:* Because civil commitment of the mentally ill on a dangerousness-to-others basis involves the same imprecise area of human behavior and the same prediction of future conduct, why is a requirement of clear and convincing proof more "unreal" for insanity acquittees than it is for civil committees?[140]

Paradoxically, jurisdictions that separately categorize insanity acquittees as individuals who are not entitled to civil commitment safeguards may be compelled by *Addington* to justify the insanity acquittee's commitment by the most stringent proof standard. In *Addington,* the

---

[132]*In re* Scelfo, 170 N.J.Super. 394, 406 A.2d 973, 975 (1979).
[133]*In re* Rose, 109 Misc. 2d 960, 441 N.Y.S.2d 161 (Sup. Ct., Kings Co. 1981); People v. Escobar, 110 Misc. 2d 1089, 443 N.Y.S.2d 534 (Sup. Ct., Bronx Co. 1980).
[134]People v. Plaksin, 107 Misc. 2d 696, 435 N.Y.S.2d 894 (Sup. Ct., Kings Co. 1981).
[135]State v. Wilcox, 92 Wash. 2d 610, 600 P.2d 561 (1979).
[136]Thompson v. Yuen, 623 P.2d 881 (Hawaii 1979).
[137]In Ashley v. Psychiatric Security Review Bd., 53 Ore. App. 333, 632 P.2d 15 (1981), the Oregon Court of Appeals discussed, and rejected, *Addington's* applicability to insanity acquittees. In the court's view, the findings in the criminal trial—commission of a criminal act, mental illness, and dangerousness—meant that the risks of an erroneous commitment decision for insanity acquittees is less than that for civil committees. Such a distinction warranted a preponderance of the evidence standard for commitment of insanity acquittees.
[138]State v. Wilcox, 92 Wash. 2d 619, 600 P.2d 561, 563 (1979).
[139]*Id.*
[140]In *In re* Harris, 94 Wash. 2d 430, 617 P.2d 739 (1980), the Washington Supreme Court ruled that the preponderance of the evidence burden was applicable also to insanity acquittees who had only been charged with crimes against property.

patient had urged adoption of a requirement of proof beyond a reasonable doubt. The Court rejected that burden, noting, "In a civil commitment state power is not exercised in a punitive sense."[141] The attempt by some jurisdictions to deny insanity acquittees full civil commitment safeguards establishes the punitive exercise of state power necessitating a higher burden of proof than is required for civil commitments generally. The resolution of this dilemma is for states to accord full civil commitment safeguards and full civil patient status to insanity acquittees.

If, as recommended, insanity acquittees are not distinguished from others for purposes of civil commitment, then the length of a hypothetical prison term that could have been imposed if the insanity acquittee had been convicted is irrelevant to the length of his or her detention as a civilly committed patient. Achievement of the therapeutic goals of hospital confinement should determine eligibility for release.[142] However, jurisdictions that attempt to distinguish insanity acquittees from other civil committees have been compelled to confront the punitive basis underlying the acquittee's confinement. Characterization of insanity acquittees as an exceptionally dangerous class of persons whose past conduct permits lesser procedural protections must of necessity evaporate whenever an insanity acquittee is confined for the maximum term prescribed for the crime that served as a basis for the insanity acquittal. The Supreme Court of California ruled that the constitutional demands of equal protection require a shifting of the burden of proof to the government whenever the insanity acquittee has "served" a period of time in institutional confinement equal to the maximum term that he could have been punished if he had been convicted of the underlying offense.[143] The

---

[141]Addington v. Texas, 441 U.S. 418, 428 (1979).

[142]Jones v. United States, 396 A.2d 183, 189 (D.C. Ct. App. 1978), *opinion vacated on rehearing*, 411 A.2d 624 (D.C. Ct. App. 1980).

[143]*In re* Moye, 22 Cal. 3d 457, 584 P.2d 1097, 149 CAL. RPTR. 491 (1978). After the maximum term, and consistent with laws that were then applicable to mentally disordered sex offenders, the insanity acquittee may be subjected to a further period of extended commitment only if the state establishes that the individual remains a danger to the health and safety of himself or others. The extended commitment period is for one year, subject to annual renewals following notice and a hearing. *Id.* at 467, 584 P.2d at 1103–4, 149 CAL. RPTR. 497–98.

The legislature responded to the *Moye* decision by enacting CAL. PENAL CODE § 1026.5 (West Supp. 1982). The statute expands the extended commitment periods to two years but limits extended commitment to those who were acquitted by reason of insanity of violent felonies "and who by reason of a mental disease, defect, or disorder represents a substantial danger of physical harm to others." *Id.* § 1026.5(a)(1). Notwith-

court noted that under existing California law, insanity acquittees were the only individuals who faced "a potential lifetime confinement, imposed without regard to the nature of the underlying offense or the maximum punishment prescribed for it, and without the additional protection of periodic review and recommitment hearings."[144]

An approach that delays complete civil commitment safeguards until the insanity acquittee's confinement reaches the length of a hypothetical maximum sentence cannot be justified.

> If those committed civilly are not presumed to become safe after some set period of time, one could not presume insanity acquittees to become safe simply because the time they would have spent in prison had elapsed. That courts commit insanity acquittees under lower standards and then feel obliged to release them after the maximum prison term shows instead that they view the insanity acquittee's term in a mental hospital not as normal preventive detention, but as something more akin to a prison sentence.[145]

The United States Supreme Court has agreed to hear a case challenging the District of Columbia statute.[146] The patient, who had been acquitted by reason of insanity of a misdemeanor punishable by a maximum sentence of one year,[147] sought release or civil commitment after he had been confined at St. Elizabeth's Hospital as an insanity acquittee for more than one year. A divided District of Columbia Court of Appeals rejected the assertion that the statute, by placing the burden of proof on the insanity acquittee and by authorizing continued confinement of the individual in the status of an insanity acquittee beyond the maximum that could have been imposed if he had been convicted of the underlying

standing the "dangerousness to others" commitment criteria clearly established in section 1026.5(a)(1), a California Court of Appeal has ruled that an insanity acquittee who was only dangerous to his own safety could be subjected to the extended commitment provisions. People v. Blackwell, 117 Cal. App. 3d 372, 172 Cal. Rptr. 636 (1st Dist. 1981). In my opinion, this decision attempts to punish an insanity acquittee by extending commitment without any justification. California's concept of extended commitment, if it is valid at all, is valid only to protect others from the insanity acquittee, not to protect the insanity acquittee from himself. See also People v. Smith, 120 Cal. App. 3d 817, 175 Cal. Rptr. 54 (5th Cir. 1981) wherein the court ruled that in establishing the maximum term for the underlying offense, the insanity acquittee was entitled to credit for the actual time he spent in precommitment confinement. However, he was not entitled to "good time" conduct credit.

[144]In re Moye, 22 Cal. 3d 457, 465, 584 P.2d 1097, 1102, 149 Cal. Rptr. 491, 496 (1978).

[145]Note, supra note 7, at 622.

[146]Jones v. United States, 432 A.2d 364 (D.C. Ct. App. 1981), cert. granted, 50 U.S.L.W. 3547 (U.S. Jan. 11, 1982) (No. 81-5195).

[147]Id. at 382 n.6.

offense, denied him equal protection of the laws. The court's majority declared repeatedly that the statute was not punitive in nature.[148]

In a well reasoned dissenting opinion, Judge Ferren demonstrated through legislative history and legislative result that in enacting the statute, Congress manifested a punitive objective:

> [Insanity acquittees'] criminal conduct continues to play a decisive role in the nature of their treatment and their chances for release after initial confinement. Congress and the courts have justified this harsher treatment precisely because acquittees have committed crimes.
>
> [A]cquittees are not confined to mental institutions for medical reasons alone. They are confined there in part because society is unwilling to allow those who have committed crimes to escape without paying for their crimes. The intent of the statute is partially punitive, and thus the procedures under [the District of Columbia statute] reflect this added burden on the defendant. Because of this punitive purpose, the maximum statutory period of confinement becomes relevant, for at that point society no longer has a valid interest in continued confinement on the basis of a shortcut procedure.[149]

Another procedural device used in many jurisdictions to distinguish insanity acquittees from civilly committed patients is the requirement of judicial review only of decisions to release insanity acquittees. In *Bolton,* the court upheld the District's statute that imposed the additional procedural hurdle to release of insanity acquittees. The court stated: "We do not think equal protection is offended by allowing the Government or the court the opportunity to insure that the standards for release of civilly committed patients are faithfully applied to [insanity acquittee] patients.[150] In a subsequent opinion reaffirming this aspect of *Bolton,* the United States Court of Appeals for the District of Columbia Circuit expressed its belief that the requirement of court approval does not disadvantage insanity acquittees.[151] Apparently, the court believed that if the insanity acquittee can establish to his doctor's satisfaction that he is entitled to release, he should have no difficulty in convincing a court as well. However, as one author noted, if courts always agreed with doctors, the trial court function would be superfluous. If the trial court disagrees

---

[148]*Id.* at 368 ("[W]e deem it necessary to reject any suggestion that confinement pursuant to subsection 301(d) is punitive in nature." "We conclude that there is no basis for finding § 301(d) punitive in any respect.") and 376 ("[T]he commitment scheme for acquittees is not intended to attribute any guilt or imply any social indebtedness in the excuse of a criminal offense.").

[149]*Id.* at 381 (Ferren, J., dissenting).

[150]Bolton v. Harris, 395 F.2d 642, 652 (1968).

[151]United States v. Ecker, 543 F.2d 178, 194–99 (D.C. Cir. 1976), *cert. denied,* 429 U.S. 1063 (1977).

with the doctor's decision—as frequently occurs—then this procedural barrier inhibits release of insanity acquittees.[152]

The circuit court has admitted that the requirement of judicial review of insanity acquittee release decisions is premised on the need to protect society from those whom the hospital is ready to release.[153] However, release decisions, just as initial commitment decisions, involve questions of mental illness and dangerousness for both classes of patients. *Baxstrom* and court decisions applying *Baxstrom* to cases involving insanity acquittees prohibit proof of past criminal activity from serving as a basis for fewer procedural safeguards in the commitment process. *A fortiori*, proof of past criminal activity cannot have greater effect *subsequent* to commitment, permitting greater procedural barriers to the release of those insanity acquittees who were committed following their insanity acquittals.

The United States Court of Appeals for the Fifth Circuit attempted to explain its decision upholding court review of insanity acquittee release decisions by stating that the issue of dangerousness "presents a mixed question involving both a legal and social judgment as well as a medical opinion."[154] The court failed to explain how the issue differed when release was permitted without court review of a person civilly committed as mentally ill and dangerous to others.

The Illinois Supreme Court upheld the validity of a statute requiring judicial review of release decisions prior to the expiration of the maximum period that defendant would have been required to serve had he been convicted instead of acquitted by reason of insanity.[155] Rejecting the implications of *Baxstrom*, the court stated simply that the criminal act committed by the insanity acquittee justified the additional release requirement of judicial review. The Illinois approach is another example of a state rejecting civil commitment of insanity acquittees and using the post-NGI commitment as a sentencing alternative to penal incarceration. This approach, if permissible at all, necessarily must terminate at the end of the hypothetical sentence that could have been imposed if the insanity acquittee had been convicted.

Professor David Wexler has suggested a practical justification for the judicial review requirement. Hospitals, fearful of adverse publicity and

---

[152]Note, *Constitutional Standards for Release of the Civilly Committed and Not Guilty By Reason of Insanity: A Strict Scrutiny Analysis*, 20 ARIZ. L. REV. 233, 269 (1978).

[153]United States v. Ecker, 543 F.2d 178, 197 (D.C. Cir. 1976), *cert. denied*, 429 U.S. 1063 (1977).

[154]Powell v. Florida, 579 F.2d 324, 333 (5th Cir. 1978).

[155]People v. Valdez, 79 Ill. 2d 74, 402 N.E.2d 187 (1980).

public reaction, may be reluctant to release insanity acquittees whom the hospital staff view as clinically ready for discharge. By diffusing the release decision through requiring judicial approval prior to release, hospitals may be less inhibited in recommending patients for release. In most cases, courts would rely on the hospital psychiatric reports and would approve the hospital release decision without a full hearing. Only in the most questionable cases would the courts fully review the hospital's release recommendation.[156]

Professor Wexler's proposal to reduce hospital decision makers' inhibitions may have just the opposite effect. Courts have not hesitated to overrule even unanimous psychiatric judgment to deny an insanity acquittee patient release.[157] A psychiatrist whose recommendation has been rejected may well be influenced to be more conservative in his or her future evaluations.

The perceived problem of timid release decision making can be better addressed through placing a short durational limit on the initial commitment order. Thereafter, if the state wishes to continue the insanity acquittee's detention, it should be required to establish by clear and convincing proof the basis for a subsequent commitment order. Each additional commitment order also should be limited in time. Many states require periodic recommitment determinations for their civil patients, but few extend the safeguard to insanity acquittees. A special committee of the Association of the Bar of the City of New York noted that insanity acquittees were the only individuals denied periodic recommitment in New York State. The committee recommended that this unfounded discrimination be eliminated.[158]

In Arizona, which utilizes the civil commitment process to secure the detention of insanity acquittees in appropriate cases, confinement of persons dangerous to others is limited to a maximum period of 180 days.[159] A recommitment order must be obtained to confine the person thereafter.[160] However, to avoid discharging demonstrably violent persons—including insanity acquittees—after only 180 days, Arizona law permits recommitment based on the *original* pre-commitment dangerous act when the act is categorized as "grievous or horrendous"[161]. In essence,

---

[156]D. WEXLER, *supra* note 61, at 53–55.

[157]*See* cases cited in note 28, *supra*. "Experience shows that more often the courts frustrate realistic expectations of release than do the psychiatrists." GERMAN & SINGER, *supra* note 7, at 1061.

[158]ASSOCIATION OF THE BAR OF THE CITY OF NEW YORK, *supra* note 97, at 39.

[159]ARIZ. REV. STAT. § 36–540(B) (Supp. 1981).

[160]*Id.* § 36–542.

[161]*Id.* § 36–501(3).

Arizona eliminates the requirement that the state establish current dangerousness as a basis for continued commitment. The Arizona scheme has been strongly criticized.[162]

In recommending that court-approved release be utilized for insanity acquittee patients, Professor Wexler noted that the crucial distinction for release-structure purposes should be drawn between *dangerous* and *nondangerous* patients.[163] Apparently, he would require judicial approval for release of all insanity acquittee patients and for those civil patients who were committed as mentally ill and dangerous to others. Even if Professor Wexler's proposal is ultimately adopted, at the current time only insanity acquittees are subjected to judicial review of hospital release decisions. Until civil patient release decisions are also subjected to court scrutiny, the existing practice is susceptible to an equal protection attack.

Even if a jurisdiction requires court approval for release of all dangerous mental patients, insanity acquittees should not, as a group, be classified in the dangerous category. Some have been acquitted of nonviolent crimes and should be released through hospital decision making that is utilized for all other nonviolent civil committees. The special committee of the Association of the Bar of the City of New York accepted this distinction and recommended that only those insanity acquittees who had been acquitted of violent crimes be subjected to release through a court order.[164]

Although I have recommended that for purposes of commitment, treatment, and release, insanity acquittees should not be distinguished from other individuals, the civil commitment approach is no panacea. The American Bar Foundation reports that civil commitment statutes

> are so broadly worded that they fail to identify with clarity or precision the type and degree of mental illness for which involuntary hospitalization, with the accompanying deprivation of many personal and civil rights, is justified. The statutory language in this area is almost universally obscure or tautological.... [For example] New York law permits hospitalization of a person who is "afflicted with mental disease to such an extent that for his own welfare or the welfare of others, or of the community, he requires care and treatment." Even those statutes which rely on the concept of dangerousness as a justification for hospitalization are in significant aspects vague.

---

[162]D. WEXLER, MENTAL HEALTH LAW: MAJOR ISSUES 149–50 (1981).

[163]D. WEXLER, *supra* note 61, at 56.

[164]ASSOCIATION OF THE BAR OF THE CITY OF NEW YORK, *supra* note 97, at 37. *See also* Benham v. Edwards, 501 F. Supp. 1050 (N.D. Ga. 1980) in which the court held that the state may require only those insanity acquittees who were charged with serious violent crimes to obtain court approval of their release.

In application, such a standard can become as broad as the ingenuity of the
person who must apply it allows.[165]

Thus, virtually all insanity acquittees who would be confined under a
mandatory, indeterminate commitment statute also could be confined
under a civil commitment statute. The elimination of mandatory, indeterminate commitment would be an illusory reform.

In recent years, many states have limited their civil commitment
standard to mental illness plus dangerousness to self or others. The traditional *parens patriae* basis of commitment—that the person is mentally
ill and in need of care and treatment—has been criticized and to some
extent supplanted by the preventive detention model. Reformers have
successfully urged that a recent, overt, dangerous act be proven in order
to establish a basis for commitment.[166]

However, even though some states have tightened their civil commitment criteria, subsequent legislative amendments have weakened the
initial reforms. For example, for civil commitment, the state of Washington requires that the person "presents a likelihood of serious harm to
others or himself, or is gravely disabled."[167] However, in 1979, the "likelihood of serious harm" criterion was broadened to include persons who
are a risk to inflict property damage.[168] The "gravely disabled" definition
was expanded to include persons undergoing deterioration in routine
functioning.[169]

Some court decisions also have inhibited the civil commitment
reform movement. A federal district court construing Nebraska law
imposed a "dangerousness" test for civil commitment and required proof
of a recent, overt act or threat.[170] However, the court added: "The threat
of harm to oneself may be through neglect or inability to care for oneself."[171] The passively dangerous person, previously committed under
Nebraska's vague and overbroad *parens patriae* approach, now may be
committed under the court's broadly defined "dangerousness" umbrella.
Similarly, a federal district court construing Utah law restricted *parens
patriae* commitments to those individuals who pose an immediate danger

---

[165]AMERICAN BAR FOUNDATION, *supra* note 7, at 39 (footnotes omitted).

[166]*E.g.*, J. KLEIN, *Mental Health Law: Legal Doctrine at the Crossroads.* 11 *The Mental Health Law
Project Summary of Activities* 7 (Mar. 1976). For statutes and cases requiring proof of overt
dangerous behavior as a prerequisite to involuntary civil commitment, see note 29
supra.

[167]WASH. REV. CODE §§71.05.150, 71.05.240 (1979).

[168]*Id.* § 71.05.020(3).

[169]*Id.* § 71.05.020(1).

[170]Doremus v. Farrell, 407 F. Supp. 509 (D. Nev. 1975).

[171]*Id.* at 515.

to themselves, but added that such danger may include the inability to provide the basic necessities of life.[172]

A detailed examination of civil commitment is beyond the scope of this chapter. It suffices to say that articulation of unambiguous, narrowly defined criteria and imposition of increased procedural safeguards for civil commitment are being advocated and, to some extent, accepted by courts and legislatures. If these trends continue, civil commitment becomes an even more desirable and proper approach to the disposition of insanity acquittees.

CONDITIONS OF CONFINEMENT

The problem of confinement conditions involves the question of equalizing treatment for insanity acquittees and other civilly committed patients. In recent years, various treatment rights of the civilly committed have been widely accepted. These rights include the right to adequate treatment,[173] the right to refuse treatment,[174] and the right to be treated in the least restrictive setting.[175] The principle of the least restrictive alternative requires the state to explore noninstitutional alternatives to hospitalization. Thus the right "does not prevent the state from achieving any of the objectives it seeks through commitment, but merely asks courts to ensure that the state imposes no greater constriction of freedom than necessary to serve the objectives."[176]

The practice of confining insanity acquittees in maximum security wards or hospitals and thus imposing special treatment restrictions on them based solely on their label as insanity acquittees may be constitutionally impermissible as violating both equal protection and due pro-

---

[172]Colyar v. Third Judicial Dist. Ct., 469 F. Supp. 424 (D. Utah 1979).

[173]*See, e.g.,* Wyatt v. Stickney, 325 F. Supp. 781 (M.D. Ala. 1971), *on submission of proposed standards by defendants,* 334 F. Supp. 1341, *enforced,* 344 F. Supp. 373 & 378 (1972), *aff'd in part, remanded on other grounds sub. nom.* Wyatt v. Aderholt, 503 F.2d 1305 (5th Cir. 1974); Rouse v. Cameron, 373 F.2d 451 (D.C. Cir. 1966).

[174]Scott v. Plante, 323 F.2d 939 (3d Cir. 1976); Winters v. Miller, 446 F.2d 65 (2d Cir.), *cert. denied,* 404 U.S. 985 (1971); Rogers v. Okin, 478 F. Supp. 1342 (D. Mass. 1979) *modified,* 634 F.2d 650 (1st Cir. 1980), *cert. granted sub. nom.* Mills v. Rogers, 49 U.S.L.W. 3788 (U.S. Apr. 20, 1981) (No. 80-1417); Rennie v. Klein, 462 F. Supp. 1131 (D. N.J. 1978), *preliminary injunction granted,* 476 F. Supp. 1294 (D. N.J. 1978).

[175]Lake v. Cameron, 364 F.2d 657 (D.C. Cir. 1966); Dixon v. Weinberger, 405 F. Supp. 974 (D.D.C. 1975). *See* Hoffman & Foust, *Least Restrictive Treatment of the Mentally Ill: A Doctrine in Search of Its Senses,* 14 SAN DIEGO L. REV. 1100, 1105–22 (1977), which discusses the evolution of judicial and legislative acceptance of this right.

[176]Chambers, *Alternatives to Civil Commitment of the Mentally Ill: Practical Guides and Constitutional Imperatives,* 70 MICH. L. REV. 1107, 1111 (1972).

cess. The rationale underlying the United States Supreme Court's *Baxstrom* and *Jackson* decisions implies that because insanity acquittees are not sentence-serving convicts they have no special "criminal" patient status. Other civilly committed patients are not initially admitted to the maximum security wards or hospitals but are transferred there only after they engage in some dangerous conduct in the "regular" wards. Arguably, to deprive an insanity acquittee patient of regular ward treatment without requiring any proven dangerous conduct in a regular ward cannot be constitutionally condoned.

In *Covington v. Harris*,[177] the United States Court of Appeals for the District of Columbia Circuit held that a civil patient, confined in the maximum security ward of the District's mental hospital as dangerously mentally ill, could properly petition the court by a writ of habeas corpus to obtain a transfer to a less restrictive ward within the same hospital. Chief Judge Bazelon, writing the opinion of the court, noted that although a mere request for a change of dormitories or for a transfer between substantially similar wards would not sustain a petition for habeas corpus, facilities for the criminally insane

> have, in the past, notoriously rivalled maximum security prisons in the pervasiveness of their restraint upon liberty and the totality of their impositions upon dignity. . . . Thus, there is reason to believe that confinement in John Howard [the maximum security ward] is not normally contemplated for civilly committed patients and entails extraordinary deprivations of liberty and dignity which make it, in effect, more penitentiary than mental hospital, even if it also provides some treatment. . . .
>
> It makes little sense to guard zealously against the possibility of unwarranted deprivations [of liberty] prior to hospitalization, only to abandon the watch once the patient disappears behind hospital doors. The range of possible dispositions of a mentally ill person within a hospital, from maximum security to outpatient status, is almost as wide as that of dispositions without. The commitment statute no more authorizes unnecessary restrictions within the former range than it does within the latter.[178]

Subsequent decisions in the same jurisdiction have specified protective procedures that would extend due process to maximum security transfers.[179]

In 1972, New York enacted legislation[180] that was even more protective of the mental patient's right not to be transferred into maximum

[177]419 F.2d 617 (D.C. Cir. 1969).

[178]*Id.* at 622–24.

[179]Jones v. Robinson, 440 F.2d 249 (D.C. Cir. 1971); Williams v. Robinson, 432 F.2d 637 (D.C. Cir. 1970).

[180]N.Y. Sess. Laws 1972, ch. 251, § 29.13.

security confinement.[181] An individual could be transferred only if he was a "dangerous" patient, defined by the statute as one who

> has committed or is liable to commit an act or acts which, if committed by a person criminally responsible for his conduct, would constitute homicide or felonious assault or is so dangerously mentally disabled that his presence in the department hospital or school is dangerous to the safety of the other patients therein, to the officers or employees thereof, or to the community.[182]

Prior to transfer, the allegedly dangerous patient was entitled to notice and a court hearing at which he was represented by counsel.[183] If the patient was adjudged dangerous, transfer could be ordered only for a period not to exceed six months. Subsequent orders authorizing retention in maximum security for similar six-month periods required new court hearings and determinations that the patient continued to meet the statutory criterion of dangerousness. Although the New York legislation was held unconstitutional on other grounds,[184] the standard and procedures articulated in the legislation serve as a model worthy of emulation.

Recent judicial activity involving prison administration may support the requirement of due process protections prior to the placement of insanity acquittees into maximum security confinement. In *Wolff v. McDonnell*,[185] a prison revoked a convict's good-time credits because of its determination that he had engaged in serious misconduct. Because the prison's decision extended the length of the prisoner's confinement, the United States Supreme Court required that minimum due process protections be accorded. The precedent of *Wolff* has been weakened by subsequent Supreme Court cases authorizing administrative transfers between prisons, even when the changes in the conditions of confinement have a substantial adverse impact on the prisoner.[186] However, when the "consequences visited on the prisoner are qualitatively differ-

---

[181]In Kesselbrenner v. Anonymous, 33 N.Y.2d 161, 305 N.E.2d 903, 350 N.Y.S.2d 889 (1973), the statute was held to violate the patient's constitutional right to due process. Notwithstanding the procedural protections provided by the statute, a finding that the civilly committed mental patient was "dangerous" resulted in his transfer from a facility administered by the Department of Mental Hygiene to Matteawan State Hospital, administered by the Department of Correction. Because the patient was neither charged with nor convicted of a crime, such a result was "constitutionally invidious."

[182]N.Y. Sess. Laws 1972, ch. 251, § 29.13(a).

[183]Pending the hearing, however, the court was also empowered to "forthwith order" the transfer of the patient if the transferring hospital was not able to care properly for the patient and the "patient was in need of immediate treatment." *Id.* at (h).

[184]*See* discussion in note 181, *supra*.

[185]418 U.S. 539 (1974).

[186]Meachum v. Fano, 427 U.S. 215 (1976); Montanye v. Haymes, 427 U.S. 236 (1976).

ent from the punishment characteristically suffered by a person convicted of crime,"[187] the Supreme Court and lower federal courts have continued to impose due process safeguards.[188]

Increased recognition of rights of mental patients can be anticipated as courts begin to draw obvious analogies between the two groups. The Supreme Court has ruled that a convict-prisoner may not, by administrative fiat alone, be placed in solitary confinement.[189] By analogy, a mental patient should not be subject to administrative placement in maximum security because such placement visits consequences on him or her that are qualitatively different from the treatment accorded other patients. To the extent that sentence-serving convicts are entitled to due process protections, surely nonconvict mental patients—including insanity acquittees—are entitled to no less.

Several court decisions have specifically required treatment in the least restrictive setting for insanity acquittees.[190] Some decisions have gone beyond the issue of maximum security institutionalization and have assured insanity acquittees all treatment rights accorded other involuntary patients. For example, a federal district court noted that under Texas law, civil committees are entitled to "receive care and treatment in accordance with the highest medical practice."[191] No standards or requirements for treatment were established for insanity acquittees. Unlike civil committees, insanity acquittes under Texas law could not be transferred from the state's maximum security facility to a less secure facility unless the committing court's permission was obtained. They were also ineligible to receive home furloughs, were not allowed hospital grounds privileges even when it was deemed medically advisable, and were not allowed to enroll in correspondence school rehabilitation and education programs. The court concluded that the ultimate goal of confinement was the same for both groups—namely, the rehabilitation of the individual as a functioning and productive member of society. The

---

[187]Vitek v. Jones, 445 U.S. 480, 493 (1980).

[188]Vitek v. Jones, 445 U.S. 480 (1980) (transfer from a prison to a mental hospital); Greenholtz v. Nebraska Penal Inmates, 442 U.S. 1 (1979) (parole revocation); Enomoto v. Wright, 434 U.S. 1052 (1978) (solitary confinement); Gagnon v. Scarpelli, 411 U.S. 778 (1973) (probation revocation). See also cases listed in Robbins v. Kleindienst, 383 F. Supp. 239, 247–48 (D.C. Cir. 1974).

[189]Enomoto v. Wright, 434 U.S. 1052 (1978).

[190]See, e.g., State v. Krol, 68 N.J. 236, 344 A.2d 289 (1975); Kesselbrenner v. Anonymous, 33 N.Y.2d 161, 305 N.E.2d 903, 350 N.Y.S.2d 889 (1973); People v. Lally, 19 N.Y.2d 27, 224 N.E.2d 87, 277 N.Y.S.2d 654 (1966); Ashe v. Robinson, 450 F.2d 681 (D.C. Cir. 1971).

[191]Reynolds v. Neill, 381 F. Supp. 1374, 1383 (N.D. Texas 1974), vacated and remanded on other grounds, sub. nom., Sheldon v. Reynolds, 422 U.S. 1050 (1975).

differences in treatment created a denial of due process and equal protection to insanity acquittees.[192]

As could be anticipated, not all authorities agree that insanity acquittees should have all treatment rights accorded civilly committed patients. Although the Association of the Bar of the City of New York advocated extending the least restrictive alternative doctrine to insanity acquittees and recommended that the insanity acquittee status should not in itself serve to allow maximum security institutionalization,[193] this recommendation was rejected by the state's Law Revision Commission. The commission's proposal,[194] accepted without modification by the New York Legislature,[195] creates three alternative tracks based on the court's determination of the defendant's mental condition at the time of his postinsanity acquittal hearing. The court may find that the insanity acquittee: (1) has a dangerous mental disorder; or (2) does not have a dangerous mental disorder but is mentally ill; or (3) does not have a dangerous mental disorder and is not mentally ill. If the first finding is made, the insanity acquittee is committed to a secure facility for six months[196] and may not be transferred to a nonsecure facility[197] or granted a furlough[198] without a court order. Subsequent retention orders for more lengthy periods of time may be obtained.[199] If the second finding is made, the insanity acquittee's confinement is governed by the state's civil commitment laws.[200] If the third finding is made, the insanity acquittee is discharged.[201] Under all three findings, the court is empowered to issue an order of conditions.[202] This order directs the insanity acquittee to comply

---

[192]*See also* Rouse v. Cameron, 373 F.2d 451 (D.C. Cir. 1966) in which the United States Court of Appeals for the District of Columbia Circuit announced a right to treatment for insanity acquittees.

[193]ASSOCIATION OF THE BAR OF THE CITY OF NEW YORK, *supra* note 97, at 33.

[194]STATE OF NEW YORK, REPORT OF THE LAW REVISION COMMISSION TO THE HONORABLE HUGH L. CAREY, GOVERNOR, ON THE DEFENSE OF INSANITY IN NEW YORK STATE 40 (1980).

[195]N.Y. Sess. Laws 1980, ch. 548, § 11, codified as N.Y. CRIM. PRO. § 330.20 (McKinney 1981).

[196]N.Y. CRIM. PRO. §§ 330.20(6), 330.20(1)(f).

[197]*Id.* § 330.20(11).

[198]*Id.* § 330.20(10).

[199]*Id.* §§ 330.20(8), 330.20(9), 330.20(1)(g) (first retention order authorizes continued custody for up to one year), 330.20(1)(h) (second retention order authorizes continued custody for up to two years), 330.20(1)(i) (subsequent retention orders authorize continued custody for up to two years).

[200]*Id.* § 330.20(7).

[201]*Id.*

[202]*Id.* §§ 330.20(7), 330.20(8). The court *may* issue an order of conditions if the insanity acquittee was found not to have a dangerous mental disorder and not to be mentally ill. The court *must* issue an order of conditions if the insanity acquittee was found to have a dangerous mental disorder or to be mentally ill.

with his prescribed treatment plan or any other condition that the court determines to be reasonably necessary or appropriate.[203] The order is valid for five years and may be extended for an additional five years for good cause.[204] At any time during the effective period of an order of conditions, the district attorney or commissioner of mental hygiene may apply to the court for a recommitment order if he believes that the defendant has a dangerous mental disorder. If, after a hearing, the court finds that the insanity acquittee has a dangerous mental disorder, the court must issue a recommitment order directing the insanity acquittee to be committed to a secure facility for six months. Subsequent recommitment orders may be obtained.[205] Under the New York statute, an insanity acquittee who was not mentally ill at the conclusion of his criminal trial is subject to security confinement for up to 10 years after that finding. This regressive legislation cannot be countenanced. The author of the supplementary practice commentary opined that the new statute may be struck down as imposing greater periods of confinement, creating more difficult qualitative bases for altering statutes and for stigmatizing the insanity acquittee as a social outcast more publicly and for a longer time than under the previous law.[206]

A Michigan statute exemplifies another questionable development to deal with the consequences of an insanity defense trial. Less than one year after the Michigan Supreme Court eliminated that state's automatic, indeterminate commitment statute,[207] the Michigan legislature created a new verdict of "guilty but mentally ill."[208] Under the statute, a defendant who has pleaded the insanity defense may be found either guilty, not guilty, guilty but mentally ill, or not guilty by reason of insanity. If the defendant is found guilty but mentally ill, the court may impose any sentence that could have been imposed if the defendant had been convicted. In fact, the guilty but mentally ill defendant is convicted. The statute merely provides that the guilty but mentally ill defendant is committed to the custody of the Department of Corrections where he shall undergo further evaluation and be given such treatment as is psychiatrically indicated for his mental condition. Treatment may be provided by either the Department of Corrections or the Department of Mental

---

[203]*Id.* § 330.20(1)(o).

[204]*Id.*

[205]*Id.* §§ 330.20(14), 330.20(1)(f).

[206]Bellacosa, Supplementary Practice Commentaries (to § 330.20), N.Y. Crim. Pro. § 330.20 (McKinney 1980), 15.

[207]People v. McQuillan, 392 Mich. 511, 211 N.W.2d 569 (1974).

[208]Mich. Comp. Laws Ann. § 768.36 (West Supp. Pamphlet 1980) (Mich. Stat. Ann. § 28.1059 (Callaghan Supp. 1981).

Health.[209] These treatment provisions largely duplicate other statutes that provide psychiatric evaluations and mental health services for all convicts.[210]

Although the treatment of insanity acquittees is not directly affected by Michigan's guilty but mentally ill legislation, the existence of the new option may well result in fewer insanity acquittals. Juries may be confused by the overlap between definitions of mental illness and legal insanity and thus return guilty but mentally ill verdicts instead of NGI verdicts.[211] The guilty but mentally ill verdict offers a perfect compromise for a jury permitting it to ignore substantial evidence that the *mens rea* element of the crime has not been proved.[212] As one author noted: "By convicting the defendant, the jury can condemn his behavior and keep a potentially dangerous individual in custody. However, by also finding the defendant mentally ill, the jury may believe that their verdict will ensure special treatment for him and will carry a lesser stigma than a regular 'guilty' verdict."[213]

Although the Michigan Supreme Court upheld the constitutionality of the guilty but mentally ill statute,[214] in my opinion this approach should be rejected as an insidious attempt to erode the defendant's right to an insanity acquittal. Nevertheless, Indiana,[215] Illinois,[216] and Kentucky[217] have recently enacted guilty but mentally ill statutes, and a bill has been introduced in Congress to apply the concept to federal prosecutions.[218]

The ultimate step has been taken by Montana and Idaho. By abolishing the insanity defense and convicting all defendants who might have successfully relied on it, those states have eliminated their concern about

---

[209]MICH. COMP. LAWS ANN. § 768.36(3) (West Supp. Pamphlet 1980). (MICH. STAT. ANN. § 28.1059(3) (Callaghan Supp. 1981).

[210]*See, e.g.,* MICH. COMP. LAWS ANN. §§ 330.2001–2006 (1980) (MICH. STAT. ANN. §§ 14.800(1001–1006) (Callaghan 1980)), MICH. COMP. LAWS ANN. § 791.267 (1968) (MICH. STAT. ANN. § 28.2327 (Callaghan 1978).)

[211]Note, *The Constitutionality of Michigan's Guilty But Mentally Ill Verdict,* 12 U. MICH. J.L. REF. 188, 196 (1978).

[212]Comment, *Guilty But Mentally Ill: An Historical and Constitutional Analysis,* 53 U. DET. J. URB. L. 471, 492–93 (1976).

[213]Note, *supra* note 211, at 196.

[214]People v. McLeod, 407 Mich. 632, 288 N.W.2d 909 (1980).

[215]IND. CODE ANN. §§ 35-5-2-3(4), 35-5-2-6 (Burns 1980).

[216]Ill. Pub. Act 82-554, 1981 Ill. Legis. Serv. (West).

[217]H.32, Ky. Gen. Ass., reg. sess. 1982, was enacted into law on March 26, 1982, effective July 15, 1982.

[218]H.R. 5395, 97th Cong., 2d Sess. (1982).

proper handling of insanity acquittees.[219] Both states do admit into the criminal trial evidence on the defendant's state of mind whenever it is an element of the offense.[220] Whether these new laws will withstand constitutional scrutiny is questionable. Two state legislatures—Washington in 1909 and Mississippi in 1928—attempted to eliminate both the insanity defense and the requirement of *mens rea.* The statutes, struck down almost immediately by the states' supreme courts, were held to unconstitutionally deny due process of law by depriving defendants of a jury trial on defenses that had always been considered by the jury.[221] In 1928, Louisiana enacted a statute providing for a trial before a lunacy commission if the defendant pleaded insanity. If the commission found the defendant sane, he was precluded from raising the insanity defense at a subsequent trial before a jury. One year after its enactment, the Louisiana Supreme Court held the statute unconstitutional as violating both due process and the right to a jury trial.[222]

CONCLUSION

Each development of the law to improve the plight of the insanity acquittee has been accompanied by a counterdevelopment designed to continue his or her "neither-fish–nor-fowl" status. Virtual elimination of automatic, indeterminate commitment following insanity acquittal has been replaced in some jurisdictions by the creation of "release" hearings with the burden of proof placed on the insanity acquittee. The attempt to utilize civil commitment release proceedings for insanity acquittees has been obstructed by the requirement of court review of release decisions. The effort to extend to insanity acquittees the right to treatment and the right to be treated in the least restrictive treatment setting has been stymied by the requirement of segregation and maximum security institutionalization and by devices, such as the guilty but mentally ill verdict, designed to avoid insanity acquittal altogether.

A criminal trial that results in an insanity acquittal absolves the defendant from criminal responsibility. Simply put, an insanity acquittee

---

[219]MONT. REV. CODES §§ 45-2-101(34), 46-14-102, 46-14-201 (1980); S. 1396, 46th Idaho Leg., 2d reg. sess. 1982, repealing existing IDAHO CODE § 18-207 and adding new § 18-207(a): "Mental condition shall not be a defense to any charge of criminal conduct."

[220]MONT. REV. CODES § 46-14-102; S. 1396, 46th Idaho Leg., 2d reg. sess. 1982, repealing existing IDAHO CODE § 18-207 and adding new § 18-207(c).

[221]State v. Strasberg, 60 Wash. 106, 110 P. 1020 (1910); Sinclair v. State, 161 Miss. 142, 132 So. 581 (1931).

[222]State v. Lange, 168 La. 958, 123 So. 639 (1929).

is an acquittee.[223] He has been excused for his act. Conceptually, commitment, release, and treatment distinctions between insanity acquittees and other nonconvict citizens cannot be justified. The author of a recent law review article asserts that discrimination against insanity acquittees in the postacquittal process is motivated by "the deeply felt but seldom acknowledged belief that insanity acquittees deserve something approaching punishment for their actions."[224] He labels this notion "the cleanup doctrine."[225] Mistakes in processing insanity acquittees are "justified by their effect of 'cleaning up' mistakes of criminal trials."[226] Relying on society's "visceral disbelief in the possibility of acts without choice,"[227] the doctrine sacrifices "those who, under traditional views, do not deserve punishment or involuntary hospitalization. The cleanup doctrine rests on the assumption that a defendant must either be responsible enough to merit punishment or insane enough to merit detention."[228]

I realize that utilizing the civil commitment process to handle insanity acquittees jeopardizes recent reforms of that process. For example, would society be willing to limit civil commitment to 60 or 90 days, if to do so would result in the release of an insanity-acquitted mass murderer after that period? Of course not. Such a result would provoke a legislature into maintaining or restoring indeterminate commitment of all dangerous, civilly committed persons. While I offer no perfect solution to the quandary, I believe that civil commitment reforms can be harmonized with insanity acquittal reforms. For example, the "danger to others" commitment criterion could be expanded to include individuals who would commit acts that would be crimes if committed by sane persons. An insanity acquittee whose mental condition has not changed since his or her last criminal act would then be civilly committable at the completion of the criminal trial. If civil commitment is limited to those who can be identified as currently dangerous, then perhaps commitment should not conclusively terminate after only 60 or 90 days. Periodic recommitment determinations appropriately balance the individual's liberty interest and society's security interest.

---

[223]Benham v. Edwards, 501 F. Supp. 1050, 1064 (N.D. Ga. 1980).
[224]Note, *supra* note 7, at 623.
[225]*Id.* at 618.
[226]*Id.*
[227]*Id.* at 607.
[228]*Id.* at 619–20. Additionally, the doctrine uses the trial and commitment processes interchangeably, demonstrating "a nonchalance about whether the defendant is incarcerated through a civil or criminal process." *Id.* at 623.

In the final analysis, society must decide whether any individuals should be absolved from criminal responsibility because they are unable to conform to the demands of the criminal law. I believe such individuals exist. If the insanity defense is to continue to serve as an appropriate device for dealing with them, discrimination against and stigmatization of insanity acquittees cannot be tolerated.

4

Defendants Not Guilty by Reason of Insanity

HENRY J. STEADMAN AND JERALDINE BRAFF

In 1974, discussing the state of empirical data available in the United States on the criminally insane we said:

> In the research literature on the mechanisms that process the criminally insane ... there are some consistencies such as recidivism rate comparisons. ... However, such consistencies and even studies that allow such comparisons do not dominate the area. Rather, non-cumulative studies, which barely begin to meet the needs in these problem areas, are the norm. Unfortunately, even less adequate data is available on the personal characteristics of those people who pass through these processing points. (Steadman & Cocozza, 1974, p. 38)

In a similar vein Cooke and Sikorski in the same year reported, "the only statistical study of NGRIs concerns an estimate of the size of the NGRI population. ... Unfortunately, however, there have been no empirical studies delineating the characteristics of persons acquitted by reason of insanity nor of the factors affecting their lengths of hospitalization" (p. 251). While this is a slight exaggeration and overlooks the seminal work of Morrow and Petersen (1966), it does point to the same state of affairs we had mentioned, that is, the extreme paucity of material available in the mid-1970s about persons acquitted by reason of insanity.

HENRY J. STEADMAN AND JERALDINE BRAFF ● Special Projects Research Unit, New York State Department of Mental Hygiene, 44 Holland Avenue, Albany, New York 12229.

The intent of this chapter is: (1) to assess the scope of the problem using our recently completed national survey of admissions to and residents of facilities for NGRIs in 1978; (2) to review what the state of knowledge was in 1974 and how it may have improved since 1974; (3) to present data we are just now analyzing dealing with factors associated with the successful use of the plea and a comparison of successful and unsuccessful defendants; and (4) to identify what appears to be the substantial gaps in available information that still exist as they relate to the critical legal and administrative issues continuing to swirl around one state legislature after another.

SCOPE OF THE PROBLEM

From our national survey data (Steadman, Monahan, Hartstone, Davis, & Robbins, 1982), it was readily apparent that the number of insanity acquittals in the United States each year is much smaller than the volume of legal scholarship on the topic might indicate. Of the 19,971 admissions to facilities for mentally disordered offenders in 1978, only 1,625 (8.1%) were NGRI. The only group with fewer admissions was the MDSO category. NGRIs made up a much higher percentage of residents in these facilities due to their longer stays as compared to other groups. Of the 14,069 residents on an average day in 1978, 3,140 (22.3%) were NGRI. Thus, from the standpoint of institutional administration and program, NGRIs are a very significant problem, while comprising only a relatively small portion of dispositions in any given year. This is not to say that the policy and jurisprudence issues these 8% raise are not disproportional to their volume. Rather, it is simply to point out that the amount of resources that NGRIs consume is much less than is often thought (cf. Pasewark & Lanthorn, 1977).

The one source of data with which our recent data can be compared is that reported by Scheidemandel and Kanno (1969). Their national survey found that 4% of the patients admitted to facilities they identified for mentally disordered offenders were NGRIs. It is unclear whether our 8% finding results from actual system change or differences in methodology. One suggestion that it may indicate an increase is the New York data (Steadman, 1980) showing increases in that state from an average of 8 NGRIs per year 1965–1971 to 47 per year 1971–1976 to 55 per year from 1976–1978. More data are needed before firm conclusions can be drawn. At this time what is clear is that the volume of insanity acquittals is not near the level of notoriety of certain cases, such as Charles Manson and Mark David Chapman, where the plea is raised.

RESEARCH BEFORE 1974

By far the major research piece at the time of our earlier review was that of Morrow and Petersen (1966). Their basic question came from the observation that officially NGRI acquittees were considered both psychiatric patients and criminals. Their question was whether "they resemble one category more than the other in recidivism rates and prognostic background variables" (p. 31). To answer this question they looked at samples of 44 NGRI patients and 43 persons detained as criminal sexual psychopaths in Missouri and compared them with data available for psychiatric patients and prison inmates. What they reported about the sociodemographic, diagnostic, and criminal history information on the NGRIs was the only descriptive information available through 1974.

They found a group older than would be expected to be found in the criminal court system, and slightly younger than were then in many state mental hospitals. Their average age was 33. They were predominantly white (66%). Only 23% were currently married. Their mean level of educational attainment was ninth grade and 88% were unskilled or semiskilled workers. About two-thirds had no prior mental hospitalization (66%) and 34% had no prior criminal history. The majority of current offenses were economic (54%), with assaults (18%) and homicides (11%) second and third in frequency. As we shall see below, these descriptors are amazingly similar to those on populations of NGRIs in other states for other time periods.

Although in many ways it is the study's descriptive information that makes it so valuable, the researchers also carried out a very thorough follow-up to answer their primary research questions. What they found, which was to be confirmed by other researchers on both insanity acquittees and incompetent defendants, was that over three years, 37% of the NGRI's were rearrested. They concluded that this was "not significantly greater than the corresponding rate of 35% for a large Federal prisons sample" (p. 33). Based on the similarity of these rearrest rates and the lack of relationship between recidivism and either diagnosis at time of acquittal or number of previous mental hospitalizations, Morrow and Petersen concluded that NGRIs are more like criminal offenders than psychiatric patients.

The other report available in 1974 offering some data about insanity acquittees was Rubin's (1972). The major thrust of his analysis was a demonstration of the inordinate detention of 17 men in Menard State Hospital, a maximum security facility for the criminally insane in Illinois. Of these 17, 8 were insanity acquittees, 8 were found incompetent to stand trial, and 1 was found incompetent to be executed. Case specific descriptive data on the NGRIs are reported in one table, but these are never aggregated. Their major utility is to show how the absence of procedural safeguards before the early 1970s resulted in inordinately long detention for both NGRIs and incompetent defendants. In this instance, the 17 men spent an average of 25 years in a correctional facility after legislative remedy permitted their placement in mental health or community settings. Rubin's observations were supported by data reported by Lewin (1968) who found that in comparing NGRIs who had private counsel with acquittees who did not the latter's detentions were decreased by an average of 5 years and 9 months.

Aside from the steady flow of legal analyses of various aspects of the plea, only three other reports offered empirical glimpses of persons acquitted by reason of insanity. Arens (1969) described the courtroom processes before the bench, in chambers, and in the corridors and psychiatric wards. Matthews (1967, 1970) dealt with the relative infrequency of the plea; relative in terms of incompetent defendants (14 of 756 admissions in Ionia State Hospital in 1964) and in terms of all criminal cases handled within a jurisdiction (2 of 515 homicide cases disposed of in Detroit from 1959 to 1963, and 5.1% of all felony cases in Washington, D.C., in 1962).

A study closely allied with Arens's was Simon's (1967). In this instance an experiment was conducted with a sample of 1,176 persons drawn from a pool of prospective jurors. They were asked to participate in a study in which two experimental conditions varied the rule of law for the trial and the instructions to the juries. While these data were not drawn from actual case deliberations, actual recordings of real trials involving the insanity defense were used. She found that the particular rule of law employed made little difference in the outcome of the case. Judicial instructions were important, but basically whatever the jury was going to do, it would do regardless of the particular rule in effect in a given jurisdiction.

This, then, was the extremely limited picture of the persons acquitted by reason of insanity and the process by which this occurred in 1974. The one comprehensive study by Morrow and Petersen suggested that these defendants were more like criminals than mental patients. Rubin found them to be as susceptible to overly long detention as incompetent defendants. Matthews showed that the plea was infrequently raised and was rarely a disposition. Arens depicted some of the dynamics of the hearings in which the plea was raised in Washington, D.C. It remained for the studies after 1974 to confirm the picture of persons acquitted by reason of insanity and of the consequences of this determination for both defendants and society.

RESEARCH SINCE 1974

The seven major studies completed since 1974 deal with four primary issues: (1) the *characteristics of persons acquitted* by reason of insanity; (2) their *lengths of hospitalizations* and factors related to length of stay; (3) the *frequency, actual and perceived, with which the plea is used;* and (4) *recidivism* of the acquittees.

CHARACTERISTICS OF PERSONS FOUND NGRI

Cooke and Sikorski studied a group of 167 insanity acquittees. It included all persons housed in the Michigan Forensic Center in 1967 plus those admitted through 1972. These 167 acquittees averaged 37 years of age, were predominantly white (68%), male (87%), with less than high school education (56%), and were either unemployed (38%), unskilled, or semiskilled (53%). Only 29% were currently married. Of the 167, 43% had previous mental hospitalizations. The most frequent charge of which they had been acquitted was murder (57%), followed by some type of assault (20%), and rape or attempted rape (5%). As we will see below the picture that emerges from this group is remarkably similar to acquittees we later studied in New York. Morrow and Petersen's sample was quite similar in age (33), race (66% white), marital status (23% married), and occupational skills (88% were unskilled or semiskilled). The major dissimilarity was in the current offense. Most of Morrow and Petersen's group were acquitted of economic offenses (54%) compared to the much more serious charges in Cooke and Sikorski's study group.

The major research question of Cooke and Sikorski was to what extent the demographic, criminal and hospitalization history, and clinical factors were related to length of stay. As would have been expected, a nonpsychotic diagnosis, no previous mental hospitalizations, no prior criminal record, less serious current offense, and psychometric test data indicating a denial of pathology were associated with shorter hospitalizations. Not so expectedly, married, educated, and skilled workers were more apt to be released. The research left open the question as to whether these latter results suggested a middle-class bias in releasing acquittees or whether, in fact, these factors in this population were actually associated with a lessened probability of dangerousness, the major criterion for release. This latter explanation has been suggested by Monahan (1981).

The next study focusing on characteristics of persons involved with the defense relates not to acquittees, but to persons entering the plea. This study by Pasewark and Lanthorn (1977) relates minimally to acquittees, because of 22,101 felony indictments in Wyoming between 1970 and 1972, only 102 (.46%) had the insanity plea entered and only one person was successful. Thus their information is very important for understanding the legal processes, but tells us nothing about the persons who are actually acquitted. They found that the plea is entered in more serious offenses, that most of the persons so pleading had no prior mental hospitalizations (67% of the women and 52% of the males), and that most had some police record (62% with at least one prior arrest). However, since only one person was acquitted by reason of insanity, little in the way of policy implications about the administration of the plea evolve.

A number of reports on the issues of the characteristics of the acquittees and their lengths of stay have emanated from our continuing analyses of New York State acquittees from 1965 through 1978 (Pasewark, Pantle, & Steadman, 1979a,b; Steadman, 1980). Our first effort compiled information on all persons acquitted by reason of insanity from 1965 through 1976. The second effort extended the first study two more years, 1976 through 1978. The first compiled recidivism data while the second tracked the acquittees only until their hospital discharges.

Although the volume of successful pleas ($N = 278$) increased dramatically over the 13 years studied (8 per year 1965–1971, 47 per year 1971–1976, and 55 per year 1976–1978), the characteristics of the acquittees varied very little and remained amazingly like Morrow and Petersen's and Cooke and Sikorski's earlier findings in other states.

The average age of the 278 acquittees was in the mid-thirties (36 during the 1965–1976 era and 33 from 1976–1978). Men made up the vast majority of cases (86% and 87%, respectively), almost exactly the same proportion as in the two prior studies. In our New York data, the acquittees were predominantly white (65% and 60%, respectively, for the two time periods) and thus were greatly overrepresented when compared to the state prison population (60% vs. 31%). As with the earlier findings, the majority of acquittees in the two time periods had no prior state mental hospitalizations (56% and 58%). Following this same pattern, the most frequent charge of which they were acquitted was murder (53% and 44%), not very disparate from Cooke and Sikorski's 57%. In all studies reporting crime information, assault was the second most frequent acquittal charge (15% and 8%). In sum, our two New York studies developed a picture of acquittees as white males with fairly serious charges and without previous mental hospitalizations. This is very similar to the data from other states. It should be noted, however, that despite women making up just over 10% of most acquittee groups studied, in New York they are greatly overrepresented when compared to prison populations. In New York, they made up 13% of the acquittees for all 13 years, while comprising only 4% of the inmates in the state prisons. The reasons for the overrepresentation of women is entirely unclear from the available data.

More recent data on the characteristics of NGRIs is Petrila's (1981) study on 1978 acquittees in Missouri. The two major differences among these 67 cases and the previous New York and Ontario data (*see* Greenland, 1979 reported below) occurred in criminal charges and the proportion of acquittees with prior mental hospitalizations. Again, the groups were predominantly male (94%) and not previously arrested (61%), and the targets of violence tended to be family or friends. However, of their offenses, only 10% were for murder or manslaughter. The largest number were for assault (27%), followed by burglary (18%) and robbery (16%). Auto theft accounted for 6% as did weapons possession. Overall, the level of seriousness was very much lower. Fully 79% of the Missouri acquittees had prior psychiatric hospitalizations. This is in sharp contrast to the 44% in New York. Given the recency of the cohort little could be said about their courses of hospitalization.

The most recent study is that of Rogers and Bloom (1981). Their work focused on 440 defendants NGRI in Oregon who were supervised by a five-person Psychiatric Security Review board created on January 1, 1978. Again, males made up most (91%) of the acquittees active in the system as of January 1, 1978, or admitted through 1980. The mean age of all acquittees was 31. The criminal charges of which they were acquitted were much more similar to Petrila's Missouri data than to our New York data. Only 5% (24) were acquitted of murder with another 5% (22) acquitted of attempted murder and 2% (10) of manslaughter. Assault was the single largest category (14%, 62 cases) followed by burglary (11%) and unauthorized use of vehicle (11%). Overall, the demographics of the Oregon acquittees are comparable to other studies, but the criminal charges suggest the seriousness of New York and New Jersey acquittees' criminal charges may be more serious than those of acquittees in other jurisdictions.

Lengths of Hospitalizations

The second major focus of our New York studies has been the length of hospitalizations after acquittal and the factors related to release. Fully 40% of the 278 persons found NGRI between 1965 and 1976 were still hospitalized in 1978. Their average length of stay was three and a half years (1,701 days). For the 47% who were released without supervision, the average length of stay was 406 days. The remainder had escaped (4%), were living in the community under supervision (4%), or had died

(4%). From the 1976–1978 group, fully 89% were still hospitalized at the end of the follow-up period, averaging 402 days of detention. Only 6% had been released after an average of 189 days. Five persons had escaped and one had died. By the time 47% of the 1976–1978 group is released their average length of stay will considerably exceed the 406 days of the prior study group.

In these length of stay data, there was a clear trend for more severe crimes to be associated with longer stays. For example, the mean length of stay for the two persons acquitted of rape who were released from the 1965–1976 group was 1,102 days, the 55 acquitted of murders who were released averaged 500 days, and the 25 acquitted of assault and released averaged 398 days. In contrast, the 6 acquitted burglary cases who were released averaged 288 days, the 2 for resisting arrest 218 days, and the 1 for criminal mischief 71 days. The follow-up on the 1976–1978 group was not sufficiently long to provide trend data in these regards.

It should be noted that the data gathered in these studies cannot address the question of the appropriateness of longer hospitalizations for more serious charges. Whether such defendants are "sicker" and thus require longer terms of treatment or whether these detention patterns represent a retributive model is entirely unclear from the research data.

Most of these findings from the New York data were similar to data reported by Singer (1978) from New Jersey. The background character-istics of her study group were very similar in all respects and the rela-tionship between the severity of the offense of which the person was acquitted and length of stay also was similar. The major difference in findings was the type of offense for which they were acquitted. Her study group had much less serious offenses overall. Only 26% were acquitted for murder, but 35% were acquitted of assault. Beyond these two offenses the distributions were quite comparable to ours and the other studies discussed above.

Also similar in many respects to the New York data are those reported from Ontario (Greenland, 1979). On only two dimensions were the 88 Lieutenant Governor Warrant (LGW) commitments in Ontario from 1961 to 1970 substantially different from the New York findings. Among the 70 men and 18 women studied, they were younger (28 and 34, respectively, as compared to 36 and 34 among the 1965–1978 New York sample) and had much longer hospitalization periods after acquittal (1,574 and 1,376, respectively, as compared to 406 days). In terms of the sex distributions, offenses of which they were acquitted, victims of these offenses, and diagnostic groupings, the total lengths of stay were very different between the two groups though the relationship of longer stays to more serious offenses seemed somewhat consistent.

These studies, then, provide the full complement of data currently available in the research literature about persons acquitted by reason of insanity. As should be apparent, there are many consistencies from one state to another. What thus far cannot be very well addressed from any of these data are how the characteristics of the persons acquitted may be like or unlike those of all persons entering the plea. The Pasewark and Lanthorn study examined this question, but only one of the 102 cases in which the plea was entered was successful. Whether, as we have argued elsewhere (Pasewark, Pantle, & Steadman, 1979a), these data suggest strong middle-class biases in the operations of the courts in regard to the insanity plea really awaits more comprehensive data from a variety of jurisdictions comparing persons entering the plea successfully and unsuccessfully.

PERCEPTIONS OF THE USE OF THE PLEA

Another content area relevant to insanity acquittals that is especially important when dealing with public policy is the perceptions by various groups of the frequency with which the plea is entered and is entered successfully. The two major studies done in this regard were by Pasewark and Seidenzahl (1980) and Pasewark and Pantle (1979). In the first, a group of college students were asked to estimate how many of the 22,102 felony indictments in Wyoming between 1971 and 1973 had pleas of NGRI entered and how many of the pleas were successful. The average estimate from this group was that 8,150 of the cases had an insanity plea entered (37%) and that it was successful in 3,599 of these cases—a 44% success rate and the ultimate disposition in 16% of all felony indictments. As the reader may recall, the actual data from Wyoming was that only 102 of the 22,102 cases actually entered the plea (.46%) with only 1 case being successful. At first glance the tendency may be to reject such inordinate overestimations by college students as the result of ignorance of the "real world." Such an outright rejection is tempered by the findings of their second study.

In their next study, Pasewark and Pantle (1979) surveyed state legislators in Wyoming asking their estimates for the same 22,102 cases. While somewhat more conservative than the college students, they were still unrealistically high. The legislators estimated that 4,458 of the cases had the insanity defense entered (20%) with 1,794 being successful—a 40% success rate and an 8% overall disposition rate for felony indictments. Thus, it is clear that even state legislators badly overestimated the volume of cases involving the insanity defense and the number of cases in which it is successful.

These data from Wyoming are the only data documenting the discrepancy between the actual and perceived use of the insanity defense. Data we previously reported from New York (Burton & Steadman, 1978) offer only estimates by attorneys, district attorneys, and judges of the proportion of cases employing the defense and its success rate. The average estimate was 5% of all criminal court cases. The mean success rate was estimated to be 22%. Unfortunately no data exist against which to compare these estimates. Given the similarity of the estimates of the number of cases in which the plea is entered to the data reviewed by Matthews (1970), the 5% figure seems to be reasonable. The success rate cannot be measured against anything within state and to take actual success rates from other jurisdictions would not seem appropriate. But one example can suffice. Fukunaga (1977) reports that in Hawaii during the years 1969–1976, 458 defendants plead NGRI. Of these, 86 were acquitted (19%) and 31 were *nolle prosequi* (7%) and thus released. The huge differences in these actual numbers and Wyoming's indicate the inappropriateness of direct comparisons of jurisdictions without additional data.

What is strongly suggested by Pasewark's two studies, but which remains to be confirmed in other more populous states, is that the public and legislators may radically overestimate the volume of use of this defense and thereby be misled in making policy decisions relating to the legal statuses and administrative arrangements for persons acquitted by reason of insanity.

RECIDIVISM AND REHOSPITALIZATION

The final area that has been a major focus of the recent research studies on NGRIs has been their criminal recidivism. As we indicated above, of the pre-1974 studies only Morrow and Petersen's offered any data on this topic. They found that over their follow-up period 37% of their sample was rearrested. Of the more recent studies only Pasewark *et al.* (1979a) includes comparable data. Of the 278 persons acquitted between 1965 and 1976 in New York, 107 were discharged. Of these, 21 (20%) were subsequently arrested. All 21 were from the 88 discharged men. None of the 19 women discharged were rearrested through 1976. The 21 men rearrested totaled 66 arrests. Property crimes comprised the largest proportion of the 66 arrests, 24 (36%), followed by crimes against persons, 13 (20%), drug charges, 9 (14%), other felonies, 5 (8%), and misdemeanors, 15 (23%). The crimes with which these discharged acquittees were charged were for the most part less serious than the offenses of which they were acquitted. Whether their recidivism rate is considered high or low would depend on one's standard. From Morrow and Petersen's perspective of comparing these rates with those of felons released from the prison system, it would be low, that is, less than 35%. When compared to the arrest rates of patients recently released from New York State mental hospitals, it would be somewhat higher. Elsewhere (Steadman, Cocozza, & Melick, 1978) we reported that 9.4% of the recently released patients were arrested during their first year and a half in the community. Although the follow-up periods in the NGRI samples were longer, the additional time at risk would not seem to offset the difference in rates. This would suggest that in terms of arrest, contrary to Morrow and Petersen's conclusions, insanity acquittees look like neither mental patients nor offenders.

But two studies have reported on the subsequent mental hospitalizations of insanity acquittees. Morrow and Petersen (1966) determined that 37% of their sample was rehospitalized. Pasewark and associates (1979a) found that among New York's NGRIs released from 1965–1976, 22% were subsequently hospitalized. These figures tend to be lower than those for incompetent defendants who also tend to have more prior hospitalizations.

The studies reviewed here represent the sum total of knowledge developed since 1974 about persons acquitted by reason of insanity and public perceptions of the plea. At best, the information is limited. At worst, it could be terribly misleading, given the few jurisdictions for which even the most basic information is available. There is, however, some reason for optimism in making more informed public policy decisions that now may need to be made. This optimism stems from an expanding picture of both the characteristics and offense patterns of persons acquitted. The areas in which it is much less easy to be confident about progress are those that involve questions about the success rate of the plea and the actual results of raising the plea both for those who are successful and for those who are not. As we will see below, some efforts are underway to address some of these gaps, but the agenda that remains indicates the limited extent to which past and ongoing efforts have provided a data base adequate to inform the core issues of public policy and jurisprudence that swirl around the insanity defense.

ONGOING RESEARCH

We have two major efforts underway to supplement the current data base. The first represents continuing work on the data gathered by Pasewark. The thrust of this work is a comparison of the institutionalization experiences of insanity acquittees with a similar group of felons. The series of research questions revolve around the popular but unfounded conception by legislators and the public that insanity acquittees are dangerous and that acquittal by reason of insanity is an "easy way out" for defendants who "should" be detained for much longer periods. Currently, there are no empirical data with which these perceptions can be measured since there is no baseline against which to contrast the known hospitalization times of the acquittees. Our earlier data did show how long patients were hospitalized and that lengths of stay varied by the seriousness of the acquittal crime. What has been missing is a standard against which these stays could be compared. In our current work we are seeking to add such baseline.

This work is comparing two distinct groups in each of two time periods. The first includes all insanity acquittals 1965–1971 and a comparison group of felons convicted of the same offenses. Since the administrative arrangements for the care and detention of the acquittees changed in 1971, a second time period was selected, 1971–1973. In this second time period, also, all insanity acquittees plus a second group of felons convicted of the same offenses are being followed.

Our findings (Pasewark, Pantle, & Steadman, 1982) suggest somewhat different results across the two time periods. Among the 46 1965–1971 acquittees, 40 have been released, while 44 of the 46 felons have been released. For both males and females, the NGRI and felon groups had almost exactly the same lengths of detention. For the males it was 1,021 versus 955 days and for the females 638 days for the NGRIs compared to the felons' 789 days. Neither difference was statistically significant. The initial findings for the second time period, 1971–1973, when the full responsibility for care and detention of insanity acquittees fell to the State Department of Mental Hygiene rather than to the Department of Correctional Services, suggest a dramatic decrease in the detention time of both the NGRI and felon groups, but considerably more for the NGRI group. The 42 NGRI men accumulated an average of 533 hospital days as opposed to the 42 felons' 837 prison days. Likewise, the 8 women in the NGRI group averaged 435 hospital days as compared to the 565 prison days of the 8 comparison felons. Thus, the NGRI group admitted after 1971 had detention times substantially less than their earlier cohort (48% less) and less than their comparison group of felons (36% less). These findings, while limited in their generalizability, could be interpreted as lending support to the belief by the public that acquittal by reason of insanity is an easier way out than conviction. Such an interpretation would be based on the premise that the crime of which the defendant was acquitted had an associated sentence that should be comparable to the length of hospitalization after acquittal. Both because hospitalization is supposed to be dependent on therapeutic as well as protective rationales, and because few defendants do time for their arrest charges due to plea bargains, the premise of such reasoning by the public would be faulty. The data on detention periods probably will fuel such reasoning nonetheless.

The second project on these topics currently underway focuses on all insanity pleas in Erie County, New York between 1970 and 1980. There were 205 such cases of which 65% were convicted, 25% were NGRI, 8% were dismissed, 1% were acquitted, and 1% were either pending, withdrawn, or the defendant was deceased prior to disposition. Thus far our analysis has concentrated on the convicted and acquittee groups.

The average age of both the convicted (i.e., unsuccessful NGRI pleas) and NGRI groups was 29, somewhat younger than the statewide acquittees from 1965–1978, and the acquittees reported on by Morrow and Petersen (1966) and Cooke and Sikorski (1974), but similar to Petrila's (1981) Missouri data. Both acquittees and those convicted were predominantly male (88% and 92%, respectively), white (69% and 62% respectively), currently unmarried (88% and 77%, respectively), and either unemployed or unskilled (72% and 73%, respectively). The majority of the acquittees and the convicted in our study group had no prior state psychiatric hospitalization (67% and 74%). Although proportionally few of those in our study group had any prior state mental hospital admissions, the NGRIs averaged a slightly higher but statistically significant number of prior admissions (3.3 and 2.0) although for shorter periods. The acquittees averaged fewer days in residence than the convicted (756 and 1,245) although the difference was not statistically significant. Prior local hospitalization data for the two groups are similar, with only 22% of the NGRIs and 15% of the convicted having had prior local admissions.

The prior arrest history for the two groups reversed the trend for prior hospitalizations. While the majority of both groups had prior arrest histories (57% NGRIs, 70% convicted) and the acquittees averaged fewer arrests (3.5 and 4.7), the findings were not statistically significant.

As regards current offense, analysis focused on seriousness, victim involvement, and weapon use. Both groups were charged most frequently with violent or potentially violent crimes (80% acquittees; 69% convicted), but, proportionally more acquittees than convicted were so charged. The most frequent offense charged in both groups was murder/ manslaughter (35% acquitted, 41% convicted).

Victims were involved in a majority of the offenses (80% acquitted; 71% convicted). Analysis of victim involvement failed to differentiate between our two groups on all but one item. While not statistically significant, in the NGRI group they were mostly female (56%), and in the convicted group, mostly male (63%). Otherwise, they were predominantly white (67% and 70%), and almost identical in age (33 and 34). Lastly, acquittees tended more often than the convicted to use a knife or a gun in perpetrating the offense (61% and 44%).

Comparisons of the experiences following court disposition revealed few differences between the NGRIs and convicted defendants. Only small proportions of either group had state mental hospitalizations subsequent to their disposition related detention (acquitted, 10%; convicted, 20%). Each group averaged almost the same number of subsequent admissions (2.2 and 1.9). Both groups had similar subsequent arrest rates (35%, acquittees; 39%, convicted) which closely paralleled the rate for acquittees reported by Morrow and Petersen (37%), but which was substantially greater than the rate reported for the 1965–1976 New York State acquittees.

The only other meaningful findings revealed in our preliminary analysis focus on symptomatology and consensus between the court and mental health evaluation in the determination of insanity. Symptomatically, statistically significant differences were present in 4 of the 14 psychiatric impairments reported. Acquittees were considered by forensic staff to be more psychotic (28% and 5%), depressed (53% and 36%), and agitated (24% and 12%) than the convicted. Only alcohol and drug indulgence was more prevalent among the convicted, 12% as compared with none for the acquitted group. Finally, there was agreement between the court and the mental health evaluators in an overwhelming majority of cases. Ninety-four percent of those determined NGRI by the court were also found insane by the mental health clinic, while 92% of the convicted were found to be sane. Except on a few variables, the profile developed thus far for defendants in Erie County who pled NGRI between 1970 and 1980 was very similar regardless of whether they were acquitted or convicted. Overall, it is quite difficult to determine from these data on what basis the court's decisions were made other than simply the recommendations of the mental health clinic.

RESEARCH AGENDA

In developing and proposing any research agenda, the initial question must be, "toward what ends?" That is, it may be nice scientifically to say that more data are needed; that we simply should know more. This, however, is insufficient justification by most cost-benefit standards to justify the implementation of any study. What difference will it make if the agenda is implemented? Here the agenda is presented both to fill gaps in the knowledge base that are evident when the research studies reviewed above are evaluated and, particularly, to lead to informed policymaking about the insanity defense. We have argued elsewhere (Steadman, 1980) that legal precedent is an inadequate base in itself on which to build appropriate public policies about the insanity defense. It is essential to understand what happens to the people who are acquitted in the mental health and correctional systems into which they are placed. So, the research topics listed below are offered with an eye to improving what is known about the operation of the insanity defense so that empirically based policy decisions, reflecting necessary legal precedent, may be more informed than often has been the case in the past.

Trends in the Use of the Insanity Plea

With the exception of New York and Wyoming data, there are no data reported on trends in insanity acquittals in the United States. In New York, the data that we have reported deal only with successful pleas. No information is available about trends in the use of the plea. In New York there has been a dramatic increase from the late sixties when 8 cases per year were NGRI through the early 1970s with 47 per year to the mid 1970s when the volume had increased to 55 per year. From the planning perspective it becomes crucial to be aware of and to foresee such developments. Further, through trends such as those observed in New York, fundamental and important changes in the judicial realm may become evident. In other words, basic changes in the functioning of the judicial process may only become apparent through cumulative data that provide unobtrusive insights leading to inferences about altered practices that may serve as hypotheses for direct studies. Thus, it would appear beneficial both directly, in the more effective planning and administration of services for acquittees, and indirectly, in the understanding of the operation of the criminal court systems, to gather information systematically about trends in the volume and types of cases in which the insanity plea is entered and in which it is both successful and unsuccessful.

Rates and Trends in Success of the Plea

A set of questions related to the volume of pleas and acquittees is the success rate of the plea and its trends. Only in Wyoming and Hawaii, for periods during the 1970s, is there information reported about the proportion of cases in which the insanity defense was entered that resulted in an NGRI determination. An understanding of the characteristics of those cases that are successful as compared to unsuccessful pleas may indicate substantial biases in the court system. For example, while our New York data looked only at successful pleas, it suggested a significant overrepresentation of white women and certain occupational categories such as police officers. Comparative data on those pleas that were unsuccessful would have enabled us to substantiate or refute a "mother love" and police protection bias as Pasewark *et al.* (1978) have suggested.

Given the limitations of the data, it is premature to postulate possible infringement of equal protection standards in regard to the insanity defense. Yet, the little data that is thus far available lends some credence to such an assertion. Accordingly, it is very important to develop substantial amounts of data dealing with groups of persons over longer periods of time in numerous jurisdictions who have raised the plea. This group then needs to be studied to assess what factors distinguish the successful from the unsuccessful cases. Further, the unsuccessful cases need to be followed to determine what impacts raising the plea in the first place may have within the correctional system. This latter point is important given the suggestions from Cooke and Pogany (1975) from a mixed group of persons evaluated for both competency to stand trial and for insanity acquittals that the evaluation may have influenced whether bail is granted and the severity of sentences for those found fit to stand trial. Thus, considerable work in longitudinal studies of persons entering the insanity plea is badly needed. Currently, we are aware of only our Erie County study discussed above and one in progress by Pasewark and colleagues using Connecticut data. These efforts should be fruitful, but much more is required.

Public Perceptions of the Use and Success of the Plea

W. I. Thomas observed that, "if men define situations as real, they are real in their consequences" (Coser & Rosenberg, 1964, p. 232). The application of this observation to this context means that if the public thinks that murderers are being acquitted by reason of insanity and are routinely released from state mental hospitals within two or three months, they will pressure their legislators to stop what they perceive as a miscarriage of justice. All too often, in the interest of reelection or because legislators are no better informed than their constituents, legislation is pressed forward to rectify the situation. The fact that this is not the situation at all makes little difference, often until either much time is wasted in draft legislation and committee hearings or worse, inappropriate legislation is established. Pasewark's Wyoming data demonstrated that legislators were more conservative than were college students in their estimates of the frequency of the plea and its success. However, their more conservative errors reduced the overestimation only from 80 to 44 times more than the actual use of the plea and from 3,599 to 1,794 times the actual successful use of the plea.

What is suggested under this item in our research agenda is that it may make for much more understandable and adequate public policy formation in regard to the insanity defense to know more accurately what the public and special interest groups believe is occurring with the use of this plea. It may well be that much of the concern for its application results from misinformation rather than disagreements with actual, current practices. At this time, however, such assertions are purely speculative outside of Wyoming. Clearly, the administration of the insanity defense could greatly profit from increased research attention to the public perceptions about how the defense is used and the implications of its successful application.

WOMEN AND THE INSANITY DEFENSE

The New York data that we reported (Pasewark et al., 1979a) suggested that the women acquitted by reason of insanity had committed quite different crimes than the men and had shorter lengths of hospitalization. Cooke and Sikorski (1974) found similar results in their length of stay study in Michigan. Our data suggested that murder was by far the most prevalent offense among women acquittees. Further, the murders tended to be infanticide or spousal. However, the numbers from 1965 to 1976 in our studies were very small. It is really tentative speculation as to whether certain cultural transgressions are made easier for women than men. Until additional research is conducted this speculation will remain exactly that—speculation.

Another, closely related set of questions for which no data have been reported is the availability of services and facilities for women acquitted by reason of insanity. As we noted from the national survey data (Steadman et al., 1981), there are very few women found NGRI (5.3% of all 1978 admissions in the United States). They are underrepresented relative to their presence in the prison population, which would seem to indicate that there is not a question of unequal protection. In fact, the contrary might be argued. It may seem either easier or more humane to the court to hospitalize a woman than to incarcerate her. As such, an NGRI determination becomes convenient. Were this the case, rather than a potential infringement of rights under unequal protection issues, the overuse of insanity acquittals might represent the inappropriate medicalization or psychiatrization (Monahan, 1973) of criminal behavior. Again, however, these musings remain in the realm of speculation. More data are needed before inferences may be made with any sort of assurance.

THE USE OF CIVIL COMMITMENT AFTER ACQUITTAL

An area that is clear neither in statute nor in practice is how, to what extent, and with what effects various jurisdictions use civil commitment standards and practices to detain insanity acquittees. For example, in New York an acquittee is committed under a criminal order and cannot receive ground passes or transfer from one Office of Mental Health facility to another, let alone release, without approval of the convicting court or the court in the county where the acquittee is hospitalized. At the same time, in Arizona after an NGRI determination an acquittee is committed under the civil involuntary commitment statute.

The first question such practices raise is a descriptive one of how many jurisdictions do it which way or in some combination. A second set of questions is more important, however. What difference does it make? Do acquittees receive differing types and quality of treatment under one mode of commitment or another? In what ways are their lengths of detention affected? Do differences in language really transfer to differences in practices or is it simply the "old wine in new bottles"? All of the questions switch the focus of inquiry from one of precedent and statute to one of impact and administrative practice. Such a shift in approach would be most useful in making progress toward a more rational system for accomodating defendants acquitted by reason of insanity.

ACQUITTEES'S RESEMBLANCE TO CRIMINAL OR MENTAL PATIENTS

The seminal study by Morrow and Petersen was premised on the question of whether insanity acquittees more resembled inmates or mental patients. This question stemmed from their interest in determining what type of treatment/detention setting might be more appropriate. From the data thus far available, there is the suggestion that they may resemble neither. In most studies, over half of the acquittees have never been hospitalized and most have no prior police records. Some special classes of acquittees were identified, such as women and police officers. It may well be that in developing appropriate programs for NGRIs, standard models for prisoners or mental patients both are inappropriate. They may be a class unto themselves. Like much else about the insanity acquittee, these possible program implications are quite speculative.

There is simply insufficient descriptive information about acquittees' demographic, criminal, and mental hospital history, and current clinical characteristics from which rational program development can proceed. Since in all states acquittees currently are housed in facilities operated either by departments of corrections or mental health, the question posed by Morrow and Petersen remains as important today as it was 20 years ago when they raised it. It remains to develop the empirical data it demands.

These, then, are what seem to be the major questions that emerge from the current state of knowledge about the use of the insanity defense and the people who are acquitted under it. One area that may seem conspicuous by its absence is any reference to recidivism studies. No mention of this area is included in our agenda because the value of such follow-up is unclear. What are the implications of knowing what the recidivism rates are absolutely and relatively to either offenders or ex-mental patients? It is the type of information that the public may want to see. State legislative committees, law reform commissions, and the like may prefer to have such information at their disposal, but to what good? Reduced recidivism is not an appropriate clinical treatment goal. Clinicians are supposed to be treating various types of symptomatology. Any relationship of these symptoms to criminal behavior after release may be quite incidental, if extant. It is, in fact, quite possible that good clinical intervention could increase an acquittee's ability to function in the community in ways that would make him or her a more efficient criminal. To then say that a subsequent arrest marks a treatment failure would be most inaccurate. This is not to say that in some instances there may be direct links between symptoms and criminal behavior, but to use recidivism rates routinely as direct measures of the success of treatment programs is quite inappropriate. Thus, we are hard-pressed to set such information high on any research agenda given the uncertainty of what real use either in the administration of the courts or in programs for acquittees such data can have.

What we have highlighted in this agenda and what emerges from the limited data are two generic types of needs. The first is a much clearer picture of who the people are who are acquitted and what happens to them after acquittal. Second, much is needed about the total range of cases in which the plea is raised to ascertain factors related to its successful and unsuccessful use. Such information is critical to understanding the role of the plea in the United States judicial system and in informing both the prosecution and defense as to the real implications that such a plea has for both the state and the defendant. Currently, neither party sufficiently understands the implications of raising the plea and the sequela of it's success. Both the state and the defendant deserve better information and, surely, state legislators must demand better empirical data upon which to base their deliberations on potential revisions of existing statutes.

REFERENCES

Arens, R. *Make mad the guilty.* Springfield, Ill.: Charles C Thomas, 1969.

Burton, N., & Steadman, H. J. Legal professionals' perceptions of the insanity defense. *Journal of Psychiatry and Law,* 1978, *6,* 173–187.

Cooke G., & Pogany, E. The influence on judges' sentencing practices of a mental evaluation. *Bulletin of the American Academy of Psychiatry and the Law,* 1975, *3,* 245–251.

Cooke, G., & Sikorski, C. Factors affecting length of hospitalization in persons adjudicated not guilty by reason of insanity. *Bulletin of the American Academy of Psychiatry and the Law,* 1974, *2,* 251–261.

Coser, L. A., & Rosenberg, B. *Sociological Theory: A Book of Readings.* New York: Macmillan, 1964.

Fukunaga, K. *The criminally insane.* Honolulu: Hawaii State Department of Health, 1977.

Greenland, C. Crime and the insanity defense, an international comparison: Ontario and New York State. *The Bulletin of the American Academy of Psychiatry and Law,* 1979, VII(2), 125–138.

Lewin, T. Disposition of the irresponsible protection following commitment. *Michigan Law Review,* February 1968, *66,* 721–736.

Matthews, A. R., Jr. Mental illness and the criminal law: Is community mental health an answer? *American Journal of Public Health,* September 1967, *57* (9), 1571–1579.

Matthews, A. R., Jr. *Mental disability and the criminal law: A field study.* Chicago: American Bar Association, 1970.

Monahan, J. The psychiatrization of criminal behavior: A reply. *Hospital and Community Psychiatry,* February 1973, 24(2), 105–107.

Monahan, J. *The Clinical Prediction of Violent Behavior.* Washington, D.C.: USGPO, 1981.

Morrow, W. R., & Petersen, D. B. Follow-up on discharged offenders—"not guilty by reason of insanity" and "criminal sexual psychopaths." *Journal of Criminal Law, Criminology and Police Science,* 1966, *57,* 31–34.

Pasewark, R. A., & Lanthorn, B. W. Disposition of persons utilizing the insanity plea in a rural state. *Journal of Humanics,* 1977, *5,* 87–98.

Pasewark, R. A., & Pantle, M. L. Insanity plea: legislator's view. *American Journal of Psychiatry,* 1979, *136,* 222–223.

Pasewark, R. A., Pantle, M. L., & Steadman, H. J. Characteristics and disposition of persons found not guilty by reason of insanity in New York State, 1971–76. *American Journal of Psychiatry,* 1979, *136,* 655–660. (a)

Pasewark, R. A., Pantle, M. L. & Steadman, H. J. The insanity plea in New York State 1965–1976. *New York State Bar Journal,* 1979, *51,* pp. 186–189, 217–225. (b)

Pasewark, R. A., Pantle, M. L., & Steadman, H. J. Insanity acquittees and felons: A control study of their detention and rearrest. *American Journal of Psychiatry.* 1982, *139,* 892–897.

Pasewark, R. A., & Seidenzahl, D. Opinions concerning the insanity plea and criminality among mental patients. *Bulletin of the American Academy of Psychiatry and Law,* 1980, *1,* 199–202.

Petrila, J. *Intersections between the criminal justice and mental health systems.* Paper presented at the 6th International Symposium on Law and Psychiatry. Charlottesville, Va., June 11–13, 1981.

Rubin, B. Prediction of dangerousness in mentally ill criminals. *Archives of General Psychiatry,* September 1972, *27,* 397–407.

Scheidemandel, P. L., & Kanno, C. L. *The mentally ill offender: A survey of treatment programs.* Washington, D.C.: Joint Information Service, 1969.

Simon, R. J. *The jury and the defense of insanity.* Boston: Little, Brown & Co., 1967.

Singer, A. Insanity acquittals in the seventies: Observations and empirical analysis of one jurisdiction. *Mental Disability Law Reporter,* 1978, *2,* 406–417.

Steadman, H. J. Insanity acquittals in New York State, 1965–1978. *American Journal of Psychiatry,* March 1980, *137*(3), 321–326.

Steadman, H. J., & Cocozza, J. J. *Careers of the criminally insane.* Lexington, Ma.: D.C. Heath, 1974.

Steadman, H. J., Cocozza, J. J., & Melick, M. E. Explaining the increased arrest rate among mental patients: The changing clientele of state hospitals. *American Journal of Psychiatry,* July 1978, *135*(7), 816–820.

Steadman, H. J., Monahan, J., Hartstone, E., Davis, S. K., & Robbins, P. C. Mentally disordered offenders: A national survey of patients and facilities. *Law and Human Behavior,* 1982, *6,* 31–38.

III

MENTALLY DISORDERED
SEX OFFENDERS

5

Special Dispositional Alternatives for Abnormal Offenders

DEVELOPMENTS IN THE LAW

GEORGE E. DIX

Other chapters of this book deal with what might usefully be regarded as "indirect" methods of diverting criminal offenders into the mental health system. None of the procedures discussed in the other chapters permit a convicting court to determine that a particular defendant, although criminally responsible, is most appropriately dealt with by the mental health system and to implement that determination by committing the offender to a mental health program. Incompetency to stand trial, covered in Chapter 1, comes into play before the defendant's guilt or innocence is considered. Commitment following acquittal by reason of insanity, addressed in Chapter 3, assumes the absence of criminal responsibility and thus "guilt." Transferring imprisoned offenders from correctional to mental health placements, considered in Chapter 7, does not involve the convicting court. But a number of jurisdictions traditionally have provided a "direct" means of accomplishing diversion by authorizing convicting courts, in lieu of standard sentencing, to commit certain convicted defendants to mental health programs. These programs for direct diversion during the dispositional stage of the criminal trial are the subject of the present chapter.

GEORGE E. DIX • School of Law, University of Texas, Austin, Texas 78705.

The programs with which this chapter is concerned have limited the offenders subject to diversion to those who are viewed as psychologically abnormal or impaired. Frequently they have further restricted diversion to those defendants regarded as sexually dangerous. Many label those within the programs' criteria "mentally disordered sex offenders" or MDSOs. There is no reason, of course, why such programs need to be limited to the sexually dangerous and in fact a few programs—most notably the Maryland Defective Delinquency program—have not been so restricted. This chapter, therefore, will consider all provisions for direct diversion of convicted abnormal defendants, whether sexually dangerous or not. For convenience, persons subject to diversion under these programs will be referred to as abnormal offenders and the programs will be referred to as abnormal offender programs. Those abnormal offender programs limited to persons regarded as sexually dangerous will be referred to as sex offender programs. Because the concern of this book is with diversion, the present chapter does not cover sentencing options which permit the sentencing court, on a determination that an offender is abnormal and dangerous, to impose a longer period of *correctional* detention.

DEVELOPMENT OF ABNORMAL OFFENDER PROGRAMS

Programs for abnormal offenders did not seem to find their basis in the indeterminate sentencing movement, which saw enactment of numerous indeterminate sentencing provisions following the initial Michigan statute in 1869. By 1922, 37 states had such provisions and 7 others had parole procedures that provided functionally the same result (Dershowitz, 1978, p. 66). The intellectual basis for the movement did not distinguish among offenders, but rather assumed that all were susceptible to the benefits of processing through a correctional program in which treatment personnel controlled release. Lewis's classic 1899 brief for the indeterminate sentence, for example, contained no suggestion that he or others saw it as especially appropriate for any subgroup of convicted persons (Lewis, 1899).

The first statutory authorization for a program limited to selected abnormal offenders was the Massachusetts Biggs Law, passed in 1911, which provided for special processing of the undefined group labeled "mental defectives." Only a single brief and unsuccessful effort was made at implementation before 1922, when a department for mentally defective men was established at the State Farm, located at Bridgewater (Robinson, 1933, p. 363). A similar program was established by 1919 New

York legislation which authorized commitment following examination of a person arraigned on criminal charges, before or after trial or conviction. The phrase *defective delinquents* has been widely used to describe those subject to the Massachusetts and New York programs. It apparently was not formally incorporated in the New York statutory scheme, however, until 1923 legislation was passed creating an institution at Napanoch for these persons.

While this is not entirely clear, the motivation for these programs seems to have been the discovery that a significant number of convicted persons were not receptive to rehabilitative efforts under indeterminate sentencing and in fact tended to be a disruptive element in programs for the general prison population (Ricker, 1934; Robinson, 1933, at 352). There was no widespread acceptance of the early programs. Robinson, writing in 1933, noted only the Massachusetts and New York statutes, although he observed that New Jersey had incorporated the concept into its classification system, the federal prison system's mental hospital then under construction contemplated accommodating such persons, and several other states were making "movements" toward these programs. Perhaps anticipating future objections, he noted that there was no uniform meaning for the identifying label, *defective delinquents*, and opined that several years of experimental work would be necessary before a clear-cut definition would emerge.

The limited enthusiasm for these early broad "defective delinquency" programs stands in contrast to the vigor with which the states embraced subsequent proposals for programs limited to the sexually dangerous. The first such statute was that of Michigan, enacted in 1937, and during the next few years many states enacted similar provisions. The Massachusetts statute, for example, was enacted in 1947; California's original "sex psychopath" legislation was passed in 1939, although the switch to "mentally disordered sex offender" terminology did not take place until 1963. Sutherland, writing in 1950, observed that 12 states and the District of Columbia had enacted so-called sex psychopath laws (Sutherland, 1950, p. 142).

Sutherland's classic study of the diffusion of these statutory provisions attributed their acceptance to a pattern of developments. Typically, the community was frightened by a series of highly publicized sex offenses. This was followed by agitated community activity, focusing on sex crimes. Next, a committee frequently was formed to study the situation and the psychiatric profession often was extremely active in this stage of the process. These committees, Sutherland reported, tended to collect the evidence of the popular concern, to examine approaches taken by other jurisdictions, and to formulate a sex psychopath statute to present as a community response to the anxiety-producing situation. This response was especially attractive because it not only promised community protection from what was perceived to be an almost unique source of danger but also was consistent with the trend toward treatment and rehabilitation of offenders. The result of this diffusion process, Sutherland concluded, was uncritical acceptance of sex psychopath programs in the name of science, despite the fact that the underlying assumptions were either demonstrably false or questionable (Sutherland, 1950, p. 142).

The early defective delinquency legislation constituted a first stage in the development of abnormal offender programs; the rapid acceptance of sex psychopath legislation was a second (Kittrie, 1971, pp. 178–179). A third less well defined stage also must be identified. Some jurisdictions adopted provisions similar to the sex psychopath legislation but not limited to those regarded as sexually dangerous. Yet there appears to have been no rush toward such programs similar to the rush into sex psychopath legislation. In 1933, the Pennsylvania Greenstein Act authorized indefinite commitment to a psychiatric facility of convicted defendants found not insane but so mentally ill or deficient "as to make it advisable for the welfare of the defendant or the protection of the community that he or she be committed to some institution other than [a correctional facility]." Ohio's Ascherman Act was enacted in 1939 (Penn. L. 1933, No. 78 § 3, p. 225). The Maryland Defective Delinquency statute, creating the most significant of the programs, was enacted in 1951. In 1955, the Patuxent Institution was opened at Jessup, Maryland, to house persons committed under the statute. The Maryland program has been recognized as an experimental effort to apply psychiatric principles and knowledge to the task of identifying, treating, and disabling the abnormal and dangerous offender (Boslow & Kohlmeyer, 1963) and has given rise to much litigation and discussion (Hodges, 1971; Schreiber, 1970).

The history of programs for abnormal offenders clearly seems now to have entered a fourth stage, characterized by repeal and abolition. The Michigan sex offender program was abolished in 1968, and similar repeals occurred in Iowa in 1976, Vermont in 1977, Minnesota in 1978, Indiana and Wisconsin in 1979. (See also Addendum.) The broader programs have experienced a similar fate. Ohio's Ascherman Act was repealed in 1978. In 1977 the Maryland Defective Delinquency Program was dramatically modified; offenders now cannot be compelled to enter or remain in the program and must be released at the expiration of their "regular" sentence (Kohlmeyer, 1979). These abandonments of programs for abnormal offenders apparently are a result of a combination of factors, including growing sensitivity to the danger of arbitrary and over-long detention, disillusionment with rehabilitation programs, and increasing complexities caused by developing legal requirements (Ransley, 1980). Provisions for diversion of abnormal offenders in general appear to have almost totally disappeared. A few vestiges still are in effect. Kansas, for example, authorizes commitment of a convicted defendant to a mental health facility if a psychiatric examination reveals that the defendant is in need of psychiatric treatment and such a commitment is not likely to endanger either society or the defendant.[1] While a number of sex offender programs remain, there is clearly a trend toward their repeal.

Programs for abnormal offenders, then, have had a complex history. The initial programs, which received only limited acceptance, apparently arose out of problems generated by some offenders in indeterminate sentencing programs. More widespread acceptance was found for programs limited to the sexually dangerous, although there is reason to doubt the rationality of the decision to embrace such programs. A number of broader programs developed, apparently in response to interest generated in particular jurisdictions rather than as part of a trend such as that underlying sex offender legislation. Finally, recent abandonment of the program leaves primarily a reduced number of sex offender programs as the subject of current concern.

PRESENT ABNORMAL OFFENDER PROGRAMS

In stark contrast to the early defective delinquency procedures, contemporary abnormal offender programs are procedurally quite complex and varied. Virtually all are limited to the "sexually dangerous," so a discussion of present abnormal offender programs is necessarily one of sex offender programs. An overview of the programs, their similarities, and their differences can be accomplished by examining five reasonably representative programs, selected to include those most frequently utilized and to provide a significant range of provisions. The five statutes that will be examined include the California program for Mentally Disordered Sex Offenders,[2] the "sexually dangerous persons" programs of Illinois,[3] Massachusetts[4] and Oregon,[5] and Washington's Sex Psychopath

[1]KAN. STAT. ANN. § 22–3429 et seq.
[2]CAL. WEL. & INST. CODE, § 6300 et seq.
[3]ILL. ANN. STAT., ch. 38, art. 105.
[4]MASS. GEN. L. ANN., ch. 123A.
[5]ORE. REV. STAT. ANN. § 426.675.

procedure.[6] Several aspects of these procedures will be examined and compared: the condition that must exist for the procedure to begin (the "triggering condition"), the criteria for commitment, the petition that must be filed to begin the proceedings and the discretion—if any—to begin inquiry into the subject's condition on the filing of a petition, the hearing itself, the commitment terms and discretion to sentence an offender under regular provisions despite a finding that the sex offender criteria are met, provisions for review of the propriety of continued retention and for discharge, rights of committed persons during commitment, and the possibility of retention beyond the term of the initial commitment.

TRIGGERING CONDITIONS

Virtually all of the programs require, as a prerequisite to the advent of proceedings, that the subject occupy a certain status concerning criminal charges. They differ, however, in regard to the specific status required and the charges that must be involved.

The Illinois procedure requires only that the subject be charged with a criminal offense. Most other programs require conviction.

There is widespread variation in the offenses that can trigger the proceeding. As noted, Illinois requires only that it be a criminal offense. Most procedures, however, require some sexual aspect to the conduct. Washington requires a "sex offense." This same requirement in the California statute is defined as any felony or misdemeanor committed primarily for purposes of sexual arousal or gratification. Oregon also requires conviction of a "sexual offense," which is defined as including rape, sodomy, sexual abuse, public indecency, and incest.

COMMITMENT CRITERIA

Substantively, the most important part of the statutory schemes is the criteria for determining whether a subject comes within the scheme, that is, properly can be committed. It is useful to consider four possible aspects of these criteria, although few if any statutes contain criteria embodying requirements in all four categories. The first is essentially clinical: What nature or degree of psychological impairment must exist? The second addresses the danger that must exist as a result of the impairment: What kind and how great a danger must the subject pose to others?

[6]WASH. REV. CODE ANN. § 71.06.010 et seq.

The third consists of any special requirements concerning the evidence that is necessary to prove that either or both of the first two portions of the criteria are met. The final category consists of requirements concerning the extent to which the subject's condition is subject to treatment.

Impairment

The statutes are at some variance concerning the impairment required. California demands a "mental defect, disease, or disorder." The Illinois statute requires a mental disorder but adds that it must have existed for a period of not less than one year immediately before the filing of the petition. The Oregon statute, on the other hand, requires either a "mental disease or defect" or "repeated or compulsive acts of misconduct in sexual matters." The Washington criterion contains a distinct clinical flavor; it requires that the subject be "affected in a form of psychoneurosis . . . or psychopathic personality." Most of the statutes, however, make no effort to define the impairment required in clinical or diagnostic terms.

Danger

There is also substantial variation concerning the danger that the subject must pose to others before commitment is appropriate. Washington requires that the subject's impairment "predisposes him to the commission of sex offenses in a degree constituting him a menace to the health or safety of others." The required finding under the California statute is similar; the subject must be "predisposed to the commission of sex offenses to such a degree that he is dangerous to the health and safety of others." Under the Oregon statute, the defendant must be "deemed likely to continue to perform [sexual] acts and be a danger to other persons." The Illinois statute requires a conclusion that the subject has "criminal propensities to the commission of sex offenses."

Special Evidentiary Requirements

A few statutes impose specific requirements concerning the nature or quantity of evidence that will suffice for a finding that commitment is appropriate. Strictly speaking, these are not parts of the criterion for commitment because they do not concern the ultimate issue to be addressed by the committing court. Rather, they impose minimal requirements that must exist before it is appropriate to consider whether the ultimate standard has been met. It is somewhat unclear whether these are requirements concerning the evidence showing impairment, that demonstrating the resulting danger posed by the subject, or both.

The Illinois statute requires that the subject have "demonstrated propensities towards acts of sexual assault or acts of sexual molestation of children." Massachusetts requires that the subject's lack of control over sexual impulses be indicated by "misconduct in criminal matters" and be "evidenced by repetitive or compulsive behavior and either violence, or aggression against a victim under the age of sixteen years." This is in interesting contrast to the Oregon statute, which makes a showing of "repeated or compulsive acts" of sexual misconduct necessary only when there is no showing of "mental disease or defect."

It is important to note that almost all of these statutes require conviction for some criminal offense. While this is not spelled out, the requirement of a criminal conviction to some extent serves the purpose of the special evidentiary requirements in the Illinois and Massachusetts statutes. But under these other schemes, there is no specific and direct relationship required between the conduct constituting the underlying offense and the finding that the subject meets the ultimate standard for commitment.

Treatability

A few statutes require that the committing court specifically find that the defendant's condition is appropriately within the concern of the program. The California statute, for example, requires that the court conclude that the subject "could benefit from treatment in a . . . mental health facility." Oregon requires that the committing judge find that treatment is available that will reduce the risk of future sexual offenses by the defendant.

PETITION AND DECISION TO PROCEED WITH INQUIRY

The procedures generally require the filing of a petition to begin inquiry into whether the subject is committable. Illinois and Washington authorize the filing of a petition by the prosecution; Massachusetts provides for petition either by the state or on the court's own motion. Some jurisdictions, California and Washington, for example, provide for the defense to begin the inquiry.

There is considerable difference in the degree of flexibility or discretion that the court has under the various programs. This discretion may be exercised at two points. One is in deciding to bring the inquiry into play, which is covered here. The other concerns discretion to decline to process the subject even if he or she is found within the statutory criterion; this is addressed on page 142.

Some statutes give the trial judge virtually no discretion as to whether or not to begin inquiry into the subject's condition. The Illinois procedure, on the other hand, directs that the judge "may" hear the allegations of sexual psychopathy, suggesting that the judge may, in the exercise of discretion, decline to do so. Oregon provides that on a determination that "probable cause" exists to believe that the defendant is within the statute, the trial court may conduct further inquiry. The California procedure is more complex. An inquiry is mandatory upon conviction for certain offenses; in other situations the judge has discretion but is directed to begin inquiry only if probable cause exists to believe the defendant within the statutory criterion.

EXAMINATION AND DECISION TO PROCEED TO HEARING

Substantial differences also exist as to the manner in which the "clinical" inquiry into the subject's condition is conducted and the conditions under which the matter is to go to a formal hearing on whether the subject is within the statutory criterion.

Some jurisdictions merely provide for a court-ordered examination by clinical personnel without specifying the manner in which this is to occur. California and Illinois fall within this group. Under this type of procedure, the examination may be conducted at the jail where the subject is being held or the subject may be taken by law enforcement personnel to the examiner's office. Other jurisdictions provide for a commitment to a designated facility for observation and examination; this is provided in both the Massachusetts and Oregon statutes. Under the Washington procedure, an observational commitment for no longer than 90 days is directed if a preliminary hearing results in a finding of probable cause to believe the subject a sexual psychopath.

Under some procedures, a negative finding by the clinical personnel must end the inquiry. The Oregon statute provides that if the result of the observational commitment is affirmative, a hearing must be held; the implication is that on a negative report no further proceedings are authorized. On the other hand, the Washington procedure seems to contemplate a determination by the court as to whether the subject is a sexual psychopath whatever the nature of the conclusion drawn by clinical personnel during the observational commitment. Massachusetts provides somewhat more flexibility; a hearing on the petition is to be held only if the examiner's report "clearly indicates" that the subject is a sexually dangerous person.

Hearing

The heart of the procedure is the hearing at which a formal determination is made as to whether the subject will be processed as an abnormal sex offender. In California, Illinois, and Washington, jury trial on the issue is available; in Massachusetts and Oregon it is not.

The statutory schemes seldom contain comprehensive provisions relating to the procedure at these hearings. Provisions for representation by counsel, provided by the state if the defendant is indigent, are common. The California statute directs that the hearings are to be held "as provided by law for trial of criminal cases." Illinois, on the other hand, makes the state's Civil Practice Act applicable. Illinois and California specifically provide that the burden of proof on the state is to show beyond a reasonable doubt that the subject comes within the statutory criteria. Washington's legislation states that nothing in the statute "shall be construed to prevent the defendant, his attorney, or the court of its own motion, from producing evidence and witnesses at the hearing."

Commitments and Discretion Not to Commit

Provisions for further processing of those cases in which the subject is found within the statutory criteria vary in several respects. The court may or may not be given discretion as to whether to process the offender as a special offender. If the offender is processed under the special offender program, there are important differences in the duration of the commitment and the entity to which the subject is committed.

Under the Illinois and Washington procedures, the court is required to commit the subject if it determines that the statutory criteria are met. Under the California, Oregon, and Massachusetts statutes, however, the court has discretion—even if it determines that the statutory criteria are met—to sentence the defendant under regular penal provisions.

Jurisdictions are split concerning the duration of the commitment. Illinois, Massachusetts, and Washington follow the traditional pattern of providing an indefinite commitment. California and Oregon, on the other hand, place an upper limit on the duration of commitment, determined by the maximum sentence that might be imposed for the crime of which the subject was convicted. This, of course, must be viewed in light of the provisions for retention beyond the original commitment; these are discussed at page 145.

Generally, the commitment is to the state department of mental health or its equivalent. Massachusetts provides for commitment to a specific center established by the Commissioner of Mental Health for treatment of "such persons." Under the Oregon procedure, the defendant receives a standard prison sentence to the Correctional Division containing a directive to assign the defendant to a program for sex offenders. The Mental Health Division is directed by statute to establish and operate a treatment and study program for sex offenders, which may be housed in either a Correctional Division institution, a Mental Health Division institution, or elsewhere. Illinois provides for commitment to the Director of Corrections, but with directions to place the subject in a facility set aside for the care and treatment of sexually dangerous persons. Provisions for commitment to a mental health agency must be considered in light of authorization for transfer to other agencies, including correctional facilities; this is discussed at page 146.

Provisions are sometimes made for court-ordered treatment other than full-time hospitalization in a state institution. California authorizes, as an alternative to commitment to the department for placement in a state hospital, commitment to the county mental health director for placement in an "appropriate public or private mental health facility." In an apparent effort to assure that alternatives to restrictive placements in state hospitals are thoroughly considered, the California statute mandates that a sex offender be evaluated by the county mental health director or his designee before admission to a state hospital or any other facility.

Somewhat the same results could be accomplished under the Massachusetts and Oregon provisions for probation. The Massachusetts procedure authorizes the court, *if* the department of health has recommended the person as a suitable subject for outpatient treatment, to suspend the commitment or grant probation on conditions, including the condition that the person receive outpatient treatment. Similar provision is made under the Oregon statute.

Several abnormal offender programs previously had provisions for indefinite commitment of untreatable but dangerous offenders, sometimes to correctional rather than mental health facilities. Under pre-1976 California law, a person found to be a mentally disordered sex offender but further determined to be unable to benefit from treatment in a state hospital could be committed for an indeterminate period to a correctional institution designated for such persons. This could be done at the time of initial commitment or after a period of treatment (or attempted treatment) under the regular penal code provisions. Similarly, Nebraska law provided for the court to consider whether one found to be a sexual sociopath could benefit from treatment. If this was determined negatively, the court was mandated to commit the offender to the correctional system, where he was to be kept separate from other inmates and where adequate provisions "to detain, house and care for him" were to be made. This commitment was indefinite. In 1979, however, the statutory scheme was redrafted and untreatable offenders are now to be sentenced under regular penal provisions.

DISCHARGE AND PERIODIC REVIEW

There are a variety of ways in which persons placed into abnormal offender programs can be removed from them. Unlike "civil" commitments, commitments under abnormal offender programs are not subject to termination by treating facilities or personnel. Ultimate responsibility rests on the court.

The classic pattern is that used in the Washington procedure, under which proceedings to end a sexual psychopath commitment are begun by the superintendent of the institution to which the defendant was committed. The superintendent is to make a report to the committing court when, in the superintendent's opinion, the defendant is "safe to be at large," has received maximum benefits of treatment, or is not amenable to treatment. The committing court then has several options. One is to reject the superintendent's conclusion and to return the subject to the institution. A second is to release the subject, either conditionally or unconditionally. A third is to impose the sentence attached to the crime for which the subject has been found guilty. In this event, time spent in custody under the commitment is to be credited on the defendant's sentence. Where this last option is available, as it also is in California, the abnormal offender program is not a substitute for a regular criminal sentence but rather a course of action that can be tried without loss of the ability to invoke normal correctional programs should experience with the abnormal offender program be unsatisfactory.

In those states that impose a limit on the duration of the commitment—California and Oregon—the defendant is of course entitled to discharge at the end of that period unless special procedures for imposing an additional period of commitment are available and invoked; these are discussed at page 145.

Several states also provide for the possibility of conditional release on parole, with the decision on this to be made by an authority other than the committing court. Massachusetts provides for consideration of parole pursuant to the same procedures used for other imprisoned defendants. Oregon makes no specific provisions for parole of persons processed under the statute, but apparently the standard parole procedures and criteria are applied to these individuals.

A variety of provisions also are made for review of a committed person's status. Some of these must be invoked by the defendant; others are "automatic." Some involve reconsideration of the person's status by the committing court; others place primary responsibility on the treatment program. Massachusetts, for example, requires the department to undertake annual reexamination of committed persons and to provide reports to the district attorney and to the parole board. California requires that the commitment order direct the filing of periodic reports with the court; the first is to be within 90 days and the remainder at intervals not to exceed six months.

Provision usually is made for committed persons to seek review by the committing court of their retention periodically. California, Massachusetts, and Illinois provide for a petition to be filed with the committing court and for the court then to review the propriety of the person's continued retention under the program. California limits the frequency of these proceedings to one every 6 months, while Massachusetts permits only one every 12 months. Washington has no statutory provisions permitting committed persons to seek review, but the state courts have created such procedures.[7]

Rights during Commitment

The statutory schemes seldom contain comprehensive provisions defining the committed subject's rights. California law contains two apparently contradictory provisions. One mandates that mentally disordered sex offenders shall have full patients' rights as those are defined in the civil hospitalization provisions; the other provides that a facility "may" extend to a mentally disordered sex offender any privileges granted to other patients "as are not incompatible with his detention or unreasonably conducive to his escape." Massachusetts takes the qualified position that committed persons are entitled to the rights and privileges of other inmates "in so far as may be compatible with . . . treatment."

Illinois provides a special right to treatment. The Director of Corrections "shall provide care and treatment for the person committed to him designed to effect recovery." It is likely that language or the general statutory policy of other statutes would be read as implying a similar promise of treatment.

Retention beyond Term of Commitment

California limits commitments to the maximum period of imprisonment that could be imposed for the crimes committed but also pro-

---

[7]State v. McCarter, 17 Wash. App. 319, 562 P.2d 995 (1977); State *ex rel.* Terry v. Schubert, 74 Wis.2d 487, 247 N.W.2d 109 (1976).

vides a procedure by which the subject can be "recommitted." Thus the limit on the initial detention can be avoided, but it is necessary to pursue a new and perhaps more stringent procedure to do so. The procedure is complex. Jury trial is available. Further retention is possible only if the subject originally was committed on the basis of a felony offense. The court must find that the subject is predisposed to the commission of sex offenses to such a degree that he presents a *substantial* danger of *bodily* harm to others. This is a more stringent standard than that applicable at the initial commitment hearing. The danger required is not sufficient. Moreover, the danger posed, that is, the likelihood of such harm being caused, must be "substantial." Although the precise meaning of this may be less than obvious, it seems certain to require a higher likelihood than will suffice for initial commitment. A 1979 amendment to the statute made clear that amenability to treatment is not required for recommitment under this section.

A compromise position was engrafted on the Washington scheme by the Washington Supreme Court in *State v. McCarter*.[8] Noting that defendants acquitted of their crimes by reason of insanity could be hospitalized only for a period no longer than the maximum term of imprisonment applicable to the offense involved, the court held that indefinite incarceration of sex offenders would violate equal protection requirements if those offenders could secure release only by affirmatively proving their nondangerousness. But the court saved the statutory scheme by holding that if a committed sex psychopath seeks judicial review of his continued retention after the expiration of the maximum sentence applicable to the crime of which he was convicted, continued retention is permissible only if the state affirmatively proves beyond a reasonable doubt that the offender is still dangerous.

Transfer to Correctional Institutions

Some programs that provide for initial commitment to the state mental health agency also provide, in varying ways, for the possibility of transfer from the mental health system to correctional institutions. Washington permits transfer to a correctional institution in the event that the superintendent of the mental hospital to which the subject has been committed determines that the subject is "a custodial risk or hazard to other patients." The correctional institution must be one "which has psychiatric care facilities."

California's provisions are more complex. Transfer is possible only

[8] 91 Wash.2d 249, 588 P.2d 745 (1978).

for those subjects who have been committed to an additional term beyond the period of original commitment and who are not amenable to treatment in existing hospital programs or who "need" stricter security or custody measures than are available in the state hospitals. Further, it is permitted only after the subject has been accorded the right to a prior, that is, pretransfer, hearing on "whether he may be confined and treated in a state hospital." Apparently an affirmative finding on this precludes transfer. Any person who is transferred "shall be entitled to treatment of a kind and quality similar to that which he would receive if confined by the State Department of Mental Health."

MAJOR LEGAL ISSUES POSED BY ABNORMAL OFFENDER PROGRAMS

It is clear that there are important questions presented by abnormal offender programs, including the basic issue of whether such programs are desirable at all. As in many areas of policy concern, there has been a tendency to translate these questions into constitutional challenges, in large part because such a formulation of them is often necessary to place the issues before the courts. In this section, *legal*—as it describes the issues with which the chapter will deal—will be defined broadly. It will include interpretation of existing statutory provisions for abnormal offender programs, constitutional questions raised by such programs, and the legislative issues of whether such programs should be retained and, if so, how they should be structured. Obviously, complex statutory schemes such as those of many abnormal offender programs present more issues than can be covered here. Therefore, those selected are the ones most basic to the programs and which raise the most important questions of the relationship between empirical information, clinical needs, and legal issues.

The major constitutional issues are defined and, to some extent, resolved by five United States Supreme Court decisions relating to abnormal offender programs. These will be discussed in more detail later, but at this point it is useful to identify them. *Minnesota ex rel. Pearson v. Probate Court*,[9] decided in 1940, is widely regarded as settling the constitutional acceptability of such programs and as establishing the validity of the criteria used for selecting persons for processing through them. *Specht v. Patterson*,[10] decided in 1967, on the other hand, holds that in the

[9]309 U.S. 270 (1940).
[10]386 U.S. 605 (1967).

judicial hearing to determine whether a convicted defendant is to be processed through such a special program a number of procedural safeguards must be utilized. *Humphrey v. Cady*,[11] decided in 1972, resolves virtually nothing but can be read as an indication that the Court regards a number of additional matters as presenting significant issues that cannot be ignored out of hand. Two other 1972 decisions reflect the Court's unwillingness to resolve issues raised under the former Maryland Defective Delinquency procedure that would have ramifications for many other abnormal offender programs. In *McNeil v. Director, Patuxent Institution*,[12] the Court declined to decide whether one being examined as a potential defective delinquent had a Fifth Amendment privilege to decline to participate in the examination. The Court instead addressed the much narrower issue of the propriety of a long-term detention for examination of a noncooperative defendant and held such detention impermissible unless certain procedures were followed. And in *Murel v. Baltimore Court*,[13] the Court reversed its earlier decision to address a number of procedural questions raised by the Maryland program and declined to consider the merits of any of them.

Differential Processing of Abnormal Dangerous Offenders

The basic question posed by abnormal offender programs is, of course, the desirability of processing these persons in a manner different from that used for other offenders. Traditionally, special programs provided two benefits. First, they resulted in offenders being channeled into a different custodial situation thought specially suited to their particular needs. Second, they provided flexibility in achieving preventive and therapeutic objectives. Unlike an offender sentenced under regular provisions, the abnormal dangerous offender did not have to be released at any particular time but rather could be retained until no longer dangerous. On the other hand, he did not need to be retained any longer than was necessary and therefore could be released when he was determined to be "cured." Of course, the possibility of long-term or lifetime incarceration made such a program a heavier burden on a defendant processed through it. But the benefits have been regarded as outweighing this intrusiveness. The basic question, however, is whether there exists an identifiable class of offenders whose behavior is sufficiently predictable and whose conduct is sufficiently "symptomatic" of a treatable "condition" so that these benefits can reasonably be expected to materialize.

[11]405 U.S. 504 (1972).
[12]407 U.S. 245 (1972).
[13]407 U.S. 355 (1972).

Sutherland (1950) and Tappan (1955) have pointed out that sex offender programs are based on a number of factual assumptions about sex offenders and their crimes: (1) sexually motivated offenses are unusually harmful to victims, especially minor victims; (2) such offenses often are the result of a clinically identifiable psychological abnormality; (3) this abnormality permits reasonably accurate prediction of the offender's future conduct, including the likelihood of his engaging in more serious criminal sexual activity; and (4) this abnormality is subject to "cure" by means of treatment techniques that are different from those properly used for normal offenders. Similar assumptions formed the foundation for the broader based programs such as the Maryland Defective Delinquency Program. The Maryland legislative counsel research report preceding adopting of the program stated:

> Studies . . . demonstrate that this class of criminal in general constitutes a particular menace to the Maryland community. On the other hand, it also seems clear that with the special kind of treatment which their needs require, some of these . . . can be rehabilitated so that they can be made law abiding members of the society to which they return. (p. 2)

If these assumptions are insufficiently supported, it is arguable that the differential processing of abnormal offenders violates the equal protection clause of the Fourteenth Amendment. Those processed as abnormal offenders may be deprived of liberty longer and under more intrusive circumstances than offenders sentenced under regular penal provisions. This distinction among offenders violates equal protection if there is no reasonable basis for it (LaFave & Scott, 1972, p. 131).

Although *Pearson* is widely regarded as having definitively rejected this argument as it concerns sex offender programs, it does not appear that the issue was placed squarely before the Court. Appellant conceded the authority of the state legislature to deal separately with the "sexual irresponsible" and claimed a denial of equal protection only in what he perceived was the statute's arbitrary exclusion of some of the sexually irresponsible. The Court's rejection of appellant's equal protection claim, therefore, did not address the basic issue. In a separate, rather confusing argument, appellant in *Pearson* also urged that the Minnesota legislature, in enacting the statute at issue, acted in haste and without adequate consideration. This was apparently in support of an assertion that the legislation was so arbitrary that it could not survive due process attack. The Court did not respond directly to this in its opinion, but the decision is certainly an implied rejection of the argument.

Lower courts generally have assumed the basic validity of abnormal sex offender programs. The comprehensive attacks on the Michigan statute in *People v. Chapman*,[14] for example, did not challenge the foundations of the program. The Court noted that although the matter was not raised, it was "satisfied that the statute is a valid and proper exercise of the state police power as a measure of public safety." In *State v. Little*,[15] the Nebraska Supreme Court upheld that state's sex offender program against equal protection attacks, urging that no meaningful distinction existed between those subject to the sex offender program and habitual offenders processed in other ways.

Courts, then, have been uncritically willing to grant the validity of at least some of the factual assumptions on which programs for abnormal—and especially sexually dangerous—offenders are based. *Pearson*, however, cannot fairly be read as a definitive rejection of the argument that these assumptions have so little basis that more intrusive programs for abnormal offenders violate equal protection. Recent repeals of abnormal offender programs in a number of jurisdictions, however, suggest that attacks on the accuracy of these assumptions are finding a more sympathetic ear in the legislative forum.

CRITERIA FOR PROCESSING AS ABNORMAL OFFENDER

There are two basic concerns regarding the criteria used to select offenders for processing as abnormal offenders; these correspond to the constitutional objections that may be raised to the criteria. First, the criteria may be insufficiently precise. Due process requires that legal criteria affecting important interests be sufficiently precise to permit one potentially affected by the situation to ascertain in advance how to avoid liability. The standards also must be sufficiently clear to reasonably discourage arbitrariness in their application by police, prosecutors, and lower courts. Second, it is sometimes urged that, insofar as the limits of the criteria can be ascertained, the criteria are "overbroad" in the sense that they encompass persons who should not be processed through the program. In constitutional terms, this argument is that the criteria embrace persons who cannot constitutionally be subject to processing as abnormal offenders. This is a more difficult legal argument to make, since it is not immediately obvious what constitutional rights particular defendants have not to be processed as abnormal offenders. As a result, most litigation has involved claims of inadequate precision, or "vagueness."

Pearson, again, is widely read as insulating many if not all abnormal offender statutes from such attacks. The statute (Minn. L. 1939, ch. 369 §1)

[14]301 Mich. 584, 4 N.W.2d 18 (1942).
[15]199 Neb. 772, 261 N.W.2d 847 (1978).

at issue in *Pearson* identified those subject to the program as "psycho-pathic personalities," and defined this as follows:

> the existence in any person of such conditions of emotional instability, or impulsiveness of behavior, or lack of customary standards of good judgment, or failure to appreciate the consequences of his acts, or a combination of any such conditions, as to render such persons irresponsible for his conduct with respect to sexual matters and thereby dangerous to other persons.

The state court, however, had read the statute as also requiring proof of three additional specific matters: (1) a habitual course of misconduct in sexual matters by the subject; (2) an utter lack of power in the subject to control his sexual impulses; and (3) that the subject consequently is likely to attack or otherwise inflict injury, loss, pain, or other evil on the objects of his sexual desires. Appellant urged to the Supreme Court that the standard was insufficiently precise in several aspects: the clinical condition of "emotional instability" was not sufficiently clear; it was too uncertain what was meant by "customary standards of good judgment"; and the requirement that the defendant be "dangerous" did not sufficiently identify the risk of harm that must be established. The Supreme Court held that it must evaluate the statute as embodying the additional requirements read into it by the state tribunal. Then, without addressing specifically the appellant's objections to various parts of the criterion, the Court rejected the vagueness challenge on the ground that the underlying conditions required by the state court "are as susceptible of proof as many of the criteria constantly applied in prosecutions for crime."

Pearson certainly does not provide reasoned support for rejection of the vagueness claim and the Court's sensitivity to assertions of imprecision may have increased sufficiently that the case is not firm precedent. But even if it resolves the constitutional question, substantial doubt nevertheless may exist concerning the desirability on general policy grounds of using criteria such as those embodied in contemporary programs. Several areas of concern are most significant.

Impairment Required

Conceptually, the adequacy of the definition of the impairment required is of major importance because the impairment justifies distinguishing abnormal offenders from other, especially repeat, offenders. As the discussion on page 139 made clear, the statutory schemes make little effort to define the required impairment. But this might be of minimal importance. There may be a "clinical condition" that is difficult or impossible to articulate in statutory language but which is nevertheless generally agreed upon by clinical practitioners. Administrative practice, in other words, may "cure" the apparent uncertainty. Or, other requirements, such as the need in *Pearson* for a showing of a "habitual" course of sexual misconduct, may substitute for a clinical definition of the impairment.

There is some reason to believe that clinical practice does not provide a well accepted and easily applied standard for determining the required impairment. The commonly used name for the programs—"sex psychopath"—suggests that the impairment required might reasonably be regarded as what in clinical practice is the personality disorder of antisocial personality, sociopathy, or psychopathy. There is evidence, however, that this is not the case in practice. Konecni, Mulcahy, and Ebbesen (1980), studying commitment under the California statute, found that none of the defendants diagnosed by the examiners as having "antisocial personality" were found mentally disordered sex offenders. Moreover the case law contains no indication that such a diagnosis is necessary. On the other hand, there are some indications that a diagnosis bringing the subject within other so-called personality disorders is sufficient. In *People v. Cooper*,[16] for example, the Illinois court held that proof that the defendant was a "passive aggressive person" and that this condition was classified as a "personality disorder" was sufficient to establish that he had the impairment required by the statute.

But the assumption that a personality disorder is sufficient runs into considerable difficulty if it is necessary to establish that the subject suffers from a mental disease, disorder, or its equivalent. In *People v. Griffes*,[17] the court held that a "mental disorder" was required for criminal sexual psychopath proceedings. But it then held that such proceedings should have been begun on the basis of testimony that the defendant's indecent exposure was the result of "a state of accumulating sexual and attention-getting tension." In explanation, the psychiatrist testified:

> [I]n our own [psychiatric] circles there is some controversy over whether this actually is an illness or whether this is a defect in personality. . . . I think that most of my colleagues regard this not as an illness but [as] a defect in personality. . . . I also would not regard this as a sickness, but rather that his innate personality is not sufficiently strong . . . to repudiate these ideas or these sexual strivings. He does not have the willpower—as we say, superego—to constraint that most of us can exercise. (13 Mich. App. at 304–305, 164 N.W. 2d at 429)

Uncertainty such as this as to whether certain "causes" of sexual misconduct constitute sufficient pathology or impairment to bring an offender

[16]64 Ill.App.3d 880, 381 N.E.2d 1178 (1978).
[17]13 Mich.App. 299, 164 N.W.2d 426 (1968).

within the criteria for processing as an abnormal offender was also noted by Dix (1976), who found examiners divided on the need to bring an offender within an accepted diagnostic category and on the pathological nature of intoxication that led to sexual misbehavior. In the absence of professional consensus on which clinically determinable "causes" constitute illness or impairment and which ones are pathological personality characteristics, it is unlikely that professional consensus can be relied on to give content to an imprecise statutory definition of the impairment required.

Resulting "Danger"

The second area of concern addresses the "danger" that the subject must be shown to pose. What impact on the victim must be anticipated? Is some physical impact or harm required, and, if so, what sort of impact or harm? If not, what sort of "psychological" harm will suffice? And further, how likely must it be that the subject will cause this impact or harm in order to bring him within the criteria? *Pearson* appears to have upheld a criterion that required anticipation of "injury, loss, pain or other evil" on the victim and that the subject was "likely" to cause this impact. It seems quite clear that this phraseology does not provide answers to the questions posed above, despite the Court's conclusion that it was acceptably precise. Few of the modern statutory criteria are more satisfactory, although this is undoubtedly due in part to legislative willingness to use broad and imprecise criteria that *Pearson* seems to insulate from constitutional attack. Even if the constitutional issue is settled by *Pearson* (however unwisely), legitimate concern properly may exist concerning the desirability of such standards.

Generally it seems clear that most statutory criteria do not require physical harm. In *People v. Cooper*,[18] the Illinois court held that under that state's statute the prosecution need not establish that the defendant had a propensity to commit sex crimes involving the use of force. The Wisconsin Supreme Court, in *State v. Torpy*,[19] upheld the commitment of the defendant on the basis that the proof showed a sufficient danger that he would seek out minors and "impose" himself upon them in the hope of establishing a homosexual relationship. In the subsequent case of *State v. Hungerford*,[20] the court confirmed that the statute does not limit concern to the danger of physical harm and suggested that "dangerousness" under the statute means a risk of either physical or "moral" harm.

[18]64 Ill.App.3d 880, 381 N.E.2d 1178 (1978).
[19]52 Wis.2d 101, 187 N.W.2d 858 (1971).
[20]84 Wis.2d 236, 267 N.W.2d 258 (1978).

Perhaps the greatest concern has been with the extent to which persons sufficiently likely to engage in exhibitionism are covered by the statutes. The few cases on the issue demonstrate a variation in approach to this question but no court has been willing to embrace the proposition that exhibitionism never involves the sort of impact or harm required by the criteria. *People v. Stoddard*,[21] a 1964 California case, accepted an expansive view of the statute that required that the defendant be shown to be a "menace to the health or safety of others." The four medical examiners apparently agreed that the defender would expose his sex organs to young girls and that there was no likelihood of physical contact with the "victims." At least one expressed the opinion that at least "some" of the girls who were "likely" to observe this conduct would incur "serious psychological injury"; some others disagreed. The court upheld the finding that the defendant was within the statute and expressed "no hesitancy" in holding that the threat of psychological trauma is sufficient. Without considering further what sort of trauma must be shown, or how likely it must be, the court held that the evidence was sufficient to support the finding that the defendant came within the statute.

The District of Columbia Circuit Court of Appeals has generally, however, shown greater sensitivity to problems in this area. In *Millard v. Cameron*,[22] it held that in order to save the sex psychopath statute from fatal vagueness, it would read the statute as requiring proof that the defendant would engage in conduct involving either physical or psychological harm that has "a serious effect on the viewer." In *Millard v. Harris*,[23] the court applied this to the issue of exhibitionism and held that the criterion demanded a detailed inquiry into the effects of a particular defendant's conduct. On the facts before it, the court found sufficient proof that the defendant would engage in public exposure and perhaps masturbation. But the expert testimony established that serious psychological harm from viewing this could be expected only in unusually sensitive adult women or small children and, further, that the typical small child would be injured only by repeated observation of this sort of adult behavior. It also established that the "very seclusive, withdrawn, shy, sensitive" women who would be harmed by the conduct were in a minority. The evidence showed that the defendant was unlikely to engage in the anticipated conduct with great or uncontrollable frequency. On this record, the court concluded that the government had failed to show a sufficient likelihood that the defendant's conduct would

[21]227 Cal.App.2d 40, 38 CAL.REPTR. 407 (1964).
[22]373 F.2d 468 (D.C. Cir. 1966).
[23]406 F.2d 964 (D.C. Cir. 1968).

be observed with sufficient frequency by persons who might be harmed by it and the defendant was therefore not within the statute.

All of this concern addressed only the conduct that must be anticipated and not the likelihood that must exist that the conduct will be engaged in. Even less attention has been paid to this matter. The single discussion of any value is that of Judge David Bazelon in *Cross v. Harris*,[24] addressing the determination of whether an exhibitionist is "likely" to cause harm that is shown to be substantial:

> It may well be impossible to provide a precise definition of "likely" as the term is used in the statute. The degree of likelihood necessary to support commitment may depend upon many factors. Among the particularly relevant considerations are the seriousness of the expected harm, the availability of in-patient and out-patient treatment for the individual concerned, and the expected length of confinement required for the in-patient treatment. (418 F.2d at 1100)

Judge Bazelon's suggested analysis may be an admission of defeat. It appears to be based on the assumption that "likely" or similar terms in commitment criteria cannot be read as imposing statistical requirements, such as a showing of a 50% likelihood. Why he rejects this is not clear. Perhaps to interject such numbers into the statute would be to take too great a liberty with legislative intent. If this is the rationale, it is no bar to drafting statutes with such requirements (Monahan & Wexler, 1978). But more likely Judge Bazelon is recognizing that even if such numbers were drafted or read into the criterion our knowledge concerning prediction is so inadequate that we could not meaningfully work with the criterion that would now be precise on its face. He responds to this by substituting an inclusive analysis that would incorporate a variety of other concerns. Apparently, the more serious the harm anticipated and the greater the chance that the defendant could be "cured" in a short period of inpatient treatment, the lower the likelihood that he will cause the harm needs to be. Perhaps, however, this compounds rather than reduces the problem. It in no way addresses the difficulty of determining the specific likelihood of a given harm or whether any specific likelihood is sufficient under a particular statute. Rather, it substitutes an analysis that merely deflects attention and concern from these problems and obscures them by merging them with other, logically unrelated, matters. It may be true that the seriousness of the harm and the duration and intrusiveness of the treatment program may be legitimate considerations in determining whether a subject should be processed as an abnormal offender. But it is by no means clear that these factors should be consid-

[24]418 F.2d 1095 (D.C. Cir. 1969).

ered as part of the "likelihood" analysis. It may well be that the analysis required by *Cross v. Harris* is as subject to arbitrary administration as that under the more traditional dangerousness statutes, and that the complexity of the *Cross v. Harris* analysis unfortunately tends to obscure this danger which is far more self-evident under the traditional schemes.

Long-term Commitments

The traditional pattern for abnormal offender programs involved an indefinite commitment, which in many cases subjected the defendant to a potential period of incarceration longer than would have been possible under the standard penal sentencing provisions. On the facts of some cases or as a general matter, it can be argued that long-term or indefinite commitment of this sort is so disproportionate to the underlying conduct or to the risk posed by the subject that it is unacceptable on policy grounds and perhaps even unconstitutional.

The leading decision limiting indefinite commitment of sex offenders is *People v. Feagley*,[25] a 1975 decision of the California Supreme Court. Feagley had been convicted of a simple battery, a misdemeanor, and after being found a mentally disordered sex offender not amenable to treatment in a state hospital, had been committed to a correctional institution for an indefinite period. The court concluded that sex offenders confined in correctional facilities are "customarily" confined without treatment. Since no treatment is provided, the desire to treat could not justify the commitment. The remaining justification, society's need for protection, was not sufficiently at issue to justify the extremely intrusive indefinite commitment. As a result, the court held, Feagley's commitment constituted cruel and unusual punishment under both the federal and state constitutions.

The major development of *Feagley* has come under the Nebraska sex offender procedure. In *State v. Little*,[26] the 58-year-old defendant had been convicted of indecent exposure and of fondling the sexual organs of a minor boy; he had two prior convictions for sex offenses involving minor children. After being determined to be an untreatable sex sociopath, he was indefinitely committed to the correctional system. Accepting *Feagley's* result, the Nebraska Supreme Court held that on the facts of the case confinement of the defendant indefinitely without treatment and without provisions for review of "treatability" would violate the prohibition against cruel and unusual punishment. Rather than invalidating the

[25]14 Cal.3d 338, 121 Cal.Reptr. 509, 535 P.2d 373 (1975).
[26]199 Neb. 772, 261 N.W.2d 847 (1978).

commitment, however, the court implemented what it found to be the statutory directive to the correctional authorities to "care" for untreatable sexual sociopaths.

Under *Feagley* and *Little,* the legal limit on indefinite commitments is a relatively limited one. The *Feagley* holding, as stated by the court, is only that "the state may not involuntarily confine a civilly committed mentally disordered sex offender for an indefinite period in a prison setting," and involves an assumption that no treatment is provided in the prison setting. *Little* is even more limited, and permits even indefinite incarceration without treatment in a correctional setting if (1) efforts are made to treat and (2) periodic reexaminations are made to assure that the subject is still untreatable. What constitutes treatment under *Feagley* and an effort to make the possibility of treatment open to the subject under *Little* remains unclear. In *Feagley,* the state urged that the correctional program provided "treatment" because it attempted to motivate the subjects to accept treatment, which would be made available by transfer to the mental health system if the subject indicated a willingness to cooperate. The court rejected this:

> This is not treatment but coercion. It falls far short of the human, therapeutic consideration which every person civilly committed has a right to expect in exchange for giving up his or her liberty. (14 Cal.3d at 371, 121 Cal. Reptr. at 531, 535 P.2d at 395)

Insofar as these cases rest on the federal Constitution's prohibition against cruel and unusual treatment, their foundation may have been substantially eroded by *Rummel v. Estelle,*[27] in which the Supreme Court refused to invalidate a felony defendant's life sentence under Texas's habitual criminal provision. The majority's analysis strongly suggests that it would find a penalty unconstitutionally disproportionate to the defendant's situation only in very exceptional cases, perhaps only those in which there is some objective indication of disproportionality. The classification of the crime of which the defendant was convicted may provide such an indication; definite incarceration following conviction of a misdemeanor, at least in the absence of an exceptionally strong showing of the subject's long-term dangerousness, may still be subject to scrutiny under the Eighth Amendment. *Rummel,* of course, in no way precludes state courts from engaging in more rigorous proportionality review of penalties under state constitutional provisions, and it is worth noting that the California Supreme Court rested *Feagley* on both federal and state constitutional provisions.

[27]445 U.S. 263 (1980).

Whatever the availability of constitutional challenges to indefinite commitments, it is at least arguable that they are unacceptable on policy grounds. The difficulty of predicting behavior, especially that of making institutional predictions concerning a subject's likely conduct in the community, may be so great as to require some limit on the effect that will be given these predictions. This is especially so if the offender's conduct shows only relatively minor misbehavior and long-term detention is based on a prediction that if permitted to remain at large the offender will engage in misconduct of an increasingly serious nature. Both California and Nebraska have repealed the provisions authorizing long-term detention of untreatable abnormal offenders in a correctional environment. Some jurisdictions have also responded to these concerns (and probably to actual or threatened litigation) by imposing as an upper limit on abnormal offender commitments the maximum period of incarceration that could be imposed for the offense involved under regular sentencing procedures. Thus being labeled an abnormal offender cannot subject a defendant to incarceration beyond what otherwise would have been possible. The validity of the use of the statutory maximum as the upper limit on an abnormal offender commitment was sustained by the California Supreme Court in *People v. Saffell*.[28]

Of course, the propriety and desirability of these limited-term commitments must be considered in light of the provisions for extensions of detention. By invoking these authorizations for extension, the state may be able to accomplish the same objective as that provided by indefinite commitment. But the extension procedures may blunt the objections to long-term detention in several ways: First, the decision to impose long-term detention will not be made solely at the time of original disposition but rather at intervals during that detention. Since periodic decisions will be made and will focus on the defendant's current condition (rather than speculation concerning his condition at some unspecific future time), it is reasonable to expect them to be more accurate. Second, the extensions may provide—as the California one does—that long-term detention will be limited to those situations in which there are objective indications that the danger to society justifies preventive detention. Thus the California provision applies only where the defendant's initial commitment followed commission of a felony and requires a showing of a greater danger than is required for an initial commitment. On the other hand, there undoubtedly is a danger that the extension process will be no more than a *pro forma* one and that the procedural niceties will be only a facade obscuring the same sort of questionable long-term confinements possible under the traditional schemes.

[28]25 Cal.3d 223, 157 Cal.Reptr. 897, 599 P.2d 92 (1979).

The validity of the California provision for recommitment of an MDSO whose maximum prison term has expired was questioned by two intermediate California appellate courts[29] that were especially bothered by the absence of a requirement that the subjects be found amenable to treatment. 1979 legislative action made clear that recommitment does not require a finding of amenability to treatment. But nevertheless the California provision was upheld by one intermediate appellate court,[30] which distinguished *Feagley* on the ground that it involved indefinite commitment to a prison setting.

There is, then, increasing concern regarding the acceptability of long-term confinement under abnormal offender programs, especially if this takes place in a correctional rather than a mental health setting. Perhaps the basic question is whether there is sufficiently greater predictive ability or treatment possibilities concerning abnormal offenders as contrasted with other convicted defendants to justify any difference in processing at all. Is the predictability of such persons' behavior so much greater than that of others that confinement beyond the statutory maximum should be available for the abnormal offenders but not others? Are there treatment techniques available that can be expected to give reasonably effective results if—but only if—treatment personnel are given greater flexibility in retaining the subject than is available under standard sentencing and release procedures? These are questions that must be addressed in order to assess the validity of the increasing concerns regarding long-term commitment of offenders identified as psychologically abnormal.

DISCRETION AND SELECTIVITY

Virtually all abnormal offender programs involve the exercise of substantial discretion concerning whether or not to process defendants who are or well might be within the statutory criteria as abnormal offenders. To some extent, this discretion lies in the hands of the judge hearing the case. But there is at least as much and perhaps more discretion in the hands of the prosecutor who may have the power to decide whether to invoke the programs. Two major concerns are raised by the existence of this substantial discretion. The first deals with the danger of improper use of the "threat" of abnormal offender programs; the second is with potential denial to defendants of an adequate opportunity to be considered for processing as abnormal offenders.

[29]People v. Lakey, 102 Cal.App.3d 962, 162 CAL.REPTR. 653 (1980); People v. Compelleebee, 99 Cal.App.3d 296, 160 CAL.REPTR. 233 (1979).
[30]People v. Poggi, 107 Cal.App.3d 581, 165 CAL.REPTR. 758 (1980).

Improper Selection of Defendants

A major danger is that prosecutorial discretion will be exercised for improper reasons and therefore some persons processed as abnormal offenders will have been improperly selected. Prosecutors may select defendants for processing as abnormal offenders because of personal bias or unsubstantiated personal views as to what persons or conduct constitute sufficiently serious dangers to justify taking extraordinary procedural steps. But a separate concern is that abnormal offender programs will be used in the plea bargaining process as a means of "encouraging" guilty pleas. To the extent that this materializes, defendants who are processed as abnormal offenders will have been selected because of their unwillingness to waive the right to trial, a factor that clearly is unrelated to the objectives of the program. It has been reported that under the California program the threat of MDSO proceedings is often used to encourage guilty pleas and that trial judges, anxious to move their dockets, uncritically commit defendants as MDSOs in order to maintain the viability of the threat as a plea bargaining tool (Guthman, 1980).

Such selectivity in choosing defendants for processing as abnormal offenders may be objectionable for several reasons. First, "fairness" to those defendants processed as abnormal offenders arguably dictates that they be selected on the basis of objective criteria reasonably related to a significant public interest. Second, the ability of the programs to determine effectively the danger of recidivism and to treat those committed may be harmed if defendants are selected for processing on grounds unrelated to the objectives of the program. Even if the programs can be relied upon to identify defendants who are insufficiently dangerous or treatable to warrant continued retention in the program, this process is time-consuming and may detract from the programs' ability to deal with those defendants who have been "properly" committed to it.

Constitutional litigation has made clear that there are few constitutional limitations on these exercises of prosecutorial discretion. *Oyler v. Boles*[31] establishes that the mere fact that a program is applied selectively does not mean that those selected for processing through it are denied federal constitutional rights. Only if a subject can establish that the selection was for a constitutionally impermissible reason—such as race—can the selection be attacked. This is a burden almost impossible to meet. In regard to the use of "threats" to stimulate guilty pleas, *Bordenkircher v. Hayes*[32] establishes that a guilty plea is not invalidated even if a defendant was caused to enter it by a prosecutor's threat to bring more serious

[31]368 U.S. 448 (1962).
[32]434 U.S. 357 (1978).

charges if the defendant persisted in pleading not guilty. Only if the prosecutor's decision to proceed against the defendant—as by pursuing abnormal offender allegations—is a vindictive response to a defendant's plea of not guilty and the defendant has no opportunity to escape it by giving up the right to trial is due process violated.

These dangers of what reasonably might be regarded as arbitrary application of abnormal offender programs must, therefore, be evaluated with only minimal consideration of possible constitutional limits on the exercise of discretion. How heavily they weigh against the continued existence of such programs depends in part on how frequently, if at all, discretion is exercised in a manner that is "arbitrary," and the impact on the programs' ability to serve their protective and rehabilitative functions if the offenders processed through them have been selected on what may be arbitrary bases.

Prosecutorial selection may be subject to review by the judge. In some programs, as discussed above, a judge has discretion as to whether or not to proceed on a prosecutor's request that abnormal offender proceedings be pursued. This discretion, it appears, could be exercised on the basis that the prosecutor's decision to begin sex offender proceedings was an inappropriate one. There are no indications, however, that such judicial review occurs or is effective.

Denial of Access to Abnormal Offender Programs

Traditional analysis assumes that being processed as an abnormal offender disadvantages a defendant and it is therefore important to avoid improper inclusion in such programs. But there is growing concern based on the opposite assumption, that is, that being processed as an abnormal offender is an advantage for a defendant. A former California prosecutor has reported that commitment as an MDSO often is attractive to a felony defendant, as it offers "softer" time and earlier release (Guthman, 1980, pp. 76–77). A California defense lawyer, however, has cautioned that the lack of control over actual time served makes a defense decision to seek MDSO status a "calculated risk" to be taken only with care (Cronin, 1980). But to the extent that access to abnormal offender programs is perceived by defendants as an advantage, care needs to be taken to assure that defendants are not unfairly deprived of a reasonable opportunity to be so processed. This opportunity may be endangered at two points: the prosecutor's decision to invoke the program and the judge's decision to proceed under the abnormal offender statute.

If, as is the case in many jurisdictions, a defendant or someone on the defendant's behalf may begin abnormal offender proceedings by petitioning the court, the prosecutor lacks the formal ability to prevent the initiation of proceedings. But where the prosecutor has sole authority to file the petition beginning abnormal offender programs, the opportunity for unfair selectivity exists. Courts have been unwilling to interfere with prosecutors' decisions not to file such petitions. In *State v. Wheat*,[33] for example, the evidence supporting the defendant's guilt of rape and sodomy indicated that a variety of sexually oriented indignities had been forcibly performed on the victim. Nevertheless, the prosecutor refused to proceed under the Missouri Criminal Sexual Psychopath Act and the defendant was sentenced as a regular offender. On appeal, the court refused to give the defendant relief despite language in the statute arguably mandating that the prosecutor begin sex offender proceedings when evidence indicating that the defendant is within the statute exists. The court emphasized the general rule that courts will not interfere with the exercise of discretion and selectivity by prosecutors and apparently saw no justification for creating an exception for the discretionary decision to eschew sex offender proceedings.

In regard to judicial abandonment of abnormal offender proceedings once begun, there are both procedural and "substantive" issues. Whether a defendant has a right to have procedural regularity respected in the making of a decision to abandon abnormal offender proceedings was presented in *People v. Breazeale*.[34] After receiving reports from examiners appointed under the Colorado Sex Offender Act, the trial court, without a hearing, terminated the proceedings and sentenced the defendant under regular provisions. On appeal, the court found no denial of due process in the refusal to afford the defendant a hearing. *Specht v. Patterson* (discussed at page 147) was read as requiring procedural due process before a sex offender commitment is imposed but not before such a commitment is rejected. A New York Court reached an identical conclusion in *People v. Adams*.[35]

It is unclear under many statutes whether persons in Breazeale's position would be entitled to a hearing. But it is arguable that the Colorado court's result is inappropriate, both as a matter of statutory construction and constitutional due process. If the promise of rehabilitation and a potentially shorter period of incarceration held out by abnormal offender programs is a realistic one, it seems reasonable that the statutes are not intended to permit denial of this promise to one potentially sub-

[33]573 S.W.2d 126 (Mo.App. 1978).
[34]544 P.2d 970 (Colo. 1976).
[35]350 N.Y.S.2d 96, 76 Misc.2d 36 (1973).

ject to "cure," at least without a reasonably reliable determination that exclusion of the person is appropriate. Under due process concerns, it may be that for at least some persons sentencing under regular sentencing provisions rather than sex offender options is as intrusive as the opposite choice would be for others. If so, procedural due process should apply to the decision to abandon sex offender proceedings as well as to the decision to apply the special dispositional alternatives made available in such proceedings.

The "substantive" issue is whether judges may ignore evidence that a defendant is within the statutory criterion and sentence under standard penal provisions. Decisions such as *State v. Tissot*,[36] which find substantial if not complete discretion to reject recommendations for abnormal offender processing, suggest that a trial judge's decision to ignore evidence and proceed under standard sentencing options will be reviewed on appeal, if at all, only for the grossest abuses of discretion. The Florida courts, on the other hand, have shown significant sensitivity to defendants' interest in being processed under the state's sexual psychopath program where the evidence indicates that they come within the program's criteria. In *Dorman v. State*,[37] the Florida Supreme Court held that a trial judge who has probable cause to believe a defendant a sexual psychopath commits reversible error in failing to hold a hearing on the matter. In *Donaldson v. State*[38] and *Hendricks v. State*,[39] the lower Florida appellate courts found error in failing to commit the defendants as sexual psychopaths where the evidence showed that they were within the statutory standards.

Again, the extent to which this is a matter of appropriate concern depends in large part on the accuracy of some defendants' perception that they would be significantly better off being processed as abnormal offenders. This might be true because such processing would offer opportunities for treatment not otherwise available that would improve the quality of their lives. It might also be true if such processing would reduce the period of time these persons would spend in confinement. If for any reason defendants are likely to benefit in important ways from being processed as abnormal offenders, it seems reasonable to subject refusals to proceed under abnormal offender programs to review and scrutiny.

[36]152 N.J.Super. 42, 377 A.2d 761 (1977).
[37]279 So.2d 854 (Fla. 1973). See also, Rosier v. State, 374 So.2d 1041 (Fla.App. 1979).
[38]371 So.2d 1073 (Fla.App. 1979).
[39]360 So.2d 1119 (Fla.App. 1978).

PROLONGED OBSERVATIONAL COMMITMENTS AND "PARTICIPANT EVALUATION"

In *McNeil v. Director, Patuxent Institution*[40] the Supreme Court addressed a relatively narrow issue that has ramifications for other problems presented by abnormal offender programs. McNeil had been sentenced to a five-year term of imprisonment for assault; he was referred by the sentencing court to Patuxent Institution for evaluation as a possible defective delinquent. He refused to cooperate in the evaluation and the institution, reasoning that it could not arrive at a recommendation without a personal examination, retained him pending its ability to persuade him to cooperate. Six years later—and after the expiration of his prison sentence—he sought relief.

McNeil's long-term confinement, the Supreme Court held, violated due process, at least in the absence of a judicial determination of its propriety. Minimal procedural safeguards are sufficient for a brief detention for evaluation, the Court held; although disclaiming an intention to set a "precise time limit," the Court noted that the statutory scheme at issue appeared to assume that ordinarily such evaluations could be accomplished in six months or less. If the defendant's refusal to cooperate was willful, prolonged detention might be permitted. But in such cases due process requires a hearing to determine whether the refusal to cooperate was sufficiently willful to justify penalization. Even in cases of willful refusal to cooperate, the Court noted, due process may impose some outer limit upon the duration of detention for this purpose.

The direct impact of *McNeil* is minimal, as present programs do not appear to contemplate or authorize long-term detention of uncooperative persons referred for an examination. But the underlying state interest that Maryland sought to pursue has ramifications elsewhere. The detention of McNeil and of others similar to him is supportable only if a personal examination of the subject, in which the subject participates, is essential or at least important to the accurate determination of whether such persons are abnormal offenders. If such "participant evaluations" are important, long-term detention to encourage participation is more supportable. Moreover, this increases the need to avoid other positions— such as the applicability of the privilege against self-incrimination, discussed at page 166—that might interfere with such participation.

McNeil was clearly litigated on the assumption that participant evaluations were essential to the formulation of reliable clinical judgments concerning alleged abnormal offenders and that such clinical judgments were essential to reliable judicial determinations of whether particular

---

[40]407 U.S. 245 (1972).

persons came within abnormal offender criteria. Maryland's brief in the Supreme Court[41] contained affidavits from the associate director (psychiatry) and the chief psychologist at Patuxent, emphasizing the value of the personal interview in the evaluation process. In its brief, the state urged that the value of a personal psychiatric or psychological interview and other manifestations of the subject's cooperation "has been continually reaffirmed by factual studies and judicial decisions." To hold that subjects cannot be compelled to participate in such evaluations would "be the frustration of every sexual psychopath statute in the country." Diagnoses without personal examination of the subject "could be made by virtually any lay individual," and—the unstated implication is—to preclude personal examination would be to remove the opportunity for trained mental health professionals to offer information of value in the decision-making process. If personal interviews could not be compelled, Maryland argued, abnormal offender schemes would have to rely on "rigid" standards focusing upon subjects' past conduct. This would undesirably frustrate any efforts to conduct a careful inquiry into whether each particular defendant is—"clinically"—a proper and fitting subject for indeterminate sentencing.

The same underlying issue was presented in *Commonwealth v. Childs*,[42] arising under Massachusetts' Sexually Dangerous Persons Program. The legal issue was whether the reports required as a prerequisite for a petition could be based on information other than personal interviews with the subject. The court held that they could be, and stressed the potential value of testimony at past trials involving the subject, probation records, police reports, past criminal records, observation of the subject's conduct, and interviews with victims of his misbehavior. But the court carefully reserved decision on whether an ultimate finding that the subject was in fact a sexually dangerous person could be made without testimony based on personal interviews. Thus it left open the possibility that only the preliminary decisions, such as whether to bring inquiry, could be based on what was perceived to be the relatively unreliable evidence lacking a personal examination of the subject.

The extent to which a program should—and can—impose penalties for refusal to cooperate in interview as well as a number of other issues raised by abnormal offender programs, then, depends in part upon the value of participant evaluations in the inquiries required by such programs. How reliable and accurate are clinical assessments of the sorts of impairments at issue in these cases? How reliable and accurate are clini-

---

[41]Brief for Respondents, McNeil v. Director, Patuxent Institution, 407 U.S. 245 (1972).
[42]360 N.E.2d 312 (Mass. 1977).

cal assessments of the subjects' susceptibility to "treatment" and the subjects' dangerousness? Of equal importance, how comparatively reliable and accurate are alternative sources of information? If clinical personnel are required to arrive at judgments based upon nonclinical information (such as past conduct) and if courts are required to decide whether particular persons come within abnormal offender program criteria on the basis of such information, are the resulting judgments and decisions likely to be more or less reliable and accurate than decisions using the results of participation evaluations? The answers to these questions are by no means clear, yet they are essential to an informed resolution of a number of legal issues raised by abnormal offender programs.

PRIVILEGE AGAINST COMPELLED SELF-INCRIMINATION

A major question presented by abnormal offender programs is the relationship between the programs and the subjects' Fifth and Fourteenth Amendment privilege against compelled self-incrimination. The issue requires careful formulation. It is reasonably clear that in abnormal offender programs as well as in other contexts, a person cannot be compelled to disclose information that would tend to subject the person to liability for a crime of which the person has not been convicted. What is not clear is whether the subject of abnormal offender proceedings can decline to provide information on the basis that doing so would tend to cause the person to be found an abnormal offender and processed or sentenced in a manner more burdensome or intrusive than regular sentencing. This is really a part of a broader unresolved matter raised by criminal sentencing: May a convicted defendant decline to provide information that could not result in additional convictions but might increase the severity of the penalty to be imposed for crimes of which the person already stands convicted? It is important to distinguish from these questions the inquiry as to what procedural devices or rules are desirable or necessary to protect the privilege *if* it is found applicable in the sentencing or abnormal offender context.

The basic issue arises because increased severity of sentence is not literally "incrimination" within the meaning of privilege. On the other hand, it is clear that labels are not determinative. In *In re Gault*,[43] the Supreme Court held that being determined to be a juvenile delinquent was sufficiently akin to criminal conviction that the privilege protected against such a finding, even though delinquency proceedings might be labeled "civil" in nature. The question, then, must be whether increased

[43]387 U.S. 1 (1967).

severity of sentence (or being found an abnormal offender after conviction) sufficiently resembles incrimination to bring it within the privilege and, if so, whether there are overriding policy reasons why the privilege should not be construed so as to protect defendants from having to divulge this sort of information.

McNeil v. Director, Patuxent Institution[44] raised the question of the right of one referred for examination as a potential defective delinquent to decline to participate in the evaluation. The Supreme Court, however, declined to reach the question on the basis that McNeil had never been provided with a hearing on the propriety of his refusal to participate and to raise his potential privilege and therefore it was inappropriate to reach the issue for the first time at the appellate level. Lower courts generally have found the privilege inapplicable. The Michigan Supreme Court so held in *People v. Chapman*,[45] decided in 1942, and the Illinois Supreme Court reached the same result in *People v. English*,[46] decided in 1964. *Haskett v. State*,[47] decided by the Indiana Supreme Court in 1970, reached the opposite result. Stressing that the end result of sex psychopath proceedings could be incarceration for life (while criminal conviction for the crime at issue in the case carried a maximum penalty of 60 days in jail time), the court held that use of Haskett's responses in sex psychopath proceedings would constitute "incrimination" and he could not be compelled to cooperate with court appointed examiners. None of the decisions, however, carefully examine the competing considerations bearing upon the issue.

In some situations, at least, being found an abnormal offender creates a risk of deprivation of liberty substantially greater than that which would otherwise be possible. Loss of liberty was emphasized in *Gault* as a primary factor bearing on the question whether juvenile delinquency proceedings were "incriminatory." The position that a determination of whether a person—to use the facts of *Haskett*—engaged in "peeping," which permits 60 days of detention, is incrimination, but that no incrimination is involved in proceedings to extend the period of potential incarceration from 60 days to life seems absurd on its face.

But there may be overriding reasons why the privilege should not be read as applicable to abnormal offender proceedings. Perhaps the primary possibility is that if effectively implemented, the privilege frequently would prevent participant evaluations by clinical personnel and thereby deprive the programs of information essential to their fair and

---

[44]407 U.S. 245 (1972).
[45]301 Mich. 584, 4 N.W.2d 18 (1942).
[46]31 Ill.2d 301, 201 N.E.2d 455 (1964).
[47]255 Ind. 206, 263 N.E.2d 529 (1970).

accurate administration. The merits of this argument depend on a number of factual matters. Would the privilege prevent such evaluations? This might depend on how it was implemented, that is, whether and to what extent warnings concerning the privilege are required and whether counsel is required during the evaluation to protect the privilege. The privilege may be waived in all or most cases; to the extent it is waived, its impact would be minimal. Or, even if application of the privilege resulted in reduced availability of clinical judgments based on participation evaluations, this may not adversely affect the administration of the programs. Decisions based on other sources of information may be equally or more accurate and reliable.

Similar concerns must be explored concerning the applicability of the privilege at the judicial hearing. If it applies, the subject would be entitled to decline to testify on the issue of his status. It is unclear what if any impact this would have. Are defendants frequently required to testify at such hearings? When defendants are compelled to testify, how useful or essential is the information provided? It is at least arguable that the prosecution's inability to require the defendant to testify at the judicial hearing is unlikely to have any substantial impact upon the quality of the decisions at those hearings.

The issue is affected by the Supreme Court's recent decision in *Estelle v. Smith*,[48] although the impact of that case is not entirely clear. In *Smith*, a psychiatrist interviewed the defendant before trial without notice to his lawyer and without warning the defendant that he had a right to refuse to answer the questions posed. After the defendant was convicted of capital murder, a sentencing hearing was held to determine whether to impose death or life imprisonment; under the state's capital sentencing law, the major issue at this hearing was the future dangerousness of the defendant. The psychiatrist testified that the defendant was dangerous, basing this conclusion largely on the defendant's account of the crime given during the interview and the defendant's failure to express remorse concerning the incident. The Supreme Court held that this use of the results of the interview violated the defendant's Fifth Amendment rights. It rejected the state's claim that no Fifth Amendment issue was raised because the evidence was used only to determine punishment and not to establish guilt, noting the "gravity of the decision" made at the capital sentencing hearing. It then concluded that the Fifth Amendment protects a defendant against having to testify personally at such a hearing and also against the use at such a hearing of statements elicited from him during a custodial psychiatric interview conducted without first

[48]101 S.Ct. 1866 (1981).

warning him that his statements might be used against him at such a hearing and that he had a right to remain silent and then obtaining his consent to the interview.

It is unclear whether the Supreme Court will apply *Smith* to situations in which mental health professional testimony is used, not to obtain a penalty of death, but rather to establish that the defendant is an abnormal offender. Conceptually, the situations seem indistinguishable. If the Fifth Amendment protects a defendant against being compelled to provide testimonial evidence to be used to subject him to a more severe penalty this protection would not seem to be limited to cases in which the greater severity means death rather than life imprisonment. But in *Smith* the Court did emphasize the gravity of the life-and-death decision, and it ultimately may conclude that the gravity of other dispositional decisions—such as the determination of whether a defendant is an abnormal offender—is sufficiently less to render the Fifth Amendment inapplicable. If *Smith* is found to apply, testimony based on information elicited during a court-ordered custodial interview would not be admissible in an abnormal offender proceeding unless, prior to the interview, the subject was informed that the results of the interview might be used in this manner and that he had a right to remain silent. Further, the subject's voluntary consent to the interview, given such warnings, would have to be proven.

Smith also held that during the postindictment interview at issue in that case the defendant had a Sixth Amendment right to the assistance of counsel. Further, it concluded that this was violated by failing to inform the defendant's attorney of the pending interview, thus depriving the defendant of an opportunity to utilize the help of counsel in making the decision as to whether or not to submit to the interview. Again, it is unclear whether the Court will limit this holding to situations in which life-or-death is at issue. If it does not, however, testimony based on an interview conducted after the defendant has been formally charged with a serious crime will be subject to more stringent requirements than are applicable to testimony based on an earlier interview. In the postindictment interview situation, the state will have to show that the defendant was assisted by his attorney in making the decision as to whether to participate in the interview or, in the alternative, that the defendant made a knowing and intelligent waiver of this right to the assistance of counsel. But even if this aspect of *Smith* is applied to abnormal offender programs, it is unlikely to lead to a requirement that counsel be present during the actual interview. In *Smith*, the Supreme Court noted that the defendant had not argued for such a right to have counsel present and it cited with approval the statement by the lower court that "an attorney present during the psychiatric interview could contribute little and might seriously disrupt the examination."[49]

PROCEDURES AT THE JUDICIAL HEARING

The required procedural safeguards at the hearing on whether a person is an abnormal offender were addressed in *Specht v. Patterson*.[50] In *Williams v. New York*[51] the Supreme Court had held that in "ordinary" sentencing proceedings due process did not require a formal hearing or any opportunity for the defendant to participate. While "adhering" to *Williams* in *Specht*, the Court declined to extend it to the hearing stage of the Colorado sex offender program, which it characterized as a "radically different situation" than that presented in *Williams*. The Colorado procedure requires the court to determine specifically whether the person, previously convicted, either constitutes a threat of bodily harm to members of the public or is a habitual offender and mentally ill. Thus what is involved, the Supreme Court reasoned, is not merely the sentencing stage of the prior criminal proceeding but an entirely new proceeding requiring new findings of fact. Despite its emphasis on prevention, this new proceeding is "criminal" in nature, the Court held, and as a result:

> Due process . . . requires that [the subject] be present with counsel, have an opportunity to be heard, be confronted with witnesses against him, have the right to cross-examine, and to offer evidence of his own. And there must be findings adequate to make meaningful any appeal that is allowed. (386 U.S. at 610)

Specht establishes a firm requirement of substantial procedural requirements at the hearing, but the numerous technical requirements of state law permit an almost unlimited number of additional issues to be raised. For present purposes, only a few additional matters, that is, matters not resolved by *Specht*, will be noted.

Jury Trial

In a number of states, persons subject to abnormal offender proceedings have a right to jury trial on the question of whether they come within the statutory criterion. As the recent decision in *State v. Wilmoth*[52] illustrates, where no such right exists by statute, courts generally have

[49]101 U.S. at 1877 n. 14, quoting Estelle v. Smith, 602 F.2d 694, 708 (5th Cir. 1979).
[50]386 U.S. 605 (1967).
[51]337 U.S. 241 (1949).
[52]22 Wash.App. 419, 589 P.2d 1270 (1979).

been unwilling to find such a right in either the state or federal constitution. In *Humphrey v. Cady*,[53] however, the Supreme Court indicated that such a right might exist, in some jurisdictions, because of the requirement of equal protection. Under the Wisconsin sex offender procedure at issue in *Humphrey*, a defendant has no right to jury trial. Under Wisconsin "civil commitment" procedure, however, a proposed patient has a right to trial by jury. In *Humphrey*, the defendant argued that to grant proposed patients in civil commitment proceedings a right to jury trial but to deny that same right to the subjects of abnormal offender proceedings violated equal protection. The lower court had dismissed the claim without a hearing. The Supreme Court reversed, on the ground that the claim was substantial enough to warrant an evidentiary hearing. The Court's language made clear that a proper subject of inquiry at that hearing would be whether there is a meaningful difference between civil commitment and abnormal offender proceedings that permits the distinction that Wisconsin draws between them:

> Commitment for compulsory treatment under the Wisconsin Sex Crimes Act appears to require precisely the same kind of determination [as does civil commitment], involving a mixture of medical and social or legal judgments. If that is so (and that is properly a subject for inquiry on remand), then it is proper to inquire what justification exists for depriving persons committed under the Sex Crimes Act of the jury determination afforded to persons committed under the Mental Health Act.... [A] justification for the discrimination might be sought in some special characteristic of sex offenders, which may render a jury determination uniquely inappropriate or unnecessary. (405 U.S. at 510, 512)

Following the Supreme Court decision, however, Humphrey was released for reasons unrelated to the decision and no further litigation took place. The hearing on the merits of the claim, then, never was held despite the high court's holding.

Humphrey requires consideration of the same question that is posed by the policy issue of whether jury trials should be made a part of abnormal offender proceedings. It can be argued that an abnormal offender proceeding involves issues of the same sort as civil commitment and, indeed, as the trial of criminal guilt or innocence and, as a result, jury trial is equally appropriate. All involve on their face determinations of questions of fact. But in addition all necessarily involve some sort of community judgment of an "ethical" sort: Is the situation presented really the sort that justifies the significant step of commitment, conviction, or identification of the subject as an abnormal offender? To the extent that the proceeding involves this nonfactual community standard issue, jury

[53] 405 U.S. 504 (1972).

trial is especially appropriate because it poses the question to those best equipped to answer it, members of the lay community.

On the other hand, *Humphrey* suggests that something about abnormal offender proceedings might be unique enough to justify dispensing with jury trial. It is difficult to speculate as to what this might be. Perhaps it can be argued that the sorts of impairment, the dangerousness issue, and treatability questions that are placed in issue in abnormal offender programs are uniquely within the realm of clinical expertise and therefore resolution of the issues by a judge rather than a jury is appropriate. But it is hard to see how in this way abnormal offender proceedings differ from civil commitment, where many of the same matters are obviously at issue. Perhaps the argument boils down to whether the most appropriate comparison is between abnormal offender programs and civil commitment with its frequent right to jury trial or between such programs and run-of-the-mill criminal sentencing, where jury trial usually is not provided.

Precision Required of Expert Testimony

It seems clear that in abnormal offender proceedings, the courts have and will continue to place tremendous reliance on expert testimony by clinical personnel. This raises the question of the degree of precision and certainty that must characterize the expert testimony before that testimony will suffice to support a finding that a person is an abnormal offender.

The issue was raised in the Massachusetts case of *Commonwealth v. McHoul*.[54] During the defendant's service of a prison term imposed in 1967 for assault with intent to rape, proceedings were begun to have him declared a sexually dangerous person. Evidence was introduced as to a 1962 conviction for breaking and entering with intent to commit rape. Two psychiatrists testified in support of the petition. One expressed the view that there was a "strong propensity" for repetition of the defendant's conduct. The other testified that there was "a likelihood" of future violent behavior and "reason to expect" that the defendant would repeat some sort of violent sexual crime. Neither would make a definitive, categorical statement concerning the defendant's future behavior. On appeal, the defendant urged that unless the experts were willing to testify, based on adequate support, that the subject was within the statutory criterion, a finding that he was a sexually dangerous person was unsupported by adequate evidence.

[54]360 N.E.2d 316 (Mass. 1977).

The court rejected the argument. The ultimate question in abnormal offender proceedings, the court noted, is a legal and not a psychiatric one. Psychiatric testimony may be probative of the issue but "it is not conclusive." Therefore, it is not necessary that the expert witnesses specifically testify that they are convinced by the appropriate burden of proof that the defendant is within the statute.

The decision seems appropriate. To have the sufficiency of the evidence depend on the witnesses' choice of phraseology would, of course, be absurd. Moreover, the court is unquestionably correct that the issue is for the court and should not be delegated—formally or informally—to expert witnesses. But arguably the court gave insufficient significance to the witnesses' unwillingness to be more affirmative in their views. The degree of certainty or specificity that should be required must be determined in light of what is currently possible given the state of the predictive art. No brief can be made for requiring greater certainty or specificity than is ever possible by conscientious and skilled clinical practitioners who are aware of and sensitive to the debate concerning the value of clinical predictive testimony. But in those cases where such experts are unwilling to be as specific or as certain as they are in other cases, this should certainly be considered as weighing against a conclusion that the standard of proof has been met.

Standard of Proof

A major procedural question left open in *Specht* is whether at abnormal offender proceedings the prosecution must prove "beyond a reasonable doubt" that the subject is within the statutory criterion or whether some lesser standard is appropriate. In *People v. Burnick*,[55] decided in 1975, the California Supreme Court held that in mentally disordered sex offender proceedings the state and federal constitutions required proof beyond a reasonable doubt. Three years earlier, the United States Supreme Court dismissed *certiorari* as improvidently granted in *Murel v. Baltimore City Criminal Court*,[56] thereby avoiding the question of whether due process required proof beyond a reasonable doubt in defective delinquency proceedings under the Maryland statute. Justice Douglas dissented in *Murel*, urging that proof beyond a reasonable doubt be required.

In *In re Winship*,[57] the Supreme Court held that due process requires,

---

[55] 14 Cal.3d 306, 121 CAL.REPTR. 488, 535 P.2d 352 (1975).
[56] 407 U.S. 355 (1972).
[57] 397 U.S. 358 (1970).

in juvenile delinquency proceedings, that the child be proved beyond a reasonable doubt to be a delinquent. But in 1979, in *Addington v. Texas*,[58] the Court held that in civil commitment proceedings proof beyond a reasonable doubt is not required. Considering especially the nature of the issues in civil commitment proceedings, proposed patients' interest in avoiding improper commitments was held adequately served by a requirement of no more than "clear and convincing" evidence. This is an intermediate standard that imposes a somewhat higher requirement than is applied in usual civil litigation where the standard of proof requires only a "preponderance" of the evidence.

A major consideration in resolving the standard of proof question is whether the result of the abnormal offender determination is, in its impact on the subject, significantly similar to that of a finding of guilt in a criminal case. Since convicted defendants may be sentenced to confinement in the absence of a determination that they are abnormal offenders, the determination may not mean the difference between freedom and loss of liberty. For those offenders whose crimes carry high penalties, it may not substantially increase the length of possible incarceration. But for other offenders, whose crimes carry lesser penalties, a determination that the person is an abnormal offender may increase substantially the length of incarceration to which the person is subject. In *Burnick*, the court also emphasized the stigma of being determined psychologically abnormal and weighed this quite heavily in determining that the criminal standard of proof should be applied.

Several considerations that were influential in *Addington*, however, suggest that proof beyond a reasonable doubt will not be required as a matter of federal constitutional law. In *Addington*, the Court stressed that civil commitment proceedings, unlike delinquency proceedings, are not a "punitive" exercise of state power. It is arguable that abnormal offender programs are rehabilitative and perhaps preventive but—like civil commitment proceedings—not punitive. On the other hand, it seems clear that some punitive motivations affect abnormal offender proceedings and it is difficult to find less punitive motivation in them than exists in juvenile proceedings.

But perhaps more important, the Court in *Addington* stressed the nature of the issues in a civil commitment proceeding. Unlike a criminal trial—which the Court characterized as presenting "a straightforward factual question"—civil commitment proceedings involve questions of diagnosis and dangerousness. These require an evaluation of the "mean-

[58]441 U.S. 418 (1979).

ing" of facts "which must be interpreted by expert psychiatrists and psychologists." Given the state of the art in which these persons have expertise, the Court concluded, a requirement that a person be shown beyond a reasonable doubt to be within the criterion would be unrealistic. Interestingly, the California court in *Burnick* gave exactly opposite effect to the state's argument that the predictive nature of the sex offender determination justified relaxing the burden of proof upon the state. When considered in light of developing skepticism concerning the validity and reliability of clinical diagnoses and predictive judgments, the predictive nature of the task reinforced the court's inclination to require proof beyond a reasonable doubt. The unreliability of the information used increased, in the court's view, the need for a high standard of proof to assure against inaccurate prediction.

Addington reduces the likelihood that the Supreme Court will require, as a matter of federal due process, proof beyond a reasonable doubt in abnormal offender proceedings. This, however, still leaves open state constitutional issues and imposes no barrier to requiring proof beyond a reasonable doubt as a matter of legislative judgment. The most perplexing part of the analysis is the significance to give to the increasingly recognized defects in clinical evaluations. Does this mean that the burden of proof should be relaxed so as to avoid an impossible requirement? Or does it demonstrate an increased danger of unreliable determinations that demands a higher burden of proof as a preventive measure? Since a number of states have imposed the higher standard as a matter of state law, experience under these programs should be of value in determining whether such a standard unrealistically hinders an abnormal offender program or provides a potentially useful barrier to unjustified commitments.

RIGHT TO TREATMENT (AND PRISON TRANSFERS)

Perhaps the most significant right, or potential right, of abnormal offenders during the period of retention in abnormal offender programs is the right to treatment. This right may exist as a matter of federal (or state) constitutional law, or it may be recognized as a matter of statutory interpretation. If it exists, the obvious question is the nature and quality of treatment to which the offenders are entitled. The right also poses special problems when abnormal offenders may be transferred to an institution or unit that is "correctional" in nature.

The argument that abnormal offenders have a federal constitutional right to treatment draws heavily on the civil commitment analogy

(Spece, 1980). The leading development of the position that civilly committed mental patients have a right to treatment is the opinion of the intermediate appellate court in *Donaldson v. O'Conner*.[59] In that opinion, Judge John Minor Wisdom developed two theories on which patients could be said to have a "right to receive such individual treatment as will give [them each] a reasonable opportunity to be cured or to improve his mental condition." Those patients committed pursuant to the state's *parens patriae* power to act on behalf of impaired citizens must be provided treatment or their detention will amount to an arbitrary exercise of governmental power proscribed by the due process clause. Under the second theory, no distinction is drawn among patients on the basis of the nature of the commitment. In civil commitment proceedings, the state abandons a number of generally applicable limitations on the power to detain persons, most importantly the requirements that detention be in retribution for a specific offense, that it be limited to a fixed term, and that it follow a proceeding where fundamental procedural safeguards are observed. Where the state abandons these limitations, the subjects must be afforded a *quid pro quo* to justify the commitment, and the *quid pro quo* most appropriate in the civil commitment process is the provision of the promised treatment.

Whether civilly committed patients have a constitutional right to treatment was left unclear by subsequent litigation in *Donaldson*. On further appeal, the United States Supreme Court held[60] that the case did not actually present the question of right to treatment and thus left the existence of such a right an open question. Chief Justice Burger filed a concurring opinion in which he developed his view that no such federal constitutional right does or should exist.

Even if Judge Wisdom's view were to prevail in regard to civilly committed patients, it is not clear that abnormal offenders would fall within those entitled to treatment under either of his theories. Detention of abnormal offenders is arguably an exercise of the state's police power authority to protect its citizens rather than its *parens patriae* responsibility for impaired persons, so the first theory may be inapplicable. Under the second theory, it is by no means clear that the state has sufficiently abandoned the traditional limitations on the detention power to give rise to a duty to provide a *quid pro quo*. Detention under abnormal offender programs is usually in response to conviction for a specific offense. But the provision of separate procedures for those found "abnormal" suggests that the detention of such persons rests in part on their "status" and is

[59]493 F.2d 507 (5th Cir. 1974).
[60]422 U.S. 563 (1975).

not entirely a retributive response to the offense. To the extent that commitment rests on such a "status," the arguments for a right to treatment are strengthened.

In some jurisdictions, abnormal offender programs do dispense with the maximum term otherwise applicable, so the second limitation stressed in *Donaldson* is arguably abandoned. This would not hold true, of course, in those jurisdictions that provide a maximum term for abnormal offender commitments as well as penal sentences. Given the mandate of *Specht v. Patterson*,[61] it is at least arguable that abnormal offender proceedings must observe "fundamental procedural safeguards." In any case, however, an abnormal offender commitment, unlike a civil commitment, generally follows a criminal conviction in which these procedural safeguards were followed in the determination of guilt or innocence.

The existence of a federal constitutional right to treatment for abnormal offenders was left open in *Humphrey v. Cady*.[62] Among the petitioner's arguments was that due process and equal protection were violated by his detention at a prison unit labeled "Sex Deviate Facility." He urged that no treatment was provided in the prison unit but if he had been civilly committed he would have been admitted to a state hospital where treatment would have been provided. The Court held that this argument could not be summarily dismissed and that the petitioner was entitled to have it seriously considered. But since the petitioner was released for other reasons soon after the Supreme Court's action, there was no follow-up litigation in the lower courts.

Whatever the constitutional doctrine, a right to treatment may well be found in the express or implied language of the statutes providing for abnormal offender programs. In *Rouse v. Cameron*,[63] the Court of Appeals for the District of Columbia Circuit held that civilly committed patients had a right to treatment under the statute providing for commitments. In *Millard v. Cameron*,[64] the court held that "the same principles apply to a person involuntarily committed to a public hospital as a sexual psychopath." And in *State v. Harvey*,[65] the New Jersey courts found a right to treatment in a provision authorizing transfer of abnormal offenders for the purpose of providing for needs and requirements of such persons according to the individual circumstances of their cases.

The significance of a right to treatment, however, depends on how

[61]See discussion in text at note 50, *supra*.
[62]405 U.S. 504 (1972).
[63]373 F.2d 451 (D.C. Cir. 1966).
[64]373 F.2d 468 (D.C. Cir. 1966).
[65]162 N.J. Super. 386, 392 A.2d 1248 (1978), *aff'd*, 170 N.J. Super. 391, 406 A.2d 724 (1979).

treatment is defined. What is the "treatment" to which the abnormal offender, under the right, is entitled, and how will that right be enforced? The answer to this question will clearly determine the extent to which the right to treatment, insofar as it is recognized, will mitigate or obviate some of the objections to abnormal offender programs. Experience with the right to treatment in civil commitment cases suggests that the right might be applied in two different ways.

The first is a system- or institution-wide application that assures that the program will have adequate resources to provide whatever treatment the current state of the art permits. The right may also be interpreted so as to structure the clinical decision-making process in order to maximize the likelihood that appropriate treatment decisions will be made. The prime example of this application of the right in the civil commitment process is *Wyatt v. Stickney*,[66] in which the parties agreed that the right required adequately trained staff in sufficient numbers and an individualized treatment plan for each patient.

The second manner in which the right might be applied is to review the sufficiency of the treatment provided in particular cases. If the right is read as requiring that the treatment provided be certain or at least reasonably certain to change the offender's behavior within a reasonable period of time, it is arguable that the right would greatly minimize the danger of long-term detention of abnormal offenders for purposes insufficiently related to the social interest in modifying their behavior patterns. But the available case law suggests that the right will not be so read. *Millard* held that a person committed under the District of Columbia sex offender program has a right only to "reasonably suitable and adequate treatment." In *State v. Sell*,[67] the Nebraska Supreme Court similarly referred to the right of sexual sociopaths to "such care and treatment as may be appropriate to [them] under the circumstances." It is virtually certain that such standards will require only that the program make efforts that are reasonable given the current state of the clinical art.

The relatively passive nature of the right as it is likely to be developed was demonstrated by *In re Thompson*,[68] arising under the Massachusetts Sexually Dangerous Persons program. Thompson contested the adequacy of his treatment after 13 years of "experience" with the program. Evidence was introduced that he had not responded to conventional psychotherapy but that he would benefit from attendance and participation in biweekly group sessions involving persons of limited mental capacity

[66]344 F.Supp. 373 (M.D. Ala. 1972), *aff'd*, 503 F.2d 1305 (5th Cir. 1974).
[67]202 Neb. 840, 277 N.W.2d 256 (1979).
[68]362 N.E.2d 532 (Mass.App. 1977).

who have not responded to other treatments. He refused to attend these meetings on the ground that this would be "personally inconvenient" and of no value. There was evidence that he was otherwise amenable to changing his behavior. Before the court, Thompson argued that his right to treatment meant a right to treatment that would be effective and, at a minimum, that treatment is necessarily inadequate if the staff is unable to persuade the patient of the wisdom of accepting it. The court rejected this and held that Thompson was entitled only to "treatment that is suitable to him to the best of the staff's collective judgment." Evidence before the court established that this sort of treatment was being provided.

There is some indication that the courts will enforce the right to treatment with special vigor when the offender has been transferred or "sentenced" to a correctional institution. In *State v. Little*,[69] the court held that indefinite incarceration of "untreatable" sexual sociopaths in a correctional environment without efforts at treatment would, on the facts of some cases, make the detention so disproportionate as to constitute cruel and unusual punishment. Noting the statutory directive to "care" for such persons, the court held, "The 'care' of such an individual must include, at the very least, some effort to make the possibility of treatment open to him." Later, in *State v. Sell*,[70] the court made clear that even such "untreatable" offenders were entitled under the statute to "such care and treatment as may be appropriate . . . under the circumstances."

If the offender is placed in the general prison population without an authorized determination of untreatability, it seems certain that the right to treatment will be violated. *State v. Harvey*[71] illustrates this. After conviction for rape, Harvey was processed as a sex offender under the New Jersey procedure. A week after arrival at the treatment center, he committed forcible sodomy of another inmate. He was then transferred to the general prison population at state prison. No provision was made for treatment there. This was held inappropriate and the state was directed to place Harvey at an institution where his right to treatment would be respected. If this was not feasible, the state was directed to formulate such a program as would meet Harvey's needs and implement it at the institution at which he was placed.

Special sensitivity to claims raised by abnormal offenders incarcerated in the general prison population was evident in the most authoritative judicial consideration of abnormal offenders' right to treatment, *Ohlinger v. Watson*,[72] decided by the United States Court of Appeals for

[69]199 Neb. 772, 261 N.W.2d 847 (1978).
[70]202 Neb. 840, 277 N.W.2d 256 (1979).
[71]162 N.J. Super. 386, 392 A.2d 1248 (1978), *aff'd*, 170 N.J. Super. 391, 406 A.2d 724 (1979).
[72]652 F.2d 775 (9th Cir. 1980).

the Ninth Circuit. The plaintiffs were convicted of sodomy on the basis of nonforcible sexual activity with children. Neither was sentenced under the Oregon Sexually Dangerous Persons provision. Both received a life term (rather than the 15-year maximum for sodomy) under a since-repealed statute that authorized an indeterminate correctional term for offenders convicted of sex offenses involving children who were shown to have a "mental or emotional disturbance, deficiency or condition" that rendered them a menace to others. Both plaintiffs had been incarcerated at the state prison. The state conceded that plaintiffs had a constitutional right to treatment, but the court nevertheless addressed the issue. Oregon's decision to sentence plaintiffs under the life sentence provision, the court concluded, constitututed a determination that it has no interest in punishing them but only a continuing interest in treating their abnormality. The determinate incarceration of plaintiffs, then, constitutes cruel and unusual punishment as well as a violation of due process in the absence of treatment. Rejecting the trial court's conclusion that plaintiffs were entitled only to treatment that is reasonable within the budget and time constraints imposed upon the prison, the appellate court held that each plaintiff had a right to such individual treatment as will give him a realistic opportunity to be cured or to improve his mental condition. It concluded that this treatment was not available at the prison and directed the state to transfer the plaintiff to the state hospital (where, the court concluded, treatment was available) or to some other suitable facility.

In summary, although the constitutional nature of a right to treatment is questionable, such a right will often be recognized as a matter of statutory interpretation. Generally, however, the right is unlikely to be interpreted in a manner that will place significant limits on abnormal offender programs. It may mean that an abnormal offender program must be funded and staffed in a reasonably adequate manner, given the current state of the art. Further, individualized treatment plans may well be required. But an offender will be able to show a violation of the right in the offender's own treatment plan only if it can be shown that a plan is "unreasonable" given the current state of the art. This probably embodies the malpractice standard: Only if the treatment program is clearly beyond the bounds of professional discretion and judgment will it be inadequate. But violations of the right will be more readily found when the defendant is incarcerated in a correctional setting and especially if the placement is within the general population. The main impact of the right may well be to deter placement of abnormal offenders in such correctional environments.

Right to Avoid Certain Treatment Techniques

A major question posed by abnormal offender programs in operation is the extent to which, if at all, persons in such programs have a right to avoid being subjected to certain treatment techniques. Most of the case law developing this right has arisen in the context of persons civilly committed. But the fact that the leading—and only—psychosurgery case, *Kaimowitz v. Department of Public Health*,[73] concerned a person committed as a criminal sexual psychopath makes clear that these decisions are likely to find some application in abnormal offender programs as well.

It is important to note that the description of the right as one to "avoid" certain treatment techniques is somewhat misleading. The civil commitment litigation makes clear that courts may take any of a variety of positions with regard to the ability of a treatment program to administer challenged forms of treatment:

- The techniques may be absolutely prohibited, without regard to the patient's effort to "consent."
- The technique may be permitted, but only if the patient is competent and gives an "effective," that is, voluntary and intelligent, consent.
- The technique may be permitted without consent if a court order is obtained on the basis of a determination that justification exists for overriding the patient's objection.
- The technique may be permitted if certain nonjudicial procedures are followed to assure that adequate grounds exist for overriding the patient's objections.
- The court will not review the program's decision to use the technique on the basis that inclusion in the program is itself legal authorization to use the technique without regard to the patient's willingness.

The case law further suggests that courts' positions as to which of these positions will be taken with regard to a particular treatment technique will depend on several factors. One is the perceived "intrusiveness" of the technique. This will depend on the nature and seriousness of risks, side effects, and similar considerations. A second is the demonstrated effectiveness of the technique in dealing with the impairment at issue. A third is the availability of alternatives; a high risk technique of

[73]This unreported decision has been reprinted in a number of sources, *e.g.*, MILLER, F. W., DAWSON, R. O., DIX, G. E., & PARNAS, R. I., THE MENTAL HEALTH PROCESS. Mineola, N.Y.: The Foundation Press, 1976 (page 567).

questionable demonstrated effectiveness is likely to be subjected to even more stringent limitation if it appears that alternative treatment techniques are or may be available.

Three recent cases demonstrate the application of this analysis. *Kaimowitz* placed in issue the use of experimental psychosurgery to modify episodic violent outbursts of the patient, Louis Smith; he had given what purported to be an "informed consent" to the procedure. The trial court held that, despite the consent, the procedure could not be performed because the consent could not be "effective." Examining the effects of detention, the court concluded that an involuntary mental patient has a "diminished" capacity for making decisions about matters such as psychosurgery; but it did rest on the basis that this diminished ability constituted incompetency and prevented such persons, for this reason alone, from giving effective consent. The lack of available information concerning the risks involved, on the other hand, clearly established that the consent could not be informed. The subject's detention as an involuntary patient meant that the consent could not be voluntary. Assumed as apparently so obvious as not to need discussion was the proposition that the state could not use the procedure on Smith regardless of his consent.

Although this was not articulated, the court's stringent standards for evaluating the "intelligence" and "voluntariness" of the consent offered apparently were heavily influenced by several characteristics of the psychosurgery at issue: The procedure was experimental so the risks and benefits were difficult to assess. Insofar as could be determined, however, the procedure appeared to have a high-risk–low-benefit ratio. The need for experimental use of the procedure on institutionalized subjects was low, as animal experimentation and use of it on noninstitutionalized persons had not been exhausted. For procedures subject to less of such objections, the court suggested, the standards for evaluating intelligence and voluntariness would be significantly relaxed.

Rogers v. Okin[74] addressed the right of patients to refuse antipsychotic medication, arguably a less intrusive and less experimental treatment modality with a high effectiveness impact. Recognizing a "qualified right" to refuse such medication, the court held that a patient's refusal can be overridden in a nonemergency situation only after a judicial determination that the patient lacks the capacity to decide whether or not to submit to such treatment. *Price v. Sheppard*[75] involved the right to administer, over a patient's objection, electroconvulsive therapy, a treat-

[74]634 F.2d 650 (1st Cir. 1980). See also, Rennie v. Klein, 462 F.Supp. 1131 (D.N.J. 1978), 476 F.Supp. 1294 (D.N.J. 1979).
[75]307 Minn. 250, 239 N.W.2d 905 (1976).

ment technique arguably between psychosurgery and medication in terms of intrusiveness and demonstrated effectiveness. The court also recognized only a qualified right to refuse: A patient's refusal can be overridden, but only if, after an adversary hearing, a court determines that given all relevant considerations the treatment is necessary and reasonable.

The legal bases for these decisions are somewhat varied. *Kaimowitz* rested initially on state tort law; in the absence of effective consent, the psychosurgery would be a battery under tort (and perhaps criminal) law and therefore impermissible. As alternative grounds, the court relied on what it regarded as patients' first amendment right to be free of any impairment of their idea-generating capacity and the right of privacy found in a combination of the first, fourth, and fifth amendments. *Rogers* and *Price* rested more heavily on the right of privacy, which seems most likely to be the basis for future decisions limiting the availability of treatment techniques.

To what extent are decisions in the civil commitment area likely to be applied to abnormal offenders? The considerations conflict. Abnormal offenders are less likely to be diagnosed as suffering from traditional serious mental illness, so there should be less concern regarding their ability to evaluate whether to submit to a procedure. On the other hand, the long-term nature of many abnormal offender commitments suggests that the *Kaimowitz* court's concern with voluntariness and especially the coercive impact of the promise of release is probably more of a concern here than in civil commitments. Perhaps the need for an opportunity to use even experimental techniques is greater in the abnormal offender context, because there is no equivalent to the generally-effective medications widely used and available for those civilly committed. Most important, however, is the likelihood that the state's interest in overriding the subjects' objections is greater in abnormal offender programs because the subjects' dangerousness has generally been demonstrated. Conviction for a criminal offense, especially a serious one, places the abnormal offender in a different category than the civilly committed patient. This suggests that less of a showing should be required to override patient objections than is demanded in the civil hospitalization context. But this may to some extent be counterbalanced by courts' perception that effective treatment of abnormal offenders is such an illusory goal that requests for authority to treat such offenders do not bring into play a very important state interest.

The impact and development of the right (or the "qualified right") to refuse treatment in abnormal offender programs will depend not only on the content of such rights to refuse as are recognized but also on the treatment techniques that are sought to be used in such programs. It seems clear that psychosurgery will be barred or at least subject to rigorous scrutiny; it probably will be prohibited absent extremely satisfactory consent. The use of medications more "experimental" than the major tranquilizers at issue in *Rogers* will most likely be subject to even more stringent regulation than *Rogers* imposed in the civil commitment context.

Perhaps the major issues will involve aversive conditioning and "behavior modification" programs. In the absence of persuasive evidence of the demonstrated effectiveness of aversive conditioning programs, these seem likely to be effectively barred. In *Mackey v. Procunier*,[76] the use of succinycholine (which paralyzes the respiratory muscles) on prison inmates transferred to a state correctional medical facility was said to raise serious constitutional questions. And in *Knecht v. Gillman*[77] the use of apomorphine to induce vomiting in mental hospital patients was held permissible only under carefully controlled conditions and only if the patient was permitted to withdraw consent at any time, even immediately before the administration of the substance. If even the consent required here was found to be stimulated by the desire to secure release from the program, it is likely that it would be found ineffective to support the aversive conditioning program.

Whether abnormal offender programs will be limited or regulated in their use of behavior modification programs, such as those involving graded tiers offering increasing benefits and privileges to the subjects, is not clear. In *Clonce v. Richardson*,[78] the court addressed the START program (Special Treatment and Rehabilitative Training) used by the United States Bureau of Prisons. Finding that selection for such programs involved a major change in the conditions of confinement, the court held that due process requires at least an administrative hearing on the propriety of selecting particular inmates for it. But since the bureau had voluntarily terminated the program before the litigation ended, the court declined to decide whether federal constitutional doctrines gave inmates any right to avoid participation in such a program if adequate procedures were followed in selecting them. Whether such programs will be permitted over objection will probably depend on the intrusiveness of the deprivations involved in the initial stages, the demonstrated effectiveness of such programs in modifying criminal behavior, and a showing of an absence of equally effective but less intrusive forms of treatment.

---

[76]477 F.2d 877 (9th Cir. 1973).
[77]488 F.2d 1136 (8th Cir. 1973).
[78]379 F.Supp. 338 (W.D. Mo. 1974).

FUTURE OF ABNORMAL OFFENDER PROGRAMS

The future for abnormal offender programs is bleak. The most recent stage of their development has seen repeal of a considerable portion of those programs that were "on the books" several years ago. Abandonment of the programs may to some extent reflect the view that the programs are too vulnerable to legal attack or at least that they are not worth the continual litigation that they stimulate. If this is correct, it is somewhat anomalous. Although courts have been reasonably receptive to arguments concerning the procedures necessary for abnormal offender programs, there has certainly been no judicial willingness to question the basic validity of the programs themselves.

It also seems clear, however, that to a large extent the decline in the availability of such programs reflects disenchantment with the promise of institutional rehabilitation programs and with clinical predictions of antisocial conduct. The determinate sentencing movement is based on the assumption that fairness and accuracy will be best served by focusing on an offender's conduct in determining the severity of punishment. While treatment or rehabilitation might be attempted during a period of institutionalization determined by the severity of the conduct, considerations related to treatment concerns and clinical prediction of offenders' future conduct should not influence the determinate of sentence. This attitude also suggests, of course, the abandonment of abnormal offender programs, which assume the existence of clinical skills in identifying abnormal offenders, determining their dangerousness, and to some extent treating what is assumed to be their underlying pathology.

The shift is effectively illustrated by two publications of the Group for the Advancement of Psychiatry. In 1950, the organization issued a report expressing reservations concerning existing sex offender statutes but urging adoption of legislation permitting indefinite commitment to mental hospitals of convicted offenders found mentally ill or deficient and dangerous (Group for the Advancement of Psychiatry, 1950). Twenty-seven years later, in 1977, another report was issued. It concluded that sex offender statutes "can best be described as approaches that have failed" and urged that such legislation be repealed (Group for the Advancement of Psychiatry, 1977, pp. 935, 941–42). The second report noted the numerous constitutional issues raised by sex offender programs, the unreliability of predictions concerning "sexual dangerousness," the difficulty of providing effective treatment in public institutions, and the ability to provide treatment under regular correctional programs. "The paramount emphasis on community protection is still

prominent" in sex offender programs, the report concluded, but it is perpetuated by "the cloak of therapeutic help." Although the second report
did not address the issue of abnormal offender programs not limited to
the sexually dangerous, implicit in its analysis is similar condemnation
of such more inclusive programs.

It is possible that increasing adoption of determinate sentencing in
criminal cases may affect this trend toward abolition of abnormal
offender programs. If states find that they are faced with offenders who
are perceived to pose a high danger to the community but who must
nevertheless be released at the expiration of a relatively short determinate sentence, pressure may develop for special provisions for selected
offenders. Soon after California's adoption of determinate sentencing,
the state's major mental health groups proposed an exception to determinate sentencing that would permit flexible commitment of some
impaired offenders to a mental health facility (Monahan & Ruggiero,
1980, p. 115). The California legislature passed a bill[79] that would have
permitted the Director of Corrections, during the last year of a defendant's prison term, to seek the defendant's commitment as a "mentally
disordered violent offender." This was defined as "any person who by
reason of a serious mental disease, defect, or disorder represents a substantial danger or harm to others." If the convicting court found the
defendant to be such an offender, it was authorized to commit the defendant to the State Department of Mental Health for a two-year period.
Subsequent two-year commitments could be obtained by a showing that
the defendant remained a mentally disordered violent offender. The
measure was vetoed by Governor Brown on September 29, 1979.

The California proposals would have provided for diversion of
exceptionally dangerous and abnormal defendants from the correctional
system to the mental health system. But if determinate sentencing is perceived to be inadequate to deal with some offenders posing long-term
risks, the resulting pressure may be for longer periods of correctional
detention rather than diversion into the mental health system. The
Model Penal Code[80] provides for extended terms of imprisonment for
defendants found, at the time of sentencing, to be dangerous and mentally abnormal. Similar provisions have been enacted in several states.[81]
Such action would involve a conclusion that predictive skills permit
identification of abnormal and dangerous offenders but not a further

---

[79]CAL. ASSEMBLY BILL No. 29, 1979–80 Regular Session.
[80]MODEL PENAL CODE, Section 7.03(3) (P.O.D. 1962).
[81]HAWAII REV. STAT. § 706-662(3); N.H. REV. STAT. ANN. § 651:6; N.D. CENT. CODE ANN. §
   12.1-32-09(1) (a); ORE. REV. STAT. § 161.725.

conclusion that treatment is available or, if available, can best be provided in a mental health context.

The trend may also be affected by developing evidence concerning the effect of being processed through abnormal offender programs on the length of incarceration. There is reason to expect that this evidence may show that being processed through such programs reduces the amount of time an offender spends institutionalized (Dix, 1976). This may well increase the pressure for abandonment of those programs that have survived until this point. The current political climate does not seem to favor placing public safety at additional risk by reducing periods of institutionalization for convicted offenders. On the other hand, such evidence may not have this effect unless it is accompanied by further evidence that the decreased period of institutionalization increases the risk to the community, that is, that the offenders commit more offenses because of earlier release. If convinced that the programs are being applied carefully, the public may accept that these offenders' abnormality reduces their culpability and that the reduced period of incarceration is therefore appropriate.

Despite the trend toward abolition of abnormal offender programs, a significant number of jurisdictions retain sex offender programs in some form. These retained to some extent show the influence of the same attitude that has resulted in repeal of other programs. There is a trend, for example, toward limiting the commitment to the period of imprisonment that could or has been imposed for the crime of which the subject has been convicted. There is certain to be continuing concern with the breadth and precision of the criteria used in selecting persons for such programs and with procedural issues in their administration, such as the applicability of the privilege against self-incrimination. But perhaps the most significant issues will be the availability of procedural safeguards to assure defendants who perceive the programs to be an advantage fair access to them and the rights of persons in the programs. These rights will include the right to "treatment" and the right to avoid—perhaps under only certain circumstances—some treatment techniques. Use of correctional facilities is likely to be severely limited, especially if the abnormal offender is placed in the general prison population.

In short, abnormal offender programs seem certain to become less and less available. Like indeterminate sentencing in general, these programs are victims of what Francis Allen has called "the decline of the rehabilitative ideal in American Criminal Justice" (Allen, 1978).

One consideration often is overlooked. Experience with schemes for imposing the death sentence on convicted murderers suggests that a diagnosis of personality disorder increases the likelihood of the ultimate penalty (Dix, 1978). Offenders sentenced to death would probably be prime candidates for abnormal dangerous offender programs if such programs were available. Problems posed by at least selective programs of this sort may—if capital punishment develops as the alternative—become less convincing to some of their long-standing opponents.

ADDENDUM

Following preparation of this chapter, the trend towards repeal and abolition of abnormal offender programs noted above (see p. 136) was confirmed by the California legislature's dramatic revision of that state's Mentally Disordered Sex Offender Program.[82] Under 1981 California legislation, the program is no longer a dispositional alternative available to convicting courts. Sex offenders are to be sentenced under generally applicable penal provisions. If imprisonment is ordered, they are to be incarcerated under the supervision of the Department of Corrections. An offender convicted of a sex offense who receives a prison sentence of three or more years and who has no more than two prior felony convictions for nonsex crimes may, at the beginning of the third year prior to release, be transferred to an appropriate state hospital for evaluation. If that evaluation results in a recommendation for treatment and the offender consents, the offender may be transferred to the state hospital for treatment. Insofar as the program survives, then, it is a treatment program available to convicted offenders during the term of their imprisonment. It does not affect the duration of their incarceration. The change seems to have been the result of a widespread perception that the previous program released dangerous offenders too soon (Bower, 1982; Luther, 1981). The legislation contained express statements of the legislature's intention:

> It is the intention of the Legislature that persons committing sex offenses . . . have the opportunity during their time of incarceration to participate voluntarily in a state hospital program. The program shall be established according to a valid experimental design in order that the most effective, newest, and promising methods of treatment of sex offenders may be rigorously tested. . . . [T]he Legislature recognizes and declares that the commission of sex offenses is not in itself the product of mental diseases. It is the intent of the Legislature that persons convicted of a sex offense . . . who are believed to have a serious, substantial, and treatable mental illness shall be transferred to a state hospital for treatment. (West's Cal. Leg. Service 1981, Ch. 928, pp. 3367–68)

---

[82]WEST'S CAL. LEG. SERVICE 1981, Ch. 928.

REFERENCES

Allen, F. A. The decline of the rehabilitative ideal in American criminal justice. *Cleveland State Law Review*, 1978, *27*, 147–156.

Boslow, H. M., & Kohlmeyer, W. A. The Maryland Defective Delinquency Law: An eight year follow-up. *American Journal of Psychiatry*, 1963, *120*, 118–124.

Bower, B. California reverses: Sex offenders to prison. *Psychiatric News*, Feb. 19, 1982, *17* (4), 6.

Cronin, D. J. Defending the sex offender. *Criminal Justice Journal*, 1980, *4*, 85–94.

Dershowitz, A. The role of psychiatry in the sentencing process. *International Journal of Law and Psychiatry*, 1978, *1*, 63–78.

Dix, G. E. Participation by mental health professionals in capital murder sentencing. *International Journal of Law and Psychiatry*, 1978, *1*, 283–308.

Dix, G. E. Differential processing of abnormal sex offenders: Utilization of California's mentally disordered sex offender program. *Journal of Criminal Law and Criminology*, 1976, *67*, 233–243.

Group for the Advancement of Psychiatry. *Psychiatrically deviated sex offenders*. Topeka: Group for the Advancement of Psychiatry, 1950.

Group for the Advancement of Psychiatry. *Psychiatry and sex psychopath legislation: the 30s to the 80s*. New York: Mental Health Center, 1977.

Guthman, D. H. MDSO law: The assumption challenged. *Criminal Justice Journal*, 1980, *4*, 75–83.

Guttmacher, M. S., & Weihofen, H. *Psychiatry and the law*. New York: W. W. Norton & Co., 1952.

Hodges, E. F. Crime prevention by the indeterminate sentence law. *American Journal of Psychiatry*, 1971, *128*, 291–295.

Kittrie, N. N. *The right to be different*. Baltimore: Johns Hopkins Press, 1971.

Kohlmeyer, W. A. The first year of operation under the new Patuxent law. *Bulletin of the American Academy of Psychiatry and the Law*, 1979, *7*, 95–102.

Konecni, V. J., Mulcahy, E. M., & Ebbesen, E. B. Prison or mental hospital: Factors affecting the processing of persons suspected of being "mentally disordered sex offenders." In P. D. Lipset & B. D. Sales (Eds.), *New directions in psycholegal research*. New York: Van Nostrand Reinhold, 1980.

LaFave, W. R., & Scott, A. W. *Handbook on criminal law*. St. Paul: West Publishing Co., 1972.

Levy, S. S. Interaction of institutions and policy groups: The origin of sex crime legislation. *The Lawyer and Law Notes*, 1951, *5* (no. 1), 3–12.

Lewis, C. T. The indeterminate sentence. *Yale Law Journal*, 1899, *9*, 17–30.

Luther, C. Prison terms for sex crimes urged. *Los Angeles Times*, March 31, 1981, Part I, p. 22.

Miller, F. W., Dawson, R. O., Dix, G. E., & Parnas, R. I. *The mental health process*. Mineola, N.Y.: The Foundation Press, 1976.

Monahan, J., & Ruggiero, M. Psychological and psychiatric aspects of determinate criminal sentencing. *International Journal of Law and Psychiatry*, 1980, *3*, 105–116.

Monahan, J., & Wexler, D. A definite maybe: Proof and probability in civil commitment. *Law and Human Behavior*, 1978, *2*, 37–42.

Ransley, M. T. Repeal of the Wisconsin Sex Crimes Act. *Wisconsin Law Review*, 1980, *1980*, 941–975.

Reiblich, G. K., & Hubbard, H. H. An indeterminate sentencing law for defective delinquents, Research Report No. 29, Baltimore: Legislative Council of Maryland, 1950.

Ricker, C. S. A critique of the Defective Delinquency Law. *Law Society Journal*, 1934, *6*, 94–111.

Robinson, L. N. Institutions for defective delinquents. *Journal of Criminal Law, Criminology & Police Science*, 1933, *24*, 352–399.

Schreiber, A. M. Indeterminate therapeutic incarceration of dangerous criminals: Perspectives and problems. *Virginia Law Review*, 1970, *56*, 602–634.

Spece, R. G. Preserving the right to treatment: A critical assessment and constructive development of constitutional right to treatment theories. *Arizona Law Review*, 1978, *20*, 1–47.

Sutherland, E. H. The diffusion of sexual psychopath laws. *American Journal of Sociology*, 1950, *56*, 142–148.

Sutherland, E. H. The sexual psychopath laws. *Journal of Criminal Law & Criminology*, 1950, *40*, 543–554.

Swanson, A. H. Sexual psychopath statutes: Summary and analysis. *Journal of Criminal Law, Criminology & Police Science*, 1960, *51*, 215–235.

Tappan, P. W. Some myths about the sex offender. *Federal Probation*, 1955, *19* (No. 2), 7–12.

6

Mentally Disordered Sex Offenders

JOHN MONAHAN AND SHARON KANTOROWSKI DAVIS

"Sex," Havelock Ellis (1936) once wrote, "is the central problem of life." While it may not be the central problem, it is surely a major problem of law as well. Since Michigan enacted the first "sex psychopath" statute in 1937, the diversion from the criminal justice system to the mental health system of those who have committed a sexual offense and are believed to be mentally disordered has been fraught with controversy. Conservatives have charged that the indeterminate confinement that accompanies such diversion results in offenders being released "too soon," while liberals have argued that it results in a confinement that is "too long." A recent legislative hearing in California, the state with the largest program for mentally disordered sex offenders (MDSOs), heard a staff psychiatrist at an MDSO facility testify that "What I feel quite often is this guy ought to be in the slammer." When a legislator stated that "*any* sex offender is mentally messed up, so let's lock the SOBs up and get on with the business of the people of California," the hearing room resounded in applause (Luther, 1981, p. 22).[1] When the Wisconsin legislature consid-

---

[1]The legislature and governor went on to repeal California's mentally disordered sex offender statute effective January 1, 1982.

JOHN MONAHAN • School of Law, University of Virginia, Charlottesville, Virginia 22901.   SHARON KANTOROWSKI DAVIS • Department of Behavioral Science, University of La Verne, La Verne, California 91750.

ered whether to abolish that state's Sex Crimes Act in 1979 not a single witness could be found to defend the statute. The repeal was passed unanimously by both houses of the legislature and promptly signed by the governor (Ransley, 1980).

Professional, no less than legislative, assessments of MDSO statutes have been highly critical. The most influential report on the subject, by the Group for the Advancement of Psychiatry (1977, p. 935) concluded: "First and foremost, sex psychopath and sexual offender statutes can best be described as approaches that have failed." The Task Panel on Legal and Ethical Issues of the President's Commission on Mental Health (1978, p. 132) likewise reached the conclusion that "Laws authorizing the involuntary confinement of sexual psychopaths and other 'special' offenders (such as 'defective delinquents') should be repealed."

Arguments in favor of and opposed to the existence of MDSO statutes are most often made on philosophic grounds with recourse to anecdotal data. As Ransley (1980, p. 951) notes with regard to the repeal of the Wisconsin statute, "there seemed to have been little if any attempt to . . . support the arguments with facts." This chapter will review the known "facts" about the operation and effects of programs for mentally disordered sex offenders. With a few sporadic exceptions, the studies have all been done within the past five years. The focus here will be on studies of mentally disordered sex offender *programs* and not on "basic" research into the etiology, description, and modification of sexual misconduct (e.g., Dietz, 1978). Brodsky, Hobart, Skinner, Bender, and Polyson (1979) have surveyed 1,472 works in this latter area published in English between 1965 and 1977 and provide a 145-page summary and analysis.

MDSO STATUTES AND THEIR INVOCATION

As of January 1, 1980, 20 states of the United States had mentally disordered offender statutes in effect (*see* Chapter 9). Seven additional states had such procedures in 1978, but had repealed them by 1980. There is, as Dix (*see* Chapter 5) noted, a clear trend toward repeal.

The national survey of Steadman, Monahan, Hartstone, Davis, and Robbins (1982) found that 1,203 persons in the United States were admitted to mental health facilities as mentally disordered sex offenders in 1978, accounting for 6% of all "mentally disordered offenders" admitted (i.e., 6% of the group that includes those not guilty by reason of insanity, incompetent to stand trial, and prison transfers, as well as MDSOs). As far as could be determined, all were male. The average daily census of mentally disordered sex offenders on any given day in 1978 was 2,442. If one assumes that prior years' rates of admission and release were similar to 1978, the average length of institutionalization for mentally disordered sex offenders in mental health facilities was 24.4 months.

Konečni, Mulcahy, and Ebbesen (1980) found that approximately three cases were formally evaluated for MDSO status for each case of MDSO adjudication. Should this figure be generalizable to other states with similar statutes, it would yield an estimate of approximately 3,600 mentally disordered sex offender evaluations nationwide in 1978.

Selection of Offenders for MDSO Processing

Forst (1978) provides a comprehensive "ethnomethodological" picture of mentally disordered sex offender processing in three California counties. He found a uniform perception among both prosecuting and defense attorneys that MDSO commitment resulted in less time spent confined than did a sentence to state prison and more time than a sentence to a county jail. Thus, for a serious sex offense, where the alternative to MDSO processing was state prison, the defense attorney would generally argue in favor of his or her client being an MDSO, with the prosecutor generally opposing it, while for a relatively minor sex offense, where the option was a jail sentence, the defense attorney would argue against MDSO processing and the prosecutor for it.

Virtually all (85 of 87) of the MDSO adjudications in the three counties studied by Forst (1978) were a result of plea bargaining, which proceeded in three phases. In the first, the "reality" of the case is negotiated. Here, what actually happened in the instant offense, the extent of the offender's prior record, and the nature of his "character" (e.g., the presence of mental illness) are established. In the second phase, the quantity and quality of evidence available to sustain the above "facts" are considered. Even when a defense attorney agrees with the prosecutor's assessment as to what actually happened, for example, the defense attorney may point out that the defendant's confession was obtained through unconstitutional means and so could not be admitted were the case to go to trial. Finally, in the context of the facts and the evidence to support them, direct negotiation on the disposition of the case—prison, MDSO facility, or jail—is entered. Forst (1978) thus concludes that MDSO procedures which, in theory, are supposed to present a "civil" *alternative* to criminal processing, are in fact completely *integrated* into the criminal justice process. They provide those who have committed sex offenses with an interstitial disposition—confinement in a mental hospital—that is viewed as a less severe sanction than prison and a more severe sanction than jail. As could be expected from the role requirements, prosecutors try to use this mid-level sanction to raise what otherwise would be a lower (jail) sentence and defense attorneys try to use it to lower what would, if MDSO procedures were not available, be a sentence to state prison.

Whereas Forst (1978) used interviews with the participants and observations of them to arrive at his conclusions, Konečni, Mulcahy, and Ebbesen (1980) relied on a statistical analysis of written documents (psychiatric evaluations, probation reports, etc.) in their study of MDSO determinations. They found that a simple decision-rule could account for who was and who was not found to be MDSO. If a person alleged by one side or the other to be an MDSO had no prior history of sex-related criminal behavior, he was usually diagnosed by the examining psychiatrists as an "antisocial personality" or received no diagnosis at all. The psychiatrists then concluded that these people were not MDSOs and the judge almost automatically agreed and sent them forward for criminal processing. If, on the other hand, the person being considered for MDSO status had a record of prior sex-related crime, he was likely to be diagnosed as a "sexual deviant" and found to be an MDSO by the judge. The authors ironically note that the results of their study support the following "optimal defense strategy" for a person who wishes to be classified as MDSO: "After committing and being arrested for an offense of the type that would likely lead to the suspicion that the defendant were an MDSO, he should (unless, of course, he already has a prior, sex-related criminal record) get himself released on bail and quickly commit additional sex-related crimes. Such behavior would presumably sufficiently impress the psychiatrists and the judge to classify the defendant, after he has been convicted, as an MDSO" (p. 118).

Dix's (1976) study of random samples of MDSOs committed to California's Atascadero State Hospital supports the conclusions of Konečni et al. (1980) in several respects. Of those committed as MDSOs, 85 to 90% had a prior history of sex offenses (although often these had not led to formal conviction). The most significant aspect of the psychiatric reports on which the courts had based their MDSO determination was their reliance on the "social history" that often was obtained from the report of the probation officer. "There was relatively little reliance on 'clinical observations,' that is, characteristics of the defendant or his behavior observed during the examination or interview which might reasonably be expected to have been elicited or noted only by a person with clinical skills" (1976, p. 236).

The studies by Forst (1978), Konečni et al. (1980), and Dix (1976) are the only empirical investigations of the process of adjudicating MDSO status that we have been able to find. Although one focused on the perceptions of the legal participants and the other two on the written record, and therefore are noncomparable in many regards, they converge on the conclusion that MDSO determinations are hardly the "scientific" triage envisioned by the statute. The behavior of the mental health evaluators, according to Konečni *et al.* and Dix is determined largely by the type of the offender's criminal history. The behavior of prosecuting and defense attorneys in MDSO cases, according to Forst, is indistinguishable from their behavior in other criminal cases.

Two other studies, while they did not examine the initial selection process *per se,* provide data that reflect on it. Sturgeon and Taylor (1980) compared 260 MDSOs in California with a group of 122 persons convicted of sexual crimes, not found to be MDSOs, and released from California prisons. Although whites who committed sex crimes were more likely to be found MDSO and sent to a hospital than they were to be found guilty and sent to prison, blacks and hispanics who committed sex crimes were almost twice as likely to be sent to prison as to be found MDSO. The type of sex offense, as well as race, distinguished the MDSO and prison groups. Sex offenses involving children (i.e., male and female pedophilia and incest) comprised 78% of the MDSO group, but only 44% of the prison group.

Although a relationship between the choice of victim (adult or child) and the presence of mental disorder in an offender is not implausible, the racial disparity in MDSO processing may represent an additional selection bias, one found in the following study as well.

Pacht and Cowden (1974) compared 380 persons evaluated by the Wisconsin Department of Health and Social Services and found to be mentally disordered sex offenders with 121 persons evaluated but found not to be MDSOs, who were then given a prison sentence. Results indicated that those found to be MDSO, compared with the group found to be criminal, were older, more often white, had a higher frequency of prior sexual offenses and a higher frequency of both prior mental health treatment and correctional incarceration. The relationship between the MDSO and his victim was closer (e.g., relative or friend) and of longer duration than that between the average "criminal" sex offender and victim. The MDSO also was less likely than the nonMDSO to be drunk at the time of the sex offense.

The "Mental Disorders" of MDSOs

The report of the Group for the Advancement of Psychiatry (1977) noted that the circularity of the relationship between crime and mental illness in MDSO cases "is repeatedly demonstrated by identifying the special sex offender on the basis of minimal evidence of psychopathology and instead inferring mental illness from the act itself" (p. 867). Data from Sturgeon and Taylor's (1980) study of MDSOs in California makes this point rather emphatically. Forty-nine percent of all psychiatric diagnoses given to persons on their admission as MDSO were "sexual deviation" (DSM 302). Thirty-six percent were "personality disorders" (DSM 301). Only 11 of the 260 MDSOs studied received any psychotic diagnosis. Thus, "significant pathology such as psychosis, retardation, or major affective disorders, usually found among mental hospital patients, is uniformly lacking within the sex offender population" (p. 42; see also Dix, 1976, p. 266). Within the "sexual deviation" category, the specific diagnosis simply reflected the commitment offense: rapists were most frequently diagnosed as "aggressive sexuality" (DSM 302.80) and child molesters whose victims were female were most frequently diagnosed as "female pedophilia" (DSM 302.20). "In sum," Sturgeon and Taylor (1980, p. 43) conclude, "these psychiatric diagnoses described the crime for which the patient was committed." The GAP report (1977, p. 936) put it even more strongly. "Sex psychopathy is a questionable category from a legal standpoint and a meaningless grouping from a diagnostic and treatment standpoint."

THE CONTENT OF INSTITUTIONALIZATION

Although there are numerous studies on the process and pitfalls of psychotherapy with mentally disordered sex offenders (Cohen, Groth, & Siegel, 1976; Kozol, Boucher, & Garofalo, 1972), there are few accounts of the actual institutional experience of MDSOs. Most reports focus on one factor: the relative safety of the MDSO in special segregated treatment facilities (or units), compared to the victimization of the offender who committed the same act as an MDSO (e.g., child molestation) but was sent to prison.

Consider the fate of sex offenders (and some other prisoners, such as informers) who were housed in Cellblock 4, the "protective custody unit" of the Penitentiary of New Mexico—a state that does not have a special MDSO statute—when their fellow prisoners rioted and took over the prison in 1980. The prisoners did not have keys to this unit, so they burned their way in with blowtorches. The following account describes what happened next:

> Most of those killed in Cellblock 4 were first brutally beaten and stabbed, then thrown to the floors below. In one case . . . the inmates couldn't get into an inmate's cell, so they cut it open with blowtorches. The inmate

shrieked with fear as the work progressed. When they got the cell open, they beat the man. Then they tied one end of a rope to the cell bars and another around his neck. They threw him off the tier. His neck snapped and he died immediately. They dragged him back up onto the tier and slashed his body with knives.

In another case, the killers were not able to get into a cell, so they threw a can of gasoline on the inmate inside and set him on fire. A reporter later viewed the body. Only a shinbone remained uncharred. At least three victims were killed in this way.

The most grisly murder was that of James Delbert Perrin. Perrin was convicted of raping two little girls and their mother and then murdering all three. Inmates reportedly dragged him out of his protective custody cell and turned a blowtorch on him. As he screamed with pain, they first burned off his genitals and then moved the torch up his body to his face and burned his eyes out. Several other victims, both dead and alive, were reported to have had their eyes either burned or gouged out . (Serrill & Katel, 1980, pp. 12–13)

Priestley (1980) notes similar, if less graphic, harassment of sex offenders in British prisons.

RELEASE FROM MDSO STATUS

Dix (1976) observed professional staff meetings at the major treatment facility for MDSOs in California concerned with the issue of whether treatment had been a success and the offender could be released into the community or whether the offender was still "dangerous" and needed additional confinement. He concluded that eight factors entered into the staff's release decisions:

1. *Acceptance of guilt and personal responsibility for the offense.* It was essential for a judgment that treatment was successful for the offender to admit factual and moral guilt for his offense.
2. *Development of ability to articulate resolution of stress-producing situations.* The successfully treated person was one who could give a reasonable solution to situations that in the past he had mishandled.
3. *Fantasies.* Those who revealed that they still fantasized committing sexual offenses were not viewed as successfully treated.
4. *Behavior during hospitalization.* "Good" adjustment in the hospital was a positive sign of treatment working.
5. *Duration of hospitalization.* Some staff believed that serious sex offenders had to spend a certain "minimum" period in the hospital, regardless of progress in treatment.
6. *Achievement of maximum benefit from hospitalization.* Regardless of the level of outcome achieved, staff were influenced in their deci-

sions by whether they thought the offender would continue to progress in treatment.

7. *Change in community circumstances.* If a change in the environment to which he would be released (e.g., his family) lessened the fear of recidivism the offender was more likely to be viewed as non-dangerous, even though *he* had not changed at all.

8. *Seriousness of the anticipated conduct.* The more serious the staff thought an offender's recidivism might be, the higher the standards they set for judging treatment a success.

One of the most comprehensive descriptive studies published to date on the release of mentally disordered sex offenders is that of Sturgeon and Taylor (1980). They analyzed pre-hospital, hospital, and post-hospital data on 260 MDSOs released from Atascadero State Hospital in California (the same facility studied by Dix, 1976) in 1973, 180 of whom had been released as successfully treated and "not a danger to the health and safety of others" and 80 of whom were "not recovered" and "still a danger to the health and safety of others." While only a "few" of the former patients were sent to prison upon their release from Atascadero to complete their sentence, 68% of the latter group were transferred to prison upon release from the hospital.

A substantially higher proportion of patients released from Atascadero as still dangerous had a history of prior convictions for sex crimes (55%) than was the case for patients released as nondangerous (32%). The groups did not differ in terms of prior convictions for nonsexual crimes against persons (11% and 10% respectively) or property crimes (55% and 58% respectively).

A follow-up five years after release from the hospital showed patients predicted to be dangerous to be twice as likely (24%) to be reconvicted for a sexual crime as patients released as nondangerous (12%), while there was no difference in reconviction rates for nonsexual crimes against persons (11% and 8% respectively) or for property crimes (6% and 8% respectively). Staff recommendations, therefore, were much more predictive of sex crimes than of other forms of criminal behavior. These results are even more impressive when one takes into account that most of the group released as dangerous were sent to prison and therefore were "at risk" in the community for a much shorter period.

Consequences of MDSO Versus Prison Disposition

Sturgeon and Taylor (1980) compared the 260 MDSOs released from Atascadero State Hospital in 1973 with 122 persons convicted of sex crimes, not found to be MDSOs, and released from California prisons in that year. The prison group spent much more time in prison (a mean of 54.0 months) than the MDSO group spent in the hospital (17.7 months for the MDSOs found nondangerous and 21.5 months for those found dangerous). These figures for MDSOs, however, do not include any prison time added at the end of hospitalization. Considering that additional prison time was given to only a "few," of the 180 MDSOs found to be nondangerous and that 32% of the 80 MDSOs found to be dangerous received no additional prison time, the data still indicate that being an MDSO results in drastically less "time confined" than being convicted and imprisoned for a sex offense.

This difference in "time confined" cannot be accounted for by differences in prior convictions for sex offenses, since the prison group, which spent much *more* time in confinement, had *fewer* prior convictions for sex crimes (30%) than either the MDSO nondangerous (32%) or dangerous (55%) groups. The prison group did, however, have more prior convictions for nonsexual personal crimes (and for property crimes) than the MDSOs.

Finally, the post-release reconviction rate for sex crimes (25%) and nonsexual personal crimes (12%) for the prison group was almost precisely the same as that of the MDSOs predicted by the staff to be still dangerous. The prison group, however, was much more likely to be reconvicted for a property crime (24%) than were the MDSO dangerous (6%) or nondangerous (9%) groups.

Sturgeon and Taylor (1980, p. 62) are careful to note that "none of these data prove that any particular treatment is effective in helping to rehabilitate sex offenders" and that "[t]he initial discriminating process which channels offenders either to prison or to the hospital may account for more of the outcome differences between these two groups than differences in treatment."

Ransley (1980) reports a similar, though less drastic difference in total "time confined," between prison and MDSO processing for sex offenders in Wisconsin, prior to the 1979 repeal of the Sex Crimes Act. Persons found to be mentally disordered sex offenders spent, on the average, four to six months less time institutionalized than did persons sent to prison for a sex crime.

RESEARCH PRIORITIES

"It is difficult," Greschler (1980, p. 20) has noted, "to reach any conclusions with regard to an area of the law in which significant changes occur with such profound regularity." If the trend toward repeal of MDSO statutes continues, it will soon be impossible to study them.

Unlike some other procedures for "mentally disordered offenders," such as incompetence to stand trial and the insanity defense, MDSO statutes are not even arguably required by the Constitution. Their enactment or repeal, therefore, are purely questions of legislative *policy*. It is in this policy framework that we believe future research efforts should take place. We see three types of studies that could clarify the choice of whether to maintain or abolish MDSO statutes in the 20 states that have them and of whether to enact or not to enact them in the 30 states that do not now have such provisions.

Confirming the Findings of Existing Research

There are some data currently available to support the following assertions about MDSO programs: (1) they are well integrated into standard criminal justice plea bargaining procedures, rather than being an alternative to these procedures; (2) they are invoked primarily on the basis of a record of prior sexual offenses; (3) there may be a significant racial bias in their application; (4) they are applied to persons for whom serious mental disorder is at best dubious; (5) they may protect the physical safety of institutionalized sex offenders better than imprisonment; and (6) they allow for a shorter period of institutionalization than is the case with imprisonment. What is to be emphasized here is the "softness" of the data base on which these assertions rest. Rarely do more than two studies address a given conclusion. The overwhelming amount of all research on the topic of MDSOs has been done in one jurisdiction (California) and therefore the generalizability of these findings is even more tenuous. Replication of the existing studies, particularly in MDSO jurisdictions outside California, would greatly help to buttress confidence in what is becoming the received wisdom about MDSOs.

Comparative Studies of MDSO and NonMDSO Jurisdictions

We have reviewed some studies that compared MDSO and non-MDSO sex offenders *within* a given jurisdiction in terms of factors distinguishing placement in the two groups. We have found no studies, however, that compared procedures for dealing with sex offenders *between* jurisdictions. How, for example, does the length of time spent institutionalized for a given sex offense differ between California, which has an MDSO law, and New York, which does not? Is the time a sex offender spends in a New York prison more comparable to the time a (nonMDSO) sex offender spends in a California prison than to the time an MDSO spends in a California mental hospital? To the extent that Forst's (1978) finding that the MDSO classification serves as a mid-point on the sanction gradient, one might expect that jurisdictions without this "compromise" verdict would be characterized by greater variability in sanctioning. The comparative approach also could bring information to bear on one of the central arguments of the defenders of MDSO statutes (e.g., Forst, 1978): that sex offenders (especially pedophiles) would be brutalized if housed in the general prison population. Are sex offenders, in fact, more than "regular" prisoners, being subject to harm in the general prison populations of nonMDSO states? Or do nonMDSO states mitigate this problem by providing separate "protective" wards for sex offenders and, if so, how often does this "protection" break down as it did in the New Mexico prison riot?

Comparative studies should take place not only between jurisdictions but between periods when MDSO laws are in effect and periods when they are not in effect in the same jurisdiction. Thus one of the most pressing research priorities, from a policy perspective, is an evaluation of the effects of repealing MDSO statutes in those states that have recently done so (e.g., Wisconsin). Comparing these states before-and-after repeal in terms of (1) plea bargaining procedures; (2) treatment options available for institutionalized offenders; (3) rates of institutional violence; (4) time spent institutionalized; and (5) recidivism of sex offenders would provide precisely the kind of data of which legislators in states contemplating repeal should be appraised.

The Effects of Determinate Sentencing upon MDSO Procedures

There is, in the United States, a growing movement away from sentencing "normal" criminals to prisons for relatively indeterminate periods (e.g., 1 to 10 years) and toward sentencing them for determinate periods (e.g., 5 years). Part of the reason for this change in sentencing policy lies in an abandonment of faith in the efficacy of prison rehabilitation programs and the validity of the predictions of "dangerousness" and recidivism that parole boards rely on to judge when rehabilitation has occurred. Another part relates to the renewed philosophical interest in "just deserts" for past crime as the principal justification for state intervention (e.g., Hirsch, 1976; Morris, 1974).

Although the movement toward determinacy in sentencing is of too recent origin to permit a comprehensive evaluation of its effects, preliminary results may have interesting ramifications for MDSO procedures. One early review of studies on determinate sentencing (Austin &

Krisberg, 1981) has concluded that it has resulted in a substantial increase in the number and length of prison sentences. In California, for example, persons who under the state's old indeterminate sentence law would have been placed on probation or in jail are now more likely to be sent to state prison. First-time felony offenders in Indiana are projected to spend almost 50% more time in prison under determinate than under indeterminate sentencing. Thus, "the most immediate result of determinate sentencing has been severe prison overcrowding and reduced discretionary release power to relieve the situation in a parole" (p. 182).

How will states adapt to this prison overcrowding? One possibility is to "divert" more offenders to the mental health system through MDSO-type statutes. Early in 1979, shortly after California's determinate sentencing law went into effect, the California Conference of Local Mental Health Directors and the California Psychiatric Association issued a joint position statement entitled "The Mentally Disordered Offender." In this document, these two influential groups recommended that the existing state statute allowing the involuntary treatment and (relatively) indeterminate sentencing of mentally disordered sex offenders be abolished. They argued that the MDSO statute is "over-inclusive" since it defines mental disorder so broadly as to include "many social failures who are not seriously mentally ill and for whom no adequate treatment methods now exist," and "discriminatory" since the law "diverts to treatment persons charged with sex offenses while excluding seriously mentally disordered persons charged with other crimes."

The statement hastened to add, however, that it recommended the abolition of the MDSO statute if and only if it were replaced by a "more generic" mentally disordered offender (MDO) statute.

Under the proposed MDO commitment an offender who had "a *substantial* and *treatable* mental disorder (which may predispose him to the commission of dangerous offenses)" (italics in original) could be committed to a mental health facility in lieu of sentencing by a trial judge after conviction for *any* crime, not just a sex crime. This commitment would be "flexible enough to allow outpatient as well as inpatient care," thus effectively reducing the time-in-instituion. Likewise, "The MDO commitment could be used to extend inpatient or outpatient treatment beyond the end of the determinate sentence with full due process if the MDO presents a serious threat of substantial harm to others as now exists with the MDSO and NGRI [Not Guilty by Reason of Insanity]."

Thus, following closely on the heels of California's move to limit the involvement of mental health professionals in sentencing by eliminating the predictions of dangerous behavior they offer, the state's major mental health groups propose (and are offering into legislation) a plan to expand the category of persons exempt from the usual criminal sentencing process altogether, because psychological disorder places their culpability into question. Predictive considerations ("which may predispose him to the commission of dangerous offenses") will then be given more free reign in determining their period of institutionalization, very similar to the way "normal" offenders were treated under the old indeterminate sentence law.

The position of these California mental health groups have many adherents in other states. The manner in which the adoption, repeal, and use of MDSO statutes relates to larger changes in the criminal justice system is one of the most interesting research priorities in the field.

REFERENCES

Austin, J., & Krisberg, B. Wider, stronger, and different nets: The dialectics of criminal justice reform. *Journal of Research in Crime and Delinquency*, January 1981, 165–196.

Brodsky, S., Hobart, S., Skinner, L., Bender, L., & Polyson, A. *Sexual assault: An annotated bibliography and literature review.* Microfilm available from the Institute of Criminology, Cambridge, England, 1979.

Cohen, M., Groth, N., & Siegel, R. The clinical prediction of dangerousness. *Crime and Delinquency*, January 1978, 28–39.

Dietz, P. Social factors in rapist behavior. In R. Rada (Ed.), *Clinical aspects of the rapist*, New York: Grune & Stratton, 1978.

Dix, G. Differential processing of abnormal sex offenders: Utilization of California's mentally disordered sex offender program. *Journal of Criminal Law and Criminology*, 1976, 67, 233–243.

Ellis, H. *Studies in the psychology of sex* (Vol. 1). Philadelphia: F. A. Davis, 1936.

Forst, M. *Civil commitment and social control.* Lexington, Mass.: Lexington Books, 1978.

Greschler, A. California's law concerning mentally disordered sex offenders: A model of ambivalence. *Criminal Justice Journal of Western State University, San Diego*, 1980, 4, 3–30.

Group for the Advancement of Psychiatry, *Psychiatry and sex psychopath legislation: The 30s to the 80s.* New York: Group for the Advancement of Psychiatry, 1977.

Konečni, V., Mulcahy, E., & Ebbesen, E. Prison or mental hospital: Factors affecting the processing of persons suspected of being "mentally disordered sex offenders." In P. Lipsitt & B. Sales (Eds.), *New directions in psycholegal research.* New York: Van Nostrand Reinhold, 1980.

Kozol, H., Boucher, R., & Garofalo, R. The diagnosis and treatment of dangerousness. *Crime and Delinquency*, 1972, 18, 371–392.

Luther, C. Prison terms for sex crimes urged. *Los Angeles Times*, March 31, 1981, pp. 1,22.

Morris, N. *The future of imprisonment.* Chicago: University of Chicago Press, 1974.

Pacht, A., & Cowden, J. An exploratory study of five hundred sex offenders. *Criminal Justice and Behavior*, 1974, 1, 13–20.

Priestley, P. *Community of scapegoats: The segregation of sex offenders and informers in prisons.* London: Pergamon Press, 1980.

Ramsley, M. Repeal of the Wisconsin Sex Crimes Act. *Wisconsin Law Review*, 1980, 941–
975.

Serrill, M., & Katel, P. New Mexico: The anatomy of a riot. *Corrections Magazine*, 1980, *6*,
6–24.

Steadman, H., Monahan, J., Hartstone, E., Davis, S., & Robbins, P. Mentally disordered
offenders: A national survey of patients and facilities. *Law and Human Behavior*, 1982,
6, 31–38.

Sturgeon, V., & Taylor, J. Report of a five-year follow-up study of mentally disordered sex
offenders released from Atascadero State Hospital in 1973. *Criminal Justice Journal of
Western State University, San Diego*, 1980, *4*, 31–64.

von Hirsch, A. *Doing justice: The choice of punishment.* New York: McGraw Hill, 1976.

IV

PRISON–MENTAL HOSPITAL TRANSFERS

7

The Transfer of Inmates to Mental Health Facilities

DEVELOPMENTS IN THE LAW

MICHAEL J. CHURGIN

INTRODUCTION

Issues concerning the rights of persons confined under state authority have been the subject of increasing litigation during the past two decades. Prisoners and mental hospital patients have sought relief from the judiciary for perceived constitutional errors in the manner of confinement and the actual treatment in the institutions. Usually, prisoner and mental health cases are treated separately, each with its own developing body of law. However, there is at least one area of concern that crosses the boundaries: the transfer of an inmate from a correctional facility to a mental health facility.

In 1980, the United States Supreme Court issued a decision in *Vitek v. Jones*[1] and indicated that the transfer of an inmate from a penitentiary to a mental health hospital required, at minimum, an administrative hearing to determine whether such a transfer was appropriate. This decision broke new ground in the area of corrections law since the Court found that at least one change in a prisoner's status, by its very nature,

---

[1] 445 U.S. 480, 100 S.Ct. 1254 (1980).

MICHAEL J. CHURGIN ● School of Law, University of Texas, Austin, Texas 78705.

could not be accomplished without some formal fact-finding procedure. However, the Court's opinion leaves many unanswered questions. In order to place this important decision in perspective, I will first review the basic legal theories and their development in the area, discuss *Vitek*, and indicate the important aspects of the issue that remain to be resolved during the current decade.

Corrections authorities in both state and federal governments have all recognized the presence of inmates whose medical problems cannot be treated within the confines of the normal institutional facility. Special medical units often have been established to handle these cases, or in the alternative, contract arrangements were developed with hospital facilities within the jurisdiction. However, the inmate diagnosed as mentally ill generally was perceived as needing special attention since he or she might require prolonged inpatient services away from the prison population. As a result, almost every state and the federal government enacted special statutory authority permitting the transfer of mentally ill prisoners to mental health facilities. The general rubric was to have a prison doctor certify to the prison director that the individual inmate was mentally ill and required hospitalization in a mental health facility. With the concurrence of the director of the mental hospital, the inmate was then transferred and remained in the mental health facility until such time as the inmate was deemed to be an appropriate subject for the prison once again. The transfer simply was an administrative decision by the prison authorities. No hearing, either internal or external, formal or informal was required.[2]

The change in physical setting usually was not the only difference between confinement in the prison and confinement in the mental health facility. Often, parole consideration would be delayed. Parole boards would take the attitude that an individual deemed unable to function in a prison certainly was not able to function in the community.[3] Good-time credits, which materially reduce a prisoner's length of incarceration, would be denied to the inmate transferred to a mental health facility. If the prisoner were mentally ill, he or she could not conform his or her behavior to that expected of the "normal" inmate.[4] The routine of the mental hospital was often quite different, and occasionally, more

[2]*See* statutory appendix at p. 283.

[3]*See, e.g.*, People ex rel. Slofsky v. Agnew, 68 Misc.2d 128, 326 N.Y.S.2d 477 (1971) and Chesney v. Adams, 377 F.Supp. 887, 894 (D. Conn. 1974).

[4]"Constitutional Rights of the Mentally Ill," Hearings Before the Subcommittee on Constitutional Rights, Committee on the Judiciary, United States Senate, 87th Cong., 1st Sess., pt. 1, pp. 242, 244 (1961) (testimony of James V. Bennett, Director, United States Bureau of Prisons).

restrictive than that found in the prison.[5] As an individual who is both a "criminal" and mentally ill, the person had to be supervised more closely and restricted in his or her activities. Furthermore, having been labelled as mentally ill could result in long-term confinement in a mental health facility. Any misbehavior would be perceived as some manifestation of the mental illness, and there would be a strong possibility that the individual would remain in the mental health facility for the duration of his or her confinement. To protect society from this mentally ill person, who also had been convicted of a crime, jurisdictions enacted special statutes providing for the civil commitment of these individuals once the prison term was over. In many situations, the individual would simply remain in the same facility.[6]

CONSTITUTIONAL CHALLENGES TO TRANSFER STATUTES

Early litigation in this area showed little promise of success for the inmate challenging his or her confinement in the mental health facility. The most prevalent reported challenges involved inmates initially serving sentences in federal prisons who were transferred to a special medical facility at Springfield, Missouri, maintained by the United States Bureau of Prisons as a general medical facility and mental hospital. The United States Court of Appeals for the Eighth Circuit consistently found that the transfer simply was a matter of administrative discretion and raised no legal issue:

> Whether a federal prisoner is a suitable subject for hospitalization at the Medical Center is, in our opinion, a question for the Attorney General and the prison authorities, and not for the courts. It is not conceivable to us that every inmate of the Medical Center who considers himself to be sane and ineligible for confinement in that institution can, by asserting that to be the fact, require the District Court to conduct a hearing and investigation to determine whether the prisoner should be in the Medical Center or in some penitentiary or correctional institution.[7]

The prisoner was in the custody of the attorney general during his period of confinement. The attorney general was charged with providing adequate medical care for each inmate, and the prison officials had decided that the Medical Center was the appropriate place to provide this care. No further inquiry would be required by the courts.

[5]*See, e.g.,* United States *ex rel.* Schuster v. Herold, 410 F. 2d 1071, 1090 (2d Cir.), *cert. denied,* 396 U.S. 847 (1969).
[6]*See, e.g.,* Baxstrom v. Herold, 383 U.S. 107 (1966).
[7]Garcia v. Steele, 193 F.2d 276, 278 (8th Cir. 1951).

This basic view was echoed by other courts as well. In 1965, the United States Court of Appeals for the Ninth Circuit indicated that a California prisoner had presented no substantial federal question in challenging his placement in a mental health facility. It was the judgment of conviction that deprived the inmate of liberty, not placement in a mental health facility. The person was not being held beyond the prison term and any treatment during that term was a matter for prison personnel and not the courts.[8]

These early cases basically were grounded on the due process clauses of the fifth and fourteenth amendments, for federal and state prisoners, respectively, of the United States Constitution. The underlying theory was that a protected interest existed in not being confined in a mental health facility without a hearing. The early courts never even addressed the adequacy of the procedure for the transfer since they held there was no interest at stake worthy of constitutional protection. A new approach, the equal protection clause, developed to challenge the transfer process following the United States Supreme Court decision of *Baxstrom v. Herold*[9] in 1966.

The issue in *Baxstrom* was not the transfer of an individual from a prison to a mental health facility, but the disposition of that individual following the completion of his sentence. Under New York law, there was a special commitment procedure for persons completing sentences at the mental health facility. This civil commitment differed significantly from the procedure followed for all other persons facing civil commitment in that no jury trial was allowed for prisoners. The Supreme Court concluded that the special procedure for persons who already had completed their prison terms violated the equal protection clause. Speaking for the Court, Chief Justice Earl Warren succinctly stated the issue:

> Classification of mentally ill persons as either insane or dangerously insane of course may be a reasonable distinction for purposes of determining the type of custodial or medical care to be given, but it has no relevance whatever in the context of the opportunity to show whether a person is mentally ill *at all*. (emphasis in original)[10]

Thus, New York could not have a special procedure for civil commitment for one class of individuals just because these individuals happened to be transferred from a prison to a mental health facility during the course of serving their sentences. *Baxstrom* opened the door to consideration of new issues. If the ordinary civil commitment procedures

[8]Darey v. Sandritter, 355 F.2d 23 (9th Cir. 1965).
[9]383 U.S. 107 (1966).
[10]383 U.S. at 111.

had to be applied to determine the issue of committability when the person had completed his prison sentence, might not a court also require that the ordinary civil commitment procedure apply as to the issue of committability for a person currently serving his sentence? Any comparison between civil commitment methods utilized for civilians and those utilized for persons confined in prison revealed an almost total lack of procedural safeguards for persons in the latter category.

In 1969, two federal circuits took this judicial leap and applied *Baxstrom* to persons currently serving criminal sentences. Each concluded that where the person was at the time of commitment was irrelevant to the basic issue of committability. It might be relevant to the question of confinement or treatment, but not to the question of whether or not the person should be placed in a mental health facility.

In *United States ex rel. Schuster v. Herold*,[11] the United States Court of Appeals for the Second Circuit in 1969 extended *Baxstrom* to cover persons currently serving criminal sentences and struck down the New York prison to mental hospital transfer statute as being in violation of the equal protection clause. Ironically, New York courts had been one of the few to recognize the special character of a transfer of a prisoner to a mental health facility. In a 1961 decision, the Court of Appeals, New York's highest court, indicated that an inmate could challenge his or her placement in a mental health facility through use of habeas corpus action. The court found that the transfer was a *"further* restraint *in excess* of that permitted by judgment [of conviction and] . . . should be subject to inquiry. . . . [A] denial of a writ, thereby precluding a hearing to test sanity, would be egregious" (emphasis in original).[12] Of course, in a habeas proceeding the burden would be on the inmate to show that he did not require the transfer. Furthermore, there was no automatic procedural rights accompanying any transfer.

Mr. Schuster was a particularly appealing petitioner. According to the court's opinion, he had been transferred to the mental health facility after charging prison officials with corruption. It was alleged that this charge was part of a delusional system and the state continued this position despite the fact that several prison officials had been discharged shortly after Schuster had presented his allegations. Once transferred in 1941, he remained in the corrections mental health facility until ultimately ordered released through federal court intervention. Although eligible for parole in 1948, Schuster was never seriously considered in accord with state practice of not releasing persons incarcerated in the

---

[11]Schuster, n. 5 *supra*.

[12]People *ex rel.* Brown v. Johnston, 9 N.Y.2d 482, 485 (1961).

corrections mental health institution. (Based on the description of Schuster's crime and his pre-transfer prison record, one can reasonably conclude that he likely would have been paroled.) After a tortured series of hearings in state and federal court, Schuster finally achieved success in the Second Circuit.[13]

In a sweeping decision, Judge Kaufman applied *Baxstrom* to Schuster's situation and required that he be given a hearing on the question of committability with "substantially the same procedures ... as are granted to civilians when they are involuntarily committed to a mental hospital."[14] Using Mr. Schuster's case, Judge Kaufman carefully and extensively described the differences of being confined in the prison and the corrections mental health institution, concluding that a wrongfully committed person might well become mentally ill in the latter setting. He buttressed his negative comments concerning the hospital institution by reference to a devastating report prepared by a prestigious bar committee.[15] Having presented Schuster's plight, Judge Kaufman next approached the law and concluded that *Baxstrom* encompassed Schuster's situation:

> *Baxstrom* clearly instructs that the *procedures* to be followed in determining whether one is committable must be unaffected by the irrelevant circumstance that one is or has recently been under sentence pursuant to a criminal conviction. ... Whether a man should be committed for mental illness has no relevance to the place where he happens to be at the time he becomes ill. This much we have surely learned from *Baxstrom* and its progeny. (emphasis in original)[16]

The court never defined what it meant by "substantially" the same procedures utilized in civil commitment other than to suggest that a commitment to a maximum security mental health facility might be appropriate for prisoners.[17] The United States Supreme Court declined review.

Relying on *Schuster*, the United States Court of Appeals for the District of Columbia Circuit judicially rewrote the local prison to mental health facility transfer state in *Matthews v. Hardy*[18] the same year. Noting the stigma of mental illness, the restrictions of a mental health facility, the possibility of longer confinement, and the risk of an improper decision, the court concluded that a judicial hearing was necessary and that

---

[13]*See generally* Schuster, n. 5 *supra*, United States *ex rel.* Schuster v. Vincent, 524 F.2d 153 (2d Cir. 1975).
[14]Schuster, n. 5 *supra* at 1084.
[15]Schuster, n. 5 *supra* at 1078.
[16]Schuster, n. 5 *supra* at 1081, 1083–84.
[17]Schuster, n. 5 *supra* at 1084.
[18]420 F.2d 607 (D.C. Cir. 1969), *cert. denied* 397 U.S. 1010 (1970).

the safeguards provided for in normal civil commitment proceedings would apply to prisoners as well. Once again, the United States Supreme Court declined review.

In two cases decided by the United States Supreme Court in 1972 concerning special mental health statutes, the Court indicated a recognition of the prison to mental hospital transfer issue. In one decision, the Court indicated that the government position claiming that as long as the duration of the confinement was not lengthened, there was no need for procedural safeguards "arguably has force," although *Schuster* and *Matthews* had implied the contrary.[19] However, in a second case, the Court recognized the equal protection argument of *Schuster* and *Matthews*. "[P]etitioners' challenge to the Maryland Defective Delinquency Law should be considered in relation to the criteria, procedures, and treatment that the State of Maryland makes available to other persons, not 'defective delinquents,' committed for compulsory psychiatric treatment."[20]

In recent years, attacks on transfer statutes based on the equal protection clause have been successful in several jurisdictions. A federal court in Connecticut noted that "the doctrine of *Schuster* and *Matthews* is not beyond challenge or criticism," and that the Supreme Court "has studiously avoided deciding the issue," but then proceeded to strike down the Connecticut procedure as unconstitutional.[21] Similar decisions have been rendered by federal courts in Pennsylvania,[22] West Virginia,[23] and Virginia,[24] as well as by the Supreme Court of Washington.[25] In each instance, the decision has been based on the equal protection clause and not the due process clause. The only decision based on the due process clause concerned the Nebraska transfer statute. The federal district court concluded that it could not easily undertake an analysis based on the equal protection clause since during the period in question, the Nebraska civil commitment statute had been found unconstitutional.[26] Since the United States Supreme Court chose to review and basically affirm the Nebraska federal district court, it is worthwhile reviewing the state of due process law and this case in detail.

---

[19]Humphrey v. Cady, 405 U.S. 504, 510–11 (1972).
[20]Murel v. Baltimore City Criminal Court, 407 U.S. 355, 357–58 (1972).
[21]Chesney, n. 3 *supra.*
[22]United States *ex rel.* Souder v. Watson, 413 F.Supp. 711 (M.D. Pa. 1976).
[23]Sites v. McKenzie, 423 F.Supp. 1190 (N.D. W. Va. 1976).
[24]Evans v. Paderick, 443 F.Supp. 583 (E.D. Va. 1977).
[25]Harmon v. McNutt, 587 P.2d 537 (1978).
[26]Miller v. Vitek, 437 F.Supp. 569, 575 (D. Neb. 1977).

DUE PROCESS AND CONFINED POPULATIONS

Beginning in 1972, the Supreme Court had decided a series of cases involving the due process rights of persons convicted of criminal offenses. The first question in due process analysis is one of the nature of the interest involved. Initially, the court concluded that a state statutory system providing for parole gave the person paroled a liberty interest in maintaining his status of conditional liberty.[27] Similarly, an inmate receiving good-time credits under a state regulatory scheme had a liberty interest in not having accrued time forfeited.[28] However, since an individual had no right to be paroled, an inmate had no protected interest in the initial parole decision and accompanying procedures unless the statutory scheme provided for a presumption of parole at a certain time in one's sentence.[29]

The more difficult issues concerned questions of status and placement. The Court found that "solitary confinement" implicated a liberty interest because such a placement "represents a major change in the conditions of confinement and is normally imposed only when it is claimed and proved that there has been a major act of misconduct." This confinement requires "minimum procedural safeguards as a hedge against arbitrary determination of the factual predicate for imposition of the sanction."[30] More recently, the Court summarily affirmed a district court ruling that a California regulation granted prisoners a liberty interest concerning nonplacement in administrative segregation.[31] However, a transfer from a medium to a maximum security institution would not generally implicate any liberty interest:

> [N]o due process clause liberty interest of a duly convicted prison inmate is infringed when he is transferred from one prison to another within the state, whether with or without a hearing, absent some right or justifiable expectation rooted in state law that he not be transferred except for misbehavior or upon the occurrence of other specified events.[32]

Most recently, the Supreme Court has focused on the broad authority of prison officials to regulate inmate life without any judicially mandated restrictions. "[M]aintaining institutional security and preserving internal order and discipline are essential goals that may require limitations or retraction of the retained constitutional rights of both convicted

---

[27]Morrissey v. Brewer, 408 U.S. 471 (1972).
[28]Wolff v. McDonnell, 418 U.S. 539 (1974).
[29]Greenholtz v. Nebraska Penal Inmates, 442 U.S. 1 (1979).
[30]Wolff. n. 28 *supra*, at 571–72 n. 19.
[31]Enomoto v. Wright, 434 U.S. 1052 (1978), *aff'g* 462 F.Supp. 397 (N.D. Calif. 1976).
[32]Montanye v. Haymes, 427 U.S. 236, 242 (1976).

prisoners and pretrial detainees."[33] "The fact of confinement as well as the legitimate goals and policies of the penal institution limit these retained constitutional rights."[34] While there might be "no iron curtain drawn between the Constitution and the prisons of this country,"[35] the current Supreme Court has not been very congenial to the extension of constitutional rights for prisoners.

The Court has been somewhat more receptive to the rights of the mentally ill. However, the rulings have not been exceptional. "[A] state cannot constitutionally confine without more a nondangerous individual who is capable of surviving safely in freedom by himself or with the help of willing and responsible family members or friends."[36] Commitment had been described as "a massive curtailment of liberty,"[37] which requires due process protection. In addition, the Court has recognized that involuntary confinement "can engender adverse social consequences to the individual. Whether we label this phenomenon 'stigma' or choose to call it something else is less important than that we recognize that it can occur and that it can have a very significant impact on the individual."[38] The constitutional significance of this "stigma" is less clear. At least, with regard to juveniles, little in the way of constitutional protection is required other than "a neutral fact finder to determine whether the statutory requirements for admission are satisfied," and that individual must make an inquiry into the juvenile's background, conduct an interview, and have the discretion to refuse admission. Some comparable form of periodic review also must be provided.[39]

The Nebraska statute challenged in *Vitek* was typical of the statutory procedures in existence in states that did not face challenges to their transfer laws at the time of the Supreme Court's 1980 decision. On a finding by a physician or psychologist that an inmate was mentally ill or retarded and that proper treatment could not be given within the correctional facility, the director of the state department was authorized to arrange for treatment in another facility. As in many jurisdictions, one particular mental health facility appears to have been designated as the receiving institution for penal transfers. The inmate remained in this facility until such time as it was determined that the individual could be returned to the penal institution.[40]

---

[33]Bell v. Wolfish, 441 U.S. 520 (1979).
[34]Jones v. North Carolina Prisoners' Labor Union, 433 U.S. 119, 125 (1977).
[35]Wolff, n. 28 *supra* at 555–56.
[36]O'Connor v. Donaldson, 422 U.S. 563, 576 (1975).
[37]Humphrey, n. 19 *supra* at 509.
[38]Addington v. Texas, 441 U.S. 418, 425–26 (1979).
[39]Parham v. J.R., 442 U.S. 584, 606–7 (1979).
[40]Vitek, n. 1 *supra* at 1258–59.

The district court concluded that the inmates had a liberty interest in remaining at a penal institution based on the state statute that required findings of "mental disease or defect" and an inability to be given "proper treatment" in the prison complex prior to a transfer, as well as because the transfer was a most significant alteration in the nature of the confinement. Once the protected interest was found, the district court addressed the question of what procedural safeguards were necessary. The judgment specified seven: written notice, a hearing, opportunity to present witnesses and to cross-examine witnesses with certain limitations, an independent decisionmaker, written fact-finding, availability of counsel (and free counsel, if indigent), and notice of these rights. Nebraska appealed to the United States Supreme Court, which in turn remanded the case for a determination of mootness since the named plaintiffs no longer were confined in the mental health facility. The district court concluded that the case was not moot and the Supreme Court addressed the merits.[41]

VITEK V. JONES

Against this background, the Supreme Court addressed the question of whether the Nebraska statute providing solely for an administrative mechanism to transfer prisoners from correctional to mental health facilities without any hearing was constitutional. As a result of a procedural dispute within the Court, only five members—a bare majority—reached the merits of the case. The only remaining named plaintiff in the litigation currently was confined in a correctional rather than a mental health facility. He previously had been transferred to the mental health facility, but subsequently had been returned to the psychiatric ward of the correctional facility, paroled on condition that he accept psychiatric treatment, and returned to the correctional facility on a finding that he had violated parole. Noting that he remained subject to the transfer procedures, and that he would lose the benefit of having received a judicial determination that there had been "an inadequate basis for declaring Jones to be mentally ill," the majority concluded that the case was not moot.[42] Four members of the Court dissented on the question of mootness, and they would have dismissed the case.[43]

This procedural ruling is quite important in its ramifications for future litigation. It will often be the case that persons subject to a transfer statute who actually are transferred to a mental health facility will be

[41]Vitek, n. 1 *supra* at 1259–60.
[42]Vitek, n. 1 *supra* at 1260.
[43]Vitek, n. 1 *supra* at 1267–70.

returned to the correctional institution by the time of a judicial decision concerning any challenge to the process. In *Matthews,* the inmate faced three transfers during the course of litigation, while, in the Connecticut case, the individual had been transferred twice. In each instance, the inmate was confined in a correctional facility at the time of the actual decision; however, each court concluded that in light of the past practices and the insistence of the government as to its prerogative to transfer the inmate to a mental health facility, the merits of the case should be reached.[44] It is likely that in future litigation, many inmates will be in the same posture. The ruling in *Vitek* will permit future courts to rule on the substantive questions as they arise.

In his opinion for the Court, Justice White followed the approach of the Nebraska federal district court. The first question addressed was "whether the involuntary transfer of a Nebraska state prisoner to a mental hospital implicates a liberty interest that is protected by the due process clause."[45] The Court accepted the lower court's analysis of the state statute and concluded that an inmate had a protected interest in staying in the correctional facility until such time as there was a finding of mental illness and that the inmate could not be treated in the penal complex. Furthermore, the Court concluded that even without the special state statute, an inmate retained a liberty interest in not being sent to a mental health facility.[46] This aspect of the decision is somewhat surprising. Having already concluded that the statute created a liberty interest, there certainly was no necessity to reach out and decide the alternate ground provided by the district court. In so doing, the Supreme Court explicitly recognized the special nature of confinement in a mental health facility and the accompanying stigma that often attends a commitment. Mere confinement, however, might not be sufficient. The district court had found that the inmate was exposed to mandatory behavior modification programs at the mental health facility. Coupled together, the commitment and the forced treatment constituted such a substantial change in the conditions of confinement that a liberty interest was implicated.[47]

The state argued that a transfer to a mental health facility was within the range of treatment alternatives given to a prison administrator to effectuate basic penological goals. Just as an inmate has no say as to which particular correctional facility he may be placed based on an administrator's determination, an inmate could not complain about being housed in a mental health facility. The Court directly rejected this

[44]Matthews, n. 18 *supra* at 612–13; Chesney, n. 3 *supra* at 890.
[45]Vitek, n. 1 *supra* at 1261.
[46]Vitek, n. 1 *supra* at 1261–1264.
[47]Vitek, n. 1 *supra* at 1264.

argument and concluded, "that involuntary commitment to a mental hospital is not within the range of conditions of confinement to which a prison sentence subjects an individual."[48] A state may not so easily classify an inmate as mentally ill and transfer him to a mental health facility.

Having concluded that a protected liberty interest was at stake, the Court now approached the second question: What procedures were due? The state had a simple answer. The certification by the physician or psychologist pursuant to the Nebraska statute would either extinguish the inmate's interest or adequately protect it. The Court, in strong language, rejected this contention, and indicated that it was a question of federal constitutional law and not state law that governed the approach to the question of the procedures to be employed.[49] Similarly, Justice White easily dismissed Nebraska's position that since the basic question was one of mental illness, the issue to be determined was a medical or psychological one and not a legal decision. While accepting the premise, the Justice noted that "[i]t is precisely 'the subtleties and nuances of psychiatric diagnosis' that justify the requirement of adversary hearings."[50] The Court proceeded to adopt six of the seven requirements stated by the district court.

The one exception was the lower court's requirement that legal counsel had to be provided indigent inmates. Four members of the five-man majority were willing to adopt this procedural safeguard as well, concluding that an individual thought to be mentally ill required legal assistance to exercise his constitutional rights in the hearing process.[51] However, Justice Powell, as the fifth vote necessary for a decision on the merits, concluded that "[the] essential requirements are that the person provided by the State be competent and independent, and that he be free to act solely in the inmate's best interest."[52] A licensed attorney was not required. The question not answered was whether an inmate with sufficient means can provide his own counsel.

In sum, the following minimum procedural safeguards are now necessary before an inmate can be transferred from a prison to a mental health facility:[53]

1. Written notice to the prisoner that a transfer to a mental hospital is being considered

[48]Id.
[49]Vitek, n. 1 *supra* at 1262.
[50]Vitek, n. 1 *supra* at 1265.
[51]Id.
[52]Vitek, n. 1 *supra* at 1267.
[53]Vitek, n. 1 *supra* at 1264.

2. A hearing, sufficiently after the notice to permit the prisoner to prepare, at which disclosure to the prisoner is made of the evidence being relied on for the transfer and at which an opportunity to be heard in person and to present documentary evidence is given

3. An opportunity at the hearing to present testimony of witnesses by the defense and to confront and cross-examine witnesses called by the state, except upon a finding, not arbitrarily made, of good cause for not permitting such presentation, confrontation, or cross-examination

4. An independent decisionmaker ("This person need not come from outside the prison or hospital administration")[54]

5. A written statement by the fact-finder as to the evidence relied on and the reasons for transferring the inmate

6. Availability of "qualified and independent assistance,"[55] furnished by the state, if the inmate is financially unable to furnish his own

7. Effective and timely notice of all the foregoing rights

A DIFFERENT ANALYSIS

There are certain striking characteristics of the Supreme Court's decision that require some notice. Not a single lower court case, other than the decision being reviewed, is cited despite the fact that the question of the constitutionality of transfer statutes had been considered by numerous courts including four federal appellate tribunals. While the issue of the constitutionality of the Nebraska statute measured against the equal protection clause was not at issue, the Supreme Court studiously avoided any mention of the evidence amassed in *Schuster* and other decisions concerning the interests at stake in the transfer of an inmate from a correctional to a mental health facility. Nor did the Court cite any secondary materials.

The trial court in *Vitek* explicitly utilized the balancing test developed by the Supreme Court for application in due process cases to determine the appropriate procedural safeguards. While never mentioning the test in his decision, Justice White indicated that the district court had "properly identified and weighed the relevant factors in arriving at its judgment."[56] Applying this same balancing test, in light of the evidence

---

[54]Vitek, n. 1 *supra* at 1265.
[55]Vitek, n. 1 *supra* at 1267.
[56]Vitek, n. 1 *supra* at 1264.

presented in the full gamut of transfer cases, results in the requirement of more procedural safeguards. The items to be weighed are:

> [F]irst, the private interest that will be affected by the official action; second, the risk of an erroneous deprivation of such interest through the procedures used, and the probable value, if any, of additional or substitute procedural safeguards; and finally, the Government's interest, including the function involved and the fiscal and administrative burdens that the additional or substitute procedural requirement would entail.[57]

Basing its decision largely on stigma and compelled treatment, the Supreme Court recognized the substantial interest an inmate has in not being transferred to a mental health facility. There are two additional factors to be considered that tip the scales even more strongly in favor of an inmate staying in a correctional facility. There is a strong likelihood that an inmate transferred to a mental health facility will be paroled later than a like inmate who remained in the correctional facility. As was noted in *Schuster,* the New York Board of Parole would not even consider releasing persons currently at the mental health facility. While a state court has struck down this particular practice,[58] it is not unreasonable to believe that New York illustrated a common phenomenon. (For example, the Connecticut transfer case revealed a somewhat similar practice.[59]) Even without any restriction, it is likely that most parole authorities would be wary of releasing a person from a mental health facility directly to the community. The more common practice would be to wait until the individual had been returned to the correctional institution. For persons unable to post bond and who are confined in jails, a transfer can have disastrous effects. Trials can be delayed significantly and the individual often would be confined for a longer period prior to plea or trial than he would have served if convicted and sentenced on the day of initial incarceration.

In at least one jurisdiction, the District of Columbia, persons transferred are denied good-time credits.[60] As a result, the period of incarceration is significantly longer for these individuals than for other convicted persons. According to the federal statute authorizing transfers to the Bureau of Prisons Facility at Springfield, Missouri, good time is denied all such persons.[61] However, to avoid this harsh result, federal

---

[57]Matthews v. Eldridge, 424 U.S. 319, 335 (1976), quoted in Miller v. Vitek, n. 26 *supra* at 573.

[58]Slofsky, n. 3 *supra.*

[59]Chesney, n. 3 *supra.*

[60]Dobbs v. Neverson, 393 A.2d 147 (D.C. App. 1978).

[61]18 U.S.C.A. § 4241.

inmates often are brought to Springfield under the general federal transfer statute rather than the special mental health provision.[62]

The second factor to be considered in the balancing test is the possibility of a wrong conclusion being reached. The United States Supreme Court only requires that an "independent decisionmaker" be used to determine the transfer issue. This may include an official of either the prison or the mental health system. Giving this discretion to institutional personnel, however structurally isolated, raises the risk of an erroneous decision. If the individual decisionmaker is responsible to either the mental health or corrections department in terms of promotion, salary, and perquisites of office (*e.g.*, work space, secretarial assistance, etc.) and must work with the individual officials of the department who are actually making the recommendation to transfer, the "independent" decisionmaker's role would be compromised. No doubt, the somewhat isolated individual would be better than a system that places absolute discretion in the administrator. A 1978 study undertaken by the New York Department of Mental Hygiene revealed "a tendency to transfer to these facilities those inmates who, whether or not mentally ill, were too troublesome for the prisons."[63] Research undertaken following the Court decision in *Baxstrom* and related lower court decisions releasing large numbers of persons from maximum security mental health institutions showed a significant overcommitment under an administrative rubric. It appeared that many inmates transferred to mental health facilities simply did not belong there.[64] In the area of the civil commitment of children, the Court permitted the decisionmaker to be a hospital psychiatrist.[65] However, in so doing, the focus was on the parent–child (or surrogate parent–child) relationship in the parental decision to seek mental health services and not the commitment itself. In the transfer situation, the Court is requiring adversary hearings; a decisionmaker from either the prison or the hospital does not easily fit into this model.

The alternative to the administrative proceeding is a judicial hearing. On the surface, this might appear as an unduly cumbersome mechanism to handle transfers from a prison to a mental health facility, but on further reflection, it might well be the most effective and efficient mechanism. The seriousness of the civil commitment process for adults has been emphasized in recent court decisions. Every jurisdiction has rejected a purely medical model to determine involuntary commitment

---

[62]18 U.S.C.A. § 4082; correspondence with U.S. Bureau of Prisons on file with the author.

[63]NEW YORK DEPARTMENT OF MENTAL HYGIENE, THE INSANITY DEFENSE IN NEW YORK 120 (1978).

[64]*See, e.g.*, H. STEADMAN & J. COCOZZA, CAREERS OF THE CRIMINALLY INSANE (1974); T. THORNBERRY & J. JACOBY, THE CRIMINALLY INSANE (1979).

[65]Parham, n. 39 *supra*.

for more than emergency situations pending a hearing. Even in the transfer context, the Court explicitly recognizes "the requirement of adversary hearings."[66] Presumably, the judicial system for civil commitment already fits this mode. (This does not ignore the fact that many courts and appointed counsel do not properly carry out their responsibilities under state civil commitment statutes and that an abdication to hospital authorities sometimes is the norm.[67])

In the transfer situation, it is unlikely that the judge would have a tendency to overcommit and to rely too heavily on the judgment of the prison or hospital officials. There is no question as to the release of the individual inmate to the community at large. Rather, the issue is mental illness and whether he should be confined in the mental health facility or the prison.

Focusing the argument on administrative and fiscal burdens does not yield a pro-administrative hearing result. The procedure articulated by the Nebraska district court, and approved by the Supreme Court, is unlike any other procedure within the prison walls. The model chosen is based on the parole revocation process which involves an entirely separate agency with an extensive hearing component.[68] It is unlikely that there will be an overwhelming number of transfer cases. Yet, somehow, a trained independent decisionmaker must be located, a qualified, independent advocate for the inmate must be found, and adversary proceedings must be introduced to the prison populace. This process is in sharp distinction to the disciplinary procedure utilized within correctional facilities. In the transfer context, the contemplated hearing is adversarial, far more complicated, and involves the provision of significant additional constitutional rights. Introducing a new mode of decision making into the correctional facility might well cause disruption of the normal routine.

In contrast, the judicial mechanism is already in place. Adding a few more cases to the docket of the court that handles civil commitments is unlikely to overburden the judicial system. There already exists a system of representation by counsel. It would be unnecessary to train any new cadre of personnel. Presumably, there is a system providing for the statutory appointment of counsel to represent persons facing civil commit-

---

[66]Vitek, n. 1 *supra* at 1265.

[67]*See, e.g.,* Cohen, *The Function of the Attorney and the Commitment of the Mentally Ill,* 44 Tex. L. Rev. 44 (1966); Dix, *The Role of the Lawyer in Proceedings Under the Texas Mental Health Code,* 39 Tex. B.J. 982 (1976); and Andalman & Chambers, *Effective Counsel for Person Facing Civil Commitment: A Survey, A Polemic, and A Proposal,* 45 Miss. L.J. 43 (1974); *see* State *ex rel.* Memmel v. Mundy, 249 N.W.2d 573 (Wis. 1977).

[68]Miller v. Vitek, n. 26 *supra* at 574.

ment. The decisionmaker already has experience with "the subtleties and nuances of psychiatric diagnoses"[69] and would be able to evaluate the need for involuntary commitment. Once you require a full adversary hearing, it is difficult to perceive the reluctance also to require a judicial hearing and counsel.

The Court requires that the inmate be given adequate time to prepare and to consult with an independent, qualified counsel substitute. Speed is not the goal since it is likely that most correctional facilities have some type of short-term holding cells that could be utilized for any type of medical or psychiatric emergency. Since the dockets of commitment courts are kept current and it rarely takes more than a few weeks to move through the entire process, these courts represent an efficient method of handling the transfer cases. Furthermore, it is quite possible that a large proportion of the inmates proposed for transfer will agree to the placement in a mental health facility. (It is the author's experience that this is the case.) Since the number of cases is unlikely to be very large, the development of a new administrative mechanism within corrections facilities is likely to be more cumbersome than it is worth. Utilizing the due process balancing test, a judicial hearing is the more appropriate outcome. It is quite conceivable that states will turn to the judicial model, already utilized in some, rather than create a new system to handle just transfer cases.

The recent President's Commission on Mental Health and other advisory groups that have addressed the question of the prison to mental hospital transfer issue generally have favored a hearing procedure to effect the transfer. In its 1978 report, the commission recommended that "each state should enact a prison–hospital transfer law with procedures to protect those prisoners who become patients." In the accompanying commentary, the commission concluded that the procedural safeguards for a transfer should be "equivalent" to those utilized in civil commitment hearings for the nonprison population.[70]

THE TRANSFEREE

Little attention has been paid to the question of the rights of the inmates while in the mental health facility or the question of the procedure to return the inmate to the correctional facility. In *Vitek*, the Court

---

[69]Vitek, n. 1 *supra* at 1265, quoting Addington, n. 38 *supra*.

[70]1 President's Commission on Mental Health, Report to the President 73 (1978). *See also* National Advisory Commission on Criminal Justice Standards and Goals, Corrections, Standards 2.13 & 16.12 (1973).

noted that the Nebraska mental health facility had a requirement of participation in a behavior modification program. In fact, both the district court and the Supreme Court indicated that it was such types of mandatory treatment that, when coupled with the transfer itself, "constitute the kind of deprivations of liberty that require procedural protections."[71] In another context, the Supreme Court has indicated that a state has the "obligation to provide medical care for those whom it is punishing by incarceration."[72] The right of civil patients to refuse treatment has not been firmly established, although there is some evidence of movement in that direction.[73] However, it is possible that courts would conclude that prisoners transferred according to a proper adversary procedure lose some of their rights to be free from intrusions on personal security.

The "right" to remain at the mental health facility or to return from the mental health to the correctional facility has rarely been the subject of litigation. There are two reported cases, each reaching an opposite result.[74] It is likely that today courts would treat this decision as one committed to the discretion of the administrators. Presumably, the initial transfer to the mental health facility would be conducted in accord with the procedures announced in *Vitek*. The decision to return the inmate basically would be a medical one just as the decision to terminate any commitment. The only remedy would be if the decision making was done in an arbitrary and capricious manner. The constitutional right concerning medical care for inmates is limited. Correction officials may not show "deliberate indifference to serious medical needs of prisoners."[75] The only appellate court that has addressed this standard in the psychiatric context declared that the standard is "medical necessity and not simply 'a desirable' treatment."

> [An inmate] is entitled to psychological or psychiatric treatment if a physician or other health care provider, exercising ordinary skill and care at the time of observation, concludes with reasonable medical certainty (1) that the prisoner's symptoms evidence a serious disease or injury; (2) that such disease or injury is curable or may be substantially alleviated; and (3) that the potential for harm to the prisoner by reason of delay or the denial of care would be substantial.[76]

---

[71]Vitek, n. 1 *supra* at 1262.

[72]Estelle v. Gamble, 429 U.S. 97, 103 (1976).

[73]*See, e.g.*, Rogers v. Okin, 478 F.Supp. 1342 (D. Mass. 1979), *affirmed in part, vacated in part* 634 F.2d 650 (1st Cir. 1980), *vacated*, 162 S. Ct. 2442 (1982); Rennie v. Klein, 476 F.Supp. 1294 (D. N.J. 1979); In re K.K.B., 609 P.2d 747 (Okl. 1980).

[74]*Compare* Burchett v. Bower, 355 F.Supp. 1278 (D. Ariz. 1978) with Cruz v. Ward, 558 F.2d 658 (2d Cir. 1977) (with a strong dissent by Kaufman, the author of Schuster).

[75]Gamble, n. 72 *supra*.

[76]Bowring v. Godwin, 551 F.2d 44, 47, 49 (4th Cir. 1977).

The burden would be quite difficult for any inmate to meet. Great deference would be given to the medical authorities. An inmate has no vested interest in staying at the mental health facility; after all, it was to the prison that he was sentenced.

REMAINING ISSUES

Vitek was the first pronouncement of the United States Supreme Court on the issue of transfers from a correctional to a mental health facility. Many aspects of the issue remain undecided. Perhaps, the most basic concerns the applicability of the equal protection clause to the transfer process. As indicated earlier, the major transfer cases decided by lower courts prior to *Vitek* never really addressed the due process clause issue.[77] Rather, the transfer procedure was compared to the civil commitment procedure and found wanting. Jurisdictions were ordered to match "substantially" the general civil commitment procedure. The viability of these decisions is now in question.

The district court in *Vitek* never directly addressed the equal protection issue, although it strongly hinted that its analysis would have been somewhat more restrictive than that employed by *Schuster* and other courts:

> Even under an equal protection analysis, the ultimate question of the propriety of differentiating procedures for prisoners and nonprisoners probably depends upon a weighing of the factors discussed in this opinion regarding due process. Whether the Nebraska legislature ultimately decides to use a procedure for transferring prisoners to a mental hospital that differs from that for committing nonprisoners must be left to the good judgment of the legislature, remedied only by constitutional strictures.[78]

How similar are prisoners and nonprisoners when the basic question is committability to a mental health facility? Did *Schuster* overread *Baxstrom* in concluding that where you are at the time of the commitment is irrelevant to the committability issue? Even if it is appropriate to compare prisoners to nonprisoners for commitment purposes, the actual procedures employed may be different. "Substantially" the same might simply mean the seven rights articulated in *Vitek*. After all, the Supreme Court has indicated in recent years that the "retained constitutional rights" of inmates are quite restrictive. The basic protections of the civilian commitment procedure might well be pared down to conform with

---

[77]*See* text accompanying notes 13–25.
[78]Miller v. Vitek, n. 26 *supra* at 575.

"the legitimate goals and policies of the penal institution." It is unlikely that the Supreme Court would expand the list of rights announced in *Vitek* simply by reference to a different clause of the Constitution.

It is one thing to conclude that you must have a hearing to be transferred from a correctional to a mental health facility. What if the transfer is simply between two correctional institutions, one of which is essentially a hospital facility? Probably, whether the facility is under the jurisdiction of the department of mental health or the department of corrections makes little difference. It is the nature of the institution itself that has constitutional significance. There is, however, a broad grey area. Where the institutions are all within the corrections framework, will a court be willing to go behind the reason given for a transfer? The named plaintiff in *Vitek* had been confined in a psychiatric wing of the penal complex. No one argued that this implicated a liberty interest. If a corrections department has its own medical facility, it is likely that the court would have to be presented with substantial information concerning the differences between life in a "normal" prison unit and the medical facility before finding a protected interest. The mere transfer would not be sufficient; some additional deprivation or "stigma" must be identified.

One consequence of *Vitek* might be increased movement in the direction of the provision of psychiatric services within the corrections facilities themselves. While a transfer might have once been the easy way out for a correctional administrator, in the post-*Vitek* world there are added costs in terms of the new type of hearing required. In addition, the transfer might not be particularly beneficial to the inmate, even the inmate requiring mental health treatment. One study concluded that the transfer "may submerge potential for survival and change."[79] It often has been said that the best place to provide mental health services for the civilian population is one's own community. Similarly, the prison might be the best place to provide mental health services to a convicted individual. The use of on-site treatment might obviate the need for the *Vitek* procedure as long as the inmate is not so isolated from normal prison operations so as to be considered in the equivalent of a separate facility with special increased restrictions.

The line-drawing to determine when a *Vitek* hearing is necessary will be an evolving process. Of course, unless corrections facilities have improved medical staffing, the provision of on-site services will be difficult, if not impossible. The traditional level of all medical care in prisons has not been high and the specialized state mental health unit might be the only option available to provide adequate mental health services

---

[79]THURRELL, HALLECK, & JOHNSEN, *Psychosis in Prison*, J. CRM. L.C. & P.S. 271, 276 (1965).

for at least some inmates. Due process hearings would have to accompany any such transfers. It is quite possible that a dual system will develop of short-term acute care with medication maintenance within the prison and long-term care for the more chronic cases at the specialized mental health facility. Presumably, the greater number of inmates would be treated within the prison facilities.[80]

The one population often ignored in discussions of the transfer issue is the pretrial detainee. The ideal would be the provision of services in the jail facility rather than a transfer to a different location. Any transfer might well result in a delay in trial or plea and would probably lead to confusion of competence to stand trial with the need for mental health services. However, the ideal is not often possible in the nation's jails which usually are dependent on financially-strapped local governments for their funding; this funding rarely includes comprehensive mental health services.[81] The pretrial detainee presumably has even a greater legally cognizable interest in not being transferred to a mental health facility than the convicted inmate. This individual is awaiting trial, has not been convicted, and is being held because of an inability to post bond. A strong argument could be made that the full panoply of rights accorded a civilian faced with civil commitment should apply to the pretrial detainee since there is no sentence of imprisonment. Furthermore, administratively, if only a *Vitek* hearing is held, there might be the necessity of a full commitment hearing shortly thereafter when the criminal charges are resolved and the individual is released or placed on probation. Unless state law bars it, there is no reason to prevent an individual charged with a crime from being committed to a mental health facility under ordinary procedures. The mental health facility, of course, might choose a more restrictive setting than used for other patients since the person is awaiting trial and was not released on his own recognizance. The crucial element for the pretrial detainee is time. There is a real danger of a transfer resulting in a period of being lost in the criminal justice system. Coordination between the mental health facility and the court is a necessity. In addition, there must be an understanding that the need for mental health services does not automatically mean that the individual is incompetent to stand trial.

The standard to be applied in making the determination to transfer has not been identified. Since the person's liberty has already been taken

---

[80]*See generally,* JAMES & GREGORY, *Improving Psychiatric Care for Prisoners,* 31 HOSPITAL AND COMMUNITY PSYCHIATRY 671 (1980).

[81]Two reports by the Comptroller General describe the plight of the nation's jails. See #GGD–80–77, September 15, 1980, and #GGD–78–96, December 22, 1978.

away as a result of the criminal conviction, is it necessary to show "dangerousness" in order to transfer the individual to a mental health facility? Once a proper procedure is utilized and the individual inmate is found to be both mentally ill and in need of some treatment, any other requirement might be superfluous. The Supreme Court hinted as much in *Vitek* by repeated references to the determination required by the Nebraska statute, a finding of mental illness and a benefit in being transferred to the mental health facility.[82] It would appear that once the basic findings are made, the choice of programs and facility to be utilized would be left to the mental health/prison professionals and generally not subject to judicial review.

The Court never discussed the procedural evidentiary standard necessary for the transfer of the inmate from a prison to a mental health facility. In the civil commitment context, the state must meet a burden of clear and convincing evidence.[83] In this area, the relationship of the prisoner to nonprisoner seems close.

> Concededly, the interests of the state in segregating and treating mentally ill patients is strong. The interest of the prisoner in not being arbitrarily classified as mentally ill and subjected to unwelcome treatment is also powerful, however, and ... the risk of error in making the determination required ... is substantial enough to warrant appropriate safeguards against error.[84]

Thus, clear and convincing evidence would appear to be the appropriate standard in the transfer context as well. Of course, much of this discussion is in a vacuum because the Supreme Court has never tied the evidentiary standard to the substantive standard.[85] If the state need only prove mental illness and possible benefit from treatment in the prison to mental health facility transfer context, perhaps the evidentiary burden should be higher than the normal civil commitment context where the state might have to show propensity for dangerousness or a recent overt act in order to justify a commitment.

As noted earlier, the Supreme Court was quite cryptic in its discussion of "the independent decisionmaker" who would be the fact-finder at the transfer hearing. The Court approvingly noted that since this individual could come from either the prison or hospital administration, the trial court had "avoided unnecessary intrusion into either medical or cor-

---

[82]Vitek, n. 1 *supra* at 1265, 1267.

[83]Addington, n. 38 *supra*.

[84]Vitek, n. 1 *supra* at 1264.

[85]*See* MONAHAN & WEXLER, *A Definite Maybe: Proof and Probability in Civil Commitment*, 2 LAW & HUMAN BEHAVIOR 49 (1978), ironically cited by the Supreme Court in Addington.

rectional judgments."[86] It is difficult to imagine how this intrusion can be avoided and still result in a truly independent fact finder. Exactly who fulfills this role is uncertain, and only time will reveal the type of individual assigned the task. Probably, some supervisory medical person will be chosen, such as the chief of medical services of the department of corrections.

The question of legal counsel is also a troublesome issue. In a previous decision, the Supreme Court indicated that legal counsel would not be required in all probation revocation proceedings, but only where factual matters were complex and where the probationer would have difficulty "effectively" presenting his case.[87] Authorities have serious difficulty making these determinations. Some have found it easier to provide counsel in all such situations. Similarly, it might be expected that a state would find it most difficult to locate individuals, who are not lawyers, who can satisfy Justice Powell's requirement that the person be "independent and . . . be free to act solely in the inmate's best interest." He further indicated that "a licensed psychiatrist or other mental health professional" would be preferred.[88] It probably would be most difficult for the state to locate these individuals, especially when the transfer hearings might be conducted at prisons, some distance from population centers. The other question is whether or not a person can provide his own attorney or psychiatrist as his representative if he can afford it. A strong case can be made that it would be unreasonable for the state to restrict an inmate in his selection of representative. The Court has indicated that the transfer hearing is adversarial in nature and that due process requires some assistance for the inmate. Therefore, there is no question as to the intrusion of another party to the proceeding. Courts might well be willing to recognize the right of an individual to have assistance of his own choice as long as he is paying the bill.

One of the conditions necessary for constitutionally satisfactory legal assistance is that the individual "be free to act solely in the inmate's best interest."[89] This "best interest" standard is fraught with problems. Does the representative serve as a surrogate decisionmaker or does this individual carry out the inmate's wishes? The parallel situation is prevalent in most civil commitment proceedings where the role to be performed is often left ambiguous.[90] The basic decision making should be

---

[86]Vitek, n. 1 *supra* at 1265.
[87]Gagnon v. Scarpelli, 411 U.S. 778, 790–91 (1973).
[88]Vitek, n. 1 *supra* at 1267.
[89]*Id.*
[90]*See* Note, *Role of Counsel in the Civil Commitment Process; A Theoretical Framework*, 84 YALE L.J. 1540 (1974).

the province of the inmate and not the representative, similar to free world attorney–client relationships. Otherwise, the inmate is deprived of the advocate he or she needs in this proceeding. The fact that the Court has designated this administrative hearing as "adversary" in nature lends support to placing an obligation on the representative to act as advocate and not as guardian or surrogate decisionmaker.

The Nebraska corrections system contained a psychiatric wing in a penal complex. As a result, any emergency situation presumably could be handled, and the inmate housed in the psychiatric wing pending an administrative hearing to decide the transfer issue. This situation, however, is not universal in American corrections. Often, units are isolated from emergency psychiatric facilities and padded isolation cells or worse might be the only alternative placement pending a hearing unless some type of emergency transfer procedure is permitted. The psychiatric services level in many corrections facilities is quite low.[91]

Most civil commitment statutes permit the emergency hospitalization of persons certified as mentally ill and likely to cause harm to self or others if not immediately restrained.[92] Although the inmate is already isolated and presumably can be kept from causing harm to self or others if not immediately restrained, a holding cell might not be the appropriate setting for the confinement pending the assembly of the machinery necessary to conduct the administrative hearing. A reasonable approach might be an emergency short-term commitment, as provided for in state civil commitment statutes, pending the hearing where holding facilities are not present. The Supreme Court previously has indicated that these emergency commitments pass constitutional muster.[93] Similarly, the emergency transfer pending the hearing would likely be approved.[94]

Every mental health code contains a provision authorizing voluntary treatment in a mental health facility upon application and approval by the requisite mental health official.[95] It might well be advisable to allow such a procedure for the inmate. Voluntary treatment generally is recognized as preferable to involuntary hospitalization. The prison system would benefit by not having to hold the adversary administrative hearing contemplated by the Supreme Court in *Vitek*. Of course, the prisoner could not be the sole decisionmaker. The judgment by the prison officials to turn down such a request would be governed by the broad

---

[91]*See generally,* CHURGIN, *Mental Health Services and the Inmate,* in PRISONERS' RIGHTS SOURCE-BOOK, Vol. 2 (I. ROBBINS, ed.) (1980) at 295–300.

[92]*See* S. BRAKEL & R. ROCK, eds., THE MENTALLY DISABLED AND THE LAW (1971).

[93]Briggs v. Arafeh, 411 U.S. 911 (1973), *aff'g* 346 F.Supp. 1265 (D. Conn. 1972).

[94]*See, e.g.,* Chesney n. 3 *supra.*

[95]Brakel, n. 92 *supra.*

constitutional standard concerning health care which only prohibits "deliberate indifference."[96] Presumably, a decision to treat an individual within the prison complex rather than a mental health facility would be one of medical discretion. Presently, at least one state has such a voluntary procedure for the inmate.

As indicated earlier, the effects of the transfer can be serious. Good-time credits may be lost or not earned, parole opportunities limited, programs restricted, and other deprivations occur. The questions remain as to which differentiations are medically or legally justified and which constitute discrimination against the mentally ill. In one district court decision, a federal judge concluded that the denial of certain workmen's compensation-like payments to persons transferred while providing payments to inmates with other long-term medical conditions was a denial of equal protection.[97] The provisions of the various federal acts related to the handicapped[98] have not been tested in the prison context and their applicability is unknown, although they might indicate "the evolving standards of decency that mark the progress of a mature society" for purposes of eighth amendment "cruel and unusual punishment" analysis.[99]

Lastly, but most important to the inmate, is the question of duration of confinement in the mental health facility. *Vitek* and most statutes provide no guidance. The question of periodic review has received slight attention in mental health litigation.[100] One possible parallel for inmates is the constitutional requirement of periodic review in the case of parental placement of juveniles in mental health facilities. "[A] subsequent, independent review of the patient's condition provides a necessary check against possible arbitrariness in the *initial* admission decision."[101] Presumably, a review by a mental health administrator at the mental health facility at reasonable intervals would satisfy any requirement in the prison context as well. In the appropriate case, the inmate could be sent back to the correctional facility. It is likely that most state mental health agencies have regulations requiring some form of periodic review; some states have more elaborate statutory systems that might apply to inmates. Although everyone would agree that the maximum sentence provides the end point of the period of confinement unless the inmate is then civilly committed, this consensus provides little solace for the inmate; most prisoners are released from confinement long before.

---

[96]Gamble, n. 72 *supra.*
[97]Delafose v. Manson, 385 F.Supp. 1115 (D. Conn. 1974).
[98]*See, e.g.,* 29 U.S.C.A. § 794, 20 U.S.C.A. 401 et. seq., 42 U.S.C.A. § 6001 et seq.
[99]Trop v. Dulles, 356 U.S. 86, 101 (1958).
[100]*See* Fasulo v. Arafeh, 378 A.2d 553 (Conn. 1977), for one of the few cases.
[101]Parham, n. 39 *supra* at 607 n. 15.

As noted earlier, the open questions of parole and good-time credits are the crucial determining factors. For the pretrial detainee who is transferred, the duration is as long as the criminal charge is pending unless returned to jail. Most will have the charges resolved within some relatively short, but often prolonged, period. For the forgotten ones, lost in the system, resort to statutory speedy trial provisions or to the constitutional speedy trial guarantee might be necessary to prod the system to take action.

In *Vitek v. Jones*, the Supreme Court recognized the significance of the issue of the transfer of inmates from corrections to mental health facilities. In answering one aspect of this multifaceted issue, the Court left undecided many significant questions that have been described briefly. During this decade, corrections officials and legislators will have to revise the statutory structure for transfer and it is likely that inmates will challenge the constitutionality of many of these provisions, thus setting the stage for new decisions by courts in this evolving area of law.

8

Prisoners Transferred to Mental Hospitals

JOHN MONAHAN, SHARON KANTOROWSKI DAVIS,
ELIOT HARTSTONE, AND HENRY J. STEADMAN

It is becoming commonplace for the United States Supreme Court to cite social science research when it decides cases of relevance to the criminal justice *(Ballew v. Georgia)*[1] or mental health systems *(Addington v. Texas)*.[2] Against this background, the first thing to strike a social scientist in the *Vitek*[3] prison-to-mental hospital transfer case is that the Court cited not a single piece of psychological or sociological data. This lack of attention to research on "social facts" (Saks, 1980) regarding prisoners who are transferred to mental hospitals bespeaks no general retreat by the Court from the incorporation of social science in judicial decisions. Rather, the more probable explanation is that the justices and their clerks simply could find no relevant empirical data on which to rely. Indeed, in our extensive search for material for this chapter, we have found very few studies directed explicitly at the topic of prison-to-mental hospital trans-

---

[1]Ballew v. Georgia, 435 U.S. 223 (1978).
[2]Addington v. Texas, 441 U.S. 418 (1979).
[3]Vitek v. Jones, 445 U.S. 480, 100 S. Ct. 1254 (1980).

JOHN MONAHAN ● School of Law, University of Virginia, Charlottesville, Virginia 22901.   SHARON KANTOROWSKI DAVIS ● Department of Behavioral Science, University of La Verne, La Verne, California 91750.   ELIOT HARTSTONE ● URSA Institute, Pier 1½, San Francisco, California 94111.   HENRY J. STEADMAN ● Special Projects Research Unit, New York State Department of Mental Hygiene, 44 Holland Avenue, Albany, New York 12229.

fer. We shall, therefore, consider in some detail the results of our own recent national survey (*see* Introduction), as well as an in depth interim study of transfer procedures in six states.

EXISTING STUDIES

We have been able to locate only four studies with data relevant to transfer issues. Gearing, Heckel, and Matthey (1980), in one of the few comprehensive reports of prison–mental hospital transfers, describe the procedure used in South Carolina since 1976 for transferring inmates to a 48-bed psychiatric unit operated by the Department of Corrections. One "contact person" at each state prison was made responsible for referring inmates. The contact people included nurses, wardens, social workers, and chaplains. They initially were instructed to refer for a transfer evaluation any inmate who seemed "fit for a state hospital." The staff of the psychiatric unit "shaped" the contact persons for making transfer referrals the staff believed to be appropriate by discussing any inappropriate referrals with the referral source and explaining the problem.

> If any institution attempted to take advantage of the psychiatric unit by deliberately making inappropriate referrals (e.g., troublesome, acting-out types) or by refusing to accept an undesirable inmate back after psychological treatment had been completed then the institution was punished. This punishment consisted of . . . advising the institution in question that if the situation was not rectified immediately, the . . . psychiatric unit would refuse to accept other referrals from this institution. (p. 850)

Under these contingencies, the authors report that only 6% of all referrals for transfer are inappropriate and that part of this 6% consists of "malingerers" who mimic disordered symptoms to get access to medication. They conclude that "the cost of hiring more highly trained personnel [as referral agents] is not worth the minuscule reduction in the number of inappropriate referrals that would be possible" (p. 854). They seem not to consider, however, the possibility that more highly trained personnel might increase the number of *appropriate* referrals. That is, while untrained wardens and others may indeed be accurately screening out the great bulk of those who would not benefit from transfer, they may be overlooking many other prisoners, with less flagrant symptomology, who would benefit. Indeed, the "shaping" procedure adopted seems much more likely to be effective at screening "out" the wrong kinds of referrals than in screening "in" the right ones. In addition, the technique of blacklisting an institution that refuses to accept back a successfully treated inmate seems to be less a punishment of "the institution" than of the mentally ill inmates in it who are thereby deprived of the opportunity for transfer.

Data from Wisconsin reported by Halleck (1966) provide more indirect support for the appropriateness of prison-to-mental hospital transfer decisions. Half of 60 inmates transferred from the Wisconsin State Prison to the Wisconsin State Hospital for the Criminally Insane had a history of mental hospitalization predating their imprisonment. An additional 20%, while having no history of mental hospitalization, revealed such disordered symptoms that the issue of mental illness had been raised in the probation officer's presentence report. Some of these people were transferred to the mental health facility immediately after their arrival at prison.

Dell (1980), in the only study available for a country other than the United States, examined the process of transferring prisoners from maximum security special hospitals to the open wards of regular National Health Service (NHS) hospitals in Britain. She did not investigate the process by which the prisoners got transferred from prison to the special hospitals in the first instance. Dell found that the regular civil NHS hospitals were very resistant to accepting patients transferred from the special hospitals, despite the fact that the special hospitals automatically readmitted any patient the NHS hospitals wished to return. The waiting period between the time transfer procedures were formally initiated and a placement in NHS hospital was available was a mean of 9.3 months for mentally ill transfers and 17.9 months for the mentally retarded. The NHS hospitals gave many reasons for refusing to accept the transfers. "The impression often conveyed," however, "was that the everchanging string of objections was simply an attempt to make acceptable the basic and uncomfortable truth—that the hospital did not want to take a patient they feared might turn out to be difficult or even dangerous" (Dell, p. 227). The data did not bear out these fears. Of 105 persons transferred from special hospitals to NHS hospitals (two-thirds of whom were originally transferred from prisons), only 7 were returned by the NHS hospitals and only 3 had been prosecuted for criminal acts within two years of the transfer.

The only report on transfers of civil patients *from* mental hospitals to prisons is that of Stelovich (1979). Under Massachusetts' law, male patients can be transferred from the Department of Mental Health to the security hospital operated by the Department of Corrections (Bridgewater State Hospital) "if keeping the patient in the civil facility would create a likelihood of serious harm because of his mental illness, and that his violent behavior constitutes an emergency" (p. 618). These hospital-to-prison transfers increased from 41 in 1974 to "well over 100" in 1978.

Stelovich attributes this increase to the change in state hospitalization policies brought about by deinstitutionalization. Stelovich's survey of the clinical opinions of the civil hospital staff indicated that the transferred patients did indeed require more security than the civil hospitals could provide, but that the majority of the patients "were readily treatable, and that if alternative treatment options had been available, they would not have need to be transferred to a prison" (p. 619).

There are two other large-scale research projects that indirectly relate to these issues. Both (Steadman & Cocozza, 1974; Thornberry & Jacoby, 1979) followed large groups of patients transferred from maximum to regular security hospitals as a result of court decisions finding their detentions violated equal protection rights. Both study groups included many transferred prisoners along with ISTs, NGRIs, and "dangerous" civil patients. Among the 967 *Baxstrom* patients studied by Steadman and Cocozza 67% were transfers and among Thornberry and Jacoby's 586 *Dixon* patients 52% were transfers. Unfortunately these two studies did not separately analyze the data for the transferred prisoners. Steadman and Cocozza (1979) did not since there were not significant statistical differences on the major variables of interest between the transfers and the other groups. Nevertheless, the mixing of groups does not permit direct comparison to the transfer studies mentioned above.

NATIONAL SURVEY

Our mail survey of forensic directors in all 50 states and the federal system found that 10,895 prisoners were admitted to mental health facilities in 1978, and that on any given day in that year 5,158 prisoners resided in mental health units. These figures constitute 54.1% of all "mentally disordered offenders" (i.e., persons incompetent to stand trial, not guilty by reason of insanity, and mentally disordered sex offenders, as well as transfers) admitted to mental health facilities in the United States in 1978, and 36.5% of the census for this group (Steadman, Monahan, Hartstone, Davis, & Robbins, 1982). Data on these admission and census figures are present in Table 1, disaggregated by gender, and by the type of the mental health facility. It can be seen that approximately the same number of people were admitted to, and resided in, out-of-prison mental health units as in-prison mental health units; that the Department of Corrections administered the facility in approximately three out of four transfer cases; and that female prisoners constituted only 4.1% of the admissions and 5.1% of the census of these facilities. This latter figure is slightly in excess of the 4.0% of the 1978 prison census of the United States that was female (Weis & Henney, 1980).

TABLE 1. ADMISSION AND CENSUS OF PRISON–MENTAL HEALTH FACILITY TRANSFERS BY GENDER AND TYPE OF FACILITY, 1978

	Male	Female	Gender unknown	Total
Admissions				
Department of Corrections facilities				
In-prison units	5,061	186	0	5,247
Correctional hospitals	2,381	4	0	2,385
Department of Mental Health facilities				
Maximum security hospitals	1,321	72	50	1,443
Civil hospitals (regular units)	237	99	0	336
Civil hospitals (forensic units)	1,374	85	14	1,473
Private hospitals	10	1	0	11
Total admissions	10,384	447	64	10,895
Census				
Department of Corrections facilities				
In-prison units	2,334	140	0	2,474
Correctional hospitals	1,368	1	0	1,369
Department of Mental Health facilities				
Maximum security hospitals	589	21	42	652
Civil hospitals (regular units)	182	81	0	263
Civil hospitals (forensic units)	364	18	10	392
Private hospitals	7	1	0	8
Total census	4,844	262	52	5,158

If one makes the assumption that prior and subsequent years' rates of admission and release were similar to 1978, it is possible to estimate the average length of stay in these transfer facilities. Dividing the admission figures into the census figures and multiplying by 12 produces an average length of stay in transfer status of 5.7 months. This figure is precisely the same for out-of-prison as for in-prison units. Female prisoners' length of stay differs from male prisoners' length of stay only for transfer for in-prison mental health units, where the female average is 9.0 months and the male 5.5 months.

Not reflected in any of the above figures are the numbers of prisoners in regular prison units who may be receiving "outpatient" mental health care (e.g., voluntary psychotropic medication, counseling from social workers, etc.). At the risk of stating the obvious, in no sense are these figures to be taken as an index of the "true" prevalence rates of mental illness in the prison population of the United States. There were 278,141 persons in United States prisons on the first day of 1978 (Weiss & Henney, 1980). Our survey found that 10,895 of them were transferred to a mental health facility at some point during that year. This is a "transfer rate" of 3.9%. Roth (1980, p. 668), in the leading review of correctional psychiatry, concluded that "approximately 15 to 20% of prison inmates manifest sufficent psychiatric pathology to warrent medical attention. . . . The number of prisoners manifesting psychoses or otherwise severe psychiatric disturbances is, however, considerably less than 20%, probably on the order of 5% or less of the total prison population." The extent to which the "treated" prevalence rate for mental illness among prisoners of 3.9% that we have found is drawn from the "true" prevalence rate of "5% or less" reported by Roth for "psychoses or otherwise severe psychiatric disturbances" is unknown (Monahan & Steadman, 1983).

Our national survey also found great discrepancy among the states in terms of the transfer options made available for prisoners. Table 2 displays the number of states that had each transfer option available for male prisoners, and the number of states in which a given option was the one most frequently used for transfered prisoners. Forensic units within civil mental hospitals were the most popular transfer option, both in terms of the number of states having the option available and the number of states using it as the preferred option. The reason that forensic units within civil mental hospitals ranks first of the six transfer options in terms of the number of states having them and the number of states using them most frequently (Table 2), yet ranks only third of the six options in terms of the number of prisoners transferred to it (Table 1) is that the various types of transfer facilities differ substantially in size. Although only 7 states have special correctional hospitals run by the Department of Corrections, for example, compared with 32 states having

TABLE 2. AVAILABILITY AND USE OF MENTAL HEALTH TRANSFER FACILITIES FOR MALE PRISONERS, 1978

	Number of states with transfer facility	Number of states in which facility is most used transfer option
Department of Corrections facilities		
In-prison facilities	17	12
Correctional hospitals	7	4
Department of Mental Health facilities		
Maximum security hospitals	19	10
Civil hospitals (regular units)	21	2
Civil hospitals (forensic units)	32	22
Private Hospitals	5	0

forensic units in civil mental hospitals, the correctional hospitals tend to be much larger facilities than the forensic units and thus to account for a disproportionate share of the patient population. The relative smallness of forensic units within civil mental hospitals may reflect the relative lack of receptivity on the part of departments of mental health to providing services for convicted offenders.

INTERVIEW RESULTS

To supplement the quantitative information obtained in the national survey, interviews were conducted in six states chosen for geographic diversity and differences in the size of the transfer population.[4] These "transfer interviews" were conducted between October 1980 and January 1981. They focused on three separate issues: (1) the factors that result in inmates being *identified* for transfer to a special mental health setting, (2) the *procedures* involved in transferring these inmates, and (3) the *everyday operations* of the mental health facilities. A total of 98 interviews were conducted by a two-person interview team. This approach was used in order to insure the reliability and validity of written responses. The interviews averaged 90 minutes and ranged from one-half hour to three hours, depending on the respondent's position, knowledge, and communication style. The interview schedule was a standardized, written document covering factual information (e.g., procedural, staffing, and historical issues), along with the attitudes and opinions of the respondents (e.g., evaluations of procedures and programs).

Respondents were selected from both the mental health and correctional fields and included administrators, treatment staff, and security staff at both the mental health facilities *to which* the largest number of mentally ill inmates were transferred, and the state prisons *from which* the largest number of mentally ill inmates were selected. In addition, administrators at the central offices of the DOC and the DMH were also interviewed. At the mental hospitals we interviewed the facility director, the chief of security, two clinical service providers, and a line staff representative, for a total of five respondents. The five persons interviewed at each of the prisons were the warden, the treatment director, two direct clinical service providers, and a correctional officer. At the agency central offices we interviewed four people: each agency's commissioner (or a deputy commissioner), the DMH forensic director, and the DOC mental health treatment director.

We restricted the range of our inquiry to *male* transfers only, since

[4]The six states were New York, Massachusetts, Iowa, Texas, Arizona, and California.

they accounted for 95.8% of all transferred cases. Overall, in 1978 there were approximately 4,850 males transferred in our six states. These transfers clearly were not evenly distributed among the six. One state transferred only 10 inmates each during the year (Arizona); three states transferred approximately 250–300 inmates each (Iowa, Massachusetts, and Texas); one state transferred almost 600 prisoners (New York); and one state actually placed approximately 3,500 inmates into mental health settings (California). Although the size of inmate population clearly had some impact on absolute numbers of inmates transferred (California and New York ranking second and third in the nation on inmate population), it does not explain all the differences. In fact, while Texas has the largest inmate population (over 30,000), three of the five other target states transferred more inmates to mental health facilities. Furthermore, while California has about 7.7% of the country's state prisoners (approximately 24,000 inmates), transfers in California accounted for over 30% of the total number of transfers in the United States. Clearly, different states define "mentally ill" inmates differently and select different placements for those inmates they so define. These differences in policy and philosophy appear to account for a larger percentage of the differences in transfer practices across states than differences in inmate population.

To date, only the interview data for *intraagency* transfers—that is, transfers from the general prison population to a correctional hospital operated by the Department of Corrections—has been partially analyzed (Hartstone, Davis, & Clark, 1981). There is some indication that this form of transfer may be accelerating: three of the six states included in our sample recently had switched the bulk of their transfer cases from facilities operated by the Department of Mental Health to those operated within the jurisdiction of the Department of Corrections.

The three principal findings of the interviews on intraagency transfer procedures were as follows:

First, the decision to transfer an inmate from the general prison population to a correctional mental hospital typically is made either by the prison psychiatrist or as a result of a negotiated settlement between the prison psychiatrist and a psychiatrist at the correctional hospital. Although in some cases there is a requirement of official approval from either the Department of Corrections central office (either the director or a "classification committee") or from a judge, this merely amounted to a "rubber stamping" of the psychiatric decision. As the treatment director at one correctional mental hospital noted, "The psychiatrists make the decision. The judge's approval is just a formality. He depends totally on the expertise of the psychiatrists."

The second pattern observed was that the correctional mental hospitals admitted virtually all inmates officially referred by the state prisons. The hospitals deviated from this norm primarily when they were overcrowded and bed space was at a premium. In those situations, some facilities engaged in the "trading" of inmates; for each new hospital admission an inmate was returned to the prison. For the most part, however, the correctional hospital took, *without a preadmission screening,* those inmates formally referred by the prison psychiatrists. The most obvious reason for the receptivity displayed by the correctional hospital was that, provided there were beds available, these facilities typically had no formal authority to refuse referrals. Once formal action was taken to move an inmate into the hospital, these facilities usually were mandated to accept the inmate. However, the absence of formal intake decision-making power did not preclude the use of informal and indirect actions that served the same ends. Our research found that such facilities could, when they desired, use other channels to keep undesired inmates out of the facility. This was accomplished primarily by quickly discharging and returning those inmates the hospital director felt to be inappropriately transferred. This "right to discharge" appeared to us to be the most important factor causing the observed correctional hospital receptivity. The ability to return to the general prison population those inmates the hospital directors felt to be inappropriately placed enabled these directors to show prison officials which inmates the officials could and could not expect to place into the hospital for a "normal" period of time. The returning of "inappropriate" transfers to the prison ultimately generated prison referrals that satisfied the criteria of the hospital staff. Furthermore, this "right to discharge" enabled hospital directors to know that regardless of how inappropriate an admission might be they always had the right to use their discretion to return the inmate quickly to the general prison population. As one correctional hospital director said, "I recognize that the director of the Department of Corrections can transfer within any of his prisons. If he has a problem he should be able to have access to all the prisons. I have no problem with that as long as I have the right to discharge."

The third major similarity cutting across the states studied was that none of the states appeared to have a due process hearing for those inmates transferred to Department of Corrections' mental hospitals. Although staff in most states said it was very rare that inmates objected to such a transfer, there were no formal procedures set up for those who did object. The clinical director at one correctional mental hospital stated, "The inmate has no say in whether he comes or goes. At the present time he has no right to refuse transfer. We would only put a note in his chart that an objection was made."

RESEARCH PRIORITIES

In an area where so little research exists, almost any study would be as welcomed. We see four generic types of research as essential for completing the descriptive and theoretical study of transfer decisions:

Structural studies: The effect of the *Vitek* decision on the organizational structure of prison-to-hospital transfers is, for us, the most pressing research priority in the area. Given that there is at least some ambiguity as to whether *Vitek* procedural protections apply to transfers to facilities operated by the Department of Mental Health, prison administrators may have an incentive to place facilities under the auspices of the Department of Corrections and thus avoid the cost and time of legal review. Should this occur (and our interview study noted a trend in this direction) the impact of *Vitek* would be severely vitiated. The decision would have the unintended result of switching a line item in the budget of the Department of Mental Health to a line item in the budget of the Department of Corrections. Inmates would be deprived of their "*Vitek* rights" to a hearing. The treatment that these inmate/patients would receive would be provided by staff of the Department of Corrections rather than by the Department of Mental Health. Whether the traditional difference in priorities between these two agencies—security versus care—would affect the quality of services rendered is unknown, but warrants efforts to become known.

As an alternative to simply changing the lines of administrative authority, legislators, anxious to avoid the increased costs occasioned by *Vitek* hearings, might be tempted to write laws *sentencing* certain types of offenders to "civil" mental hospitals in the first place. In this manner, transfer issues would not arise. *Vitek* might, therefore, have the result of increasing reliance on the kind of "abnormal offender" sentencing procedures described by Dix (*see* Chapter 5).

Intake studies: The study reported here presented data from interviews with mental health and criminal justice personnel concerning transfer decisions. While useful, this information clearly needs to be supplemented by the observations of independent observers. Perhaps the primary question in this regard concerns whether and to what extent the prisoners being transferred are *actually* diagnosable as mentally ill (compared with others in the prison population) and whether and to what extent system concerns such as the control of disruptive prisoners, availability of bed space, and interagency rivalry between Departments of Corrections and Departments of Mental Health come into play.

Content studies: Although several studies (e.g., Steadman & Cocozza, 1974; Steadman, 1979; Thornberry & Jacoby, 1979) provide systematic descriptions of the *content* of the hospitalization experiences of the "criminally insane," no study has addressed as its central concern what actually happens to prisoners transferred to mental hospitals. Several famous studies exist of the content of mental hospitalization for civil patients (e.g., Goffman, 1961; Rosenhan, 1973), but none concern what actually goes on in transfer facilities, such as the type and frequency of treatments given and the relations between staff and inmates/patients (e.g., is the relationship of the staff to the transferees more like the doctor–patient relationship in civil hospitals or the guard–inmate relationship in prisons?). Our own impression from visiting several transfer facilities is that they are "hospitals" in name only. In particular, the content of hospitalization as a "prison transfer" in facilities operated by Departments of Correction bear comparison with the content of hospitalization in facilities operated by Departments of Mental Health.

Outcome studies: Finally, the purpose of transferring prisoners to mental health facilities presumably is to cure their perceived mental illness. It would seem imperative to evaluate the extent to which such treatment has the desired effect. If prisoners return from transfer better able to cope with the stresses of the prison "community," there may be therapeutic justification for maintaining or expanding such procedures. If, however, transferred prisoners revert with regularity to their pretransfer (disordered) behavior, the case for transfer is more difficult to make. In this regard, a randomized study in which, from a pool of equally disordered inmates, some were transferred, some were maintained with "outpatient" treatment in regular prison units, and some were untreated, would appear not only feasible but highly desirable.

Should these four types of studies find their way into the social science literature, the Supreme Court should have no difficulty finding footnotes in its next *Vitek*-type transfer case.

REFERENCES

Dell, S. Transfer of special patients to the NHS. *British Journal of Psychiatry,* 1980, *136,* 222–234.

Gearing, M., Heckel, R., & Matthey, W. The screening and referral of mentally disordered inmates in a state correctional system. *Professional Psychology,* 1980, *11,* 849–854.

Goffman, E. *Asylums: Essays on the social situation of mental patients and other inmates.* Garden City, N.Y.: Doubleday, 1961.

Halleck, S. A critique of current psychiatric roles in the legal process. *Wisconsin Law Review,* 1966, *1966,* 379–401.

Hartstone, E., Davis, S., & Clark, P. Prison to mental health transfers post-*Vitek:* A six state survey. Unpublished manuscript, 1981.

Monahan J., & Steadman, H. Crime and mental disorder: An epidemiological approach. In N. Morris & M. Tonry (Eds.), *Crime and justice: An annual review of research.* Chicago: University of Chicago Press, 1983.

Rosenhan, D. On being sane in insane places. *Science,* 1973, *1979,* 250–258.

Roth, L. Correctional psychiatry. In W. Curran, A. McGorry, & C. Petty (Eds.), *Modern legal medicine psychiatry, and forensic science,* Philadelphia: Davis, 1980.

Saks, M. The utilization of evaluation research in litigation. *New directions for program evaluation,* 1980, *5,* 57–67.

Steadman, J., & Cocozza, J. *Careers of the criminally insane.* Lexington, Mass.: Lexington Books, 1974.

Steadman, H., Monahan, J., Hartstone, E., Davis, S., & Robbins, P. Mentally disordered offenders: A national survey of patients and facilities. *Law and Human Behavior,* 1982, *6,* 31–38.

Stelovick, S. From the hospital to the prison: A step forward in deinstitutionalization? *Hospital and Community Psychiatry,* 1979, *30,* 618–620.

Thornberry, T., & Jacoby, J. *The criminally insane: A community follow-up of mentally ill offenders.* Chicago: University of Chicago Press, 1979.

Weis, J., & Henney, J. Crime and criminals in the United States. In E. Bittner & S. Messinger (Eds.), *Criminology Review Yearbook* (Vol. 2). Beverley Hills: Sage Publications, 1980.

V

A COMPENDIUM OF UNITED STATES STATUTES ON MENTALLY DISORDERED OFFENDERS

9

Mental Disability in the American Criminal Process

A FOUR ISSUE SURVEY[1]

ROBERT J. FAVOLE

INCAPACITY TO STAND TRIAL: MENTAL DISABILITY AT TIME OF TRIAL

"Incapacity to stand trial" is a traditional common law concept prohibiting prosecution of those who lack the capacity to understand the criminal proceedings against them and to assist in their own defense. It differs from "not guilty by reason of insanity" in that incapacity at the time of trial does not excuse criminal responsibility. Instead, it recognizes that regardless of one's mental condition at the time of the offense one should not face the criminal justice system while presently incapable of comprehending the proceedings. The traditional ban on proceeding against one

[1]The four tables in this chapter represent a survey of the 50 American states, the District of Columbia, and the federal jurisdictions with regard to four mental disability issues. The first table carries the title *Incapacity to Stand Trial: Mental Disability at Time of Trial*, and is a survey of both case and statutory law. The second table, also covering case and statutory law, is *Excusing Criminal Responsibility: Mental Disability at Time of Offense (Not Guilty by Reason of Insanity)*. The third represents a survey of what are commonly referred to as *Mentally Disordered Sex Offender Statutes*. The fourth is a survey of *Prison to Mental Hospital Transfer Statutes*. Each table is preceded by an introductory narrative of historical information, constitutional mandates, and current trends.

ROBERT J. FAVOLE ● Orrick, Herrington & Sutcliffe, A Professional Corporation, 600 Montgomery St., San Francisco, California 94111.

who is incapable has been viewed as a by-product of the common law maxim that one has the right to be present at his own trial. Foote, *A Comment on Pre-Trial Commitment of Criminal Defendants*, 108 U. Pa. L. Rev. 832, 834 (1960). In effect, this view holds that one who is without comprehension is essentially absent.

Today the ban on proceeding against one suffering that incapacity is based in the Fourteenth Amendment to the United States Constitution. *Pate v. Robinson*, 383 U.S. 375, 378 (1966). A state's failure adequately to protect one from trial while incompetent deprives him of his due process right to a fair trial. *Drope v. Missouri*, 420 U.S. 162, 171 (1975).

Although the right is of constitutional dimension, the states are free to adopt any test that adequately protects the right. Some have followed the test adopted by the United States Supreme Court for use in all federal courts. In *Dusky v. U.S.* 362 U.S. 402 (1960), the Court held that it is not enough that the defendant is oriented to time and place and has some recollection of events. The test must be "whether he has sufficient present ability to consult with his lawyer with a reasonable degree of rational understanding—and whether he has a rational as well as factual understanding of the proceedings against him." Table 1 reports the tests adopted by the states, the District of Columbia, and the federal court system.

TABLE 1. INCAPACITY TO STAND TRIAL: MENTAL DISABILITY AT TIME OF TRIAL

State	Test	Citation
Alabama	"whether at the time of the trial he has sufficient present ability to consult with his attorney with a reasonable degree of rational understanding and whether he has rational as well as factual understanding of the proceeding against him." *Id.* at 35, citing *Dusky v. U.S.*, 362 U.S. 402, 1960.	*Atwell v. State*, 354 So.2d 30 (Ala. Cr. App. 1977)
Alaska	"as a result of mental disease or defect lacks capacity to understand the proceedings against him or to assist in his own defense."	Alaska Stat. § 12.45.100
Arizona	"as a result of mental illness or defect, he is unable to understand the proceedings against him or to assist in his	17 Ariz Rev. Stat. Ann., R. Crim. P., Rule 11.1

TABLE 1. *(continued)*

	own defense." Although not identical in language, this standard is intended in application to be identical to the one adopted for federal courts in *Dusky v. U.S.*, 362 U.S. 402 (1960). *See* Comment to Rule 11.1, 17 Ariz. Rev. Stat. Ann. at 142.	
Arkansas	"as a result of mental disease or defect, lacks capacity to understand the proceedings against him or to assist effectively in his own defense."	Ark. Stat. Ann. § 41–603
California	"as a result of mental disorder or developmental disability, he is unable to understand the nature of the proceedings taken against him and to assist counsel in the conduct of a defense in a rational manner."	Cal. Penal Code § 1367
Colorado	"a mental disease or defect which renders him incapable of understanding the nature and course of the proceedings against him or of participating or assisting in his defense or cooperating with his defense counsel."	Colo. Rev. Stat. § 16–8–102(3)
Connecticut	"unable to understand the proceedings against him, or to assist in his own defense."	Conn. Gen. Stat. § 54–40
Delaware	"because of mental illness or mental defect, is unable to understand the nature of the proceedings against him, or to give evidence in his own defense or to instruct counsel on his behalf."	Del. Code Ann. tit. 11, § 404
District of Columbia	"of unsound mind or is mentally incompetent so as to be unable to understand the proceedings against him or properly to assist in his own defense."	D.C. Code Ann. § 24–301(a)
Florida	"does not have sufficient present ability to consult with his lawyer with a reasonable degree	Transition Rule 23(a)(1), 375 So. 2d 855 (Fla. Oct. 9, 1979)

continued

TABLE 1. *(continued)*

State	Test	Citation
	of rational understanding or if he has no rational as well as factual understanding of the proceedings against him." This *Dusky* formulation was adopted as a temporary measure pending final recommendation from the Criminal Rules Commission of the Florida Bar Association.	
Georgia	"of understanding the nature and object of the proceedings against him, and rightly comprehends his own condition in reference to such proceedings, and is capable of rendering his attorneys such assistance as a proper defense to the indictment preferred against him demands." *Id.* at 620. Restated, *Spain v. State,* 252 S.E.2d 436 (Ga. 1979).	*Brown v. State,* 113 S.E.2d 618 (Ga. 1960)
Hawaii	"as a result of a physical or mental disease, disorder or defect lacks capacity to understand the proceedings against him or to assist in his own defense."	Hawaii Rev. Stat. § 704–403
Idaho	"as a result of mental disease or defect lacks capacity to understand the proceedings against him or to assist in his own defense."	Idaho Code § 18–210
Illinois	"if, because of a mental or physical condition he is unable: (1) to understand the nature and purpose of the proceedings against him; or (2) to assist in his defense."	Ill. Rev. Stat. ch. 38, § 1005-2–1(a)
Indiana	"lacks the ability to understand the proceedings and assist in the preparation of his defense."	Ind. Code Ann. § 35–5–3.1–1
Iowa	"suffering from a mental disorder which prevents him or her from appreciating the charge, understanding the proceedings, or assisting effectively in the defense."	Iowa Code Ann. § 812.3

TABLE 1. *(continued)*

State	Test	Citation
Kansas	"because of mental illness or defect is unable: (a) to understand the nature and purpose of the proceedings against him; or (b) to make or assist in making his defense."	Kan. Stat. Ann. § 22–3301(1)
Kentucky	"as a result of mental disease or defect, lacks capacity to appreciate the nature and consequences of the proceedings against him or to participate rationally in his own defense."	Ky. Rev. Stat. § 504.040(1)
Louisiana	"as a result of mental disease or defect, a defendant presently lacks the capacity to understand the proceedings against him or to assist in his defense."	La. Code Crim. Pro. Ann. art. 641
Maine	"capable of understanding the nature and object of the charges and proceedings against him, of comprehending his own condition in reference thereto, and of conducting, in cooperation with his counsel, his defense in a rational and reasonable manner." *Id.* at 66.	*Thursby v. State,* 223 A.2d 61 (Me. 1966)
Maryland	"unable to understand the nature or the object of the proceedings against him or to assist in his defense."	Md. Ann. Code art. 59, § 23
Massachusetts	"whether he has sufficient present ability to consult with his lawyer with a reasonable degree of rational understanding—and whether he has a rational as well as factual understanding of the proceedings against him." *Id.* at 895, quoting *Dusky.*	*Commonwealth v. Vailes,* 275 N.E.2d 893 (Mass. 1971)
Michigan	"incapable because of his mental condition of understanding the nature and object of the proceedings against him or of assisting in his defense in a rational manner. The court shall determine the capacity of one to	Mich. Stat. Ann. § 14.800(1020) (1)

continued

TABLE 1. *(continued)*

State	Test	Citation
	assist in his defense by his ability to perform the tasks reasonably necessary for him to perform in the preparation of his defense and during his trial."	
Minnesota	"mentally ill or mentally deficient so as to be incapable of understanding the proceedings or making a defense."	Minn. Stat. Ann. § 611.026
Mississippi	"mentally capable of conducting a rational defense by intelligently conferring with counsel." *Id.* at 364.	*Tarrants v. State,* 236 So.2d 360 (Miss. 1970)
Missouri	"as a result of mental disease or defect lacks capacity to understand the proceedings against him or to assist in his own defense."	Mo. Rev. Stat. Ann. § 552.020(1)
Montana	"as a result of mental disease or defect, is unable to understand the proceedings against him or to assist in his own defense."	Mont. Rev. Codes Ann. § 46–14–103
Nebraska	"whether the defendant has the capacity to understand the nature and object of the proceedings against him, to comprehend his own condition in reference to such proceedings and to make a rational defense." *Id.* at 825, citing Weihofen, Mental Disorder as a Criminal Defense, 429–31.	*State v. Klatt,* 188 N.W.2d 821 (Neb. 1971)
Nevada	"(1) whether he has sufficient present ability to consult with his lawyer with a reasonable degree of factual understanding—and (2) whether he has a rational as well as factual understanding of the proceedings against him." *Id.* at 208, adopting *Dusky's* as a constitutional standard. *See also,* Nev. Rev. Stat. § 178.450: "of sufficient mental ability to be able to understand the nature of the criminal charge against him	*Doggett v. Warden Nevada St. Prison,* 572 P.2d 207 (Nev. 1977)

TABLE 1. *(continued)*

State	Test	Citation
	or her and, by reason thereof, is able to aid and assist his or her counsel in the defense interposed upon the trial or commencement of judgment thereafter."	
New Hampshire	New Hampshire is without an authoritative definition but the *Novosel* court referred to "competency to stand trial and to assist counsel in the defense of the case." *Id.* at 128.	*Novosel v. Heglemoe,* 384 A.2d 124 (N.H. 1978)
New Jersey	"a. No person who lacks capacity to understand the proceedings against him or to assist in his own defense." "b. a person shall be considered mentally competent to stand trial on criminal charges if the proof shall establish: (1) that the defendant has the mental capacity to appreciate his presence in relation to time, place and things; and (2) that his elementary mental processes are such that he comprehends: (a) that he is in a court of justice charged with a criminal offense; (b) that there is a judge on the bench; (c) that there is a prosecutor present who will try to convict him of a criminal charge; (d) that he has a lawyer who will undertake to defend him against that charge; (e) that he will be expected to tell to the best of his mental ability the facts surrounding him at the time and place when the alleged violation was committed if he chooses to testify and understands the right not to testify; (f) that there is or may be a jury present to pass upon evidence adduced as to guilt or innocence of such charge or, that if he should choose to enter	N.J. Stat. Ann. § 2C:4-4

continued

TABLE 1. *(continued)*

State	Test	Citation
	into plea negotiations or to plead guilty, that he comprehend the consequences of a guilty plea and that he be able to knowingly, intelligently, and voluntarily waive those rights which are waived upon such entry of a guilty plea and (g) that he has the ability to participate in an adequate presentation of his defense." This is adapted from the Model Penal Code of the American Law Institute, § 4.04.	
New Mexico	"the capacity to understand the nature and object of the proceedings against him, to comprehend his own condition in reference to such proceedings, and to make a rational defense." *Id.* at 443, citing Weihofen, Mental Disorder as a Criminal Defense, 431. *See also, State v. Gardiner,* 509 P.2d 871, 873 (N.M. 1973), adopting the *Dusky* standard.	*State v. Upton,* 290 P.2d 440 (N.M. 1955)
New York	"1. 'Incapacitated person' means a defendant who as a result of mental disease or defect lacks capacity to understand the proceedings against him or to assist in his own defense." *See also, People v. Francabandera,* 310 N.E.2d 292 (N.Y. 1974), adding "assisting counsel with a modicum of intelligence."	N.Y.C.P. Law § 730.10
North Carolina	"when by reason of mental illness or defect he is unable to understand the nature and object of the proceedings against him, or to comprehend his own situation in reference to the proceedings, or to assist in his defense in a rational or reasonable manner."	N.C. Gen. Stat. § 15A–1001(a)

TABLE 1. *(continued)*

State	Test	Citation
North Dakota	"as a result of mental disease or defect, lacks capacity to understand the proceedings against him or to assist in his own defense."	N.D. Cent. Code § 12.1–04–04
Ohio	"because of his present mental condition he is incapable of understanding the nature and objective of the proceedings against him or of presently assisting in his defense."	Ohio Rev. Code Ann. § 2945.37
Oklahoma	"whether the accused has sufficient present ability to consult with his lawyer with a reasonable degree in relational understanding and whether he has rational as well as actual understanding of the proceedings against him." *Id.* at 597, para. 6 of the syllabus by the court.	*Roberson v. State,* 456 P.2d 595 (Okl. Cr. 1968)
Oregon	"if, as a result of mental disease or defect, he is unable: (a) to understand the nature of the proceedings against him; or (b) to assist and cooperate with his counsel; or (c) to participate in his defense."	Or. Rev. Stat. § 161.360(2)
Pennsylvania	"substantially unable to understand the nature or object of the proceedings against him or to participate and assist in his defense."	50 Pa. Cons. Stat. § 7402(a)
Rhode Island	"unable to understand the character and consequences of the proceedings against him or is unable properly to assist in his defense."	R.I. Gen. Laws § 40.1–5.3–3(3)
South Carolina	"lacks the capacity to understand the proceedings against him or to assist in his own defense as a result of a lack of mental capacity."	S.C. Code § 44–23–410
South Dakota	"incapable of understanding the charge against him or the	S.D. Codified Laws Ann. § 23A–10A–1

continued

TABLE 1. *(continued)*

State	Test	Citation
	proceedings, or of participating in his defense."	
Tennessee	"mental condition such that he lacks the capacity to understand the nature and object of the proceedings against him, to consult with counsel and to assist in preparing his defense." *Id.* at 707.	*MacKey v. State,* 537 S.W.2d 704 (Tenn. Cr. App. 1975)
Texas	"does not have: (1) sufficient present ability to consult with his lawyer with a reasonable degree of rational understanding; or (2) a rational as well as factual understanding of the proceedings against him."	Tex. Code Crim. Proc. Ann. art. 46.02, § 1(a)
United States	"unable to understand the proceedings against him or to properly assist in his own defense. . .", construed in *Dusky v. U.S.,* 362 U.S. 402 (1960): "test must be whether he has sufficient present ability to consult with his lawyer with a reasonable degree of rational understanding—and whether he has a rational as well as factual understanding of the proceedings against him."	18 U.S.C. § 4244
Utah	"if he is suffering from a mental disease or defect resulting either: (1) in his inability to comprehend the nature of the proceeding against him or the punishment specified for the offense charged; or (2) In his inability to assist counsel in his defense."	Utah Code Ann. § 77–15–2
Vermont	"ability to comprehend the nature of the proceedings against him and to participate rationally in the decisions relating to his own defense." *Id.* at 290.	*In re Russell,* 227 A.2d 289 (Vt. 1967)
Virginia	"cannot understand the proceedings or confer intelligently about the case." *Id.* at 938.	*Thomas v. Cunningham,* 313 F.2d 934 (4th Cir. 1963)

TABLE 1. *(continued)*

State	Test	Citation
Washington	"to understand the proceedings against him and assist in his own defense."	Wash. Rev. Code. § 10.77.090 (1)
West Virginia	"whether or not the individual is capable of participating substantially in his own defense and understanding the nature and consequences of a criminal trial." *See also, State v. Milam*, 226 S.E.2d 433 (W. Va. 1976).	W.V. Code § 27–6A–2(b)
Wisconsin	"as a result of mental disease or defect is unable to understand the proceedings against him or to assist in his own defense."	Wis. Stat. Ann. § 971.13
Wyoming	"as a result of mental illness or deficiency, he lacks the capacity to: (i) comprehend his position; (ii) understand the nature and object of the proceedings against him; (iii) conduct his defense in a rational manner; and (iv) cooperate with his counsel to the end that any available defense may be interposed."	Wyo. Stat. § 7–11–302(a)

EXCUSING CRIMINAL RESPONSIBILITY: MENTAL DISABILITY AT TIME OF OFFENSE (NOT GUILTY BY REASON OF INSANITY)

Table 2 reports a survey of tests used in American jurisdictions to determine whether one's mental disability at the time of the commission of an offense warrants exculpation.

Born in 1843 England, the traditional or *M'Naghten* test permits exculpation if "at the time of the committing of the act, the party accused was labouring under such a defect of reason, from disease of mind, as not to know the nature and quality of the act he was doing; or if he did know it, that he did not know he was doing what was wrong." *M'Naghten's Case*, 10 Clark & Fin. 200, 210, 8 Eng. Rep. 718, 722 (1843). The *M'Naghten* test was readily adopted in this country and was the predominant test for many years.

Some jurisdictions, finding *M'Naghten* by itself inadequate, supplemented it with the "irresistible impulse" test. The perceived inadequacy arose in a situation where one might have known the nature of his act or been conscious of right and wrong but was powerless to do right in the face of an uncontrollable impulse. *See Parsons v. State*, 2 So. 854 (Ala. 1886).

The individual states were not restricted in the development of their mental disability tests. The United States Constitution does not mandate the use of a particular test for determining criminal responsibility. The choice is left to each state as a reflection of scientific knowledge and basic policy. *Leland v. Oregon*, 343 U.S. 790, 801 (1951). Because the United States Supreme Court never has adopted a test applicable in all federal courts, each of the 11 circuits has also been left to adopt the test it deems best. For this reason, the table has an entry for each of the United States courts of appeals.

In 1954 the United States Court of Appeals for the District of Columbia Circuit departed significantly from *M'Naghten* in adopting what became known as the *Durham* test: "an accused is not criminally responsible if his unlawful act was the product of a mental disease or defect." *Durham v. U.S.*, 214 F.2d 862, 874 (D.C. Cir. 1954). The *Durham* court found the traditional right–wrong test failed to take into account modern psychiatric knowledge and psychic realities. Further, the court found the traditional test underinclusive because it was based on only a single symptom of mental disability *(Id)*. Also found inadequate was the "irresistible impulse" test, for it "gives no recognition to mental illness characterized by brooding and reflection" *(Id)*. These shortcomings convinced the court to adopt the broader *Durham* test.

In 1962, the American Law Institute proposed a Model Penal Code, including § 4.01, a new test for mental disability. Not since *M'Naghten* had there been a development with such impact as the American Law Institute's Model Penal Code. Section 4.01(1) proposes that "a person is not responsible if at the time of such conduct, as a result of mental disease or defect, he lacks substantial capacity either to appreciate the criminality [wrongfulness] of his conduct or to conform his conduct to the requirements of law." Section 4.01(2) excludes from "'mental disease or defect' an abnormality manifested only by repeated criminal or otherwise antisocial conduct." The latter was intended to exclude "psychopathic personalities" from exculpation under § 4.01(1). *See* Model Penal Code, Tentative Draft No. 4, Comments § 4.01, p. 156, 160.

The ALI formulation leaves an election to those adopting it between use of "wrongfulness" and "criminality." Of the jurisdictions adopting § 4.01(1), "wrongfulness" has been the choice by a margin of two to one. The sentiment in favor of "wrongfulness" is based on the desire to include one who knows an act is "criminal but by delusion believes it to be morally justified" *U.S. v. Freeman*, 357 F.2d 606, 622 n.52 (2d Cir. 1966).

Section 4.01(2) has engendered some debate and has been expressly rejected by six of the jurisdictions otherwise adopting the MPC. One court's dissatisfaction was based on the belief that, at best, § 4.01(2) fails to achieve its purpose of excluding psychopathic personalities, and that no real abnormality could be manifested solely by repeated criminal or antisocial acts. *Wade v. U.S.*, 426 F.2d 64, 71–72 (9th Cir. 1970). In the table that follows, MPC § 4.01(1) and § 4.01(2) are referred to as MPC(1) and (2), respectively.

M'Naghten, irresistible impulse, *Durham*, and the MPC represent the major tests for determining whether one suffering from a mental disability at the time of an act should be held criminally responsible for that act.

The overwhelming trend is toward adoption of the MPC. At this writing, of the 62 American jurisdictions canvassed (including 11 U.S. courts of appeals), 39 use the MPC in some recognizable form. Only 19 still subscribe to *M'Naghten*. North and South Dakota alone, after having replaced *M'Naghten* with the MPC, subsequently have rejected the MPC and readopted modified *M'Naghten* tests. Also noteworthy is recent Montana legislation that abolishes mental disability as a defense. In Montana mental disability will hereafter be considered as a factor in the sentencing determination rather than in the resolution of an individual's guilt.

TABLE 2. EXCUSING CRIMINAL RESPONSIBILITY: MENTAL DISABILITY AT TIME OF OFFENSE (Not Guilty by Reason of Insanity)

State	Test	Comment	Citation
Alabama	MPC(1) & (2)	Replaces *M'Naghten* plus irrestible impulse test, effective January 1, 1980. In section (1) "criminality" is used.	Ala. Code § 13A–3–1
Alaska	MPC(1) & (2) in variation	Identical to MPC in section (1), using "wrongfulness"; section (2) is varied, where the MPC would exclude from the term "mental disease or defect" an abnormality manifested solely by repeated criminal or antisocial acts, Alaska's § (2) states only that the burden of proof is not satisfied solely by evidence of such abnormality. *Schade v. State*, 512 P.2d 907, 911–12 n.4 (Alaska 1973).	Alaska Stat. § 12. 45.083

continued

TABLE 2. *(continued)*

State	Test	Comment	Citation
Arizona	*M'Naghten*	Substitutes "mental disease or defect" for "defect of reason, from disease of mind."	Ariz. Rev. Stat. Ann. § 13–502
Arkansas	MPC(1) & (2)	Section (1) uses "criminality" instead of "wrongfulness" and is otherwise varied only in that defendant need only have "lacked capacity," not "substantial capacity." § 41-602 makes evidence of mental disease or defect admissible on the issue whether the defendant had the requisite culpable mental state for the offense charged, i.e., "intent," "knowingly," etc.	Ark. Stat. Ann. § 41–601
California	MPC(1)	Uses "criminality" in section (1). The court deferred decision in *Drew* on whether to adopt section (2), and has yet to act, *Id.* at 1324, n.8.	*People v. Drew*, 583 P.2d 1318 (Cal. 1978).
Colorado	*M'Naghten* plus irresistible impulse		Colo. Rev. Stat. § 16–8–101
Connecticut	MPC(1) & (2)	The defense is unavailable to one whose mental disease "was proximately caused by the voluntary ingestion, inhalation or injection of intoxicating liquor or any drug or substance" unless properly prescribed. Section (1) uses "wrongfulness" instead of "criminality."	Conn. Gen. Stat. § 53a–13
Delaware	MPC(1) plus irresistible impulse	As a result of "mental disease or defect, lacked substantial capacity to appreciate the wrongfulness of his conduct or lacked sufficient willpower to choose whether he would do the act or refrain from doing it."	Del. Code Ann. tit. 11, § 401
District of Columbia	MPC(1) & (2)	In section (1), uses "recognize" instead of "appreciate" because the latter is susceptible of varying connotations including "to enjoy"; and "wrongfulness" instead of "criminality" to avoid excluding those who are "fully aware of the law's requirements, but because of	*Bethea v. U.S.*, 365 A.2d 64 (D.C. App. 1976)

TABLE 2. *(continued)*

State	Test	Comment	Citation
		a delusion . . . believe their conduct to be morally justified." *Id.* at 79–80.	
Florida	Modified MPC–*M'Naghten*	The court refers to the test adopted as utilizing the "mental disease or defect" portion of the MPC test, and rejecting "so-called 'irresistible impulse' portion . . . which excuses . . . the defendant who 'lacks substantial capacity . . . to conform.'" 344 So.2d at 246. At the same time the court's formulation is basically *M'Naghten. Id.* at 246 n.2.	*In re* Standard Jury Instruction in Criminal Cases, 327 So.2d 6 (Fla. 1976); Wheeler v. State, 344 So.2d 244 (Fla. 1977)
Georgia	*M'Naghten* plus irresistible impulse	*See also, Gibson v. State,* 223 S.E.2d 150 (Ga. 1976).	Ga. Code §§ 26–702 and 26–703
Hawaii	MPC(1) & (2) modified	Section (1) is modified to include "physical or mental disease, disorder or defect," and uses "wrongfulness" instead of "criminality." Section (2) excludes from "physical or mental disease, disorder or defect" those abnormalities manifested only by repeated "penal or otherwise anti-social conduct."	Hawaii Rev. Stat. § 704–400(a)
Idaho	MPC (1) & (2)	Section (1) uses "wrongfulness" instead of "criminality."	Idaho Code § 18–207
Illinois	MPC (1) & (2)	Section (1) uses "criminality" instead of "wrongfulness."	Ill. Rev. Stat. ch. 38, § 6–2
Indiana	MPC (1) & (2)	In section (1) "wrongfulness" is used instead of "criminality."	Ind. Code § 35–41-3-6
Iowa	*M'Naghten*	This statute evidences a recent legislative preference for *M'Naghten*, effective January 1, 1978.	Iowa Code § 701.4
Kansas	*M'Naghten*	For a more recent reaffirmance of *M'Naghten, see State v. Levier,* 601 P.2d 1116 (Kan. 1979).	*State v. Smith,* 574 P.2d 548 (Kan. 1977)
Kentucky	MPC (1) & (2)	Section (1) uses "criminality" instead of "wrongfulness."	Ky. Rev. Stat. § 504.020
Louisiana	*M'Naghten* modified	This is the *M'Naghten* test utilizing "mental disease or defect" instead of the more traditional "defect of reason" or "disease of mind."	La. Rev. Stat. § 14:14

continued

TABLE 2. *(continued)*

State	Test	Comment	Citation
Maine	MPC(1) & (2) modified	This statute represents a repeal of the previously adopted *Durham* rule (old tit. 15, § 102). Section (1) is unchanged, using "wrongfulness" instead of "criminality." To (1) is added (1)A, that abnormal mind can negate intention, knowledge or recklessness. Section (2) is modified: "'mental disease or defect' means any abnormal condition of mind which substantially affects mental or emotional processes and substantially impairs the processes and capacity of a person to control his actions." Section (2) continues, including the paradigm MPC (2), and adding that "excessive use of alcohol, drugs, or similar substances, in or of itself does not constitute a 'mental disease or defect.'"	Me. Rev. Stat. Ann. tit. 17A, § 58
Maryland	MPC(1) & (2), modified	In sections (1) and (2) the term "mental disorder" is used in lieu of "mental disease or disorder." In section (1) "criminality" is used instead of "wrongfulness."	Md. Code Ann. Art. 59, § 25(a)
Massachusetts	MPC (1)	The Massachusetts Court views section (1) merely as a modern restatement of the traditional Massachusetts version of the *M'Naghten* plus irresistible impulse test.	*Commonwealth v. McHoul*, 226 N.E. 2d 556 (Mass. 1967)
Michigan	MPC(1) modified	Instead of "mental disease or defect," this statute uses "mental illness" or "mental retardation." "Wrongfulness" was chosen over "criminality." A section (2) is added: A person under the influence of voluntarily consumed or injected alcohol or controlled substance shall not thereby be deemed to have been legally insane.	Mich. Stat. Ann. § 28.1044
Minnesota	*M'Naghten*	MPC rejected specifically, *see* Pirsig, Comment, at § 609.07, p.90.	Minn. Stat. § 611.026

TABLE 2. *(continued)*

State	Test	Comment	Citation
Mississippi	*M'Naghten*	MPC expressly rejected.	*Hill v. State,* 339 So.2d 1382 (Miss. 1976)
Missouri	MPC(1) & (2) modified	Added to section (1) is a *M'Naghten*-like clause: "he did not know or appreciate the nature, quality or wrongfulness of his conduct." Section (2) is expanded: "whether or not such abnormality may be included under mental illness, mental disease," defect, mental abnormality or disorder. Nor do the terms "mental disease or defect" include alcoholism without psychosis, or drug abuse without psychosis or "an abnormality manifested only by criminal sexual psychopathy."	Mo. Rev. Stat. §§ 552.010; 552.030
Montana	Unique	Montana has recently acted to "[a]bolish the defense of mental disease or defect in criminal actions and to provide an alternative sentencing procedure to be followed when a convicted defendant is found to have been suffering from a mental disease or defect at the time of the commission of the offense." 1979 Montana Laws, ch. 713, p. 1979. "Mentally defective" refers to one who suffers from a mental disease or defect rendering him incapable of appreciating the nature of his conduct. The Montana scheme subscribes to MPC (2) in its paradigm form. The scheme also allows use of evidence of mental disease or defect to prove that the defendant did not have a particular state of mind that is an element of the offense charged.	Mont. Rev. Codes Ann. §§ 45-2-101 (28); 46-14-101; 46-14-201
Nebraska	*M'Naghten*	Irresistible impulse test rejected. *Id.* at 663.	*State v. Jacobs,* 205 N.W.2d 662 (Neb. 1973)

continued

TABLE 2. *(continued)*

State	Test	Comment	Citation
Nevada	*M'Naghten*		*Clark v. State*, 588 P.2d 1027 (Nev. 1979); Nev. Rev. Stat. § 178.450
New Hampshire	Unique	One who is "insane" at the time of his acts is not criminally responsible. In New Hampshire "there are no legal rules which either define a mental disease or determine when a defendant's actions are a product of such a disease. Rather these are questions of fact to be decided by the jury in each case." *Id.* at 435–36. This approach was first expressed in *State v. Pike*, 49 N.H. 399 (1870), and *State v. Jones*, 50 N.H. 369 (1871). *Id.*	N.H. Rev. Stat. Ann. § 628.2; *State v. Plummer*, 374 A.2d 431 (N.H. 1977)
New Jersey	*M'Naghten*	This statute, effective September 1, 1979, is nearly a direct quote from *M'Naghten.*	N.J. Rev. Stat. § 2C:4-1
New Mexico	*M'Naghten* plus irresistible impulse	The *White* court cited *Parsons v. State*, 2 So. 854 (Ala. 1887), the Alabama case that adopted the irresistable impulse test, in different language, as an addition to *M'Naghten*. The language adopted in New Mexico is quoted from the Royal Commission on Capital Punishment, 1949–53 Report: "was incapable of preventing himself from committing it." 270 P.2d at 731.	*State v. White*, 270 P.2d 727 (N.M. 1954)
New York	MPC-*M'Naghten* combination	The New York test combines the MPC's "as a result of mental disease or defect, he lacks substantial capacity to know or appreciate" with *M'Naghten's* "nature and consequence of such conduct; or that such conduct was wrong." The paradigm MPC was rejected. *See* Hechtman, Practice Commentaries, in note following Penal Law 30.05, p.69.	N.Y. Penal Law § 30.05
North Carolina	*M'Naghten*		*State v. Pagano*, 242 S.E.2d 825, 828 (N.C. 1978)

TABLE 2. *(continued)*

State	Test	Comment	Citation
North Dakota	Unique	This statute represents a retreat from the previously adopted paradigm MPC test. "A person is not responsible for criminal conduct if, as a result of mental disease or defect existing at the time the conduct occurs, (1) he lacked substantial capacity to comprehend the harmful nature or consequences of his conduct, or (2) his conduct was the result of a loss or serious distortion of his capacity to recognize reality."	N.D. Cent. Code § 12.1-04-03
Ohio	MPC(1)	The court adopted "does not have" in place of "lacks substantial," and "know" instead of "appreciate." The Ohio test uses "wrongfulness" instead of "criminality."	*State v. Staten,* 247 N.E.2d 293 (Ohio 1969)
Oklahoma	*M'Naghten*	*See also,* Okla. Stat. Ann. tit. 21, § 152(4)	Matter of M.E., 584 P.2d 1340, 1347 (Okla. Crim. 1978)
Oregon	MPC(1) & (2)	Evidence of mental disease or defect is admissible on the issue of intent. In section (1) "criminality" is used instead of "wrongfulness."	Or. Rev. Stat. §§ 161.295; 161.300
Pennsylvania	*M'Naghten*		*Commonwealth v. Hicks,* 396 A.2d 1183, 1185 (Pa. 1979)
Rhode Island	MPC(1)&(2) modified	The *Johnson* court rejected *M'Naghten* and adopted an alternative proposed by a minority of the ALI Council that adopted the MPC. It was supported by Professor Herbert Weschler, and is substantially similar to the British Royal Commission on Capital Punishment, 1953 proposal. It was rejected by the ALI majority because it was deemed unwise to present questions of justice to the jury: "is so substantially impaired that he cannot justly be held responsible." *Id.* at 476.	*State v. Johnson,* 399 A.2d 469 (R.I. 1979)

continued

TABLE 2. *(continued)*

State	Test	Comment	Citation
South Carolina	*M'Naghten* modified	"whether he had the mental capacity to distinguish moral or legal right from moral or legal wrong, and to recognize the particular act charged as morally or legally wrong." *Id.* at 304.	*State v. Law*, 244 S.E.2d 302 (S.C. 1978)
South Dakota	*M'Naghten* modified	In 1976 South Dakota adopted the MPC in lieu of *M'Naghten*, 1976 S.D. Sess. Laws, ch. 158, §1-1, *see also State v. Miller*, 248 N.W.2d 56 (S.D. 1976). In 1977 the MPC test was repealed and replaced, 1977 S.D. Session Laws, ch. 189, § 11. The current test is "'mentally ill,' the condition of a person temporarily or partially deprived of reason, upon proof that at the time of committing the act charged against him, he was incapable of knowing its wrongfulness."	S.D. Laws Ann. §§ 22-1-2(22); 22-3-1(3)
Tennessee	MPC(1) & (2)	The *Graham* court rejected *M'Naghten* and adopted the MPC, using "wrongfulness" over "criminality" "so that the rule requires appreciation of the wrongfulness of conduct as opposed to its criminality." *Id.* at 543.	*Graham v. State*, 547 S.W.2d 531 (Tenn. 1977)
Texas	MPC(1) & (2)	Rather than "appreciate the wrongfulness," the Texas rule adopts "know that his conduct was wrong."	Tex. Penal Code Ann. § 8.01
Utah	MPC(1) & (2)	Uses "wrongfulness" instead of "criminality."	Utah Code Ann. § 76-2-305
United States 1st Cir.	Unclear	There is no authoritative decision in this circuit but the *Amador* court refused to entertain a contention that *M'Naghten* was no longer the proper test. The court did commend *U.S.v. Currens*, infra, 3d Cir., to the lower court on remand. *Id.* at 52–53.	*Amador Beltran v. U.S.*, 302 F.2d 48 (1st Cir. 1962)
2d Cir.	MPC(1)	The 2d Circuit uses "wrongfulness" instead of "criminality" so as to include the case of one who knows his act is criminal but by delusion	*U.S. v. Freeman*, 357 F.2d 606 (2d Cir. 1966)

TABLE 2. (*continued*)

State	Test	Comment	Citation
		believes it to be morally justified. *Id.* at 633 n.52.	
3d Cir.	MPC(1) modified & (2)	The *Currens* court rejected the "to appreciate the criminality of his conduct" clause because it overemphasizes the cognitive element in criminal responsibility. *Id.* at 774 n.32	*U.S. v. Currens*, 290 F.2d 751 (3d Cir. 1961)
4th Cir.	MPC(1) & (2)	The *Chandler* court warns against rigidifying the MPC language and expects, even desires, change as the cases unfurl. *Id.* at 926.	*U.S. v. Chandler*, 393 F.2d 920 (4th Cir. 1968)
5th Cir.	MPC(1) & (2)	The *Blake* court uses "wrongfulness" instead of "criminality," citing *Freeman, supra*, 2d Cir. *Id.* at 916.	*Blake v. U.S.*, 407 F.2d 908 (5th Cir. 1969)
6th Cir.	MPC(1)	The *Smith* court refused to adopt section (2) citing the great debate over its psychiatric soundness. *Id.* at 727 n.2.	*U.S. v. Smith*, 404 F.2d 720 (6th Cir. 1968)
7th Cir.	MPC(1) & (2)	The *Shapiro* court uses "wrongfulness" instead of "criminality," citing *Freeman, supra*, 2d Cir. *Id.* at 685–87.	*U.S. v. Shapiro*, 383 F.2d 680 (7th Cir. 1967)
8th Cir.	Unique but partaking of MPC(1)	If cognition, volition and capacity to control one's behavior are emphasized in the court's jury instructions "as essential constituents of the defendant's legal sanity we suspect that the exact wording . . . and the actual name of the test are comparatively unimportant and may well be little more than an indulgence in semantics." *Id.* at 735.	*Pope v. U.S.*, 372 F.2d 710 (8th Cir. 1967)
9th Cir.	MPC(1)	The *Wade* court used "wrongfulness" for the same reasons as the *Freeman* court, *supra*, 2d cir. The *Wade* court refused to adopt section (2) because at best it does not achieve its purpose of excluding psychopathic personalities. The court felt that no real abnormality could be manifested solely by repeated criminal or antisocial acts. *Id.* at 71–72.	*Wade v. U.S.*, 426 F.2d 64 (9th Cir. 1970)

continued

TABLE 2. *(continued)*

State	Test	Comment	Citation
10th Cir.	MPC(1)	The *Wion* court adopted "wrongfulness" instead of "criminality" and instructed that the jury must be convinced beyond a reasonable doubt that the defendant was capable of controlling his conduct. *Id.* at 427, 430.	*Wion v. U.S.* 325 F.2d 420 (10th Cir. 1963)
D.C. Cir.	MPC(1) modified	The *Brawner* court rejected the *Durham* rule, and adopted the paradigm MPC test, using "wrongfulness" and added the *MacDonald* definition of mental disease or defect as "any abnormal condition of the mind, regardless of its medical label, which substantially impairs behavior controls. The term 'behavior controls' refers to the processes and capacity of a person to regulate and control his conduct and his actions." *Id.* at 1008, citing *MacDonald v. U.S.,* 312 F.2d 847 (D.C. Cir. 1962).	*U.S. v. Brawner,* 471 F.2d 969 (D.C. Cir. 1972)
Vermont	MPC(1) & (2) modified	Section (1) was adopted unchanged. Section (2) was adopted with the addition that the "terms 'mental disease or defect' shall include congenital and traumatic mental conditions as well as disease."	Vt. Stat. Ann. tit. 13, § 4801
Virginia	*M'Naghten* plus irresistible impulse	Virginia's "right and wrong" test is that one is not responsible when "unable to distinguish right from wrong and understand the nature and character and consequence of his act" or "where the accused [was] able to understand . . . and knows it is wrong, but his mind [is] so impaired by disease that he is totally deprived of the mental power to control or restrain his act." *Id.* at 291–92.	*Thompson v. Commonwealth,* 70 S.E.2d 284 (Va. 1952)
Washington	*M'Naghten*	This statute adopts "mental disease or defect" in place of the traditional "defect of reason" and "disease of mind."	Wash. Rev. Code § 9A.12.010

TABLE 2. (continued)

State	Test	Comment	Citation
West Virginia	MPC(1) and apparently (2)	The court advises against adoption of rigid language, but expressly dispenses with M'Naghten and suggests an instruction that mirrors MPC(1), using "wrongfulness." Section (2) is apparently adopted because it is quoted, id. at 645, and is favorably referred to, id. at 647.	State v. Grimm. 195 S.E.2d 637 (W. Va. 1973)
Wisconsin	MPC(1) & (2)	In section (1) "wrongfulness" is used instead of "criminality." Section (2) is adopted unchanged. Added is a section (3) making this an affirmative defense burdening the defendant to establish it to a "reasonable certainty by the greater weight of the credible evidence." This is based on §4.03 of the MPC. Prior to the adoption of §971.15, Wisconsin allowed a defendant to choose between the M'Naghten and the MPC standards. State v. Shoffner, 143 N.W.2d 458 (Wisc. 1966). Wisconsin is unique in having allowed this choice in an experiment that ended in favor of the MPC.	Wis. Stat. § 971.15
Wyoming	MPC(1) & (2)	In section (1) "wrongfulness" is used instead of "criminality."	Wyo. Stat. § 7–11–304

MENTALLY DISORDERED SEX OFFENDER STATUTES

The table that follows is the result of a survey of American jurisdictions for what are commonly called "mentally disordered sex offender" statutes. Actually, beyond a somewhat similar subject matter, the statutes have little else in common. Typically, their purpose is to provide special disposition procedures for people who have shown a tendency to commit sex offenses. The methods used to achieve this purpose are varied. For instance, California defines a mentally disordered sex offender as one who suffers from a mental defect, disease, or disorder, and Connecticut requires a finding of mental illness, while the District of Columbia requires a finding that one is not insane. In Nebraska, the hearing held to determine whether one is a mentally disordered sex offender is deemed part of the criminal proceedings against the defendant, while in Illinois it is considered a civil proceeding. Illinois will hold that hearing after the defendant is charged with a criminal offense, while Massachusets and Virginia will hold it after conviction but before sentencing. Georgia will only hold its hearing 90 days prior to the expiration of sentence or 60 days prior to parole.

Excluded from the table are what might be called "mentally disordered offender" statutes, that is, statutes that provide special disposition procedures for offenders who, though mentally disabled, have no particular tendencies toward sex offenses. *See e.g.*, KAN. STAT. ANN. § 22–3429; ME. REV. STAT. ANN. tit. 15, § 2303(1); MD. ANN. CODE art. 31B, § 1g; and OHIO REV. CODE ANN. § 2947.24 *et seq.*, repealed effective January 1, 1978.

Listed below are 27 states that have or have had mentally disordered sex offender statutes. Of the 27, 8 recently have repealed their acts, including Minnesota which repeated its Sexual Offenses Act but has retained its "psychopathic personality" statutes, and California, effective January 1, 1982. There are, therefore, 20 states (including the District of Columbia) that still have such statutes.

TABLE 3. MENTALLY DISORDERED SEX OFFENDER STATUTES

State	Definition, procedure, and consequences	Citation
Alabama	"Criminal Sexual Psychopathic Persons Act" held unconstitutional in *Davy v. Sullivan*, 354 F. Supp. 1320 (M.D. Ala. 1973). "Such legislation has been widely criticized and the [new criminal] Code makes no attempt to reinstate it." Commentary, Ala. Code §§ 13A–5–6 to 13A–5–8, p. 72, 74.	Ala. Code §§ 15–434 to 441
California	"'[M]entally disordered sex offender' means any person who by reason of mental defect, disease, or disorder, is predisposed to the commission of sexual offenses to such a degree that he is dangerous to the health and safety of others." Application of this scheme requires the conviction of a sex offense, and is within the court's discretion unless the conviction is for a felony offense involving one under 14 years of age, or for a misdemeanor offense involving one under 14 years of age and the offender has been previously convicted of any sex offense. The offender, if found to be a mentally disordered sex offender who could benefit	Cal. Welf. & Inst. Code § 6300 *et. seq.*

TABLE 3. (*continued*)

State	Definition, procedure, and consequences	Citation
	from treatment, may be committed to a mental hospital for a determinate period not to exceed the maximum sentence which could have been imposed for the offenses for which he was convicted. A person may be committed beyond that maximum only if he suffers from a mental disease, defect or disorder and as a result is predisposed to the commission of sexual offenses to a degree that he presents a "substantial danger of bodily harm to others." The court shall conduct a hearing on the prosecutor's petition for extended commitment, and the "patient" shall, by statute, be entitled to all rights guaranteed by the California and United States Constitutions for criminal proceedings. Repealed effective Jan. 1, 1982.	
Colorado	"Colorado Sex Offenders Act of 1968." The district court may, in lieu of sentencing a convicted sex offender, commit him to the department of corrections for an indeterminate period having a minimum of one day and a maximum of his natural life. Prerequisite to such commitment is a temporary commitment for examination by two psychiatrists who shall report whether the defendant constitutes a threat of bodily harm to the public, and whether he is mentally deficient, could benefit from psychiatric treatment and whether he could be adequately supervised on probation. Also prerequisite is an evidentiary hearing, after which if the court finds beyond a reasonable doubt that the defendant constitutes a threat of bodily harm to the public it shall commit him.	Colo. Rev. Stat. § 16–13–201 *et seq.*
Connecticut	When any person is convicted of a sex crime involving physical force or violence, disparity in age between an adult and a minor, or a sexual act of a compulsive or repetitive nature, the court shall, on request, or may on its own motion, order the defendant committed for diagnosis. If the defendant is found to be mentally ill, deficient or emotionally unbalanced so as to clearly demonstrate such actual danger to	Conn. Gen. Stat. Ann. § § 17–244, 17–245

continued

TABLE 3. (*continued*)

State	Definition, procedure, and consequences	Citation
	society as to require custody, care or treatment, the court shall commit him to the institution for an indeterminate period not to exceed the maximum sentencing period.	
District of Columbia	A "sexual psychopath" is "a person, not insane, who by a course of repeated misconduct in sexual matters has evidenced such lack of power to control his sexual impulses as to be dangerous to other persons because he is likely to attack or otherwise inflict injury, loss, pain, or other evil on the objects of his desire." Excluded from the purview of this scheme are those criminally charged with rape, or assault with intent to rape. After examination by two psychiatrists, unless they agree that the person is not a sexual psychopath, the court shall hold a hearing. If it determines that the person is a sexual psychopath, the court shall commit him until he has sufficiently recovered so as not to be dangerous to others.	D.C. Code Ann. §§ 22-3503 to 3511
Florida	This section was repealed effective July 1, 1981. "Those offenders who have been sentenced for the commission of a crime involving a sex offense, who are not psychotic, and who suffer from a psychosexual disorder, but are competent and amenable to treatment."	Fla. Stat. § 917. 012(b)
Georgia	Persons convicted of rape, assault with intent to rape, sodomy, kidnapping a female by a male, incest, or molesting children to gratify sex urge shall be examined no more than 60 days prior to parole, or 90 days prior to the expiration of the sentence imposed. The examination shall determine whether the subject has any mental, moral or physical impairment which would render release inadvisable. If after a hearing, the subject is determined to be mentally ill, he shall be hospitalized for a period not greater than one year, with further commitment in six month intervals depending on further court action. *See also* Mentally Retarded Offender Act of 1975, Ga. Code Ann. § 77-510c *et. seq.*	Ga. Code Ann. § 77-539

TABLE 3. (*continued*)

State	Definition, procedure, and consequences	Citation
Illinois	"Sexually Dangerous Persons" are all persons "suffering from a mental disorder, which . . . has existed for a period of not less than one year, immediately prior to the filing of the petition . . . , coupled with criminal propensities to the commission of sex offenses, and who have demonstrated propensities toward acts of sexual assault or acts of sexual molestation of children." When a person is charged with a criminal offense, a civil proceeding may be instituted to determine if that person is a sexually dangerous person. That determination, although civil in nature, must be beyond a reasonable doubt. After examination and report to the court by two psychiatrists, if the person is found to be sexually dangerous he shall be committed to the custody of the director of corrections who shall provide care and treatment until the person has recovered.	Ill. Rev. Stat. ch. 38, § 105–1.01 *et seq.*
Indiana	This section was repealed, effective September 1, 1979. "Criminal sexual deviant" meant any person over 16 years of age who had been convicted of a sexual offense or an offense which directly involved the commission of an illegal sexual act, and who was suffering from a mental disorder or defect which was coupled with a manifest tendency for the commission of sexual offenses and had been determined to be treatable.	Ind. Code Ann. § 35–11–3.1–1(a)
Iowa	This section was repealed, effective January 1, 1978. "Criminal sexual psychopaths" were all persons charged with a public offense, suffering from a mental disorder but not proper subjects for commitment as a mentally retarded or mentally ill person, who had criminal propensities toward the commission of sex offenses and who were considered dangerous to others.	Iowa Code Ann. § 225A.1
Massachusetts	A "sexually dangerous person" is any person "whose misconduct in sexual matters indicates a general lack of power to control his sexual impulses, as evidenced by	Mass. Ann. Laws ch. 123A, § 1 *et. seq.*

continued

TABLE 3. (*continued*)

State	Definition, procedure, and consequences	Citation
	repetitive or compulsive behavior and either violence, or aggression by an adult against a victim under the age of 16 years, and who as a result is likely to attack or otherwise inflict injury on the objects of his uncontrolled or uncontrollable desires." Upon the determination of guilt of the crime of indecent assault or indecent assault and battery, indecent assault and battery on a child under 14, rape, rape of a female child under 16, carnal knowledge and abuse of a female child under 16, assault with intent to commit rape, open and gross lewdness and lascivious behavior, incest, sodomy, buggery, unnatural and lascivious acts with another person or child under 16, lewd, wanton lascivious behavior or indecent exposure, or any attempt to commit any of these, the court prior to sentencing shall commit the defendant for examination by two psychiatrists. If the court finds, after a hearing, that the defendant is a sexually dangerous person, it may, in lieu of sentencing, commit him for an indeterminate period of a minimum of one day and a maximum of his natural life.	
Michigan	A "sexually delinquent person" is any person "whose sexual behavior is characterized by repetitive or compulsive acts which indicate a disregard of consequences or the recognized rights of others, or by the use of force upon another person in attempting sex relations of either a heterosexual or homosexual nature, or by the commission of sexual aggression against children under the age of 16."	Mich. Stat. Ann. § 28.200(1)
Minnesota	"Psychopathic personality" means "the existence in any person of such conditions of emotional instability, or impulsiveness of behavior, or lack of customary standards of good judgment, or failure to appreciate the consequences of his acts, or a combination of any such conditions, as to render such person irresponsible for his conduct with respect to sexual matters and thereby dangerous to other persons." Commitment	Minn. Stat. Ann. §§ 526.09 to 526.11

TABLE 3. (*continued*)

State	Definition, procedure, and consequences	Citation
	proceedings are those promulgated for judicial commitment. No offense is required, but the existence of a condition of psychopathic personality shall not constitute a defense to a charge of crime, nor relieve a person from liability to be tried unless "such person is in a condition of insanity, idiocy, imbecility, or lunacy within the meaning of the laws relating to crimes and criminal procedure." Minnesota's Sexual Offenders Act, Minn. Stat. Ann. § 246.43, was repealed, effective May 1, 1980.	
Missouri	A "criminal sexual psychpath" is defined as including "[a]ll persons suffering from a mental disorder and not insane or feebleminded, which mental disorder has existed for a period of not less than one year immediately prior to the filing of the petition . . . coupled with criminal propensities to the commission of sex offenses, and who may be considered dangerous to others." When any person is charged with a criminal offense, and a petition is filed alleging criminal sexual psychopathy, a hearing shall be held. If at the hearing *prima facie* proof of criminal sexual psychopathy is made, the court shall appoint two physicians to examine the accused. If the report of at least one of the examining physicians establishes the fact of a mental disorder, a second hearing shall be held at which the examining physicians may testify, although their written reports wlll not be admissible. Evidence of past acts of sexual deviation shall be admissible. The accused shall be entitled to counsel, to present evidence, and shall have full right of appeal. If found to be a criminal sexual psychopath, the accused may be committed until "his release will not be incompatible with the welfare of society."	Mo. Rev. Stat. Ann. § 202.700 *et. seq.*
Nebraska	"Mentally-disoriented sex offender shall mean any person who has a mental disorder and who, because of the mental disorder, has been determined to be disposed to repeated commission of sexual offenses which are	Neb. Rev. Stat. § 29–2911 *et. seq.*

continued

TABLE 3. (*continued*)

State	Definition, procedure, and consequences	Citation
	likely to cause substantial injury to the health of others." After a person is convicted of a felony sexual offense, he shall before being sentenced be evaluated. If the underlying offense is a misdemeanor the evaluation shall be discretionary with the court. Two physicians with psychiatric specialties or one physician and one clinical psychologist shall make separate evaluations. If the court determines that the defendant is a mentally disordered sex offender and that the disorder is treatable within the state, the court shall sentence the defendant, and then commit him for treatment. The commitment shall last until the defendant is no longer mentally disordered, or until he has received the maximum benefit of the treatment. The commitment shall not exceed the maximum length of the sentence imposed. The entire proceeding is deemed "a critical stage of a criminal proceeding," triggering certain procedural safeguards.	
New Hampshire	"The term 'dangerous sexual offender' . . . means any person suffering from such conditions of emotional instability or impulsiveness of behavior, or lack of customary standards of good judgment, or failure to appreciate the consequences of his acts, or a combination of any such conditions, as to render such person irresponsible with respect to sexual matters and thereby dangerous to himself, or to other persons." Whenever a person is convicted of felonious sexual assault, aggravated sexual assault, except in the case of an aggravated felonious sexual assault where a female victim is under 13 and sexual intercourse is without force and not against her will, or any attempt to commit any of these, the court shall prior to sentencing order an examination of the defendant by a psychiatrist. The examination is discretionary with the court if the conviction is for incest, sexual assault, aggravated felonious sexual assault when	N.H. Rev. Stat. Ann. § 173–A:1 *et. seq.*

TABLE 3. (*continued*)

State	Definition, procedure, and consequences	Citation
	the victim is under 13 and sexual intercourse is without force and not against her will, or if it is the second conviction for lewdness or indecent exposure or any attempt to commit any of these offenses. If the court determines that the defendant is a dangerous sexual offender he shall be committed until he has recovered or until his condition is such that he no longer presents a danger to himself and others and can no longer benefit from treatment.	
New Jersey	Whenever a person is convicted of aggravated sexual assault, sexual assault, or aggravated criminal sexual contact, or an attempt to commit any of these, the judge shall refer the person to the Adult Diagnostic and Treatment Center for a complete physical and psychological examination. If the examination reveals that the person's conduct was characterized by a pattern of repetitive, compulsive behavior, the court may sentence the offender to the Center for a program of specialized treatment for his mental condition. The judge shall nonetheless sentence the person in accordance with the regular sentencing provisions. When the person is capable of making an acceptable social adjustment in the community he is eligible for parole.	N.J. Stat. Ann. § 2C:47–1 *et. seq.*
Oregon	A "sexually dangerous person" is one "who because of repeated or compulsive acts of misconduct in sexual matters, or because of a mental disease or defect, is deemed likely to continue to perform such acts and be a danger to other persons." If voluntary, any person may be admitted and hospitalized if he is a sexually dangerous person. A defendant, or a person convicted of a sexual offense, when there is probable cause to believe he is a sexually dangerous person, may be committed prior to sentencing for evaluation. If the resulting report indicates that he is a sexually dangerous person and that treatment can reduce the risk of future offenses, the court shall order a hearing to determine by clear and convincing evidence	Or. Rev. Stat. § 426.510 *et. seq.*

continued

TABLE 3. (*continued*)

State	Definition, procedure, and consequences	Citation
	whether the person is a sexually dangerous person. If the court finds the defendant to be a sexually dangerous person and that treatment is available, it may place the defendant on probation with the condition that he participate in and successfully complete a treatment program, or impose a sentence of imprisonment with the order that the defendant participate in a treatment program, or impose any other sentence authorized.	
Pennsylvania	A person may be involuntarily committed for up to one year instead of the usual 90 day maximum if "severe mental disability is based on acts giving rise to charges of murder, voluntary manslaughter, aggravated assault, kidnapping, rape, involuntary deviate sexual intercourse, or arson and has been found incompetent to stand trial, or has been acquitted by reason of lack of criminal responsibility."	50 Pa. Cons. Stat. § 7304(g)(2)
Tennessee	A "sex offender" is any person convicted of a crime involving unlawful sexual abuse, molestation, fondling, or carnal knowledge of a child 14 or younger, or any person convicted of incest, a crime against nature, assault with intent to commit rape, or rape. Sex offenders are a "species of mentally ill persons" and where this tendency is pronounced they should have the same care and custody as mentally ill persons generally and for so long as their release would constitute a threat to them or the general public. If upon examination the convicted person is found capable of being successfully treated, that fact shall be certified to the commissioner of corrections along with suggested treatment, whereupon the commissioner of mental health and mental retardation shall provide such treatment.	Tenn. Code Ann. § 33–1301 *et. seq.*
Utah	Whenever any person is convicted of, or pleads guilty to rape, forcible sodomy, forcible sexual abuse, aggravated sexual assault, aggravated kidnapping, aggravated	Utah Code Ann. § 77–16–1 *et. seq.*

TABLE 3. (*continued*)

State	Definition, procedure, and consequences	Citation
	assault, mayhem, or an attempt to commit any of these, and it appears to the court that the person is suffering from a mental disease or defect, the court shall order a mental examination. If the court finds that the mental disease or defect substantially contributed to the commission of the offense, but not enough to preclude sentencing then the court shall order the person committed to the Utah State Hospital for an indefinite confinement for treatment.	
Vermont	This section was repealed, effective April 12, 1978. A "psychopathic personality" was a person who by a habitual course of misconduct in sexual matters had evidenced such a lack of power to control his sexual impulse that he presented a substantial risk of injury to others.	Vt. Stat. Ann. tit. 18, § 8501 *et. seq.*
Virginia	If any person is convicted "for any criminal offense which indicates sexual abnormality," the trial judge may defer sentence until a mental examination can be completed. The examination shall be by a psychiatrist. The judge may suspend the sentence in whole or in part or may place the defendant on probation.	Va. Code § 19.2–300 *et. seq.*
Washington	"'Psychopathic personality' means the existence in any person of such hereditary, congenital or acquired condition affecting the emotional or volitional rather than the intellectual field and manifested by anomalies of such character as to render satisfactory social adjustment . . . difficult or impossible." "'Sexual psychopath' means any person who is affected in a form of psychoneurosis or in a form of psychopathic personality, which form predisposes such person to the commission of sexual offenses in a degree constituting him a menace to the health or safety of others." When any person is charged with a sexual offense and it appears that he is a sexual psychopath the criminal charge shall be heard. If he is convicted or if he pleads guilty, judgment shall be pronounced but sentencing shall be	Wash. Rev. Code § 71.06.010 *et. seq.*

continued

TABLE 3. (*continued*)

State	Definition, procedure, and consequences	Citation
	deferred. If acquitted, sexual psychopathy shall be determined in a hearing. If found to be a sexual psychopath he shall be committed until safe to be at large or until he has received the maximum benefit of treatment. "Sex offense" means abduction, incest, rape, assault with intent to rape, indecent assault, contributing to the delinquency of a minor involving sexual misconduct, sodomy, indecent exposure, indecent liberties with children, carnal knowledge of children, soliciting or enticing or otherwise communicating with a child for immoral purposes, vagrancy involving immoral or sexual misconduct, or any attempt to commit any of these.	
Wisconsin	When a person is convicted of sexual assault, or attempted sexual assault the court shall commit the person for a presentence social, physical and mental examination. A person convicted of any other sex crime may be committed for examination. A sex crime is any crime except homicide or attempted homicide that probably was directly motivated by a desire for sexual excitement in the commission of the act. If the examination results in a recommendation that special treatment be provided for the defendant's mental or physical aberrations, the court shall order a hearing on the issue of need for specialized treatment. The defendant shall have the right to counsel, opportunity to appear with and compel appearance of witnesses, and right to a physician or clinical psychologist of the defendant's own choosing to examine him. If he is found in need of special treatment the court shall commit him for a period not to exceed the maximum sentence for the underlying offense.	Wis. Stat. Ann. § 975.01 *et. seq.*
Wyoming	Whenever any person is convicted of or pleads guilty to sexual assault, attempted sexual assault, incest, taking immodest, immoral or indecent liberties with any child under 18, or knowingly committing any immoral, indecent or obscene act in the presence of a	Wyo. Stat. § 7–13–601 *et. seq.*

TABLE 3. (*continued*)

State	Definition, procedure, and consequences	Citation
	child under 18 or causing or encouraging any child to commit or attempt to commit with the person convicted, any immoral or indecent act, or accosting, annoying or molesting any child under 18 with intent to commit any unlawful act, the judge shall order a mental examination of the defendant prior to imposition of sentence. The examination shall be by two disinterested physicians, at least one with a specialty in psychiatry. If it shall appear to the court that the convicted person has in "the past been characterized by a pattern of repetitive or compulsive behavior, accompanied by either violence, or an age disparity, then the court may grant probation with a condition of outpatient psychiatric treatment, or may order commitment to a hospital for treatment, or may order commitment to the state penitentiary for a specified period not to exceed the maximum provided by law for the underlying crime."	

PRISON TO MENTAL HOSPITAL TRANSFER STATUTES

The United States, the District of Columbia, and nearly every state have special statutes governing prisoner transfer and commitment to mental hospitals. Only four states do not have special statutes, leaving such changes in the disposition of mentally disabled prisoners to general civil commitment procedures.

Although nearly every American jurisdiction has such a statute, the continued viability of those statutes is in doubt. On March 25, 1980, the Supreme Court of the United States decided a case that could effectively invalidate many of the statutes listed below. In *Vitek v. Jones*, 100 S.Ct. 1254 (1980), the Court held Nebraska's prison to mental hospital transfer statute unconstitutional. NEB. REV. STAT. § 83–180 provided that when a physician or psychologist found that a prisoner was suffering from a mental disease or defect and could not be properly treated at the penal institution, the director of correctional services might transfer him for examination, study, and treatment.

The Fourteenth Amendment to the Constitution of the United States provides that no state shall "deprive any person of life, liberty, or property, without due process of law." When Nebraska attempted to transfer a prisoner under § 83–180, was it depriving him of liberty? If so, then it must respect the "due process" clause. The threshold question in *Vitek*, therefore, was whether the involuntary transfer of a prisoner implicated a liberty interest (100 S.Ct. at 1261). First, the Court noted that prisoners in Nebraska have the objective expectation, created partly by § 83–180, that they will not be transferred without being found mentally ill and in need of treatment not available within the penal institution. In that expectation the Court found a liberty interest that entitled prisoners to the benefit of adequate procedures in connection with determining the conditions that warrant a transfer (*Id.* at 1262). The Court found another liberty interest implicated in a transfer, independent of Nebraska's law. A prisoner has a "residuum of liberty," even after conviction and penal confinement, that is affected by the stigma of being labelled mentally ill and the imposition of involuntary psychiatric treatment (*Id.* at 1263–64).

Because a prisoner's liberty interests are affected by a transfer, procedural due process attaches to protect those interests. To determine the procedures necessary to protect the prisoner's liberty interests, the court must balance those interests against the state's interests. Strong are the state's interests in segregating and treating mentally disabled prisoners, but strong, too, is the prisoner's interest in not being arbitrarily classified as mentally ill and subjected to unwelcome treatment. The risk of an erroneous determination of mental illness is substantial enough to warrant appropriate safeguards against error (*Id.* at 1264). Although basically a medical or psychiatric question, it is "precisely the subtleties and nuances of psychiatric diagnosis that justify the requirements of an adversary hearing" (*Id.* at 1265).

The following procedures were held to be the minimum that would satisfy the requirements of due process. First, if a transfer is being considered, the prisoner must have written notice. A hearing must be held, permitting sufficient time after the notice to allow the prisoner to prepare. At the hearing the evidence relied on to justify the proposed transfer must be disclosed to the prisoner and he must be given the opportunity to be heard and to present documentary evidence. He also must have the opportunity to present witnesses and to confront and cross-examine the state's witnesses, unless good cause is found to deny presentation, confrontation, or cross-examination. The decisionmaker must be independent, although not necessarily from outside the penal or hospital administrations. If the decision is to transfer him, the prisoner must receive a written statement of the evidence relied on and the reasons for transfer. The prisoner has a right to competent help at the hearing, although appointed legal counsel is not necessary. He must, of course, have effective and timely notice of all the foregoing rights.

States that do not adhere to these procedures are proceeding unconstitutionally. Some states, such as New Jersey, North Carolina, and Ohio, although not expressly providing for these safeguards in their statutes, might in practice establish regulations requiring observance of them. In that way their statutes are potentially within the constitutional mandates. Other states' statutes are patently unconstitutional. Georgia's, for instance, provides no hearing at all until a transferred prisoner's sentence is completed. North Dakota's arguably fails to provide both an independent decisionmaker, and "competent help." Alaska's statute has been construed as establishing an administrative transfer procedure in which the prisoner has no due process rights beyond the expectation of fair and impartial allocation of resources. These hardly seem to stand up to the rather rigorous procedures required after *Vitek*.

Only West Virginia and Indiana have statutes that seem sure to withstand a *Vitek*-type challenge. Indeed, they seem to have been modelled after the *Vitek* procedures.

While using the following table, it is necessary to keep in mind the due process rigors mandated by *Vitek*.

TABLE 4. PRISON TO MENTAL HOSPITAL TRANSFER STATUTES

State	Procedure	Citation
Alabama	If the physician at any penal institution reports that one imprisoned there has become mentally ill, the governor shall appoint three suitable persons, one of whom is the physician who initiated the action, to examine the prisoner. If declared to be mentally ill "and fit to be sent to a mental health facility," the governor shall order the prisoner transferred.	Ala. Code § 22–52–70
Alaska	Alaska Stat. §§ 33.30.020 and 33.30.050 have been construed to mean that a prisoner has a right to psychiatric treatment if a physician or other health care provider concludes with reasonable medical certainty that the prisoner's symptoms evidence a serious but treatable condition. Decisions of prison authorities regarding classifications of prisoners are administrative matters and the prisoner has no due process rights beyond the expectation of fair and impartial allocation of resources.	*Rust v. State*, 582 P.2d 134 (Alaska 1978)

(continued)

TABLE 4. (*continued*)

State	Procedure	Citation
Arizona	The repeal of Ariz. Rev. Stat. Ann. § 31–224(A) leaves no special procedure for prisoner transfer. It leaves only the general public commitment procedures of § 36–501 *et. seq.*	Ariz. Rev. Stat. Ann. § 36–501 *et. seq.*
Arkansas	If the physician at any penal institution certifies to the superintendent that a prisoner is mentally ill, the superintendent shall transfer the prisoner to the State Hospital.	Ark. Stat. Ann. § 59–415
California	If the director of corrections is of the opinion that any mentally ill, mentally deficient, or insane person confined in a state prison can benefit from treatment in a state hospital, he shall so certify and the prisoner shall be evaluated. If the director of the appropriate department determines that the prisoner can benefit from care and treatment, the prisoner shall be transferred and kept until he can no longer benefit from care and treatment. His hospital stay shall count against his sentence.	Cal. Penal Code §§ 2684 and 2685; Cal. Welf. & Inst. Code § 7227
Colorado	If reported by the superintendent and certified by the prison physician, that any person imprisoned is mentally ill or retarded, the executive director shall transfer the prisoner for a period of not to exceed 30 days, for observation and evaluation. If, from the report, the executive director is of the opinion that the prisoner is mentally ill or retarded and cannot be well taken care of in the penal institution, he shall be confined in an institution for care and treatment, "to the extent necessary for the protection of society."	Colo. Rev. Stat. § 17–23–101
Connecticut	Any person in the custody of the commissioner of corrections may seek voluntary admission provided a physician designated by the commissioner certifies that such person is in need of observation and treatment for mental illness. If a physician certifies that any person has suddenly become in need of emergency care and treatment in a hospital for psychiatric disorder, other than drug dependence, and is a danger to self or others or to the security of the institution, or is in need of care and treatment for an acute drug dependence and is a danger to self, others or to the security	Conn. Gen. Stat. Ann. § 17–194(c), (d), (e)

TABLE 4. (*continued*)

State	Procedure	Citation
	of the institution, that person shall be temporarily hospitalized. All other transfers must be pursuant to regular civil commitment procedures.	
Delaware	The commissioner of corrections is empowered to transfer any prisoner when it has been determined that he is psychotic or mentally defective.	Del. Code Ann. tit. 11, § 6525
District of Columbia	Any person serving a sentence, who, in the opinion of the director of the Department of Corrections, is mentally ill, shall be referred to a psychiatrist. If the psychiatrist certifies that the prisoner is mentally ill, the director may order the prisoner transferred.	D.C. Code Ann. § 24–302
Florida	Mentally ill prisoners can be transferred to an appropriate institution for no longer than the remainder of their prison sentences, for specialized treatment. Regular involuntary commitment procedures must be followed. If the court, pursuant to these procedures, finds that the prisoner is mentally ill and because of the illness is likely to injure himself or others, or is in need of care and treatment without which will result neglect or a refusal to care for himself that poses a real and present threat of substantial harm to his well being, the court shall transfer him to a state mental health treatment facility.	Fla. Stat. § 945.12(1)
Georgia	A prisoner will be transferred if insane. A hearing will be held to determine the question of "lunacy" any time after his sentence is completed, but not before.	Ga. Code Ann. § 77–310(d)
Hawaii	If any resident of a state correctional facility is in need of treatment for mental illness or substance abuse, and a psychiatrist has so certified, the resident shall be transferred to a state hospital for care and treatment. If commitment is to continue beyond the duration of the sentence, regular civil commitment proceedings must be instituted.	Hawaii Rev. Stat. § 334–74
Idaho	Mentally ill convicts may be received into mental health facilities in accordance with rules and regulations adopted by the state board of health and welfare acting in conjunction with the state board of corrections.	Idaho Code § 66–335

continued

TABLE 4. (*continued*)

State	Procedure	Citation
Illinois	Any person committed to the Department of Corrections who is in need of psychiatric treatment may be treated in a separate institution within the Department or may be transferred to the Department of Mental Health and Developmental Disabilities. If the person consents he can be transferred for six months. If he does not consent, or if the period will exceed six months, or if his sentence will expire within six months, the Department of Corrections may file a petition with the court, including a physician's certificate, and a judicial hearing will be held on the matter.	Ill. Rev. Stat. ch. 38, § 1003–8–5
Indiana	A prisoner may be involuntarily committed only if a psychiatrist reports in writing that he is mentally ill and in need of care in the department of mental health, and a hearing is held to determine the need for transfer. The prisoner is entitled to ten days notice, a copy of the psychiatrist's report, representation, and to call witnesses and present evidence. He is further entitled to get a copy of the court's findings of fact and the determination shall be by a preponderance of the evidence. This statute shall take effect on October 1, 1980.	Ind. Code Ann. § 11–10–4–2
Iowa	A female prisoner suspected of being mentally ill shall be examined by the superintendent or his designee or shall be transferred to a security medical facility for examination. If found mentally ill, she shall be transferred to or retained at the state hospital. If the prisoner so suspected is male, he shall be transferred to a security medical facility for examination, diagnosis and treatment for the duration of his sentence or until he is in good mental health.	Iowa Code Ann. §§ 245.12 and 246.16
Kansas	The secretary of corrections may arrange the transfer of an inmate for observation and diagnosis or treatment to an appropriate state institution. The inmate's sentence shall continue to run. No inmate shall receive treatment beyond his sentence unless continued care and treatment is necessary at the expiration of his sentence and	Kan. Stat. Ann. § 75–5209

TABLE 4. (*continued*)

State	Procedure	Citation
	application is filed in conformance with the regular civil commitment provisions.	
Kentucky	Whenever the staff of a penal institution reports that an inmate is so mentally ill that he cannot be properly treated within the institution, the secretary of corrections shall order him examined by a physician. If found to be mentally ill and appropriate treatment cannot be properly carried out at the institution, the secretary may order him transferred to a hospital or forensic psychiatric facility. If his sentence expires during his stay and he is still mentally ill and a danger to self or others and can benefit from treatment in a hospital and the hospital is the least restrictive alternative, the staff can petition the sentencing court for involuntary commitment.	Ky. Rev. Stat. § 202A.190
Louisiana	A prisoner who becomes mentally ill may be committed to the proper institution in the manner provided for by regular judicial commitment provisions.	La. Rev. Stat. § 28:59(c)
Maine	When the warden of the Maine State Prison, or the superintendent of the Maine Correctional Center or Maine Youth Center believes that any person confined there is mentally ill, requiring hospitalization and meeting the requirements of admission, he shall make application to the court for the person's commitment. The application shall be accompanied by a certificate of a physician or clinical psychologist that the person is mentally ill and poses a likelihood of serious harm to himself or others. If the court finds the application and certificate "to be regular and in accordance with the law he shall endorse them." Upon endorsement the prisoner shall be transferred.	Me. Rev. Stat. Ann. tit. 34, §§ 136–A and 2333
Maryland	Any prisoner may be transferred in accordance with the regular involuntary commitment statutes if he has a mental disorder, needs protection for himself or others, is in need of treatment or care and will not voluntarily consent. Two physicians or one physician and one psychologist must certify that the	Md. Ann. Code art. 59, §§ 16 and 12

continued

TABLE 4. (*continued*)

State	Procedure	Citation
	person has a mental disorder, needs treatment, and poses a danger to self or others.	
Massachusetts	If the person in charge of a penal institution has reason to believe that a prisoner is in need of hospitalization for mental illness, the prisoner shall be examined at that facility by a physician. The physician shall report opinions and reasons to the court, and the court may order transfer for 30 days observation. After 30 days a written report including the physician's evaluations and supported by clinical observations shall be filed with the court. If the prisoner is in need of continued hospitalization he may be committed for six months, with one year renewals of commitment thereafter during his term of sentence.	Mass. Gen. Laws Ann. ch. 123, § 18
Michigan	If it is the opinion of the majority of the administrative hearing board that a prisoner is mentally ill or retarded and is in need of services that can be provided in a mental health facility, the officer in charge of the place of detention shall transfer the prisoner to a facility designated by the department of mental health. If any one member of the board or if the prisoner feels the transfer is involuntary then review in the probate court shall be had within five days.	Mich. Stat. Ann. § 14.800 (1000)(5)
Minnesota	If a physician or psychologist finds a prisoner to be mentally ill and in need of short term care, he may recommend transfer to the psychiatric unit of the correctional institution system. The commissioner of corrections may transfer an inmate to a state institution for the mentally ill, mentally retarded, or epileptic or to a state sanatorium for care not available at the prison. At the end of the inmate's term of sentence he shall he released, or committed pursuant to regular civil commitment procedures.	Minn. Stat. Ann. §§ 241.69 and 241.07
Mississippi	If the board of examiners, composed of a physician on the state hospital staff, a physician on the Department of Corrections staff, and an independent physician, after examination and evaluation, determine that a prisoner is suffering from psychosis, or	Miss. Code Ann. § 47–5–120

TABLE 4. (*continued*)

State	Procedure	Citation
	other mental illness or drug addiction, and is in need of, or can benefit from treatment, it can authorize transfer for observation, diagnosis, treatment and rehabilitation. The Commissioner of Corrections may transfer a prisoner for observation, diagnosis and treatment. The prisoner's sentence shall continue to run, and if it expires he shall be discharged.	
Missouri	If the person in charge of any correctional institution has reasonable cause to believe that any inmate needs care in a mental hospital, he shall certify that belief to the division of classification and assignment. The division shall transfer the inmate to the state mental hospital for custody, care and treatment as provided by law for the transfer and reassignment of inmates from one correctional institution to another. The law for transfer from one correctional institution to another provides no protective process, only that if the director shall find that an inmate is in the wrong place he shall transfer him. *See* Mo. Rev. Stat. Ann. § 216.223.	Mo. Rev. Stat. Ann. § 552.050
Montana	Montana provides no special provisions for transfer and commitment of prisoners, leaving only the regular civil commitment provisions.	Mont. Rev. Codes Ann. 53–21–101 *et. seq.*
Nebraska	This statute was declared unconstitutional in *Vitek v. Jones,* 100 S.Ct. 1254 (1980). *See* the discussion in the introduction to this table. The statute provided for transfer if a physician found the prisoner suffering from a mental disease or defect that could not be properly treated in prison.	Neb. Rev. Stat. § 83–180, held unconstitutional in *Vitek v. Jones,* 100 S.Ct. 1254 (1980)
Nevada	The director of the department of prisons may arrange for the transfer of an offender to another governmental agency for psychiatric observation, evaluation or stabilization pursuant to an agreement with that agency. When the head of the facility determines that the offender has recovered, the director shall provide for return to the department of prisons.	Nev. Rev. Stat. § 209.321
New Hampshire	The governor and council or superior court shall transfer any prisoner who is insane to	N.H. Rev. Stat. Ann. § 651:10

continued

TABLE 4. (*continued*)

State	Procedure	Citation
	the state hospital whenever they are satisfied that the transfer will be conducive to the health and comfort of the person and the welfare of the public.	
New Jersey	If it appears to the court that a prisoner is mentally ill or retarded, the court may, in an action like one for civil commitment, determine the mental or physical condition and legal settlement of the prisoner. If the court determines that the prisoner is mentally ill or retarded, it shall direct him transferred to an institution for treatment and care. When the prisoner is in a condition to be discharged he shall be remanded to the place of confinement, unless the maximum period of detention fixed by statute or operation of law has expired, in which case he shall be discharged.	N.J. Stat. Ann. § 30:4–82
New Mexico	New Mexico provides no special commitment procedures for prisoners. The citation is to the general civil commitment provisions.	N.M. Stat. Ann. § 43:1–1 *et. seq.*
New York	If the prison physician and warden certify to the director of a state hospital that a prisoner is in a state of mental health requiring involuntary care and treatment and so should be transferred to a psychiatric hospital, the director shall be responsible for providing the needed treatment. He shall have the prisoner examined and if he determines that the prisoner is in need of involuntary treatment he shall institute proceedings for commitment as provided for by the mental hygiene law. The application of admission shall be accompanied by the certificates of two physicians. The prisoner shall remain until he has improved sufficiently so that hospitalization is no longer required or until ordered by the court returned to the jail.	N.Y. Correc. Law. § 508(3)
North Carolina	If the staff psychologist executes an affidavit that a convict is mentally ill, and files it with the court, the court shall hold a hearing on the matter. The respondent (convict) is entitled to notice, as is his attorney. If the court finds by clear, cogent and convincing	N.C. Gen. Stat. § 122.85

TABLE 4. (*continued*)

State	Procedure	Citation
	evidence that the respondent is mentally ill, it shall order him transferred to a regional psychiatric facility. If his sentence expires he shall be considered as having been originally committed pursuant to regular involuntary civil commitment procedures.	
North Dakota	Whenever the warden believes that a prisoner needs treatment beyond what is available at the penitentiary, he may appoint an evaluation committee, including a psychiatrist. If the committee finds that the person's needs cannot be met at the penitentiary, but can be provided for elsewhere, it shall submit those findings to the warden. The warden shall notify the person of the results of the evaluation, and of his right to an administrative hearing if he disagrees, and of his right to be represented by the prison employee of his choice. The hearing shall be conducted by a three member board including a member of the prison counseling staff, a physician, psychiatrist or clinical psychologist and chaired by an employee designated by the warden. No member of the evaluation committee shall be included. If the board recommends, the warden may order the transfer, with a copy of the results to the person, and shall notify the person of his right to an "involuntary treatment hearing 14 days after transfer," before a magistrate of the court where the hospital is located.	N.D. Cent. Code § 12–47–27
Ohio	When a prisoner appears to be mentally ill or retarded, the managing officer may file an affidavit in the probate court, alleging that the prisoner is mentally ill or retarded. The affidavit must be filed within the regular civil commitment provisions. If the court finds that the prisoner is mentally ill or retarded, and that it will be within the least restrictive alternative, it shall commit the prisoner to the custody of the department of mental health. The prisoner shall be discharged if he ceases to be mentally ill, or hospitalization is no longer necessary or if his sentence has expired. If the latter, and	Ohio Rev. Code Ann. § 5125.05

continued

TABLE 4. (*continued*)

State	Procedure	Citation
	continued commitment is necessary, he can be committed pursuant to the regular commitment procedure, but the procedure must be accomplished anew.	
Oklahoma	When one confined in a penal institution appears to be mentally ill, the warden shall notify the director of mental health who shall have the prisoner examined. If this examination reveals that the person is in need of observation and treatment and it cannot be had at the institution of incarceration, then the director of mental health may order him transferred. Any hospitalization shall count against the person's sentence.	Okla. Stat. tit. 43A, §§ 61 and 81
Oregon	An inmate may be transferred to a state mental hospital for up to 15 days for evaluation or treatment at the request of the superintendent of the referring institution. The inmate may remain up to the duration of his sentence if he consents, and the superintendent of the state hospital recommends retention for treatment, and the superintendent of the referring institution approves. If the inmate is unwilling to consent, the superintendent of the state hospital may petition the court for a commitment hearing. The inmate shall have the rights to notice, to call witnesses, to cross-examine witnesses and to have counsel. If the court determines by clear and convincing evidence that the inmate is mentally ill he shall be committed for up to 180 days, with continued commitment subject to further court action. Time spent hospitalized shall be applied against the inmate's sentence.	Or. Rev. Stat. §§ 179.475(1) and 179.477(1)
Pennsylvania	Pennsylvania has no special statute for involuntary transfer of a prisoner. For general involuntary commitment procedures, *see* 50 Pa. Cons. Stat. § 7301 *et. seq.* For voluntary commitment of a prisoner, *see* 50 Pa. Cons. Stat. § 7407.	50 Pa. Cons. Stat. §§ 7301 *et. seq.* and 7407
Rhode Island	If the director of mental health, or the director of corrections petitions the court, the justice of the court may order such examination of the prisoner as he deems appropriate. If the	R.I. Gen. Laws §§ 40.1–5.3–6,7,8

TABLE 4. (*continued*)

State	Procedure	Citation
	justice is satisfied that the prisoner is insane he may order the prisoner transferred for the duration of his sentence.	
South Carolina	If it appears to the officer in charge of a jail that a prisoner is mentally ill, he shall cause that person to be examined by two examiners designated by the Department of Mental Health. If, in their opinions, admission to a mental health facility is warranted, the officer shall commence regular civil commitment proceedings.	S.C. Code § 44–23–220
South Dakota	Whenever it appears to the satisfaction of the warden and the board of charities and corrections that any person confined in the penitentiary has become mentally ill, the board may order that person to be transferred, confined and treated in a state hospital for the mentally ill.	S.D. Codified Laws Ann. § 24–2–24
Tennessee	Whenever the officer in charge of a penal institution determines that a prisoner requires hospitalization for mental illness, he may seek admission of the prisoner to the state psychiatric hospital pursuant to the regular civil commitment procedures. Upon the expiration of a prisoner's term of imprisonment, if examination reveals continuing mental illness creating serious likelihood of harm, the director of the department of corrections may petition the court for judicial commitment.	Tenn. Code Ann. §§ 41–1230 and 41–349
Texas	The director of the department of corrections may transfer a prisoner not under the death sentence, if a prison physician is of the opinion that the prisoner is mentally ill and would benefit from treatment in a mental hospital. A county judge may transfer a county prisoner if the county health officer certifies that the prisoner is mentally ill and would benefit from treatment in a mental hospital. Time hospitalized shall be credited against the prisoner's sentence. If upon expiration of his sentence the head of the hospital determines that the prisoner is still mentally ill and likely to cause injury to himself or others, then the head of the hospital may initiate civil commitment proceedings.	Tex. Crim. Pro. Code Ann. tit. 46.01, §§ 2,3, 6, 7, 8

continued

TABLE 4. (*continued*)

State	Procedure	Citation
United States	Upon application of the Attorney General, the Secretary of Health, Education and Welfare is authorized and directed to transfer to the Saint Elizabeth's Hospital in the District of Columbia, all persons convicted of any offense in the courts of the United States, who during their term have become insane.	24 U.S.C. § 212
Utah	The Utah State Hospital is required to receive any prisoner when ordered by the executive director of the department of social services, who shall consider the treatment needs of the prisoner and the treatment programs available at the Utah State Hospital.	Utah Code Ann. §64-7-3
Vermont	If the commissioner of the department of corrections determines a prisoner has manifested a mental illness requiring treatment, the commissioner has authority to initiate proceedings to transfer the prisoner to the department of mental health pursuant to the regular civil commitment procedures. The prisoner's sentence continues running.	Vt. Stat. Ann. tit. 28, §§ 702(b) and 703
Virginia	Any person serving a sentence in a penal institution who is declared by a commissioner of insanity to be insane or feebleminded shall be committed by the court to the proper hospital. He shall be kept there until he is restored to sanity. The time spent hospitalized shall be deducted from the term sentenced.	Va. Code § 19.2-177
Washington	When, in the judgment of the secretary of the department of social and health services, the welfare of any person confined in any correctional facility necessitates transfer to any mental illness facility for observation, diagnosis or treatment, the secretary is authorized to order and effect such a transfer. The prisoner's sentence shall continue to run, and he shall have substantially similar opportunities for parole.	Wash. Rev. Code § 72.68.031
West Virginia	When a prisoner is believed to be mentally ill, mentally retarded, or substance addicted and in need of treatment, training or other services which cannot be effectively provided at the penal institution, transfer proceedings may be initiated by the filing,	W. Va. Code §§ 28-5-31(b) and 27-6A-8

TABLE 4. (*continued*)

State	Procedure	Citation
	in court, of an application by a correctional officer, warden, a member of the institution's medical staff, or a relative, friend or the prisoner himself, stating the condition and need. The prisoner shall have appointed counsel, and notice. If the application is opposed there shall be a hearing where the prisoner has the right to be present, opportunity to present and cross-examine witnesses, the right to a court appointed medical expert if indigent, and protection from self-incrimination. He shall receive a transcript of the hearing. If he is found mentally ill, retarded, or addicted, and therefore likely to cause serious harm to self or others and needed treatment or training is not available at the penal institution then he shall be transferred. His mental condition, and the likelihood of serious harm must be proved by clear, cogent and convincing evidence and the likelihood of serious harm must be based on recent overt acts, except if the allegation is of mental retardation causing complete inability to care for himself. Time spent hospitalized shall be credited against his sentence.	
Wisconsin	If a physician or psychologist of a state prison reports that a prisoner is mentally ill, drug or alcohol dependent or developmentally disabled, and is either dangerous or in need of treatment, and the prisoner voluntarily consents, the department of corrections may transfer him. If he does not voluntarily consent, then a petition for involuntary commitment must be filed under the regular civil commitment procedures.	Wis. Stat. Ann. § 51.37(5)(a)
Wyoming	The state board of charities and reform may transfer a mentally ill prisoner to a designated hospital upon recommendation of the head of the institution.	Wyo. Stat. § 25-3-139

Index